Politics of
Guilt and Pity

By

ROUSAS JOHN RUSHDOONY

THE CRAIG PRESS
Nutley New Jersey 07110
1970

Library of Congress Catalogue Card No. 70-133083

Printed in the United States of America

TABLE OF CONTENTS

I. THE POLITICS OF GUILT

1

MASOCHISM AND ATONEMENT

The fact of *guilt* is one of the major realities of man's existence. Both personally and socially, it is a vast drain on human energies and a mainspring of human action. Any attempt at assessing either political action or religious faith apart from the fact of guilt is thus an exercise in futility.

The roots of guilt are personal and racial; the consequences are social as well. The human race, in apostasy from God, is deeply involved in a rebellious claim to autonomy and in the guilt which follows that claim. As a result of this omnipresent sense of guilt, there is an omnipresent demand for *justification*. The expression, "He's trying to justify himself," points to this demand by man for justification, an insistence on psychic or spiritual wholeness of health. A sense of guilt leaves a man feeling like a leaky, sinking ship: the energies must all be resolved to the repair of that breach. The psychology of the guilty man is thus geared to self-defense, to spiritual survival, by means of an overcoming of the breach of guilt. This concern is a demand for salvation: the sinking ego wants to save itself, to find justification by making atonement for its guilt. Atonement thus is a repair of the breach caused by guilt, and the consequence of atonement is justification. Because the need for this repair is so urgent, the whole personal, social, religious, and political life of guilty man is colored by this demand for atonement and is in fact dominated by it.

A common recourse is to self-atonement and self-justification. A modern term for such behavior is *masochism*, in the broader sense of that term. The narrower sense refers to a sexual offense, in which the masochist seeks to buy atonement by demanding punishment before the sin and as a license to the sin. In the broader sense, masochism is self-punishment as atonement for sin in order to cleanse the conscience of guilt. Theodor Reik, writing from an anti-Christian and Freudian perspective, has observed:

> The unconscious force which drives people to deny themselves enjoyment and success, to spoil their chances in life or not to make use of them, may be more accurately defined as the need for punishment. In childhood punishment is expected from parents. In adulthood God or dark forces of destiny take their place. Unconsciously these people inflict punishments on themselves to which an inner court has sentenced them. A hidden authority within the ego takes over the judgment originally expected from the parents. Analysis can show that not only are these punishments expected, but that they are even unconsciously desired, that suffering is aimed at unconsciously even if they do not know or do not want to know it. These individuals act as if they were controlled by stringent moral laws and prohibitions, and as if they were forced to punish themselves for disobeying them.[1]

A variety of human actions are deeply masochistic, and all the actions of guilty man are colored by masochism. "Neurosis is undoubtedly a masochistic formation."[2] Psychic masochism is the basic neurosis, according to Bergler.[3]

Masochistic self-punishment in atonement for sin appears in a variety of ways, a few of which can be cited, by way of illustration. *First*, psychosomatic ailments are a common masochistic recourse. The belief is simply, "If I suffer enough, I will pay for my sins."

[1] Theodor Reik: *Masochism in Modern Man, p.* 10. Translated by Margaret H. Beigel and Gertrud M. Kurth. New York: Farrar, Straus, 1941, 1949.
[2] *Ibid.,* p. 372.
[3] Edmund Bergler, M.D.: *Principles of Self-Damage.* New York: Philosophical Library, 1959.

Thus sickness is an offering of atonement for sin. Ancient medical practice, whatever its faults, often recognized this aspect of atonement. The sickness is none the less physical for having had a spiritual origin. Psychomatic medicine is now an established branch of medical knowledge.[4]

Second, gambling is a common and popular exercise in masochism. The gambler knows that the odds are against him: he gambles to lose, with an unconscious will to lose, to punish himself for his guilt and cleanse, although vainly, his conscience. The real "winnings" of the gambler, according to Bergler, "are paid in the intrapsychic coin of psychic masochism—which is, after all, what he has bargained for." [5] According to a report made to this writer by a dealer in a major Nevada gambling house, losing is the rule, and "winners" are liars. This dealer claimed that $20 could be handed to each person entering the premises without loss, that people who win insistently gamble until they lose. He stated further that he had seen only one gambler leave the premises a winner, a man who was so drunk that he passed out while still ahead. His conclusion was, "They play to lose." While this may be in part an overstatement, it is essentially true.

Third, alcoholism is another form of self-punishment, and marriage to a known alcoholic is similarly masochistic activity. When an alcoholic quits drinking, his major problem is often his wife, who is outraged at being robbed of her "cross." The result is erratic behavior on her part, and irresponsible conduct, as she seeks a new form of self-punishment and another cross to bear. Some will deliberately try to drive the man back to drink in order to regain their precarious and fallacious peace of mind.

Fourth, still another form of masochism is "burden-bearing." The burden-bearer will play the role of public saint in order to atone for private guilt. The more unpleasant the public role, the more desir-

[4] See Frank G. Slaughter, M.D.: *Your Body and Your Mind*. New York: Signet Books (1947), 1953; Therese Benedek, M.D.: *Psychosexual Functions in Women*, New York: The Ronald Press, 1952; Flanders Dunbar, M.D.: *Mind and Body: Psychosomatic Medicine*, New York: Random House, 1947; etc.

[5] Edmund Bergler, M.D.: *The Psychology of Gambling*, p. 244. New York: Hill and Wang, 1957.

able its function for purposes of atonement. As a result, the guilty rich will indulge in philanthropy, and the guilty white men will show "love" and "concern" for Negroes and other such persons who are in actuality repulsive and intolerable to them. In one academic community, the prominent public saint was a faculty wife who moved about ironing and cooking for sick or newly delivered wives of graduate students, although she had never cooked a meal for her family or done their laundry because such services were beneath her social status. Self-conscious burden-bearing, public works of virtue, worry and fretting, worship or penance, all serve as devices for self-atonement, as forms of do-it-yourself salvation.

Fifth, "injustice-collecting" has been rightly described by Reik and Bergler as an important aspect of masochism. The injustice collector systematically finds "pleasure in displeasure," places himself in positions where he will be sure to feel offended, and then self-righteously sees himself as one sinned against and hence innocent. Bergler, in the context of his Freudian faith, which we cannot accept, has described the "schedule" of the "injustice collector":

> (a) Through their behavior or the misuse of an external situation, neurotics unconsciously provoke disappointment and refusal, identifying the outer world with the "refusing" pre-Oedipal mother.
> (b) Not realizing that they themselves have brought about this disappointment, they become aggressive, seemingly in self-defense ("pseudo-aggression").
> (c) They then induldge in self-pity, unconsciously enjoying psychic masochism: "This can happen only to me."
> Consciously, these neurotics realize only their righteous indignation and self-pity. They repress the fact of initial provocation, as well as that of masochistic enjoyment of self-pity.[6]

Sixth, the will to failure is a common factor in masochism. Failure is a penalty paid, an atonement made, for sins committed.

Numerous other forms of masochistic activity can be cited. Suffice it to cite but one more: *suicidal activity*. Many persons do not reveal their personal masochism, but they do participate in mass

[6] Edmund Bergler, M.D.: *Counterfeit-Sex. Homosexuality, Impotence, Frigity*, p. 65. Second, enlarged edition. New York: Grune & Stratton, 1958.

masochism through political and economic views and activities calculated to fulfill *the urge to mass destruction*. According to Warner, the "two major dynamic factors which enter into the causation of self-and-other defeat" are *"the craving for individual power,* and *the motive of revenge."* [7] Behind this suicidal drive is a hatred of all life and a desire to destroy all life, *"to lead the living to suicide."* [8] *"Victory through defeat"* becomes the goal,[9] and the more widespread the defeat, the greater the victory. The goal unconsciously becomes mass destruction, "a mass grave for all." [10] The politics and the economics of the modern era are increasingly dominated by this unrelenting, unconscious urge to mass destruction. Masochism is thus closely related to suicide.

Masochistic activities are not only forms of self-atonement but also forms of self-deception. Thus Bergler sees homosexuality as "inner admission of the 'Lesser Crime.'" [11] The guilty person conceals a greater crime by open profession of a lesser one. For the Christian, the truest definition of sin is that it is "any want of conformity unto, or transgression of, any law of God, given as a rule to the reasonable creature." [12] Masochism is guilt atonement, but it is an atonement that both pleads guilty to the lesser crime and seeks refuge at the same time in self-justification.

A form of activity closely related to masochism and having identical roots, and some would call it a form of masochism, is sadism. In sadism, self-punishment involves also a transfer of guilt to an innocent party. It is a form of revenge against the innocent for their innocence and an attempt to reduce them to the same level of impotence and guilt. David prayed, "Keep me, O LORD, from the hands of the wicked; preserve me from the violent man; who have purposed to overthrow my goings" (Psalm 140:4). Some men go to great expense and pains to seduce a virgin, or a faithful wife, whom they actually dislike, for only one reason, to "humble" them, to

[7] Samuel J. Warner: *The Urge to Mass Destruction*, p. 19. New York: Grune & Stratton, 1957.
[8] *Ibid.*, pp. 26, 34.
[9] *Ibid.*, p. 99.
[10] *Ibid.*, p. 152.
[11] Bergler: *Counterfeit-Sex*, p. 198f.
[12] *Westminster Larger Catechism*, A24; *Westminster Shorter Catechism*, A14.

destroy their offensive innocence. A form of self-justification is thus the reduction of the world to the sinner's level. Some parents will both indulge flagrantly and then punish savagely their children as they alternate between a mood of longing for the triumph of self-indulgence and a resentment that anyone can escape the punishment when they cannot. "When a parent handles his child badly it usually means he is handling himself badly." [13] Reik, after having analyzed the problem of guilt in Freudian terms, discards the Freudian belief in its deeply instinctual nature to state:

> We all live beyond our moral means. Let us be more tolerant towards our aggressive feelings, towards our mean, cruel, and vindictive thoughts. We should at least in our daydreams dare to give the devil a fair chance.
>
> The incompatability of high moral demands on the ego with human nature manifests itself in masochism by the production of that need for punishments as a reaction to the forbidden instinctual gratification in phantasy. However, the value of the discrimination between suffering as a psychic necessity caused by biological and social factors, and as a psychic luxury, resulting from exaggerated respect for moral demands, goes beyond this point of view. We have to admit that the weak ego, having to yield to the pressure of external and, later on, introverted demands at a certain period of development, has no other outlet than instinctual satisfaction by phantasy. [14]
>
> What is this need for punishment and how does it originate? It is certainly no elementary or primary psychic formation. [15]

Freud, however, in his analysis of man, found the will to death, a demand for self-punishment and death, perhaps even stronger than the will to live. [16]

The need for atonement, the need for cleansing, and for purity, is inseparable from man, and the advertising industry is well aware of it. The clean look, the new product, the spotless modern home, new clothing, these and other forms of ritual purification are sold

---

[13] Flanders Dunbar, M.D.: *Your Child's Mind and Body*, p. 99. New York: Random House, 1949.

[14] Reik: *op. cit.*, p. 390.

[15] *Ibid.*, p. 402.

[16] See R. J. Rushdoony: *Freud.* Philadelphia: Presbyterian and Reformed Publishing Company, 1965.

by advertisers to a guilt-ridden populace in search of packaged atonement. In 1959, a new soap became a best seller with a very direct television appeal to this hunger for cleansing: "For the first time in your life, *feel really clean*—use Zest." Thus, purification was sold as a bar of soap. Reik's solution is to be tolerant towards oneself and thus avoid the sense of guilt; the answer is futile in the face of his own evidence. The answer of the advertising industry is ritual and ceremonial purification through the purchase of symbolic goods. These answers are a supplement to or a replacement of the ancient forms of works-salvation, of religions and heresies whereby man worked out his own salvation by means of self-atonement, self-righteousness, and self-justification. They share not only a common theoretical basis but a common futility.

The biblical position is radically opposed to these devices of masochistic man, of guilt-ridden man. Self-atonement is an impossibility. Reik's theological statement of masochism is revealing: "To put it theologically: first the atonement, then the sin. The discomfort is not desired as such, but it constitutes the price of pleasure." [17] The masochist seeks to buy an area of immunity and autonomy for sin from God. His thesis is that a jealous God is preventing him from enjoying his pleasure by declaring it a sin. This jealous God must be bought off and independence gained for the freedom to sin, for the privilege of living without God and without law. The masochist activity, the self-atonement, is the ostensible admission price to freedom from God and morality. It is thus a bargaining price, and, indeed, in ancient paganism the temple sacrifice was simply a payment for services rendered or expected by an autonomous man who dealt with the gods on a business basis. But this perspective is an impossibility, metaphysically and morally. Man is God's creature, totally God's creation, and man can exist only in God's world. He is totally morally liable to God, and man's every attempt to assert a claim to autonomy is not only a violation of his moral duty but a metaphysical impossibility and a mental monstrosity. Man cannot make atonement to God for his sin because he is neither capable of truly self-righteous atonement, since he is nothing in and of himself,

[17] Reik, *op. cit.*, p. 123.

nor can he add anything to God. As Paul asked the Corinthians, "and what hast thou that thou didst not receive? now if thou didst receive it, why dost thou glory, as if thou hadst not received it?" (I Cor. 4:7). Since man is totally God's act, man's justification and atonement are also of necessity totally God's acts. To give man autonomy in the sphere of atonement requires giving him autonomy with respect to his nature and origins. For man to deliver himself is tantamount to saying that man can deliver himself also from God, that he can become his own god and re-create himself after his desired pattern, and, thereby, declare not only his deliverance from sin and guilt, but also his deliverance from God. And the attempts of men to conquer death as well as to conquer sin by their own science and industry have a common impulse, their desire to conquer God and to replace Him with man.

The declaration of all Scripture is that atonement and justification are the sovereign acts of God through the work of Jesus Christ. Atonement therefore is essentially not a subjective experience but an objective fact. The primary point of reference in atonement is not the sinner's experience but God's order, God's self-propitiation. Christ pays the price to God as the representative of the sinner, so that the reconciliation and atonement are divinely initiated. Christ, by His incarnation as very man of very man, acts as man's representative in the transaction. The atonement of the elect is thus vicarious, in that it is not their work but God's work. Because man is totally a creature, he is totally passive in relationship to God; because he has been created lord over the earth, man can assume a secondary activity towards the earth. In Isaiah 52:13 - 53:12, as elsewhere, this doctrine of the atonement is clearly declared. According to the Westminster Confession of Faith,

> 1.   Those whom God effectually calleth, he also freely justi-
> fieth: not by infusing righteousness into them, but by pardoning
> their sins, and by accounting and accepting their persons as
> righteous; not for anything wrought in them, or done by them,
> but for Christ's sake alone; not by imputing faith itself, the act
> of believing, or any other evangelical obedience to them, as their
> righteousness; but by imputing the obedience and satisfaction of
> Christ unto them, they receiving and resting on him and his

righteousness by faith; which faith they have not of themselves, it is the gift of God (Rom. 8:30; Rom. 3:24; Rom. 4:5-8; II Cor. 5:19, 21; Titus 3:5,7; Eph. 1:7; Jer. 23:6; Rom: 3:22, 24, 25, 27, 28; I Cor. 1:30, 31; Rom. 5:17-19; Phil. 3:9; Acts 13:38, 39).

2. Faith, thus receiving and resting on Christ and his righteousness, is the alone instrument of justification; yet is it not alone in the person justified, but is ever accompanied with all other saving graces, and is not dead faith, but worketh by love (John 1:12; Rom. 3:28; Rom. 5:1; James 2:17, 22, 26; Gal. 5:6).[18]

Since the creative initiative is entirely of God, the only efficacious atonement is therefore entirely the act of God, and self-atonement is thus a nullity. Instead of voiding sin and guilt, self-atonement only serves to aggravate it. Bergler himself gives evidence of this from an anti-Christian perspective. For him there is no escaping masochistic activities; the Freudian concept of the infallible unconscious means that the unconscious forever demands its price for guilt. There is a new doctrine of total depravity, and this dark impulse from the unconscious always triumphs and is inescapable.[19]

The reality of man apart from Christ is guilt and masochism. And guilt and masochism involve an unshakeable inner slavery which governs the total life of the non-Christian. The politics of the anti-Christian will thus inescapably be *the politics of guilt*. In the politics of guilt, man is perpetually drained in his social energy and cultural activity by his over-riding sense of guilt and his masochistic activity. He will progressively demand of the state a redemptive role. What he cannot do personally, i.e., to save himself, he demands that the state do for him, so that the state, as man enlarged, becomes the human savior of man. The politics of guilt, therefore, is not directed, as the Christian politics of liberty, to the creation of godly justice and order, but to the creation of a redeeming order, a saving state. Guilt must be projected, therefore, on all those who oppose this new order and new age. And, because the salvation is mythical, and the enslavement real, the hatred of life and of innocence grows, and with it grows the urge to mass destruction. This urge to destroy demands

[18] *Westminster Confession of Faith*, Ch. XIII, 1, 2. Cf. Larger Catechism, Q70-71, Shorter Catechism, Q33.

[19] See Edmund Bergler, M.D.: *The Revolt of the Middle-Aged Man.* Second edition. New York: Grosset & Dunlap Universal Library (1954), 1957.

a levelling of all things, a democracy in misery, as the "rational" solution to man's problem. Because it refuses to recognize its suicidal course, and its hatred of life, this masochistic urge insists on a reversal of all norms. Its hatred is masked as love, and its slavery is declared to be liberty. The truth becomes a lie, and the lie becomes the new truth. The politics of guilt is a collective masochism whose conclusion is a self-crucifixion, a self-immolation, as the logical result of a driving will to death, an insistent inner assent to the principle that the wages of sin are indeed death even as the God liberty is denied (Rom. 6:23).

The only possible source of political liberty is on the premise of the atoning work of Jesus Christ. In ancient cultures, atonement was basic to citizenship, as Coulanges pointed out. The penalty for absence from the lustrations, except for men on military service, was loss of citizenship. "At Rome, it was necessary to have been present at the sacred ceremony of the lustration, in order to enjoy political rights. The man who had not taken part in this—that is to say, who had not joined in the common prayer and the sacrifice—lost his citizenship until the next lustration. If we wished to give an exact definition of a citizen, we should say that it was a man who had the religion of the city." [20] Citizenship rested on atonement, and, although this was a very fallacious concept of atonement, a form of self-atonement, it was at least a recognition that guilt is the destruction of society and has to be dealt with. In the modern state, in the name of democracy, there is the increasing pandering to guilt and to the hatred felt by the guilty for the innocent and for the successful. This then is the full triumph of the politics of guilt and its open enthronement. For the politics of guilt, the order of the day is mass destruction.

[20] Fustel de Coulanges: *The Ancient City*, p. 194. Garden City, New York: Doubleday Anchor Books.

2

SCAPEGOATS

Sentimental humanism asserts that man's basic need is *love*, more specifically, a passive need *to be loved*. Thus, man is seen as a passive creature whose basic problem is not a will to evil but an absence of love, so that a positive agency must be created to supply man's needs. The result is the totalitarian caretaker state. Man, being passive, needs an active agency in his life, and this agency the welfare state provides.

This perspective is clearly conducive to slavery, and it is moreover false, for man, having been created in the image of the *righteous* God, requires *justice* even more than *love*. The basic requirement of man's being is thus justice rather than love, and even the caretaker state masks its tyrannical love under the name of "social justice."

Masochism is a witness to man's need for justice. Masochism is a demand for justice, but it is also a substitution of a humanistic concept of justice for the biblical doctrine. Masochism insists that the requirements of justice must be satisfied, but it redefines justice in humanistic terms in the hopes that man can readily pay off the demands of justice and gain license to sin. The masochist gives witness to man's need for justice and justification, but, at the same time, he witnesses to man's sin in his attempt to escape justice and establish sin by redefining justice. The futility of his effort leads him only to redouble his efforts to make a sinful and counterfeit justice pass as payment for sin, so that his masochism increases.

The masochist is dominated by the unconscious drive to suicide; his masochism is a will to death, a recognition of the death sentence against himself for sin, even as it is an attempt to substitute overtly a lesser penalty. Freud saw the death instinct as basic to masochism.

Masochism for him was sadism turned back upon itself, and its origin is in guilt, not sex. He noted,

> The theory of psycho-analysis (a theory based upon observation) holds firmly to the view that the motive forces of repression must not be sexualized. Man's archaic inheritance forms the nucleus of the unconscious mind; and whatever part of that inheritance has to be left behind in the advance to later phases of development, because it is useless or incompatible with what is new and harmful to it, falls a victim to the process of repression.[1]

The more a civilization advances, the deeper will its sense of sin become, because the increase of prosperity and cultural advantages will only increase the masochistic desire to pay for progress, which the individuals unconsciously believe requires atonement before enjoyment. As a result, the very liberating forces of civilization themselves call into existence the forces of enslavement. The citizens of the civilization progressively demand political enslavement as their masochistic price for advancement. As a result, the most ruthless totalitarian enslavement is invited, and the culture uses its material liberation to forge a new slavery. The so-called "primitive" cultures are not free: they are tormented by fears, superstitions, and tabus born of a deep sense of sin. Their sexuality, so often seen as "free" and "uninhibited" by the modern liberal, is, whether in an orgy or in "normal" living, heavily surrounded by fears and often by severe restrictions. Karig's comments on Micronesia are of interest:

> The code governing sexual behavior is much more elaborate and severe in its restrictions than the celibacy-monogamy ideal of the Christian missionaries. On some islands the code of taboo is so complicated that the results approach race suicide.

> Periods of chastity are obligatory on men and women, the married and unmarried, for obscure reasons and in bewildering number. In parallel with the laws against remote consanguine matings, the average Micronesian leads a much more restricted sex life than the average American male. And the laws *are* obeyed!

[1] Sigmund Freud: "A Child Is Being Beaten, A Contribution to the Study of the Origin of Sexual Perversions" (1919), in *Collected Papers*, vol. II, p. 201; cf. 189f. Trans. by Joan Riviere. New York: Basic Books, 1959.

On Yap, for example, chastity is obligatory for a month before departing on a journey, and for a month after the return. Chastity is imposed on patient and practitioner during aboriginal medical-religious ceremonies, on pregnant women, on menstruating women, on men engaged in boatmaking and housebuilding, and while engaged in any constructive community labors. Indeed, at any given time, the greater proportion of male Yaplanders are living in a state of ritualistic celibacy. Men about to embark on any large group undertaking, such as a trading excursion or a community fishing expedition, live aloof from women during all the time the enterprise is being planned and executed.

An islander has to be crazy to dream of violating the code. Not only would he become an outcast if he could persuade or beguile some woman into being his partner in its violation, but the present and future effects of such a violation are believed terrible.[2]

It is true that in some cultures the ancient tabus are broken and disbelieved, but it is important to note that, in these broken cultures, whether on the Pacific islands or among American Indians, the consequence is a loss of ability to function, a necessity for increasing tutelage, and a regression towards an unhappy and superficial infantilism.

In the more advanced cultures, material liberation provokes the masochistic urge not only into political enslavement but into guilty sexuality. The ego demands increasing grounds and rationale for its suicidal drive, and then it rests content in a repressive political and moral bondage. Communism has used moral nihilism to prepare the way for passive political slavery: *guilty men are more docile slaves.* The Aztecs of Mexico ruled in terms of masochism, and the development of masochistic submission was basic to Aztec political enslavement. Prescott borrowed the language of poetry to describe the Aztec religious masochism, which he said resorted to cruel practices "In hopes to merit heaven by making earth a hell." [3] The Incas similarly ruled by the masochistic enslavement of the people. Although the Inca order was often a beneficent tyranny, it was

[2] Walter Karig: *The Fortunate Islands*, p. 135. New York: Rinehart, 1948.
[3] William H. Prescott: *History of the Conquest of Mexico and the Conquest of Peru*, p. 43. New York: The Modern Library.

nonetheless tyranny, a totalitarian state which brought order by
binding the conscience totally to the Inca. Baudin has observed that

> The Inca cannot be said to have given his people an ethical
> code. What he gave them was a penal law. He was concerned
> not with the individual conscience, but with a general system of
> legal regulations. And, of course, he himself was not obligated
> to conform to the laws he decreed, since he was, by virtue of
> his position, beyond good and evil.[4]

The roots of masochism are man's original sin, his desire to be as
God, knowing or determining good and evil for himself (Gen. 3:5).
Man's problem, then, is original sin, a God-centered problem, in that
it stems from man's rebellious relationship to God. Man, however,
insists on reducing the problem from *sin* to *guilt* and *shame*, from a
God-oriented meaning to a humanistic and social meaning. Wherever
theology shifts it attention from sin to "*guilt* and *estrangement*," as
in Berkouwer, the result is a man-centered and defective theology.[5]
Our purpose, then, is to analyze this false context in order to set
forth the God-centered meaning.

The reality of the human situation is man's sin, his rebellion against
God and his desire to be his own god, to establish as reality his own
existential knowledge. Because man is God's creature, his rebellion
against God is a warping of his own being; it creates a fearful inner
burden and tension. Man has different ways of expressing this inner
burden and tension, and cultures can be described in terms of their
manifestations of this inner war. Cultural anthropologists have classified various civilizations as *shame* cultures and *guilt* cultures.

In shame cultures, most commonly found in the Orient, man tries
to maintain himself in the face of his inner insecurity due to sin, by
a *surface* acceptance of himself and other men. *Face* becomes all-
important. The individual, in speaking of himself, demeans himself
as unworthy, a confession in which truth is by social convention ac-

[4] Louis Baudin: *A Socialist Empire, The Incas of Peru*, p. 40. Trans. by
Katherine Woods, edited by Arthur Goddard. New York: Van Nostrand,
1961. For a favorable view of the Incas, see Victor W. Von Hagen: *Realm
of the Incas*, New York: Mentor, 1957.

[5] See G. C. Berkouwer, "General and Special Divine Revelation," in Carl
F. H. Henry, editor: *Revelation and the Bible*, p. 23. Grand Rapids, Michigan:
Baker Book House, 1958.

cepted as modesty and humility. In speaking to and of others, and as others speak to him, social convention requires an effusive ascription of virtue, honor, and dignity to the other party. Thus, confession is made without confession, but as a social convention, and humility serves to further pride. The deep inner crisis caused by apostasy from God is covered by the accepted social lie, which ascribes honor and character to all men. *Face* is maintained, but it is precariously maintained. If the surface is cracked, and *face* is lost, i.e., if the lie is penetrated, exposed, or denounced, suicide becomes a psychological necessity. Among many Plains Indians of western America, *face* was extremely important. The United States in the twentieth century moved steadily from a guilt culture to a shame culture. The works of Vance Packard have given popular evidences of this shift, but, even more, *The Lonely Crowd*, by David Riesman, Nathan Glazer, and Reuel Denney, has carefully described it. In a *face* or *shame* culture, man becomes other-directed rather than inner-directed; the feelings of the group function as a god over the individual. There is also a shift from morality to morale.

In *guilt* cultures, the individual deals directly and personally with the inner warfare. Man, burdened with a sense of guilt and unable to enjoy life, confesses his sin, as does the man in a *shame* culture, but he pleads guilty to the lesser crime. With a fine sensitivity, he dredges up minor offenses to prove the refinement of his conscience in order to escape his capital offense against God. He may trouble himself over a stolen pencil while ignoring his open or veiled warfare against God. In the United States, as the nation has departed progressively from God, it has indulged progressively in a "debunking" of its history, in a general confession of many past faults, some often imagined. The hypocrisy of such confessions is striking: by confessing the "sins" of past generations, the present scholar or generation thereby implies its own superior virtues and its innocence of those sins. By the fact of such "debunking" or confession, it confesses also, very modestly, that wisdom is now born to us and is among us, so that confession again becomes a vehicle of pride.

The citizens of both *shame* and *guilt* cultures thus cannot escape masochistic activities. However, even in their self-punishment, they are hypocritical. The real guilt, they inwardly avow, is not theirs but God's, and, because they cannot strike sadistically at God, they find a substitute for God in the innocent. Cain was at war with God; he approached God on his own terms, without an atoning sacrifice and with only a peace-offering, i.e., peace as established on Cain's terms. When Cain was rejected, he expressed his hatred of God by killing his brother, Abel. There had been no conflict between Cain and Abel; Abel simply was God's substitute in Cain's sight by virtue of his innocence before and acceptance by God. Abel was thus Cain's *scapegoat.*

The only possible culture which autonomous man, man trying to live in independence from God, can create, is a guilt-ridden, shame-ridden culture driven by sado-masochistic urges. Such a culture lives its life under sentence of death; its way of life is an inner bondage which calls an outward slavery into being in the political and social orders. Jesus Christ, who declared that "I am the way, the truth and the life: no man cometh unto the Father, but by me" (John 14:6), affirmed himself thereby to be the only true source of culture. Orders established on any other foundation are apostate orders, ruled by "thieves" who destroy rather than establish man. "The thief cometh not, but for to steal, and to kill, and to destroy: I am come that they may have life, and they might have it more abundantly" (John 10:10). The purpose of John the Baptist's ministry was to declare the liberty from sin which was to come in the Messiah, "To give knowledge of salvation unto his people by the remission of their sins" (Luke 1:77; Mark 1:4). The purpose of Christ's coming was thus to end man's guilt and shame before God by reconciliation through His vicarious sacrifice. Such a restoration would make possible again man's creation mandate, to act as God's vice-gerent over the earth and to establish a godly culture. The call to the believer is to "enter thou into the joy of the lord" (Matt. 25:21, 23). The believer is a wedding guest (Rev. 19:6-9), and the keynote of a wedding is joy. A Christian culture has not yet been developed, because too often the clergy has worked, consciously or unconsciously, to emphasize guilt and shame before God rather than Christian grace, joy, and boldness in Jesus Christ. As a result, Christendom has seen only a partial deliverance from *guilt* and *shame* cultures and only a partial liberation of the Christian man.

The Old Testament, in Leviticus 16, set forth God's answer to man's sin, the Day of Atonement, Yom Kippur, the tenth day of the seventh month. This day gathered up and included all the sacrifices of the year. It preceded the Feast of Tabernacles, the feast of ingathering, because atonement precedes the joyful ingathering of the peoples, of all nations. The Day of Atonement was also the day of the proclamation of jubilee years, "proclaim liberty throughout all the land unto all the inhabitants thereof; it shall be a jubilee unto you" (Lev. 25:9, 10). The foundation of liberty, of the restoration of the land, the end of slavery, and the time of rest, is atonement. Ezekiel's temple (Ezek. 40-48) is a symbolic presentation of the Christian era; it has no Day of Atonement, which means that the great Atonement Day had come and gone in his vision. The high priest, on the Day of Atonement, was differently garbed, in white, to set forth the perfect purity and righteousness of Christ, whom he typified. Two goats were used, but the two were one offering. The first was sacrificed, and the second, sprinkled with its blood, was removed from the nation and set free. "All iniquities . . . all transgressions . . . all sins" (Lev. 16:21) were laid on this scapegoat and removed from the land and people, so that the burden of sin was no longer a part of the life of the people and of the land. The emphatic separation of the sin-bearer from the land and the people set forth their *utter freedom* from sin. This is to characterize godly culture: it is grounded firmly on the atonement, and it is freed basically or essentially from sin and the burden of sin. Its sanctification, its freedom, is not perfect in this life, but it is real. Liberty is the essence of sanctification and of the Christian life and culture.

Man cannot get rid of the burden of sin by himself. Man tries, *first*, either to pay for his sins himself by masochistic activity, a futile process, or *second*, to make others pay for them through sadistic activities. Both alternatives lead to sick lives and sick societies.

The biblical answer is that God removes the sin and its guilt and shame through the atonement of His only begotten Son, Jesus Christ, so that "There is therefore now no condemnation to them which are in Christ Jesus" (Rom. 8:1). What man cannot do, i.e., to cleanse himself of sin or to make atonement to God for sin, God does for man. Men, being wholly God's creation, cannot be active towards God; his relationship is derivative and passive. Man's will is not autonomous, nor is man creative in relationship to God. Hence, since God is God, the relationship between man and God is wholly a part of the eternal decree and wholly determined by the triune God.

The Day of Atonement set forth this divine initiative: it was a ceremony of God's appointing, governed by His word, and setting forth in typology the atoning work of the Messiah. Israel understood the meaning of the Day of Atonement: it signified salvation and liberation. As a result, the evening closed with a joyful feast, in token of the fact that man's liberty had been obtained by the atonement provided by God.[6] It was the day of supreme rejoicing, and, according to the Talmud,

> The daughters of Jerusalem came out and danced in the vineyards exclaiming at the same time, Young man, lift up thine eyes and see what thou choosest for thyself. Do not set thine eyes on beauty but set thine eyes on (good) family. Grace is deceitful, and beauty is in vain; but a woman that feareth the Lord, she shall be praised. And it further says, Give her of the fruit of her hands; and let her works praise her in the gates.[7]

The maidens also were clad in white garments provided for the occasion. Because the Day of Atonement was the day of liberation, it was an occasion for supreme joy. By contrast, the modern synagogue has made it a heavy and solemn day and removed the note of victory.[8] On the other hand, the apostolic note was sounded by Paul: "Rejoice in the Lord alway: and again I say, Rejoice" (Phil. 4:4). The gospel, the good news, is the remission of sins through the atoning sacrifice and saving power of Jesus Christ. The purpose of a true ministry must be the salvation of the sinner, his growth in

---

[6] A. Edersheim: *The Temple, Its Ministry and Services as they were at the time of Jesus Christ*, p. 236f. New York: Hodder and Stoughton.

[7] *The Babylonian Talmud*, Seder Mo'ed, vol. IV, Ta'anith 26b, p. 139. London: The Soncino Press (1938), 1961, 18 vol. edition

[8] Edersheim, *op. cit.*, p. 327.

sanctification, and the purging of his "conscience from dead works to serve the living God" (Heb. 9:14), i.e., his deliverance from self-righteousness and masochistic self-atonement into "a good conscience and . . . faith unfeigned" (I Tim. 1:5). The development of a good conscience and a Christian culture is thus an important aspect of the Christian life.

A contrary development is increasingly in evidence in the Western world, and especially in the United States, i.e., the development by systematic indoctrination of a *bad* conscience. The political cultivation of guilt is a central means to power, for guilty men are slaves; their conscience is in bondage, and hence they are easily made objects of control. Guilt is thus systematically taught for purposes of control. Several instances can be cited readily. For example, the white man is being systematically indoctrinated into believing that he is guilty of enslaving and abusing the Negro. Granted that some Negroes were mistreated as slaves, the fact still remains that nowhere in all history or in the world today has the Negro been better off. The life expectancy of the Negro increased when he was transported to America. He was *not* taken from freedom into slavery, but from a vicious slavery to degenerate chiefs to a generally benevolent slavery in the United States. There is not the slightest evidence that any American Negro had ever lived in a "free society" in Africa; even the idea did not exist in Africa. The move from Africa to America was a vast increase of freedom for the Negro, materially and spiritually as well as personally. The Negroes were sold from a harsh slavery into a milder one. Slavery was basic to the African way of life, to the point that slaves were the actual money of the African economy.[9] Elsewhere, gold and silver served as money; in Africa, it was slaves.

Another example of instructed guilt is with reference to the Jew. Systematic propaganda has taught the Christian that he has a "guilty past" with reference to the Jew. The reality is that the relationship has had all the diversity of tension and peace, good and evil, on both sides as exists between all conflicting groups, and very

[9] Captain Theodore Canot: *Adventures of an African Slaver*, p. 136. 1854. Malcolm Cowley, editor. Cleveland: World, 1942.

often the Jew has been the offended and also the offender. Very often too, because Christians, as witness Cromwell, have had erroneous views concerning biblical prophecy, they have assumed a respectful and reverent attitude towards the Jew. And, paradoxically, we are assured by the same theologians that the Jews are innocent of Christ's blood, even as Christians are declared guilty of the deaths of Jews who died centuries ago! Such teaching is simply the political cultivation of guilt. Christ came to free men from sin, guilt and shame, whereas the political theologians would bind men's consciences.

Again, Americans are repeatedly assured that American history is a long account of guilt, towards Indians, Negroes, minority groups, labor, Mexico, and, ultimately, all the world as well for refusing to enter the League of Nations. This is defective history and perverse politics. Its purpose is the cultivation of guilt in order to produce a submissive populace.

More basically, the subtle indoctrination of humanistic scholarship infers that the Christian, and, in America, the Protestant in particular, is guilty because he is a Christian. The inference is that the Christian has no right to his identity; he must recognize all others and their "rights," but he himself has none. The principles of the atheist must govern state and school; the wishes of all others have status before the law, and his have none.

A telling instance of the political cultivation of guilt was the assassination of President John F. Kennedy. The immediate use of it by officers of state, judges, and clergymen to assure American, and, in particular, conservative Americans, of their guilt was in proportion to their efforts to absolve the Communists of guilt, even though at least one Communist was involved in the murder of the President. This is the strategy of the politics of guilt, a strategy for the destruction of liberty and the enslavement of men. This strategy became routine with subsequent political assassinations.

Tragically, this politics of guilt is aided, not only by the apostate clergy of the left, but also by ostensibly conservative clergymen. Thus, the Rev. Donald Barnhouse, who passed for a conservative clergyman, speaking to a large congregation of Christians at a Mt. Hermon, California, conference, in a summer of the early 1950's, declared to them, "You're dung, nothing but dung." According to Scripture, these people were God's children by adoption in Jesus Christ. Barnhouse's preaching had as it goal, not a clear conscience before God in Christ, but a burdened conscience and a submissive man before priest and politician. But, by the atoning sacrifice of Jesus Christ, God's justice has been satisfied, the Christian man's record and conscience cleared, and man has been delivered into the politics and culture of Christian liberty. All who attempt to diminish that liberty or enslave the liberated conscience are either thieves and slavers, or in league with them. "Stand fast therefore in the liberty wherewith Christ hath made us free, and be not entangled again with the yoke of bondage" (Gal. 5:1).

3

THE RETURN OF SLAVERY

One of the most prevalent of errors is the tendency to regard slavery as basically an aspect of past history, surviving in the twentieth century only as a relic. But slavery, a major fact in all history, is not a finished fact. Slavery is a major fact of the human condition, a continuing factor, and an inescapable aspect of the present scene.

Three forms of slavery must be distinguished. But, before the forms of slavery can be analyzed, it is important to define first of all what slavery is. The common definition is that it is "the property of man in man." This definition, however, as John Murray has pointed out, is faulty; moreover, marriage and parenthood, as well as the powers of a state over its citizens, involve a property of man in man. But the definition is too broad, and evades the basic aspect of slavery, *labor*. According to Murray, "slavery is the property of man in the labour of another." Under certain conditions, such property in the labor of another is proper and legitimate. "Are we to say that it is improper for the creditor to have property in the debtor's labour until that debt is repaid?" Moreover,

> The property of some men in the labour of others and the property of institutions in the labour of those who are associated with them we cannot get rid of. The employer has property in the labour of his employees; the presence of contract does not eliminate this fact. Once the contract is entered into, the employee is *bound* to perform the labour as contracted. The state has property in the labour of the citizens. In this case it is not by contract; it is a necessity inherent in the institution. Sometimes large numbers of the citizenry are *compelled* for lengthy periods of time to render full-time service to the state under conditions far more stringent, and involving far more danger to life and property, than the conditions under which slaves

may be called upon to serve their masters. It is not necessary to multiply examples. Property in our labour on the part of others is a fact of our social structure. And we must not be naive enough to think that we can abstract our labour from our persons. If another has property in our labour there is an extent to which, or an aspect from which, this must be viewed as property in our persons. And we know quite well that this is no violation of our being, personality, right or privilege. It is a necessity of our nature and of the social organization of the human race. There is no need to think that the property of another in our labour or, to that extent, in the person of one involved in bond-service as such, is a violation of what is intrinsic to personality, and we are able to see the reserve of the New Testament as dictated by the principles of which the Scripture is the charter.[1]

In terms of this definition, let us examine the three forms of slavery, *first* of all, in the form of private ownership of slaves.

In the biblical form, slavery was rather a form of bond-service. The term "servant" or "slave" was used to describe anyone owing service to another, permanently or temporarily. Thus, David and Daniel described themselves as God's servants (Ps. 27:9; Dan. 9:17), and the virgin Mary described herself as "the handmaiden of the Lord (Luke 1:38). Biblical slavery was a form of feudal association and protection. The stealing of men for purposes of sale was strictly forbidden by law, so that what is popularly known as slavery was outlawed (Deut. 24:7), and Paul restated this condemnation and associated "men-stealers" with "whoremongers," homosexuals, liars, perjurers, and heretics (I Tim. 1:10). Unless the runaway were a thief, a slave could leave his master's home and could remain legally with anyone in whose home he took refuge (Deut. 23:15, 16). The slave had to be treated with respect and care (Lev. 25:39). The biblical principle, "The labourer is worthy of his reward" (I Tim. 5:18; Deut. 25:4; I Cor. 9:9; Lev. 19:13; Deut. 24:14f; Matt. 10:10; Luke 10:7), is not limited to free labor alone; it applies to all, slave or free.

A Hebrew became a slave on strictly regulated terms which re-

[1] John Murray: *Principles of Conduct, Aspects of Biblical Ethics*, pp. 97-99. Grand Rapids, Michigan: Eerdmans, 1957.

quired that a fellow believer treat him as a brother (Lev. 25:39-43, 47-55). A Hebrew became a slave, if, because he found it difficult to maintain himself as an independent citizen, he sold his labor to another (Lev. 25:39). He could become a slave also because of theft; the law required restitution, from double to fivefold, and if a thief could not meet these requirements, then he was sold for his theft (Ex. 22:3). He was thus a sold bond-servant until the restitution appointed by law was accomplished. Children assumed the condition of the parents, slave or free (Ex. 21:14). Hebrew slaves were released each sabbatical year, or every seventh year (Ex. 21:2; Deut. 15:12), and the servant had to be given some compensation to enable him to begin his liberty with some assets (Deut. 15:13, 18). Failure to observe the law of the sexennial term was a severe offense in God's sight (Jer. 34:13-17). If the Hebrew servant had no desire to be released and regarded the master's house as his sanctuary, his ear was bored in token of this subjection and he remained a slave or bond-servant (Ex. 21:6; Deut. 15:17). At the jubilee, all slaves, Hebrew and otherwise, were freed, including those with bored ears, apparently (Lev. 25:10). Non-Hebrew slaves could recover their freedom at any time, as could Hebrew slaves, on redemption by money, or if their master injured them, even if only a tooth were knocked out by a blow (Ex. 21:6; Lev. 19:20). The murder of any man, slave or free, was a serious offense (Lev. 24: 17, 29; Num. 35:31-32). The biblical law, thus, was such that it is understandable why Lindsay prefers to call it bond-service rather than slavery.[2]

From the biblical perspective, therefore, slavery is not itself intrinsically evil; the failure to live as free men, the dependency or incompetence of a slave mind is, however, regarded as an inferior way. The believer cannot revolt against his situation, but he cannot become a slave in good conscience, voluntarily, for *any form* of slavery is an infringement of Christ's total rights over him (I Cor. 7:22, 23).

[2] William Lindsay, "Slave, Slavery," Patrick Fairbairn, editor: *Fairbairn's Imperial Standard Bible Encyclopedia*, vol. 6, pp. 190-193. 1891. Grand Rapids, Michigan: Zondervan, 1957.

The private ownership of slave labor in the American South has been the subject of extensive distortion. The Negroes were slaves to their tribal heads in Africa, or prisoner-slaves of other tribes. The monetary unit in black Africa was man, the slave. The Negro moved from an especially harsh slavery, which included cannibalism, to a milder form. Much is said about the horrors of the slave ships, many of which were very bad, but it is important to remember that slaves were valuable cargo and hence property normally handled with consideration. A Canadian legislative commission member in 1847 reported that the Irish immigrants were being transported on ships loaded with twice as many passengers as the ship should hold, huddled down between decks, with too little food and water, and in conditions "as bad as the slave trade." [3] The condition of the Irish immigrants on arrival was far worse than that of slaves: they had no master to feed and clothe them or to provide shelter. The Irish moved from semi-slavery in Ireland to freedom in America only a few years before the Negro gained emancipation. After a century and a quarter, or less, the Irish are a leading power in the United States, and the Negroes remain on the lowest strata. The basic difference between the Irish and the Negro has not been color: it has been character. The Negroes demand more aid, i.e., more slavery and slave-care, and dwell on their sufferings.[4] The Irish have instead looked to the present and future and helped shape America. It is a significant difference that cannot be explained altogether by color or environment. The Chinese also came to the United States under very difficult circumstances and similarly overcame them.

It is important to note also that Southern defenders of slavery prior to the Civil War were also party to the hope of resettlement. In other words, they defended the legitimacy of American slavery while hoping to terminate it with emancipation and resettlement. Many such societies existed in the South. The title of one book of the period is revealing: *Bible Defense of Slavery; or the Origin,*

[3] Cecil Woodham-Smith: *The Great Hunger, Ireland 1845-1849,* p. 228. New York: Harper and Row, 1962.
[4] "Next: A 'Marshall Plan' for Negroes?" *U.S. News & World Report,* vol. LX, no. 10, March 7, 1966, p. 46f.

History, and Fortunes of the Negro Race, by Josiah Priest, *to which is added a Plan of National Colonization, adequate to the entire removal of the free Blacks and all that may hereafter become free,* by Rev. W. S. Brown, 1853. Alexander H. Stephens, vice-president of the Confederacy, observed that he had to work to support his slaves, some of whom were in effect his pensioners and charity cases.[5]

A picture of private slavery at its worst is usually a description of the African and Moslem worlds. The abuses of these areas are very real.[6] On the other hand, not a few masters are ruled by their slaves even in these cultures. Thus Fortie observed,

> The mild old Arabs of East Africa were ruled by their slaves. They accepted the scoldings and tantrums of their Bantu women like visitations from Allah. Those women were often the mothers of their children. Considered mere plowed fields yielding a full-blooded progeny, they were lovable human beings possessing and awakening tender feelings, so that what was an expedient fiction gave way in practice to the realities of a long life in common.[7]

The passing traveler or scholar sees the obvious evils; the man who remains sees the human factors which alter every relationship.

The private ownership of slave labor is less common and has usually been the minor aspect of human slavery. In the United States, private ownership was abolished by the Thirteenth Amendment, 1865, which stated, in Section 1, "Neither slavery nor involuntary

[5] See Myrta Lockett Avary, editor: *Recollections of Alexander H. Stephens, His Diary Kept When a Prisoner at Fort Warren, Boston Harbour, 1865,* p. 226f. New York: Doubleday, Page, 1910.

[6] See Sean O'Callaghan: *The Slave Trade Today,* New York: Crown, 1961; Robin Maugham: *The Slaves of Timbuktu,* New York: Harper, 1961. It can be added, however, that the Negro has always been in fact treated most brutally by other Negroes, and this is as true as ever today. Thus, "at the Casablanca conference of African heads of state in January, 1961, a delegate from the Republic of Mali asked the Libyan representative for the extradition of a tribal chief from Mali who was accused of leading his whole tribe on a 'pilgrimage,' selling it in the 'Holy Land,' and then retiring to Libya to live peacefully on the money he had made"; Youssef El Masry: *Daughters of Sin,* p. 127. New York: Macfadden, 1963. For slavery in Africa, see Gardiner G. Hubbard, "Africa, Its Past and Future," *The National Geographic Magazine,* vol. I, no. 2, 1889, pp. 99-124, a kindly report.

[7] Marius Fortie: *Black and Beautiful, A Life in Safari Land,* p. 72. Indianapolis: Bobbs-Merrill, 1938.

servitude, except as a punishment for crime wherof the party shall have been duly convicted, shall exist within the United States, or any place subject to their jurisdiction." By this law, private ownership of slaves was abolished, and by the Sixteenth Amendment (1913), the Federal Reserve Act, and by Supreme Court interpretations, slavery was made a state monopoly.[8]

This is the *second* form of slavery, state ownership, which is far more prevalent today, and in every era of history than the first. The "glories" of the ancient world were the products of state slave labor. Today, the communist countries make all citizens slaves. Since slavery is property in the labor of men, wherever that property in labor becomes the determinative and necessary force in the lives of a people, you have slavery. In virtually all the world today, the citizenry is moving into slavery to the state. The obligations of citizenship are being replaced by the obligations of slavery. Since involuntary servitude is defined by the Constitution as equivalent to slavery, every employer who is compelled to keep books and withhold taxes for the Federal Government is thus required to perform involuntary servitude or slave labor.

The enslaving state speaks much of the privileges of being a "free nation." The African states formed in the 1950's and 1960's were freed from colonialism, but, although they became technically free nations, they ceased to be free peoples: their citizenry became slaves of the state.

The purpose of the U. S. Constitution was to confirm the freedom of the people by binding the new federal government by the chains of the Constitution. The federal government was to be chained so that the people might be free. Today, it is the people who are progressively enslaved.

The *third* basic form of slavery is spiritual slavery, slavery to sin and to Satan. Satan has a property in the labor of the sinner: it is

[8] Liberal scholarship insists on seeing only private ownership of slaves as slavery. From this perspective, the state then becomes the savior. For liberal analyses, see David Brion Davis: *The Problem of Slavery in Western Culture*, Ithaca, New York: Cornell University Press, 1966; and Barnett Hollander: *Slavery in America, Its Legal History*, London: Bowes & Bowes, 1962. Both are able studies but with a simplistic view of slavery.

productive for him and serves him. The ground of liberty is Jesus Christ, who declared, "If ye continue in my word, then are ye my disciples indeed; and ye shall know the truth, and the truth shall make you free" (John 8:31, 32). The roots of slavery are spiritual: "Whosoever committeth sin is the servant of sin" (John 8:34). Such men are inwardly slaves, slaves to sin. A true slave always seeks a master and the security of a master. The slave mind wants security, a trouble-free, cradle-to-grave or womb-to-tomb security, and it demands a master to provide it. After the Civil War and emancipation many Negroes continued to demand that their former masters continue their care of them. One Southern family moved to New Jersey, only to be followed there by their former slaves. Until 1915, when death and the departure of sons broke up that New Jersey family, former slaves and their children and grandchildren continued to depend on that family and to return to them when ill or unemployed. They needed a master. Today, millions of Negroes, joined by millions of slave whites, are demanding that the federal government become their slave-master and provide them with security and care. Slavery is a welfare economy; private ownership is a privately maintained welfare economy, and it is not economically a sound unit of operation. Under state ownership, slavery, a social security structure, is a welfare economy which lacks the necessity for successful operation which the private owner must maintain. The private owner must make a profit somewhere; Alexander H. Stephens made it in law and supported his slaves thereby. The slave-owning state survives instead by progressive confiscation until the nation is destroyed.

Slave minds are not only sinning minds, they are guilty ones as well, guilt-ridden, shame-ridden and hence hungry for refuge and security. The politics of guilt cultivates the slave mind in order to enslave men, and to have the people themselves demand an end to liberty. *Slaves, true slaves, want to be rescued from freedom; their greatest fear is liberty.* Freedom imposes an impossible burden upon them. Lacking the inner peace of a good conscience, they seek instead the sickly peace of acceptance of and co-existence with every kind of condition and evil.

The beginning of true liberty is Jesus Christ, who delivers men from the power of sin and death and from the burden of guilt and shame, so that men have a good conscience before God and an independence in relationship to men. "If the Son therefore shall make you free, ye shall be free indeed" (John 8:36).

The deliverance and salvation of Jesus Christ is from sin and death. The salvation of Caesar is from liberty. The privilege of life in Christ is liberty; the privilege of life under Caesar is security. The security of the Christian is in Christ and in liberty under God's law. The security of the slave is in the state and in slavery. But the slave-order is not secure, nor is it permanent, as "the servant abideth not in the house for ever"; his security ends; "but the Son abideth ever," and those who are members of Him have His eternal security (John 8:35).

Basic to the Scriptures is the repeated declaration of God's absolute ownership over the world, over man, and over man's labor: "The earth is the LORD's, and the fulness thereof; the world, and they that dwell therein" (Ps. 24:1). The believer cannot become a slave of men, because he is God's property, and this is his liberty and life. He must not revolt, if he is in bondage at the time of his salvation, but he should seek freedom legitimately (I Cor. 7:21-22). But he cannot voluntarily become a slave: "Ye are bought with a price; be not ye the servants of men" (I Cor. 7:23). The Christian, having been bought at the price of the atoning blood of Jesus Christ, cannot allow sin, man, the state, or the church to own him or possess him. The Christian alone can be a true libertarian, and he is under a religious obligation to be one. Slavery is for him a legitimate way of life for an unbeliever: it is the logical conclusion of unbelief and of slavery to sin. But the life of the Christian must reflect here and now, in his every act and institution, "the glorious liberty of the children of God" (Rom. 8:21).

Slavery remains, however, a legitimate way of life, but a lower way of life. Slavery offers certain penalties as well as certain advantages. Objectively, the penalty is the surrender of liberty. Subjectively, the slave does not see the surrender of freedom as a penalty, since he desires escape from freedom. Even as a timid and fearful child dreads the dark, so does the slave mind fear liberty: it is full of the terrors of the unknown. As a result, the slave mind clings to statist or state slavery, cradle-to-grave welfare care, as a fearful child clings to his mother. The advantage of slavery is precisely this, security in the master or in the state. Socialism is thus a slave state, created by the demands of slaves for a master. The slave has the mentality of Phariseeism, he wants to live by sight, by works, manifest and visible works which will assure him of salvation. The slave saves himself by creating a slave state which offers visible assurance of womb-to-tomb salvation from the perils of manhood and liberty.

Liberty also offers penalties and advantages. The central and essential penalty of liberty is insecurity and the problems thereof. The free man lives in a world of free enterprise, of trial and error, profit and loss, success and failure. He must be prepared to take the consequences of failure as well as the prosperity of success. His security is not in the visible tokens of a guardian state or master but in the law order of the invisible and triune God. Thus, the free man must walk by faith, in the confidence that Proverbs and all of Scripture are true, that the law order of God vindicates those who walk by faith, "as seeing him who is invisible" (Heb. 11:27), who, believing that God is, "and that he is a rewarder to them that diligently seek him" (Heb. 11:6), walk in faith, wisdom, prudence, and responsibility. It is not easy to walk by faith, and free enterprise does not long endure apart from a foundation of faith. Then the business man, worker, and farmer seek statist intervention; they seek the privileges of liberty with the securities of slavery, and the consequence is socialism and slavery. The penalty of liberty is the necessity of walking by faith, but it is also a privilege. Ultimately, our faith must be in Christ or in Caesar, and it is better by far to walk by faith in Christ than to walk by sight under Caesar.

The advantage of freedom is freedom itself, the liberty of responsibility and manhood, and the security of liberty. Men will either be in service to God, or they will be in service to men, and service to God is liberty from man and the fear of man.

It is necessary that every generation be reminded of its choice:

slave or free? This is a moral choice. A man must choose between the security of slavery and the security of liberty. Slavery is a way of life: if men prefer it, let them be honest and live in terms of their choice. Liberty too is a way of life, and men who desire it must be prepared to assume its responsibilities and penalties as well as its privileges. Men cannot receive welfare aid, go through bankruptcy, or be found guilty of criminal activity, and legitimately and morally claim the privileges of citizenship and the right to participate in civil government. Such men may well be liked by many; they may be sometimes kindly men, well-meaning failures, and such men must be treated with all godly grace and charity, but they cannot morally claim the privileges of freedom. Even a good slave is still a slave.

And, for the Christian, the commandment is plain-spoken: "Stand fast therefore in the liberty wherewith Christ hath made us free, and and be not entangled again with the yoke of bondage" (Gal. 5:1). Every encroachment on liberty either by slaves or by the state must be resisted, and every personal temptation to accept the security of slavery must be seen for what it is, sin.

4

HELL AND POLITICS

Humanism in the twentieth century has progressively added a new dimension to the experience of modern Western man: terror. The progressive breakdown of law and order, and the rise of scientific weapons, steadily eroded the briefly won liberty of man from terror. A dramatic instance of the threat man faced was the atom and hydrogen bombs. One periodical observed,

> In theory, the 100-megaton bomb is a staggering conception. It is a "dirtied-up" bomb, its hydrogen core surrounded by a jacket of natural uranium to increase deliberately the amount of fallout. The chilling equations of nuclear physics can be applied to calculate its destructive force. It would dig a crater 9 miles across and knock down a brick house 19 miles from ground zero. Third-degree burns would be produced on all unprotected people within a radius of 50 miles. Grass, trees, and frame houses would be ignited 60 miles away. The fallout would persist for years over the Northern Hemisphere. . . .
>
> . . . The 2- to 5-megaton ICBM warheads now in the stockpiles of both the U. S. and the Soviet Union are already citybusters. With traditional military conservatism, both sides have adopted the "overkill" philosophy: bomb material has been produced to build an estimated 80,000 weapons (50,000 stockpiled in the U. S.; 30,000 in Russia), enough, one scientist has grimly observed, to take off the top inch of soil in both countries.[1]

Since then, General Rothschild's analysis of *Tomorrow's Weapons* has added a word on developments in other directions.

Increasingly, the mood of humanistic man has become one of increasing pessimism, anxiety, and despair. It is significant that

[1] *Newsweek*, September 11, 1961, p. 28.

Priestley cites, as a "denial" of despair, the perspective of Thomas Wolfe, the novelist,

> . . . as we may discover from his last letter to "Fox" in *You Can't Go Home Again;* this in its denial of pessimistic and fatalistic conservatism says something infinitely worth saying, once and for all: "Man was born to live, to suffer, and to die, and what befalls him is a tragic lot. There is no denying this in the final end. *But we must, dear Fox, deny it all along the way.*" [2]

That such a sentence should be seen as a triumphant one indicates the extent to which hell has become a dimension of man's life.

But, before examining hell as a dimension of man's existence, it is necessary to define hell.

The New Testament uses two words which are translated as *hell.* The first is *Hades, Sheol* in the Old Testament, the place of the departed spirits. It refers, therefore, to both heaven and hell. The sentence in the Apostles' Creed, "He descended into Hell," refers to Hades, the world of the departed spirits. Christ, in Luke 23:43, declared, "Today shalt thou be with me in paradise," a statement from the cross, so that paradise was included in the term "Hades" in apostolic usage.

The second word for *hell* is *Gehenna* or *Hinnom,* a place in Old Testament times for human sacrifice, of children in particular. It became in time the city dump for Jerusalem, a place of trash heaps and perpetual fire. The imagery of fire (Matt. 5:22; 18:19; Mark 9:43, 48) is coupled with references to the gnawing of worms, both symbols being drawn from the actual Gehenna. Both are emblems, symbols, of hell, even as thrones and crowns are images setting forth the triumphant life of the Christian. The correct meaning of the popularly used form of "hell" is the second. And the origin of the term *Gehenna* gives us an idea of what hell is like.

First of all, hell is the place of wasted lives; it is the dump-heap of the universe, a place therefore fittingly described as an area of corruption and burning. Hell is thus both a condition and a place.

[2] J. B. Priestley: *Literature and Western Man,* p. 439. New York: Harper, 1960.

Second, hell is a separation from God; it is the habitation of those men who abandon God. C. S. Lewis observed that heaven is the habitation of those who say to God, "Thy will be done," whereas hell is the habitation of those to whom God says, "Thy will be done."

Third, hell is negation of meaning and relationship. It is the conclusion of the assertion of autonomy. Man, asserting his autonomy from God, insisting on a world of brute factuality, and affirming a world without causality apart from his own will, lives in hell in terms of the full logic of his faith. In hell, all is chaos, waste, and ruin; all things are unrelated and beyond communication. There is no community in hell. It is the dump-heap and waste-pile of the universe. Nothing has any true relationship to anything else. Man, having declared himself to be his own god, lives in hell in terms of the total self-sufficiency and aseity his claim asserts. The insanity of sin is this isolation into the self which reaches its total stage in hell, where no life has any meaningful relationship to anyone or anything else, and where man lives in the eternal fire and corruption of self-exaltation and self-pity. Many people live today in the suburbs of hell. They avoid all meaningful relationships with other people, with the church, or with anything requiring something of them, lest they get "involved." One woman expressed her faith thus: an orchid, once bruised, never heals; the true way of life is to regard your heart as an orchid by allowing nothing to affect it or to hurt it, and thus to live without hurt or bruise and enjoy life to the last. But to abandon God is to abandon *all* meaning in every realm, and in every relationship, so that it means abandoning eventually family, nature, friendships, love, and life, for God, having created all things, cannot be forsaken without forsaking all things. In the words of Francis Thompson, in *The Hound of Heaven*, "All things betray thee, who betrayest Me." It is said of one famous actress that she admitted playing the role of Ophelia in *Hamlet* a hundred times before she even knew how the play ended. She was not interested in any part but her own and unconcerned with what transpired on the stage after she left. Such self-absorption is quite clearly a prelude to hell.

Hell is thus the logical conclusion of an assertion of autonomy from God and a belief in brute factuality, a universe of unrelated and meaningless facts. Hell is the logical conclusion of every denial of God and His eternal decree. For a man to deny God and to assert that the universe is one of brute factuality, of meaningless data, is to live ultimately in total meaninglessness and in terms of the only will or decree which exists for autonomous man, his own will. The resultant total isolation is hell, because man, as a creature, cannot be autonomous. The essence of his existence is his total creation by and dependence upon the triune God; denial of this dependence reduces the rebellious creature to a position of total frustration, total impotence, and total irrelevancy, and this is hell, both a condition and a place.

Hell is thus simply the end result of existentialism. Existentialism denies all meaning save that which is derived from the biology of the individual. It emphatically denies God, and it wages war on religious purpose and meaning to assert the totally existentialist dimension. Existentialism not only severs the tie between man and God but also the tie between man and man, in that it reduces all relationships to the level of feeling, existentialist feeling, and nothing more. The existentialist idea of self-realization is essentially the condition of hell. In the United States, existentialism is more commonly called Pragmatism, and its main proponents have been Charles Peirce, William James, F. C. S. Schiller, and John Dewey.

Fourth, hell witnesses to the fact that there is a fundamental difference between right and wrong. As Emory Storrs once said, "When hell drops out of religion, justice drops out of politics." [3] The denial of hell means the triumph of evil; it means that the claim of evil to be autonomous and independent of God and His judgment is upheld. Hell is a witness to the fact that a God of justice is on the throne of the universe. When people insist that they cannot believe in hell they are saying that they refuse to believe that justice has any right to exist. The denial of hell means that justice has been replaced by the total tolerance of evil, and this tolerance of evil is disguised as love. This doctrine of love involves a hatred of God and justice and an overt or covert love of evil. Ronald Brown has commented,

[3] Cited by Harry Buis: *The Doctrine of Eternal Punishment*, p. 122. Philadelphia: Presbyterian and Reformed Publishing Company, 1957.

> Those who shy away from the doctrine of eternal retribution
> will inevitably compromise the doctrine of God.
>
> All such modifications of Christian doctrine, based upon hesi-
> tancy concerning the doctrine of hell, have their reflection in
> the realm of practical Christian living. Such practical positions
> as pacifism and opposition to capital punishment are rooted in
> a denial of God's retributive justice.[4]

To deny hell is to insist, at the very least, on an ultimate dualism.
It is an assertion of the validity of *coexistence*. Since there is no
ultimate truth, varying systems have an equal right to existence, or,
similarly, since all systems are equally true and equally ultimate, they
have an equal right to existence. This means either an ultimate
dualism at the very least, or polytheism. All gods, all faiths, all ways,
are equally true and hence equally ultimate. To deny the doctrine
of hell is to restore polytheism to the world, or else it is to destroy
good and enthrone evil, the monism of evil. Modern anti-Christianity
thus moves steadily in terms of its hostility to the doctrine of hell,
and its answers waver between polytheism on the one hand, and the
monism of evil, the triumph of evil, on the other.

The "hades" of antiquity was a polytheistic doctrine. Life was
divided polytheistically into various domains. Hades belonged to
Pluto; it was under a different government than Greece or Rome,
and the law of no god was total and universal. The biblical doctrine
of hell rests on Christian theism, on the triune God and His eternal
decree. It has reference to salvation and the universal authority and
jurisdiction of God. Hell and salvation are related doctrines in the
Christian faith. If there be no hell, then there is no damnation and
there is no salvation; there is nothing to be saved from, and nothing
to be saved for. All life is then equally valid and equally moral. The
world can be destroyed by man, but there is no ultimate law to
declare this to be evil. But, because there is a hell, because the ultimate justice of God stands, man can never destroy this world or
turn it into a hell. God created the world *good*; He is redeeming it
and will recreate it. The government is in God's hands, not man's.

God's redemption involves the restoration of all things to their

---

[4] Ronald Brown, "Why Preach on Hell?" in *Torch and Trumpet*, vol. XVI,
no. 3, March 1966, p. 19.

true relationship to Him as Creator and Redeemer. The source of all things is God's eternal decree, and all things have their total and exclusive meaning in God. Heaven is that place and condition where man is totally under God, totally related to God's purposes and law, and where man finds his total meaning in and under God. Hell is that place and condition where man lives in total self-meaning, in terms of a universe of brute factuality and autonomy, and where man finds his total meaning, or total negation of meaning in his own existence, existentially.

The purpose of the politics of guilt is to enslave man. Its strategy involves the destruction of meaning. First of all, this requires an assault on religion, on biblical Christianity, in order to destroy the mainspring of meaning, faith in the triune God. It involves further an attack on the church, family, private and Christian schools, private associations, and every independent sphere, lest any independent area survive, since the purpose is to permit only one sphere to exist, the total state. In the U.S.S.R., the family exists only as a unit of the state. Charitable activities of any form for religious or other groups are "strictly prohibited." [5] Christian faith binds men to God and to one another under God, and acts of charity bind man to man. To forbid charity is to declare that men cannot have any non-statist ties. Statist welfare is designed in large measure to destroy the non-statist world of meaning and relationship. One of the most striking aspects of life in the U.S.S.R., according to visitors, is the lack of conversation on the streets. The streets are crowded with silent people because communication does not exist, and the freedom and trust which make possible meaningful communication are absent. Wherever the state works to destroy every independent sphere, it works to destroy the meaning and communication which are essential to life and to supplant it with a statist order.

Man is shattered and destroyed by meaningless living and meaningless work. The high rate of suicide among existentialists is not accidental. A world without meaning has a shattering effect on man. Convicts may grumble at hard labor, but meaningful hard

[5] St. Mary's School of Religion for Adults: *The Church and State Under Communism*, p. 14. Port Richmond, Staten Island, N. Y., 1964.

labor still gives meaning to their life. Meaningless work is shattering. Dostoyevsky, in *The House of the Dead*, describes the devastating effect on men of meaningless work. To shift boulders back and forth from one pile to another, without any purpose, has a deadly effect on man, in that it reduces not only his labor but his life to a senseless, purposeless level.

The purpose of the total state is to destroy meaningful activity on any historic foundation, to destroy all the old meanings of faith, in order to establish a meaningless world. In that meaningless world, the new meaning of the "new age" will be introduced, the purposes of the total state. By destroying meaning in every other area, the state declares that all else save the state is hell. The state then declares itself to be the new god, with a new world of meaning, and it offers life within the state as heaven.

But God's reality remains, and the total state is simply a precinct of hell, and it shall be judged, "seeing it is a righteous thing with God to recompense tribulation to them that trouble you. . . . In flaming fire taking vengeance on them that know not God, and that obey not the gospel of our our Lord Jesus Christ: Who shall be punished with everlasting destruction from the presence of the Lord, and from the glory of his power" (II Thess. 1:6, 8, 9). God's purpose is to redeem the earth, not to surrender it to the powers of darkness. Therefore, "the meek shall inherit the earth; and shall delight themselves in the abundance of peace" (Ps. 37:11).

5

BLOODGUILTINESS

Although the word "bloodguiltiness" appears only once in Scripture (Ps. 51:14), the concept itself is basic and is present throughout the Bible. Since bloodguiltiness is so basic to biblical thought, it is important that the idea be briefly analyzed in order to grasp its significance.

The first major instance (after Gen. 4:10, 11) is in Genesis 9:1-7, in which Noah is given permission to eat animals or flesh, but not the blood thereof; further, the law against murder is spelled out:

> And surely your blood of your lives will I require; at the hand of every beast will I require it, and at the hand of man; at the hand of every man's brother will I require the life of man. Whoso sheddeth man's blood, by man shall his blood be shed: for in the image of God made he man (Gen. 9:5, 6).

First, this passage asserts that the bloodguiltiness of murder requires capital punishment, both of animals killing men (Ex. 21:28, 29) as well as of men. Second, the reference to "brother" is "the equivalent of the reciprocal pronoun 'from one another,' " [1] so that all men are involved in the guilt if they neglect to punish the murderer within their country. Third, although the law is established by God, man, through civil government, must shed man's blood, must enforce God's law.

In Leviticus 17:1-7, unless every animal killed for meat is brought before the Lord, to the sanctuary, "blood shall be imputed to that man; he hath shed blood: and that man shall be cut off from among his people," i.e., he shall be excommunicated. Prior to the entry into Canaan, the necessity for the trip to the tabernacle was dropped;

[1] H. C. Leupold: *Exposition of Genesis*, p. 333. Columbus, Ohio: Wartburg Press, 1942.

the slain animals could be offered to the Lord in the field (Deut. 12:20-25). In these requirements it becomes clear that even the taking of animal life apart from God's order and without the cover of His atonement incurs bloodguiltiness.

One of the central texts on bloodguiltiness is Ezekiel 22; in the first sixteen verses, an arraignment of "the bloody city," i.e., the bloodguilty city, the word blood occurs seven times. It is important to cite Ezekiel's charges in chapter 22 in order to see what bloodguiltiness involved. The offenses are plainly stated:

1. "The first is the loss of a true conception of God." Idolatry and "uncleanness" characterize the nation in her apostasy (22:3).
2. Men's lives have been lawlessly taken (22:3, 4, 5).
3. The authority of parents was lightly regarded; widows and orphans were exploited, as were foreigners (22:7).
4. "Holy things" and the sabbath were profaned (22:8).
5. Perjured testimony prevailed even in capital criminal cases (22:9).
6. Fertility cult sexual practices were tolerated (22:9).
7. The concubines of a father were taken by his heirs, his sons, and sexual intercourse during menstruation was practiced (22: 10). Adultery and incest were practiced in open contempt of God's law (22:11).
8. Judges took bribes; men exacted "usury and interest" of their neighbors or fellow believers, and were guilty of extortion (22:12).
9. The priests violated God's law casually (22:26).
10. The leaders or princes of the people were like wolves rather than leaders of the people (22:27).
11. The prophets or preachers misrepresented the word of God, ascribing to God a word He had not spoken (22:28).
12. In the words of Skinner:

> Now the worst thing about Jerusalem was that she lacked this indispensable condition of recovery. No voice was raised on the side of righteousness, no man dared to stem the tide of wickedness that swept through her streets. Not merely that she harboured within her walls men guilty of incest and

robbery and murder, but that her leading classes were demoralised, that public spirit had decayed among her citizens, marked her as incapable of reformation. She was "a land not watered," "and not rained upon in a day of indignation" (ver. 24); the springs of her civic virtue were dried up, and a blight spread through all sections of her population.[2]

13. All this, moreover, was done "in the name of the Lord." "The form of idolatry to which Israel was most prone was the reducing of Jehovah to the level of a nature god."[3] Their idolatry was practiced in the name of God.

By the broadness of this indictment against "the bloody city," it becomes apparent what bloodguiltiness involves. It clearly deals with murder but much more than murder. Any and every control of life, whether taking or sparing life, and any and every aspect of life lived apart from the law of God incurs bloodguiltiness. Thus, secularism is bloodguiltiness, in that it asserts that vast areas of life, if not all, whether in the state, school, or vocation, can be lived apart from the law of God. *All life apart from the law of God, and the cover of His atonement, is bloodguiltiness.* Life can neither be spared nor taken apart from God's law. Again, life can be neither lived nor forsaken apart from God's law. Moreover, bloodguiltiness, a chronic condition of the modern world, calls for either judgment or atonement.

The significance of *blood* is made clear in Leviticus 17:11; "The life of the flesh is in the blood: and I have given it to you upon the altar to make an atonement for your souls: for it is the blood that maketh an atonement for the soul." Anything which mars the relationship of man to God affects man's life, and either blood atonement is offered in Christ, or bloodguiltiness is incurred. Any attempt on the part of man or of any state to establish life on man's terms is thus guilty of blood, guilty unto death.

To an age which is accustomed to secularism, and to whom God is only a word, the declaration of this biblical premise seems ridiculous and remote from reality. The irony of the situation is that the

[2] John Skinner: *The Book of Ezekiel*, p. 202f. New York: G. H. Doran, n.d.
[3] H. L. Ellison: *Ezekiel: The Man and His Message*, p. 88. Grand Rapids, Michigan: Eerdmans, 1956.

proud secularists are caught in the inexorable judgment of God on their secularism, but, in their blindness, they simply extend their planning a step further to encompass every new disaster with another opiate of planning.

The essence of planning is this attempt to be as God, to replace God and His predestination with man and his predestination. Under the opiate of planning, the dream of reason aspires to circumscribe every man and every eventuality within the omnipotent arms of the Great Society, the Kingdom of Man. The Plan is a net to ensnare God but which instead ensnares man. Its purpose is to bind the creation and its Creator within the decree of the City of Man, to make man supreme, but the only thing controlled is man: God remains sovereign. The politics of bloodguiltiness is thus statism. Since man cannot govern heaven, and since man can only govern man by compulsion, not by creation, regeneration, and inner law, man, when he seeks to be as God, must create a totalitarian state in order to rule. Man's realm is on earth, and, since every man's heart is alien ground to every other man, he must rule by force in order to gain total dominion. God's realm and sovereignty is universal as Creator. He is on home ground everywhere in the universe, as much in command in the heart of every man as in heaven. For God, there is no alien ground, and hence no compulsion: He simply exercises His will over His own domain and creation in every crevice of the universe, and in every man's heart. Wherever the state moves beyond its God-appointed grounds, it is on alien ground, as indeed all men and institutions are wherever and whenever they transgress their appointed bounds. For God, who made all men and nations, "hath determined the times before appointed, and the bounds of their habitation" (Acts 17:26).

Man has been on alien ground since his expulsion from paradise, but his every attempt to regain paradise by statist action, or by means of the anarchy of humanism, only places him further on alien ground.

The departure from God marks also the disintegration of man and his society. If man has no regard for the rights of God the Creator, he will have less regard for the rights of man, for He has denied in essence the concept of law and of right. The emphasis on blessing and social order in Malachi 3:7-12, in its demand for tithing, is essential here. God has a property right over man, and the tithe is a token of this. It is inevitable that a culture which denies God's property rights will end up by despising man's property rights also.

All of God's law is an assertion and manifestation of His property rights over man. "The nature of the law is summed up in the statement: the law is the good purpose of God. Not to be subject to the law is therefore enmity toward God (Rom. viii. 7)." [4] This enmity incurs bloodguiltiness, which only the atonement can erase, restoring man to a faith in God and obedience to His law.

The purposes of God's property rights, as manifested in His law, are totally good. Similarly, the *intentions* of the humanistic planners, as they issue their total laws over man, are totally good, but these "good intentions" do not nullify a totally evil will, a desire to be good with other people's property. It is significant that in the U.S.S.R. churches and people are forbidden to give charity to individuals. Charitable giving is strictly forbidden. In other words, honest giving, out of one's own property, is unlawful. Charity or welfare must come from property stolen by the state. Honest charity is forbidden because honest purposes are forbidden. The law of God is His good purpose toward man, His will to bring man to fulfilment, peace, and happiness in God his Creator. The purpose of statist law is ostensibly the welfare of man, but it is in actuality *power*, the aspiration to be as God. It is thus total lawlessness in relationship to God, and the essence of sin is *anomia*, this lawlessness, which incurs bloodguiltiness in its every action, because it is in its every thought and deed an offense against the life of man. When the life of man is involved in *anomia*, lawlessness, it is inevitable that his politics will be the politics of bloodguiltiness.

---

[4] Hermann Kleinknecht and W. Gutbrod: *Law*, p. 106. London: Adam and Charles Black, 1962.

6

FALSE RESPONSIBILITY

In I Chronicles 13:1-10 and II Samuel 6:1-7, an incident is narrated which is generally by-passed by clergymen as a source of embarrassment. The ark of God, captured by the Philistines and then returned, was being moved by ox-cart from its temporary location amid a national celebration. Officers of church and state, including David, were involved. Uzzah, a Levite, put out his hand to steady the ark when the oxen stumbled, and God struck Uzzah dead on the spot. This wrath of God strikes the modern mind as disproportionate to the offense. Some apologists murmur something about the "numinous," but most are silent. But few passages of the Bible are more urgently relevant to our age than this.

According to the Mosaic law, only priests could transport the ark, and then only on their shoulders. Levites were thus excluded from this responsibility (see Ex. 25:14; Num. 7:7-9, 4:2, 5; Lev. 10:2; II Chron. 15:13, 14). The Philistines had returned the ark on a "new cart" (I Sam. 6:7), and Israel had followed the example of Philistia rather than the law of God. The Philistines suffered diseases for their abuse of the ark, and Uzzah, death. This is in terms of the biblical principle: the greater the responsibility, the greater the sin. Leviticus 4 establishes the required sacrifices in terms of this principle: priest, people, and prince, in that order, were responsible to God, and the greater responsibility meant greater culpability.

Uzzah was guilty of *presumptuous responsibility*. A classic case is that of Cain, who, after murdering Abel, said, "Am I my brother's keeper?" (Gen. 4:9). Cain was not his brother's keeper, and no man is; the phrasing reveals only contempt for one's brother, as though he needed a keeper. This was a presumption on Cain's part. Again, his irresponsible concern with his brother's death is revealing: his brother's life was his *to take or to keep*. This is false responsibility, presumptuous responsibility: it is man playing God.

Although the ark was surrounded by priests and dignitaries, presumptuous Uzzah felt that without him nothing would be done properly. It was the "I must do it, or it will not be done properly" rationale. *Wherever presumption is present, the word "responsibility" is used, but what is meant is "control," i.e., I must control.* False responsibility says: I am responsible for all things, for all people, for God as well as man. In other words, "I am god, and I must control and sustain all things."

Wherever false responsibility is promoted, an ugly strategy of power is present. This strategy can be briefly summarized. *First,* make men feel *guilty* for all things and for everyone. Whatever happens on any continent or country is their responsibility and their burden. All the starving, needy, oppressed, and all the indigents, criminals, and diseased of the world are their burden, and they are guilty of evading their responsibilities if they do nothing about them.

Second, it is obvious that men cannot do much more than care for their own families. Therefore, ask them to exercise this imposed responsibility for the world by delegation, to delegate it to the state and the elite planners. Once a man is convinced that he has this world responsibility, he will want to do something about it, and this second step becomes an obvious and easy solution.

Third, by being given this world responsibility, the state and its elite planners become gods, governors of all things. They can now begin to remake the world in terms of their superior wisdom. God, after all, hardly had their superior and scientific intelligence.

Fourth, salvation has thus become the work of man. Man remakes man by statist law and action. This is the goal of false responsibility: to be gods, controlling and remaking man.

In this strategy, *guilt is necessary*, and the politics is a politics of guilt in every sense.

First, as we have noted, men are told that they are guilty if they fail to provide for all the needs of the world. The universalistic ethics and responsibility which is demanded can lead only to communism. Men who are convinced that they have this world responsibility then find it easy to delegate their presumed responsibility to the state to ease their conscience.

Second, this attempt to ease the conscience fails. Men remain feeling guilty, for a false sense of guilt has no cure save the truth, and this is not forthcoming. Since the citizens are now guilt-ridden because of their education and political indoctrination, they are more amenable to robbery, and even murder. If the white man feels guilty towards the Negro, he is less capable of defending himself against Negroes who turn into a revolutionary rabble, bent on theft and murder. The state finds it easier to rob men when men feel guilty for what they are and have, and the state drones on and on about the needs of the poor of the nation and of the world.

Fourth, since the robbed citizenry still feels guilty, and yet grumbles about the enforced giving, the planners reënforce this sense of guilt by making them feel guilty for begrudging this heavy burden of taxation and confiscation. The people grumble and complain, but with impotence and guilt, because they are without salvation.

Fifth, guilt reënforces guilt and simply increases man's slavery. The only road for guilty men who evade Christ is more guilt, and none are more burdened and more readily exploited than those with a false sense of guilt. False guilt has no true cause and hence no focus, and it is therefore more pervasive and paralyzing.

The word used by these strategists is "responsibility." The *goal* is slavery for man, and *power* for the state and its elite planners.

The only answer to this impasse is the assertion of the sovereignty of God and His saving and cleansing power. Man's responsibility is to do his duty under God, not to feel total responsibility, which is not man's business. Total responsibility means total control. Man has a responsibility to control himself, and, under God and His law, to control also his family and work. His responsibility does not extend to the world or to other men; his relationship to them is governed by the Word of God.

The incident of Uzzah is not an embarrassment to the believer: it is a promise. God will destroy the Uzzahs of every generation.

7

THE SABBATH, SLAVERY,
AND THE PROLETARIAN REVOLUTION

The concept of a Sabbath, and its introduction into history, was a revolution of amazing dimensions. There is no record of a Sabbath prior to the deliverance of Israel from Egypt, and the idea of a day of rest weekly is entirely derivative from the biblical revelation wherever found. For Israel, a slave people bound to unremitting work, the deliverance from Egypt was an event of staggering dimensions: its weekly commemoration in a day of rest, wherein work was strictly and firmly forbidden, was a continual reminder of the luxury of salvation and of liberty. Unlike all other peoples of the earth, Israel was dedicated to the luxury of rest, to the liberty from unending labor, as a religious principle. Violation of the Sabbath rest was treason to Israel and a denial of its liberty, and hence severely punishable, even by death (Num. 15:32-36; for Sabbath laws, see Ex. 20:8-11; 23:12; 31:13-17; 34:21; 35:2, 3; Deut. 5:12-15; Lev. 19:3, 30; 26:2; Num. 15:32-36. The origin of the Sabbath is specifically cited as Mosaic by Nehemiah 9:14.). The modern idea of the Sabbath and "blue laws" as an infringement of liberty exactly reverses its significance: the strict observance of the Sabbath was the essence of liberty for Israel; infringements were relapses into the bondage of Egypt. The Sabbath celebrated deliverance from slavery and servile work.

The Mosaic origin of the Sabbath is cited in Ezekiel 20:10-26, wherein it is clearly made a part of the revelation through Moses. The failure of Israel to observe the Sabbath is declared to be their failure to forsake the idolatry they had adopted in Egypt (Ezek. 20:5-9). Thus, the Sabbath violations were a mark of apostasy and of their continuing slave-nature, their spiritual captivity to Egypt.

As a result, they were returned to captivity again, this time to Babylon. They had continued in an Egyptian captivity spiritually, and so they were returned to a physical captivity.

The bondage and "abomination" of Egypt had been its religion. Egyptian religion embodied the continuity concept in a particular form. All reality was seen as one continuous whole. The world of the gods and the world of men and nature were one world with differing degrees of divinity manifested in different realms. Some were gods in the making, others gods already made, and both together were parts of one great natural process. All reality was thus basically one, although that great and essential *one* had a hierarchy of degrees and stations within it. The Egyptian world view was thus uniformitarian, and its gods were forces of nature personified. The vast variety of gods was a witness to the omnipresence of the divine process in all things and its essential oneness with all things.

The Bible presents a radically different faith: the doctrine of creation asserts, not uniformitarianism, but a radical discontinuity between the human, the created, and the divine. Reality is diverse, rich, real, and individual. Not inherent divine process but God's creative power and providence govern the universe.

Israel, as the recipient of the biblical revelation, came to accept it in a radically falsified sense. Even in the wilderness, fresh from Egypt, Israel had little confidence in God and great confidence in and fear of natural processes. The *supernatural*, seen as the *occasional*, was the realm of Jehovah, whereas the natural realm of impersonal forces normally and continually dominated history. As a result, God was honored as a backstop who occasionally intervened in history, and natural religion was depended on for daily existence. The result was syncretism.

The result ultimately was also Phariseeism and Judaism, religious moralism. Religious moralism sees life in terms of uniformitarian principles and with strict continuity. When man deals with fire, water, electricity, or any other natural force, certain consequences inevitably, naturally, and impersonally follow. It is an inevitable reaction; it is not personal, and no decision is involved. Water does not decide to drown or to spare a man: he drowns if he is submerged too long in water. Strict causality prevails. Hinduism has carried this concept to its logical conclusion with the doctrine of *Karma*: a tremendous underlying principle of causality underlies every act. Every cause will have its strict effect, and endless reincarnations are necessary to work out the effects before man can escape the fearful world of causality.

This is not the biblical concept. According to Scripture, the world is under God's absolute law, *but it is personal law, not impersonal causality*. Man is the creature of the personal and triune God, who is long-suffering, loving, merciful, and patient, and also jealous of His prerogatives. Because of His mercy, the sinner can long flourish when an automatic, impersonal process would have cut him down. Because of His wrath, man often faces total judgment: the retribution is not restricted to mere causalities, but it judges the heart and wipes out the whole man, nation, or age.

The Sabbath, besides commemorating God's salvation of Israel, also set forth His transcendence and discontinuity with man's being. God is apart from and beyond His creation, i.e., nature, and therefore true worship involves a separation from natural processes. The faith must be applied in daily life, but it cannot be found in daily life. True religion, true faith in the triune God, the Creator of heaven and earth, involves, *first*, a Sabbath, a separation, an assertion of discontinuity, a looking to the supernatural, to Jehovah, a person, not to natural processes, for salvation. Man's destiny is not a work of man or a process of nature and history; it is the ordination and fore-ordination of the sovereign and transcendental God. Man ceases from work on the Sabbath to declare thereby that his salvation is not his work but God's already accomplished work. Israel commemorated its day of salvation, the first Passover, on the Sabbath to signify its salvation from sin and bondage in Egypt. The Christian Church commemorates the first day of the week as its Sabbath (under new legislation, Colossians 2:16f.). *Second*, the application of the salvation and grace which come from beyond nature must be within nature, in the daily walk, in the Christian man's calling or vocation.

Denial of the Sabbath is an aspect of the denial of God and of His power. It is a rejection of transcendence and an insistence on total immanence. Not the transcendental and triune God, but the present and divine state is the true locale of power, and thus power, ultimate power, is transferred downward. The downward movement of power ends in Satanism. The world is the world of the fall, of evil, and, even though now in process of regeneration by the saving power of Christ, still a world in which evil is the clearly visible and immanent power in many areas. To deny God and His Sabbath rest is to deny the reality of transcendental power. The power which then looms on man's horizon is Satanic power, evil. For many men, power comes to be equated with evil, and goodness with impotence. Of the Yezidis, who worship Satan, it is said, "They knew about God and believed in Him. But they reasoned that God is good and therefore harmless. It's the Devil they worried about." [1] The Psalmist described his own temptation to fall into, i.e., to worship, evil by ascribing ultimacy to the present prosperity of evil:

> Nevertheless, my feet were almost gone, my treadings had well-nigh slipt. And why? I was grieved at the wicked: I do also see the ungodly in such prosperity. For they are in no peril of death; but are lusty and strong. They come in no misfortune like other folk; neither are they plagued like other men (Psalm 73:2-5, Book of Common Prayer translation).

For Satanism, evil is power, and power is evil. Satanism is very prevalent today, not only in occultism, communism, and other movements, but it is also present in all men who see the future as controlled by evil men who have the power to dominate the past, present, and future. Many people, who believe that they represent true righteousness, are still Satanists, because they firmly believe that the past, present, and future are controlled by a secret cabal of Jews, Germans, international bankers, secret societies, or other similar groups of conspirators. To recognize the existence of some conspiracies is one thing. To ascribe to conspiracies the power to determine history is another thing: it is blasphemy. The biblical faith is that man's conspiracies are a "vain thing" because God absolutely predestines and governs all history (Ps. 2; Rom. 8, etc.). To ascribe the govern-

[1] John Keel: *Jadoo*, p. 74. New York: Tower, 1957.

ment of history to a conspiracy is to renounce the triune God and to worship Satan. All history, including its conspiracies, move entirely in terms of God's purposes. The Scripture cites, as the classic example of man's conspiracy serving God in a total way, the condemnation of Jesus by the Sanhedrin (John 11:47-53): God, by His sovereign and total power, made Caiaphas prophesy to God's purposes and to serve Him.

The Sabbath is a reminder of God's sovereignty, of His role as creator, redeemer, sustainer, and judge. It affirms that all power belongs to God, and the redeemed rest from their labors, because their salvation depends, not on their works, but on the finished work of Jesus Christ. Man rests in His victory. The Christian works in gratitude, in confidence that the victory is accomplished and that man's labor must be, not to *attain* victory but *to manifest victory*. The Sabbath is thus an antidote to Satanism when it is kept in truth.

Israel, in its apostasy, sought to *revoke the past*, to escape from God and become a people given to a naturalistic faith and to find peace therein. Today also the Western world is seeking to revoke the past and to escape from its own history. Escapism is a growing philosophy. There is a rampant idealization of primitive peoples, Africans, Polynesians, and others, as part of a search for escape from history into the arms of primitivism. A philosopher of this demand for escapism is Mircea Eliade, and the Death of God school of thought is extensively infected by this escapism.

Israel, in its escapism, met with judgment instead. The prophets made it clear that, *first*, the past is irrevocable, in that, while it can be redeemed, it cannot be evaded. No man can escape the knowledge of God, least of all His people. *Second*, sin must be atoned for. If not atoned for by Christ, it is met with judgment. Another exodus and captivity was thus the lot of Israel and Judah. *Third*, the Scripture asserts that all things work together for good for the elect, for those who love God (Rom. 8:28). It also asserts by implication that all things work together for evil for those who reject God. The importance of Sabbath observance to Nehemiah was to maintain Jerusalem's budding liberty by total dependence in act and ritual on the sovereign God.

The Sabbath declares history to be determined by God; the Sabbath affirms transcendence by God. Man's liberty from the state and under God is affirmed by the Sabbath.

Contrariwise, the slave state works to destroy the Sabbath, which "was made for man, not man for the sabbath" (Mark 2:27), to set forth the liberty of man under God. The modern slave state has an announced goal: *total proletarianization.* As Pieper has noted, "The proletarian is the man who is fettered to the process of work." [2]

The leaders of proletarian revolution increasingly speak of the prospect of man's total freedom from the process of work by means of automation and socialist management. "Economist" Robert Theobold has held that the federal government should guarantee every American an annual income by right.[3] Work, we are told, will soon be obsolete.[4] Harvey Swados believes that modern education is obsolete because it prepares youth for a world of work.[5] The Ad Hoc Committee's "Manifesto" asks us to plan for the future in terms of the "knowledge" that the old relationship between work and income is now obsolete:

> As a first step to a new consensus it is essential to recognize that the traditional link between jobs and incomes is being broken. The economy of abundance can sustain all citizens in comfort and economic security whether or not they engage in what is commonly reckoned as work. Wealth produced by machines rather than by men is still wealth. We urge, therefore, that society, through its appropriate legal and governmental institutions, undertake an unqualified commitment to provide every individual and every family with an adequate income as a matter of right. This undertaking we consider to be essential to the emerging economic, social and political order in this country. We regard it as the only policy by which the quarter of the nation now dispossessed and soon-to-be dispossessed by

[2] Joseph Pieper: *Leisure, the Basis of Culture*, p. 50. Intro. by T. S. Eliot. New York: Mentor-Omega (1952), 1963.
[3] Nat Hentoff: "We're Happening All Over, Baby!" in *Playboy*, p. 150. March, 1966, vol. 13, no. 3.
[4] James J. Kilpatrick, "What Is Work? We Know Now—but Will We Know in a Decade?" in Los Angeles *Times*, Thursday morning, October 21, 1965, Part II, p. 5
[5] Harvey Swados, "Redefining Work," in *Cavalier*, p. 30ff., August, 1965, vol. 15, no. 146.

lack of employment can be brought within the abundant society. The unqualified right to an income would take the place of the patchwork of welfare measures—from unemployment insurance to relief—designed to ensure that no citizen or resident of the United States actually starves.

We do not pretend to visualize all the consequences of this change in our values.[6]

Ironically, this "Manifesto" calls also for "massive public works"!

Are these revolutionaries calling for the end of work, or for a new kind of work? They are clearly opposed to labor as capital, i.e., labor as a form of wealth which a man develops and sells to further his independent accumulation of other forms of wealth such as a home, money, and goods. They clearly want the break of "the traditional link between jobs and income," i.e., the destruction of labor as capital. They even more clearly want the development of labor as service to the cause of social revolution, unless, of course, a Hitler guide the social revolution. Accordingly, they are not opposed in principle to the nationalization of the labor force or of its youth. In fact, such labor is the end of labor as capital. It is, however, the fettering of man to servile work; it is the *proletarianization* of man.

State and federal welfare officials have repeatedly attacked any attempt to compel recipients of welfare to seek employment. Such an approach is regarded as cruel and inhuman.[7] Meanwhile, the Fabian Socialist American Establishment proposed the nationalization of American youth for national service in a variety of ways. The New York *Times* of May 22, 1966, cited Senator Jacob K. Javits' (New York) endorsement of "a proposal that all young Americans be asked to serve their country either in civilian duty or in military draft." Moreover, "An expanded role for women and the need to give broader access to unskilled youths to nonmilitary services was proposed here on May 6 by the first National Service Conference, an ad hoc group of prominent educators and manpower experts."[8] On June 2, 1966, Senator Javits introduced a resolution into the

---

[6] *Liberation* Magazine, editors Dave Dellinger, Sidney Lens, A. J. Muste, Bayard Rustin; April, 1964 issue, reprinted: *Triple Revolution*, p. 5.

[7] "Welfare Approach Attacked as 'Cruel,'" Santa Ana, California, The *Register*, Wednesday (m) June 1, 1966, p. A 6.

[8] *The Review of the News*, vol. 2, no. 21, p. 18f.

U. S. Senate calling for "universal national service, civilian or military, for all men under 35 years of age." [9] Defense Secretary McNamara had proposed a "universal service" plan as the opening gun of this campaign.[10] The press quickly assured Americans that the reaction of youth to the proposal was favorable,[11] an assertion which does tax credulity. Not surprisingly, a woman came out in favor of drafting women also.[12] Nothing was said about the coincidence of this plan to Communist, Fascist, and Nazi standards. Instead, the plan was presented as the essence of fairness and justice. But the essence of the plan is not any kind of national emergency, but its *destruction of liberty*, and its *confiscation of labor as capital*. The purpose of universal service is universal proletarianization.

The *purpose* of the slave state is to make all men, women, and children proletarians. This it accomplishes by three steps. *First*, the slave state works to destroy Christianity and its rest, the Sabbath. This is its least confessed but basic purpose. *Second*, the slave state works to destroy work as a holy calling in order to proletarianize man. When work ceases to be a vocation and calling, it becomes a burden. But because the state insists that this servile work is a duty and a matter of conscience, the unhappy and rebellious proletarian is made to feel *guilty* because he resents the enforced labor. As a result, *work is changed from a holy calling to a guilty burden*. But this is not all. Then, *third*, the slave state also destroys property and inheritance in order to rivet men to guilty work, to slavery. No man can independently accumulate wealth nor pass it on to his chosen heirs. By forbidding private inheritance, the state makes itself *the sole heir*. By turning work into national service, it reduces all men into proletarians and converts the state into the only capitalist.

The *results* of proletarianization are deadly. *First*, there is a rise in sickness, because man is soul-sick and guilt-ridden. *Second*, the

[9] *The Review of the News*, vol. 2, no. 23, p. 3.

[10] Robert S. Allen and Paul Scott, Allen-Scott Report: " 'Universal' Draft Starting at 17 Now Proposed," Santa Ana, California, The *Register*, Monday (e) June 6, 1966, p. A 18.

[11] John Bryan, "What About Universal Service for Youth?" in the Los Angeles *Herald-Examiner*, Sunday, June 12, 1966, Section H, p. 1.

[12] Caroline Bird, "Let's Draft Women Too!" *The Saturday Evening Post*, June 18, 1966, pp. 10, 12, vol. 239, no. 13.

state seeks to solve *all* problems by technology. Whether it be problems of health, soil exhaustion, work, man's inner conflicts, or anything else, a technological answer is forthcoming. The answer is thus manipulation, not regeneration. Technology is always the last stage of a civilization. It is man saying that man's control is the answer to all problems, so that totalitarianism results. Sin itself is reduced to a mental health problem, a question for technology to solve. Thus, one popular study of adultery concludes, "Adultery is a symptom of a social disease. We must treat it as such." [13] If adultery is a *social* disease, the answer then is social treatment and social control! *Third*, by abolishing the concept of sin, the concept of responsibility is also eliminated. Environment is the cause of social ills, and it is the function of the state to provide man with a new environment and to manipulate man into health.

The slave state, as it converts man into a proletarian, a man bound to work, i.e., tied to work, does seek also to give man leisure, but even this leisure is geared to work. It is a reprieve from work in order to make man better able to work and more amenable to social control. The slave state concerns itself greatly with "culture" as the oil in the social machine, to make it function with less friction. "Culture" in this statist sense is a kind of offering to the proletariat to demonstrate to them that now the worker has surpassed the nobility and capitalists in his social status. The worker is now the patron of "culture," and the ballet troupe exists to prove that he is the great heir and patron of "culture." No more than a cannibal dressed in a top hat, admiring himself in a newly acquired mirror, is the "proletarian culture" of the slave state an expression of culture: it is a fraud on the cannibal and on the worker, to satisfy him with trimmings and to make him agreeable to being robbed.

But, as leisure increases, man seeks to escape from the emptiness of leisure and pseudo-culture. Man without God, and without a true Sabbath rest in Jesus Christ (Heb. 4), is man fearful of rest and self-confrontation. Baudelaire wrote in his *Journal in Time*, "One must work, if not from taste then at least from despair. For, to

[13] Gary Gordon: *The Anatomy of Adultery*, p. 158. Derby, Connecticut: Monarch Books, 1964.

reduce everything to a single truth: work is less boring than pleasure." [14] The restless worker is unhappy with work, and unhappy with leisure. In one store, where the workers fought for and gained shorter hours, the next problem was the presence of employees on the premises when not working. Many workers returned to the store on their off-days to visit with working employees, and it was finally necessary to bar non-working employees from the premises. The worker wants rest, but cannot rest. The worker wants true work but is given slavery. The proletarianization of man begins not with the formal socialization of society by state ownership of the means of production, but it begins with the secularization of society. When the religious, the Christian, significance of work is destroyed or non-existent, man is reduced to a proletariat. From a God-centered, transcendental frame of reference, his life and work are reduced to a man-centered and social frame of reference. Socialization is then only a question of time.

In the biblical perspective, the Sabbath, although made for man, is the exclusive property of the Lord. It is not man's day, nor is its essential purpose man's physical rest, but rather it is man's rest in the Lord. Man must trust entirely in God for his salvation and rejoice in God's care and promises.

In early America, the church was physically and spiritually central to the community, and the Christian Sabbath had a like centrality. Sloane has described the place of the church:

> The first churches were considered to be the main support in the structure of American life. An old New England name for the summer beam—the strongest beam of a house—was the "church beam"; it was this now-waning importance that the colonists gave the church. Today, if you ask an average person why he goes to church, he will invariably say, "To gain something." But when you ask him exactly what he expects to gain, he gropes for an answer. Great-grandfather did not go to church expecting to gain anything more than he already had; he went there to give thanks for it.[15]

[14] Pieper: *Leisure*, p. 59.
[15] Eric Sloane: *American Yesterday*, p. 35. New York: Wilfred Funk, 1956.

The Sabbath involves thanksgiving for salvation, and the luxury of rest in the assurance of victory. As the day of worship, it involves obedience to the word of God, and a basic promise of obedience is healing. According to Exodus 15:26, "If thou wilt diligently hearken to the voice of the LORD thy God, and wilt do that which is right in his sight, and wilt give ear to his commandments, and keep all his statutes, I will put none of these diseases upon thee, which I have brought upon the Egyptians: for I am the LORD that healeth thee." In Deuteronomy 28, the curses on disobedience and the blessings on obedience are spelled out. The Sabbaths of the Old Testament, and the "rest" given in the promised land, were only foreshadowings of the victory and rest to be given in Christ. "Consequently, there is a Sabbath rest reserved for the people of God" (Heb. 4:9, Berkeley version). This rest Christ set forth in His resurrection and is progressively manifesting in history.

The Sabbath was early imitated by pagan monarchs, "divine" rulers, who proclaimed periodic days of rest on their birthdays. The significance of these birthday rests was the assertion by the monarch of his divine and saving power. The monarch's ostensible healing power was an aspect of the "rest" or Sabbath he provided, as witness the King's Touch in England.

Pagan temple worship was dissociated from rest; rest was instead associated with the occasional festival of the state. People worshiped at temples and shrines to and from work as a part of their work. Pagan worship was a form of work designed to save man. The concept still survives in the word *liturgy*, which meant, literally, *public work*. The Christian liturgy, the Christian public work, is the perfect law-keeping, atoning death, and triumphant resurrection of Jesus Christ, and man's response of faith and obedience.

Modern man, however, cannot find Sabbath rest because he is guilt-ridden. With more leisure than man has ever before enjoyed, he is increasingly restless and ulcerated in body and soul. In the words of Isaiah, "the wicked are like the troubled sea, when it cannot rest, whose waters cast up mire and dirt. There is no peace, saith my God, to the wicked" (Is. 57:19, 20). Man, having been reduced to a proletariat, is kept in the bondage of proletarianization by guilt. The cornerstone of the slave state is guilt, and its hostility to biblical Christianity is intense. The slave state denies that man is guilty before God; sin is called an obsolete concept. But man is steadily burdened with inescapable guilt in his relationship to the state. Proletarianization thus is the state's instrument of enslavement.

THE POLITICS OF SUICIDE

The masochism of man apart from God reaches the point of suicidal activity in its progression. The conclusion of masochism is the politics of suicide.

The denial of God is the denial of life and of wisdom. Jesus Christ identified himself as "the life" (John 14:6), as the Creator and true source of life, so that apart from Him men have only a love of death and a living death. Speaking as Wisdom in Proverbs 8:36, He said, "But he that sinneth against me wrongeth his own soul: all they that hate me love death."

According to Proverbs 8, the world was created by Wisdom; Wisdom mediates between God and man; man is a part of Wisdom's plan of creation, and Wisdom summons men to righteousness. Jesus Christ identified himself as this Wisdom (Luke 7:35; Matt. 11:19) and spoke of His pre-existence (John 8:58). According to St. John 1:13, 18, He is the Word, Logos, or Wisdom of God and very God. St. Paul called Christ the Wisdom of God (I Cor. 1:24, 30; comp. Col. 2:3).

Wisdom is the source and origin of justice and civil government: "By me kings reign, and princes decree justice" (Prov. 8:15, 16). Not only is civil government ordained by God (Rom. 13:1-10), but every principle of law, order, justice, life, community, family, economics, art, science, and all else comes from God. There is no neutral sphere of law in the universe which belongs to "Nature" rather than to God. There is no inherent and self-developed law-order in creation in which man may find refuge as a sphere of law in separation from, contradiction to, or supplementary to God's law. The only universe is God's universe, His creation, and totally under His law. There can thus be no ruling possible apart from Him, no separation conceivable from His law spheres. Hence, to hate the triune God is to love death: "all they that hate me love death" (Prov. 8:36).

Thus, the most corrupt civil government must have some element of true law and order to survive, or else it must have a subsidy from another state to maintain a temporary and artificial existence and a stay of death. There must be a measure of true reward, justice, law, order, family, and community within the state for the state to function. The humanist state seeks to make itself the sole principle of organization: it works to destroy all other allegiances, because these allegiances witness against its own claim to ultimacy and testify to a higher law sphere. Thus the Soviet Union worked to destroy the family, church, community, and private lives of its citizens, to isolate them from *all* allegiances save the allegiance to the state. Travellers to the Soviet Union have noticed, as the most immediate discernable characteristic of its people, their silence in the streets, the isolation of man even in a large group. All the same, the Soviet Union has had to allow a limited amount of family life, for example, and private agriculture on garden plots to farmers, for survival purposes. Total communization of the farmers' land would be suicidal: the major production comes from the very small privately farmed plots. By this unconfessed permission of and concession to God's ordained order, agricultural survival is made possible. Every atheist is an unwilling believer to the extent that he has any element of justice or order in his life, to the extent that he is even alive. Kirilov, in Dostoyevsky's *The Possessed*, was a logical atheist: he committed suicide as the only practical way of denying God, for he could not live without affirming God. Hell, as the total negation of all law and community, is the logical conclusion and the necessary world of anti-Christian men.

The politics of suicide leads to parasitism, since the suicidal state is not only bent on death but bent on carrying others to death also. The socialist state survives for a time either by being a parasite on its people to the point of their economic destruction, or by being a parasite on some richer state which consents to subsidize them, as the United States, after World War II, has done with much of the world. This parasitism leads also to imperialism: the parasite socialist state needs new healthy bodies to feed upon, and, as it destroys one, moves in to destroy another. The ultimate conclusion of the socialist world order is death, a goal required by its very nature.

The will to death is thus an inescapable consequence of hostility to the triune God. The will to death also characterizes anti-Christian or pseudo-Christian religions. They are joyless and lifeless, and they involve a retreat from life and law, for life and law are inseparably united. Men who are in rebellion against law are in rebellion against life, for laws, God's laws, are the necessary conditions, stays, and terms of life. Law is the blood of life, and every sphere of life is a law-sphere, and obedience to these laws is personal, moral, spiritual, and societal health and life. In Solomon's words on law, "For length of days, and long life, and peace, shall they add to thee" (Prov. 3:2). Moreover, "Where there is no vision, the people perish: but he that keepeth the law, happy is he" (Prov. 29:18). Vision is associated, as is happiness, with the keeping of the law. "Law means life." [1] "The law of the wise is a fountain of life, to depart from the snares of the wicked" (Prov. 13:14). Solomon made clear that God's law is man's life and bastion in numerous passages, as witness Proverbs 28: 4, 5. Concerning these verses, Kidner comments:

> Without revelation, all is soon relative; and with moral relativity, nothing quite merits attack. So, e.g., the tyrant is accepted because he gets things done; the pervert, because his condition is interesting. The full sequence appears in Romans 1: 18-32. [2]

Every relativistic philosophy is a rebellion against the conditions of life, and hence unconsciously against life. In relativism, man refuses in effect to accept the world as already made, as a finished product and a law system; instead, he holds that the world is a raw mass awaiting creation at man's hands, a meaningless and raw factuality which man must reduce into meaning. By his rejection of the world as it is, God's creation and an established law sphere, man rejects life as it is in favor of a dream on his terms. In doing so, man rejects

[1] Derek Kidner: *Proverbs, An Introduction and Commentary*, p. 103. Chicago: Inter-Varsity Press, 1964.
[2] *Ibid.*, p. 169.

the only life that is; he prefers death to the surrender of the dream of apostate reason.

Rebellious man is characterized by what Spengler, with another context in mind, called the "dread of reality."[3] The dread of reality is a fear of the real world of God and an insistence that the dream world of reason must supplant it because the dream is the reality. The modern anti-Christian intellectual has been the blindest person of the modern world by his studied hostility to the real world. No one has matched him in his resolute unwillingness to see man as a sinner: for a few centuries he insisted that man is naturally good or at worst morally neutral. The intellectual has been unequalled in his insistence on the total equality of all men, while at the same time maintaining that he constitutes the elite which should rule and re-make all things. He has long believed in socialism when socialism has uniformly failed, and it was held to be a mark of intelligence to see Stalin as a great and humane ruler—as long as Stalin lived. The anti-Christian intellectual has been the blindest and least educable, but he has been most insistent on educating and remaking man. President Wallace Sterling of Stanford University, a California educational institution, expressed such plans for the university in June, 1966:

> This distinguished savant, upon receiving an honorary degree from McMaster University, stated that our society is now looking toward our colleges, rather than our homes, churches, and schools, "to provide a set or sense of human and moral values as a counteraction to the drive for material success in a world that is becoming depersonalized by computers."
>
> According to him, the demand for this new set of moral and human values is stemming directly from the students as well as outsiders![4]

But the essence of apostate man's reasoning is his insistence on independence from God and the assertion of his own claim to be his own god, and therefore such an intellectual must logically claim universal jurisdiction, because he is supplanting God and the universal jurisdiction of God's law.

[3] Oswald Spengler: *The Hour of Decision, Part One, Germany and World-Historical Revolution*, p. 7. New York: Knopf, 1934, 1963.
[4] Letter by Holly Storme, in the Van Nuys, California, *News*, Thursday, July 7, 1966, p. 2A.

The politics of apostasy is therefore the politics of universal jurisdiction, of totalitarianism. The state which will not acknowledge God will not thereby leave a vacuum in the universe: the state will fill it. Universal jurisdiction, a cohesive source of unity to every sphere of activity, is a necessary principle if man's world is not to be reduced to meaningless chaos and if man is not to surrender the possibility of purposive life, of life in effect. The state, having denied God, will then make itself god; it will claim universal jurisdiction in order to make life meaningful rather than formless. It will thus become a logos incarnate, a Platonic idea incarnated in a new "republic" headed by philosopher-kings. Such a state may offer religious liberty to its citizens, but it will be increasingly at the price of shrine-worship at its own cult as the necessary condition. The other gods, Christian or otherwise, must thus be lesser gods, or they cannot exist.

But the *claim* to exercise universal jurisdiction and the *wisdom and ability* to exercise this prerogative are two different things. For a man with all the limitations of man to claim to be as God is to indulge in a dangerous fantasy; for a state, with all the limitations of man compounded, but the power of the sword added to it, to claim to be as God is desperately dangerous and suicidal as well.

The modern state is thus doubly involved in the politics of suicide. *First*, its pretensions to universal jurisdiction place the state on a suicidal course. *Second*, by its rejection of the triune God, the state is suicidal, for "all they that hate me love death."

II. THE POLITICS OF PITY

1

THE BIBLICAL DOCTRINE OF CHARITY

Basic to all actions are ideas which carry a sense of truth, necessity, or inevitability requiring action, even to the detriment of the person or society. When the ideas perish, the contingent actions rapidly wither away. The 20th century is seeing the fruition of ideas long in development and which claim, not only sanctions of humanism, but of Christianity as well. Among these is the current concept of charity.

In view of the prevalence of a sentimental and anarchistic concept of charity in our time, it is important to understand by contrast the biblical doctrine of charity. Unhappily, the subject is complicated by the fact that the contemporary concept claims to be derived from Christianity itself and indeed to be a representation of the mind of Christ. This concept of charity and of pity presents itself as basic doctrine in every aspect of political and social life. In the foreign aid program it decrees that we must have pity for all human need. In relief and welfare programs, it maintains likewise that there must be a virtually promiscuous pity and charity for all peoples. Indeed, this attitude goes so far, in the Thanksgiving season in particular, that some sermons, editorials, and cartoons often declare in effect that we dare not enjoy our abundance when others go hungry.

Is such an attitude godly, and does it have any foundation in Scripture? What precisely is the meaning of pity and compassion? The problem is one both of definition and of exegesis. *Compassion* means literally "to suffer with." In the Greek New Testament, where several words are used to convey this particular meaning, it often means "to have the bowels of yearning," as in Matthew 15:32; 20:34, and like passages. Another word, also translated as compassion, means "to suffer with another" (Heb. 10:34; I Pet. 3:8, etc.). Pity means literally "loving kindness," "to be gracious." This attitude, pity, on God's part is *never promiscuous but always selective*, and, according to Scripture, is to be selective on man's part also. Pity and charity therefore are to be extended only as far as God himself will extend them and no further. Pity to the poor in the Lord is lending to God (Prov. 19:17); on the other hand no pity must be shown to evil, nor does God himself show it, as witness Deuteronomy 8:16; 13:8; 19:13, 21; 25:12; Zechariah 11:6; Jeremiah 13:14; Lamentations 2:2, 17, 21; 3:43; Ezekiel 5:11, etc.

The implications of this promiscuous concept of pity have never been more clearly stated than by C. S. Lewis:

> The demand of the loveless and the self-imprisoned, that they should be allowed to blackmail the universe: that till they consent to be happy (on their own terms) no one else shall taste joy: that theirs shall be the final power; that Hell should be able to veto Heaven. . . . Either the day must come when joy prevails and all the makers of misery are no longer able to infect it: or else for ever and ever the makers of misery can destroy in others the happiness they reject for themselves. I know it has a grand sound to say ye'll accept no salvation that leaves even one creature in the dark outside. But watch that sophistry or ye'll make a Dog in a Manger the tyrant of the universe.[1]

What, then, is the biblical doctrine of charity? It is found, in its essential form, in Leviticus 20:30f.; Deuteronomy 12:5; 14:22-27; and 26:12-14.

1. Gleaning constituted the fundamental form of charity in biblical law. Landowners were forbidden a total harvest, that is, the corners of the field could not be reaped, the grain along the ditch banks must

[1] C. S. Lewis: *The Great Divorce*, p. 124. New York: Macmillan, 1946.

be allowed to remain, the out of reach fruits left on the tree, and thus a certain amount of produce permitted to remain unharvested. Accordingly, the landowner could then allow the poor of the community to enter in to glean the fields. This privilege was not open to all; the landowner had the responsibility of determining who was worthy in his eyes of the privilege of gleaning. We find, for example, Boaz singling out Ruth as a particularly deserving person and commanding special privileges be given her by his harvesters. A fundamental principle was thus involved in gleaning. This was indeed charity, but charity in which the recipient had to work, in that gleaning the fields was hard, back-breaking work. It was harder than normal harvesting, in that the grain reaped and the fruit picked was all the harder to secure by reason of scarcity; nevertheless, the person who gleaned had as a result of his or her work enough to provide for himself and something to sell as a source of income. Widows and orphans usually were the main recipients of the gleaning privilege. Thus, work, whereby the recipient gained self-respect and had the satisfaction of taking care of himself in the process, was essential. In conformity to this same fundamental principle, Paul declared, in II Thessalonians 3:10, "He that doth not work, let him not eat." Gleaning is referred to in the law in Leviticus 19:10; Deuteronomy 24:21, and in the book of Ruth. We have a variant form of gleaning in Deuteronomy 23:24, 25, wherein it is stated that the wayfaring, when hungry and needy, may, without permission, eat of the produce of a field but are forbidden to carry anything away, nor can they use a knife or a sickle or any instrument in the field, plucking only enough to satisfy their immediate hunger. This humane provision had in view the difficulties of travel and the hardships sometimes attendant upon it in that era.

2. The law of the tithe was an essential aspect of biblical law. The law of the tithe stipulated in part that every third and sixth year of each seven-year cycle a second tithe was to be set aside by the faithful for the purpose of a common meal. This common meal was one to which the poor of the neighborhood were invited, and the Levites as well. Note that it involved a sizeable investment of money. Consider the implications of a tithe, 10 percent of an income; translated

into modern terms, it means that a man with an income of $5,000 would every third and sixth year be obliged to spend $500 for banqueting the deserving poor and needy of the community in his own home. More than that, the presence of the Levites was a reminder of the religious orientation. As one people under God, they were mindful of one another's needs. Thus, this was indeed charity, but it involved something more in that it insisted on the unity of the rich and the poor as one people under God. The foundation of charity was therefore not sentimental or anarchistic but designed to strengthen and protect the holy commonwealth in its ties of faith. Thus, the biblical law of charity through gleaning established the working nature of the recipient and his self-respect, and then, through the common meal required every third and sixth years, furthered the solidarity of the community. Biblical charity was thus not promiscuous: it was to the deserving and it served to bind society both in work and in rest.

3. Another form of charity was the work of mercy to man and beast in cases of emergency. Scripture, as is common to its legal principles, cites the minimal case as the means of establishing a principle. In Deuteronomy 22:1-4 and Exodus 23:4, 5, the principle is established of assistance even to the livestock of a neighbor or an enemy, and thereby the basic principle of mercy to a neighbor is more than underwritten. We find this concept affirmed in the parable of the Good Samaritan, Luke 10:25-27. The term, "works of mercy," is a modern designation. The biblical terms in the two Mosaic ordinances are two different words meaning "help" or assistance. In the parable of the Good Samaritan, "compassion," "to have the bowels of yearning," is the term used. There is thus a distinction between the works of mercy and charity. Charity has as its purpose the strengthening of society and its protection. Its purpose is to unify people of a common faith and to enable the unfortunate both to care for themselves and to maintain their participation in the life of the godly commonwealth. The very process of gleaning helped determine calibre, and Ruth was quickly singled out as a woman of the highest character and integrity, whom the wealthy Boaz felt it an honor to marry.

In works of mercy, the relationship is different. The Good Samaritan, like all Samaritans, had no use for Jews as such, but he had compassion on a Jew's need, who while a traveler to Jericho had been robbed and left half dead. He made provisions for the Jew's care, and, on his return from his journey, guaranteed any additional cost, and then passed on. He was under no obligation to change his religious concepts or have further relations with the Jew. Thus, the work of mercy is a humane act, requiring no further involvement, whereas charity presupposes a fundamental identity affirmed and furthered by the donor. Moreover, since charity is an assertion of this common faith and life, it must be personal or it ceases to have meaning. With regard both to gleaning and to the tithe, another fundamental aspect appears. While the charity was personal, it was also suprapersonal, in that its fundamental aspect was religious. The godly were required to avoid total harvesting; they were required to use the second tithe each third and sixth year for a common meal, and the requirements came from God, so that the giving was essentially to God rather than to man. The money could not be used for any other purpose without robbing God, and to withhold from God His due was a fearful sin. The second tithe was unclean for any other use and was hallowed to its particular purpose, and the believer had to swear to his faithfulness in this regard to be acceptable to God (Deut. 26:12-16). The famine relief of Acts 11:27-30 was a work of mercy within the church, whereas Acts 6:1 and 9:39 refer to charity. Widows had to be supported by any relatives or in-laws, near or far (I Tim. 5:8, 16), or the relative would be regarded as "worse than an unbeliever." Widows of good repute, common sense and piety, and over the age of 60, could enter the service of the church as "widows," being assigned various duties, including visitation among women (Titus 2:3), in return for their support. Thus, the Old Testament principles are definitely the basis of church life in the New Testament church. The widows received charity, but biblical charity, in terms of which they were active, able, and profitable workers for the church as long as they were physically able, and entitled to support till death. The charity towards men is not specified, beyond the warning to feed none who will not work but rather go about as busybodies (II Thess. 3:10-15), indicating that some form of requirement to work clearly prevailed.

A false concept of pity and charity is depicted in Scripture (Mark 14:3-9; John 12:1-8) in Judas' attitude, namely, that Mary's action constituted a signal waste and misuse of money for a luxury item. Mary, declared Judas, should think of the poor; no luxury is permissible while the poor exist. We are told by John that Judas was both the treasurer and a thief, a very significant juxtaposition. False charity is always involved in theft. Jesus by way of response declared, "let her alone, why trouble ye her? She hath wrought a good work on me," continuing to say, "The poor ye have always with you, but me ye have not always." Jesus called attention to Mary's act, one of true faith, of honest feelings, of joy in his atoning work and faith in the resurrection, whereas Judas' words constituted a false faith and hypocritical religion. False charity hates joy, luxury, and abundance in every form and has a levelling demand: it denies the person's right to use his property and wealth in terms of his own conscience. The "rights" of the poor to a man's wealth exceed his own rights and wishes. Success becomes a crime to be atoned for by a required share-the-wealth program.

It is apparent from the foregoing that the modern conception of pity and of charity are by no means derived from the Bible. On the contrary, biblical laws speak with hostility towards undiscriminating pity. How, then, can men claim to have derived the concept from Scripture? This is done, not by direct appeal to Scripture, but in ostensible faithfulness to the "higher" sense of Scripture, the conception of God as love, and to the love which Jesus Christ ostensibly portrayed in his own life and teaching. That Jesus Christ taught the love of God, and the love of one's neighbor, is unmistakeable; but that it was this anarchistic conception of love is certainly to be doubted. Indeed, the very nature of the love Jesus Christ taught was both exclusive and divisive. In His own words (Luke 12:49-53, RV):

> I came to cast fire upon the earth; and what do I desire, if it is already kindled? But I have a baptism to be baptized with; and how am I straitened till it be accomplished! Think ye that I am

come to give peace in the earth? I tell you, Nay; but rather division: for there shall be from henceforth five in one house divided, three against two, and two against three. They shall be divided, father against son, and son against father; mother against daughter, and daughter against her mother; Mother-in-law against her daughter-in-law, and daughter-in-law against her mother-in-law.

The only way the sentimental concept of pity and charity can be maintained and ascribed to Jesus Christ, is by destroying his fundamental contrast between God and Satan, between good and evil, between truth and error, and between righteousness and wickedness. And, in effect, the end result of all false pity and charity is precisely the destruction of this distinction. Pity, after all, means *identification, and it is because of this very fact of identification that pity is forbidden by God in so many cases,* refused by God himself and forbidden by God to His people. The modern identification involves the confusion of good and evil. It involves a favor to evil and a furthering of it which is a manifest hostility to God and His righteousness. False charity, therefore, is essentially anti-Christian, striking as it does at the very nature of God and His being.

Consider the implications of charity. The goods, clothing, and money given to objects of charity are never created out of nothing; they are the possession of the donor. Charity therefore involves the giving of property by one person to another, and false charity therefore becomes the robbing of the godly in order to further an evil person or cause. False charity is a contribution to evil, a self-conscious espousal of evil; it is to that extent deliberately anti-Christ and anti-God. When false charity is coercive charity, as indeed so much of it is today, it constitutes a similarly anti-Christian stand on the part of the government that requires it, and, it thereby indicates that the godly and the provident must be robbed in order to provide for the wicked. We have here, therefore, a novel kind of Robin Hood, a Robin Hood who robs the godly and the provident in order to provide for the wicked and the anti-social. Not only does such a philosophy rebel against God and His righteousness, but it seeks to obscure the distinction between God and Satan, between good and evil. Consider, for example, this statement from a national

teen-age monthly published by a major church: "God loves everyone equally—the Negro, the Mau-Mau, the Puerto Rican, the Mexi-
can, and the communist, just as much as the white American." Such
statements, exceedingly commonplace, are assumed to be Christian,
and yet they strike at the very heart of all Scripture. God's love is
never spoken of as promiscuous in Scripture. God definitely indicates His hatred of many people. His love and His sovereign grace,
His predestinating counsel, His demands of righteousness, His requirement of obedience, are closely linked. To say that the Mau-Mau
and the Communist are loved by God equally with His saints is
against all biblical warrant. Up to a point there is a common provision for all of sun and rain (Matt. 5:45), and a common opportunity
to serve Him. But there are consequences for disobedience to Him,
cursing (Deut. 27, 28), and retributive justice. God hates evil
and evil actions (Zech. 8:17); more specifically, He hates "all workers of iniquity" (Ps. 5:5), and those who love the Lord must hate
evil (Ps. 97:10). God hated Israel for their wickedness (Hos.
9:15); He hated Esau (Edom) and judged him for his wickedness (Mal. 1:3). In Psalm 60, we have a strong assertion of God's
particularism with regard to the nations, and in verses too numerous
to cite, this particularity is asserted. It is an impossibility to read
Scripture in terms of its declared meaning without recognizing that,
while God's "love" with respect to certain common provisions and
opportunities is *universal*, His "love" with respect to acceptance and
blessing is definitely *particular*. To insist that God shows a common
favor in all respects to Communist, Mau-Mau, and Christian is to
insist that God has a common favor with regard to good and evil.
Such a declaration is in flagrant contempt of the whole of Scripture
and can appeal only to isolated phrases and sentences, violently
wrenched out of their context, in its support.

Every such an assertion of common favor is an attempt to destroy
all distinctions because all distinctions are seen as hateful realities,
as reminders of unpleasantly demanding moral laws. Hence the
world of the sentimental idealist must have neither high nor low, rich
nor poor, good nor evil, but all must be one in this moral blandness
and indifference. The world must be reordered in order that they

might live in it without the necessity of moral change. The distinctions must be abolished lest in some fashion they be reminded of that which they do not possess and morally refuse to possess. The false concept of charity and pity therefore is not a matter of moral indifference but involves a fundamental stand in favor of evil. It is not merely a matter of financial insolvency for the person or nation following a course of false pity, but total moral insolvency. It is precisely this moral insolvency that increasingly faces modern man. It is the culmination of a long warfare against God and His laws and must be reckoned with as such.

The moral alternative therefore must be boldly faced: godly man must recognize that he has the obligation to be without pity and without charity in dealing with some, that this attitude, however harsh it may seem in terms of modern sentimentality, constitutes moral strength and spiritual integrity. He must recognize that he cannot rob himself or others in order to feed the undeserving of the world, or the improvident who demand as their right a portion of our wealth. Property and all possessions are a stewardship from God, for according to Scripture, "The earth is the Lord's, and the fullness thereof." *Man cannot use the proceeds of that stewardship either for himself or for anyone else except as God's word allows.* Accordingly, the only effective answer to the false concept of charity is a godly concept of stewardship. Moreover, true stewardship means a humility whereby man avoids a fundamental sin common to false charity, that of trying to be God. In false charity the whole world is re-ordered and the nature of reality amended by the rebellious man, a would-be god whose societal forms and life constitute an act of warfare against God and His Word. False charity is therefore a war against reality, and every war against reality is an insanity foreordained to destruction. And when a nation involves us in such a course, we have a duty to protest, and, more than that, strengthen the only source of resistance to such a course, the true household of faith.

2

IDENTIFICATION AND ITS IMPLICATIONS

The concept of unlimited identification is increasingly a ruling principle in our culture, and its foremost Western spokesman is Albert Schweitzer, during his life-time regarded by many as the "world's greatest living man." This adulation cannot be in terms of his theological studies, long since by-passed and unsatisfactory, nor for his organ playing, commendable in the man but not comparable to that of the better professional organists. Doctors found his medical work zealous but not of the best description. Again, professional philosophers pay little attention to his philosophy, but it is nevertheless this aspect of Schweitzer which reveals the heart of the man, his missionary endeavor, and his popular appeal. Schweitzer, while nominally working within the structure of the church, in actuality found his inspiration in the Enlightenment.

The basic premise of his philosophy is reverence for life. The Christian distinction between created and uncreated being, and between good and evil, gives way in Schweitzer to an undifferentiated reverence for all life. The sovereign and triune God of Scripture being the basic premise of Christian faith, ethics is accordingly determined by the nature of God, His holiness and righteousness. But in Schweitzer's system, reverence for life being the basic premise, it becomes difficult to derive an adequate ethical differentiation from a principle which automatically raises all life into a status of holiness, makes it an object of reverence and worship, and calls for a radical identification with all being. This promiscuous worship of life Schweitzer believed will become the source of a new renaissance of society and humanity.

Schweitzer made clear the radical character of his philosophy and mysticism:

True philosophy must start from the most immediate and comprehensive fact of consciousness, which says: "I am life which wills to live, in the midst of life which wills to live." This is not a cleverly composed dogmatic formula. Day after day, hour after hour, I live and move in it. At every moment of reflexion it stands fresh before me. There bursts forth again and again from it as from roots which can never dry up, a living world- and life-view which can deal with all the facts of Being. A mysticism of ethical union with Being grows out of it.[1]

Thus, philosophy must begin with autonomous man and his will to live. This will to live, in order to survive, must recognize and reverence in others that which it reveres in itself, and the sameness of being everywhere leads to a sense of unity and "a mysticism of ethical union." How far-reaching this worship of all life must be, Schweitzer makes clear:

Ethics consist, therefore, in my experiencing the compulsion to show to all will-to-live the same reverence as I do my own. There we have given us that basic principle of the moral which is a necessity of thought: It is good to maintain and to promote life; it is bad to destroy life or to obstruct it.
. . . Life as such is sacred to him (ethical man). He tears no leaf from a tree, plucks no flower, and takes care to crush no insect. If in summer he is working by lamplight, he prefers to keep the window shut and breathe a stuffy atmosphere rather than see one insect after another fall with singed wings upon his table.
If he goes into the street after a shower and sees an earthworm which has strayed on to it, he bethinks himself that it must get dried up in the sun, if it does not get back soon enough to ground into which it can burrow, and so he lifts it from the deadly stone surface, and puts it on the grass. If he comes across an insect which has fallen into a puddle, he stops a moment in order to hold out a leaf or stalk on which it can save itself.[2]

The affinities of such thinking to Hinduism, Buddhism, and Jainism are immediately apparent. Moreover, the basic egocentricity is

[1] Albert Schweitzer: *Civilization and Ethics*, p. 246. London: Black, 1929, 2nd ed., rev.
[2] *Ibid.*, p. 246f.

also clear, and the centrality of autonomous man, who, reverencing and worshiping himself, seeks to preserve that integrity by extending to others "the same reverence as I do to my own" will to live. In biblical faith, man uses creation both as a gift and as a stewardship from God, responsibly and without guilt. In this view, man, according to Schweitzer, is perpetually bound in guilt because he must destroy even vegetable life to live as a vegetarian, and bacteria to keep his health. Thus, guilt is inescapable and unavoidable, and without release or atonement. In the biblical view, forgiveness cannot be extended to the unrepentant or be used as a cloak to excuse sin. It is *conditional* upon true repentance, and *unlimited* where true faith exists, and thus no attempt to exploit forgiveness as a license to sin (Matt. 18:15-35; I Cor. 5:1-5) can be permitted. But, for Schweitzer, forgiveness is *unconditional* and must be extended to to every man in his sin, crime, and guilt. Because we are all guilty, Schweitzer insists, we must all forgive, because to do otherwise "would be acting as if I myself were not guilty." [3] Thus, the basic reference is again man, autonomous man, who seeks to be his own god. In the biblical view, I, though myself a sinner, can withhold forgiveness because I am not the source of law whereby forgiveness and judgment are granted, but God is, and I place myself under His judgment and grace, and grant or refuse forgiveness in accordance with His word. Thus, forgiveness has a transcendental and ethical reference, whereas in Schweitzer's view its framework is purely subjective and in terms of expediency.

How, in Schweitzer's system, shall man live? He must incur guilt, he must kill to live. A monstrous and inescapable necessity to live by sinning is thus man's destiny:

> In order to preserve my own existence, I must defend myself against the existence which injures it. I become a hunter of the mouse which inhabits my house, a murderer of the insect which wants to have its nest there, a mass-murderer of the bacteria which may endanger my life. I get my food by destroying plants and animals. My happiness is built upon injury done to my fellow-man. [4]

[3] *Ibid.*, p. 252.
[4] *Ibid.*, p. 254f.

This sense of guilt cannot be compromised, or the necessity to kill made relative; it is evil. At every instant, man faces an ethical choice with regard to life. Since he must live by killing, "Whenever I injure life of any sort, I must be quite clear whether it is necessary." [5] This is "a responsibility so unlimited as to be terrifying." But the ethics of reverence for life "offers us no rules about the extent of the self-maintenance which is allowable." [6] There is no "higher court of appeal" than reverence for life. The implications thus are devastating. *Necessity* becomes the fundamental principle of *practical* action, and necessity is a dangerous principle when tied to nothing more than autonomous man. In the dedicated masochism of Schweitzer, this practical action has been zealous humanitarianism. But, in others, this principle of necessity, of suppressing lower forms of life to further higher forms, can lead to a totally ruthless and a murdering philosophy. And, after all, Nazi philosophy did spring out of the same common philosophy of the will to live as did Schweitzer, but it limited its preservation of life to the ostensibly higher Nordic forms.

Thus, the concept of identification in Schweitzer is radically anti-ethical. By embracing all life as such and worshiping it, he allows for no principle of distinction other than necessity. Schweitzer gives us thus a religion of pity (and all indiscriminate pity has behind it that egocentricity that makes self-pity central, together with a morbid pre-occupation with the self), and a philosophy which is an evasion of life and of the central problems of our time. Schweitzer did not enter a European city's slums, where he would be another man, and even a resented man, but Africa's "primeval forest," where, as a white man, he could function on a superior level and bestow grace. This is the level on which identification usually chooses to operate: it is subversive of ethical standards and distinctions, but not of the ego. But, even then, burdened constantly by a self-imposed guilt, it does not function with joy, as witness Schweitzer's own admission, "Only at quite rare moments have I felt really glad to be

[5] *Ibid.*, p. 256.
[6] *Ibid.*, p. 258.

alive." [7] Both by his withdrawal from the problems of Western culture, and by his own unhappiness, Schweitzer was characterized by the very negations of Eastern thought which he sought to avoid.

A revealing illustration of the extent of identification in Eastern thought is to be seen in a Japanese painting of the 7th century, a Buddhist youth and future Buddha, seeing a family of starving tigers, throws himself down from a cliff so that his own body might feed the tigers' hunger.[8] The Western concept of identification operates on a somewhat different level, although the foreign policy of the United States seems to suggest a similar self-destruction to feed the world's hungry tiger cubs.

In Gandhi, both Eastern and Western forms of identification were merged with tremendous popular appeal. An oft-quoted remark of Gandhi's is especially illustrative of the concept: "To the millions who have to go without two meals a day the only acceptable form in which God dare appear is food." First, consider what requirements Gandhi overlooked with regard to man. In naturally rich India, millions indeed go hungry because, in their religious folly, they refuse to kill and thereby perpetuate animal life, including tigers, monkeys, and cows, which destroy the land, eat up crops, and leave only a marginal existence for man. The natural resources also have been neglected. But God must overlook man's sin and folly and so promiscuously and radically identify himself with man as to become food for him, having no other acceptable or permissible appearance. God's sovereignty is thus set aside, and His law as well. *Identification requires that the universe function in terms of man's desires.* Second, man, as is already apparent, supplants God in primacy and sovereignty, and God is required to serve man's every need. God is thus reduced to man's servant "with no strings attached," no right to claim anything of man in return.

An interesting use of Gandhi's statement appeared in double-page advertisements in 1959 by General Dynamics Corporation.

[7] Cited from a review of George Leaver: *Albert Schweitzer, The Man and His Mind*, by Osborne L. Schumpert in *Monday Morning*, Jan. 26, 1948, p. 15.
[8] This picture, reproduced in *Time*, May 25, 1959, p. 79, is from *Japan: Ancient Buddhist Paintings*, the New York Graphic Society.

VISION: Gandhi said: "To the millions who have to go without two meals a day the only acceptable form in which God
dare appear is food." Creative uses of atomic radiation in agriculture can help give more and better food to all peoples, everywhere. Atomic contributions to the agricultural development of
undernourished nations, with "no strings attached" will offer new
proof to the world that we practice the brotherhood we preach.

REALITY: TRIGA, the inherently safe research, training
and isotope-producing reactor, conceived, designed and produced by General Dynamics Corporation's General Atomic Division, is now in use or soon will be in operation on five of the
six continents.

India: cooperative research and experiments at the World
Agricultural Fair in New Delhi:

Belgian Congo: research in bone growth and bone disease:
Republic of Korea: studies of genetic mutations in plants:
Brazil: training of engineers:
Republic of Vietnam: investigation of tropical diseases:
Japan: technical training and biological research:
Austria: programs in nuclear physics, isotopic chemistry:
Italy: research in Neutron physics:
United States: training, research in plant growth, irradiation
of seeds, cancer diagnosis and research in human metabolism.[9]

This statement is revelatory in a double sense. First of all, it is an
affirmation of faith, and the faith affirmed is not in any wise the
historic Christianity of Western culture: it is the concept of identification. This is said to be the meaning of true brotherhood. And
this faith modern science increasingly affirms. The hostility of
many scientists to matters of national security is grounded, not in
Marxist sympathies, as with a few, but in this doctrine of identification, and in terms of it many have become ardent evangelists. Second,
this statement not only affirms identification but also gives, as we
have seen, a doctrine of God, and this new god science has become.
It is the "Reality" of his appearing from the United States to the
Congo. Modern Science is increasingly messianic in temper.

However, it is when we come to contemporary writers that some
of the most vivid assertions of identification appear. Walt Whitman,

[9] In *Time*, Dec. 21, 1959, pp. 54, 55; in *The Saturday Evening Post*, Dec. 19,
1959, pp. 54, 55.

whose role was self-consciously more that of the seer than the poet, and whose success is as the spokesman of this modern mood, was insistent on his hatred of ethics, vehement in his identification with all life, including and especially the animals, because they lacked any sense of ethical separatism. Whitman's follower, Edward Carpenter, wrote *Toward Democracy*, a verbose summons to identification as the deliverance from ethical religion with all its haunting by conscience. Identification has been more thoroughly, if less ecstatically, practiced by contemporary writers. Carson McCullers has spoken very clearly of her approach to writing:

> One cannot explain accusations of morbidity. A writer can only say he writes from the seed which flowers later in the subconscious. Nature is not abnormal, only lifelessness is abnormal. Anything that pulses and moves and walks around the room, no matter what thing it is doing, is natural and human to a writer. The fact that John Singer, in *The Heart Is a Lonely Hunter*, is a deaf-and-dumb man is a symbol, and the fact that Captain Penderton, in *Reflections in a Golden Eye*, is also a symbol of handicap and impotence. The deaf mute, Singer, is a symbol of infirmity, and he loves a person who is incapable of receiving his love. Symbols suggest the story and theme and incident, and they are so interwoven that one cannot understand consciously where the suggestion begins. I become the characters I write about. I am so immersed in them that their motives are my own. When I write about a thief, I become one; when I write about Captain Penderton, I become a homosexual man; when I write about a deaf mute, I become a deaf mute, I become dumb during the time of the story. I become the characters I write about and I bless the Latin poet Terence who said, "Nothing human is alien to me." [10]

This identication, common to modern writers, is expected also of the reader, who must identify with any and all characters, all of which are "normal" because "nature is not abnormal" but only death or lifelessness is. Why death, a natural fact, is abnormal, we are not told unless it be that it constitutes a threat to this ecstatic identification. Vladimir Nabokov, in writing of the genesis of his *Lolita* from its "first little throb," specifically denies having any "moral in tow."

[10] Carson McCullers, "The Flowering Dream, Notes on Writing," in *Esquire*, December 1959, p. 163.

His one justification for any work of fiction is its production in the reader of "aesthetic bliss." [11] This "aesthetic bliss" is possible only with a moral anesthesia, for otherwise identification with perverts offers revulsion rather than bliss. But this identification is precisely the mainspring of the modern mood and its fundamental immorality. Precisely because its concept of identification has been the triumph of abnormality and disease, modern writing has by and large lost the capacity to be erotic because its image of man is too eroded to permit such activity. More than that, its concept of sex is so pathological that, as United States District Judge John M. Woolsey said, on December 6, 1933, with regard to James Joyce's *Ulysses*, the total effect "on the reader undoubtedly is somewhat emetic, nowhere does it tend to be an aphrodisiac."

In the realm of sex, the concept of identification has had earnest scientific evangelism from Kinsey, who equated normal marital intercourse, homosexuality, and animal contacts as alike natural and hence to be equated.

All this, however, is a reflection on the culture, and part of the rebellion against the law-giving God of Scripture. Identification is used as a means of negating the particularism of the law, and of reducing it to nonsense by merging all reality into one inseparable unity. *Unity, identification, is thus a substitute for law and truth by its erasure of all boundaries between right and wrong, between truth and error.* Its literary manifestations are sometimes distasteful to the public, but the fundamental faith is definitely acceptable. Moreover, in liberal neo-Protestantism, the religion of identification has largely supplanted biblical Christianity.

Identification, in social welfare, has led to the refusal, in some quarters, to require the lazy to work, or the immoral to suffer any consequences, lest it produce a "psychic trauma"; there is no concern for the psychic trauma the taxpayer suffers, or the damage to the whole of society, precisely because identification means that the whole, not the individual, must become the sin-bearer and suffer the penalties of the transgression. Redemption being identification,

[11] Vladimir Nabokov, "On a Book Entitled Lolita" in *The Anchor Review*, no. 2, pp. 105-112.

atonement is the responsibility of the group, and particularly the favored ones in the group, who must pay the penalty for their difference by a levelling atonement. Justice then ceases to become the function of government, and identification by enforced equalization is the goal. In the Negro problem in the Southern States, the concern of federal action is less and less civil justice and more and more identification. That the Negro should have justice is certain, but compulsive identification is not justice and is actually injustice, and can obscure radically the Negro's just claims before the law. In the minds of many current crusaders, identification and justice are confused, and both are sought in the Negro problem. As E. Earls Ellis, assistant professor of New Testament at the Southern Baptist Theological Seminary, Louisville, Kentucky, observed with regard to Martin Luther King, Jr.: "The 'freedom' which Dr. King envisions is not merely a freedom from domination or discrimination but a freedom from difference." [12] This is the heart of the matter, and, in every stratum of society, there is today a lust for "a freedom from difference" and a resentment against any who claim such a right. In religion, there is again this same insistence on erasing theological differences in favor of identification, and liberal neo-Protestants are especially vocal in this regard. In social life, the "different" must be suppressed; the superior persons must act like mass man, and the mentally deficient and deformed must be hidden out of sight. Differences are repellant and unpleasant to behold.[13]

But, without the moral requirements, which identification strives to undermine, the level of identification is steadily depressed, and, in various mass media of entertainment as well as in literary efforts, criminals, perverts, and psychotics have for some time been the focus of identification. Because such thinking acts on the premise that the strong must identify themselves with the weak in order to "save" them, i.e., to equalize society, it asks little of the weak and everything of the strong. Politically, it holds that unlimited foreign

[12] E. Earls Ellis, in a review of Martin Luther King, Jr.: *Stride Toward Freedom*, in *Christianity Today*, January 19, 1959, III, 8, p. 34f.

[13] For a Christian culture's acceptance of such facts, see Joseph W. Eaton and Robert J. Weil: *Culture and Mental Disorders*, Glenco, Ill.: The Free Press, 1955, a study of the Hutterites which has important observations on the ability of a strict sect to tolerate divergencies without relativism.

aid by the United States is the only hope of the world; it refuses, either on the international or individual level, to assert moral responsibility as a basic factor or to limit assistance in terms of godly and moral premises.

As a result, the inevitable outcome of the practice of identification is the growth of *moral detachment*. Since the concept is basically anti-ethical, it culminates in an unconcern with moral issues. As yet, in the West, the Christian inheritance is responsible for an extensive hangover of moralism, at present used as a facade and justification for identification. But, in Eastern thought, the logic of the position has triumphed. Identification has, to cite a dramatic example, forbidden the killing of monkeys and cows in India, but has led to a radical moral detachment between man and man in the face of frightful tragedies and sufferings. It is inevitably so. The basic orientation of identification is, as we have seen with Schweitzer, egocentric. It destroys the meaning of both particularity and universality and leaves only the self's desire for deliverance from the misery of existence. The particular loses meaning, in that the whole alone is real, and the whole, having no real differentiation, becomes an empty universal, and moral categories disappear in the face of a radical relativism. The ultimate outcome, therefore, of identification in Western society will be, if its inherent logic triumphs, the rise of a radical inhumanity and the collapse of all true progress as total relativism takes over.

In contrast to this, it is important to understand, in full focus and with none of the offense removed, the biblical doctrine of holiness and separation. The ethical emphasis of Scripture is not man-centered, as with moralism, but God-centered, in that its fundamental nature and basic structure is that the holiness and righteousness of God be manifested in man, created in God's image, and this righteousness must become the ground of fellowship with God in and through Christ, and of fellowship between man and man. Instead of identification, there is an antithesis between God and man, first metaphysical, because one is Creator and the other creature, the one uncreated being and the other created being, and, second, ethical, because of the fact of sin. The metaphysical difference is absolute and eternal; the ethical is overcome by God in Christ. God is all-holy and perfect, and man is a sinner who can never command God by his works and can only approach Him in the person of the sin-bearer and re-creator, Jesus Christ. The union with God in Christ is never a community in being but a community of life by an act of grace. Again, rather than identification between man and man, there is a call to separation in terms of the moral antithesis, and to communion in terms of membership in Christ. Holiness means, in the Hebrew, "separation" or "setting apart," and the English word holy, from the Anglo-Saxon "halig," means "whole" or "sound," also a fundamental aspect of holiness. The biblical summons to holiness and health is thus a call to separation: "Wherefore come out from among them, and be ye separate, saith the Lord, and touch not the unclean thing; and I will receive you" (II Cor. 6:17). This is the condition of adoption into the household of God (v. 18). This separation is to be in terms of the life of the church and in terms of fellowship generally; Christians are not to identify themselves with evil, although business, political, and other dealings are necessary, unavoidable, and a godly responsibility. To seek total separation is absurd, "for then must ye needs go out of the world" (I Cor. 5:10). But the Christian's calling is in the world and in terms of it; he cannot morally seek escape from it or its citizens; what he must beware of is *identification* with it. Enticers to idolatry, even if of one's own household, could not be spared: there was to be a total separation, concluding, in the Old Testament, with death (Deut. 13) as treason to the holy commonwealth.

Holiness included humane dealings, and humane laws abounded, as witness the following Mosaic laws regarding such duties towards persons (by no means an exhaustive list):

1. To widows and orphans: Ex. 22:22-24; Deut. 24:17; 27:19.
2. To neighbors: Deut. 22:4; Lev. 19:13, 18.
3. To the poor: Ex. 23:6; Lev. 19:10; 25:35, 39, 43.
4. To sojourners: Ex. 22:21; 23:9; Lev. 19:33, 34; Deut. 10:18, 19; 24:15, 27:19.
5. To the needy and defenseless: Lev. 19:14; Deut. 24:14; 27:18.

6. To slaves and servants: Deut. 24:14, 15; 15:12-15; Ex. 21:2; 23:12.
7. Reverence for the aged: Lev. 19:32.
8. To construct battlements to prevent falls: Deut. 22:8.

Humane treatment of animals was also required:

1. Beasts of burden: Ex. 23:12.
2. The threshing ox: Deut. 25:4.
3. To wild animals: Ex. 23:11; Lev. 25:5-7.
4. Mother and young: Deut. 22:6, 7; Lev. 22:28; Ex. 34:26.
5. Return of strays: Ex. 23:4, 5; Deut. 22:1-4.

An animal harming or killing a man was to be destroyed, however (Ex. 21:28-32).

But it should be noted that it is precisely in the context of a series of humane laws, and as the conclusion of them, that one of the statements most offensive to the modern mind occurs, the requirement by God that the nation Amalek be destroyed completely. Although as yet Amalek has not had the archaeological resurrection other once-forgotten states and empires have enjoyed, its significance was such that Balaam could declare, "Amalek was the first of the nations; but his latter end shall be that he perish forever" (Num. 24:20). Always a bitter foe of Israel, Amalek expressed its contempt of Israel's God, at a time when all nations feared and trembled, by attacking them at Rephidim. Whereas Moses commanded Israel, "thou shalt not abhor an Egyptian; because thou wast a stranger in his land" (Deut. 23:7), yet "thou shalt blot out the remembrance of Amalek from under heaven" (Deut. 25:19), because Amalek, in violation of all humanity, had brutally slaughtered the sick, aged, feeble, and weary who had lingered behind to revive themselves at Horeb. Amalek had "smote the hindmost of thee" (Deut. 25:18), "literally, 'and tailed thee'; i.e., cut off the tail, or rear." [14] Egypt had sought to exterminate Israel, but they must remember that they had also had their years of privilege in Egypt and were, after all, strangers or foreigners there. But Amalek had revealed a radical and basic inhumanity which, while lesser in extent than Egypt's evil, was far more serious in its

[14] W. L. Alexander in H. D. M. Spence and Joseph S. Excell: *Pulpit Commentary, Deuteronomy*, p. 393f. New York: Funk and Wagnalls.

implications. Egypt had feared their strength and warred brutally in terms of that, but Amalek had killed without provocation, purposelessly and in sheer delight in inhumane action. The inclination would be to remember the larger actions of Egypt and forget the episode with Amalek, but this would have been to neglect the fundamental principle. Subsequent history often saw Egypt on peaceful terms with Israel, and, sometimes without any compromise, a valid co-existence. This did not prove true in Amalek's case.

An important principle is involved here, and definitely raised by the text by its conjunction with humane laws and its references to Amalek's inhumanity. The alternative to identification is a concept of separation, and separation is based on religious and ethical premises which require an evaluation of every person, people, or situation in terms of them. The attitude of God is one of blessing or cursing (Deut. 27, 28), and man must echo these pronouncements and say Amen to God. With most peoples, there can and must be a separate but peaceful co-existence, but there can be no peaceful co-existence with the Amaleks of history, both because they themselves will not allow it, and neither will God. In neither Amalek's nor the Canaanite nations' cases, did God order an immediate "holy war," as some would have it, but, as the occasion arose, little by little, they must recognize the irreconcilable nature of their positions and act in the awareness that the outcome could only be death or abject surrender on the one hand, or victory on the other, with no possibility of separate but friendly co-existence. It was not God's will that an immediate attempt to force the issue take place; it would happen, by His providence, "little by little" (Deut. 7:24). Moreover, in that process and history, it became the testing of the people and their faithfulness to the premises of their culture.

The implications are very important. A nation bent on the world establishment of the concept of identification will operate on the premise that the goal must be unity or union and will work to that end, sacrificing itself constantly in terms of that hoped-for consummation. But a nation aware that some issues are irreconcilable, while avoiding any ungodly plunge into conflict, will recognize that there can be no compromise, and that peaceful co-existence in such instances is an illusion. It will seek therefore to strengthen its own life in terms of its premises and also to be prepared for the unwelcome conflict. Whereas identification, by its total pity, ultimately destroys pity and results in inhumanity, separation, by its ruthlessness towards evil and its refusal to identify itself with flagrant evil or perversions, is ultimately the only source of true pity, of which fact biblical history gives abundant witness.

The rebellion against responsibility has as an aspect of its impetus a fear of and resentment against accountability. Holiness, righteousness, responsibility, and accountability: All these terms speak also of the dread possibility of failure, and a scheme which makes failure and guilt the shadows of man's every step is presently very unpopular. Better a system of identification which removes this possibility. In Francis of Assisi an attempt to use Christianity as the vehicle of identification was very early made. Francis identified himself with Christ to the point of reproducing the stigmata, thus identifying himself with the atonement also. But he also identified himself with the animals, birds, fish, and all nature in a radical sense, including "brother worm." In his "Canticle of the Sun," he called the sun his brother, the moon, his sister, spoke of "our brother the wind," "our sister water," "our brother fire," "our mother the earth," and so on. He refused to allow any formal organization of his order, or any discipline. "I will not become an executioner to strike and punish as political governors must." The suspicions of Innocent III concerning the heresy of Francis and the movement were later verified in the thinking of the minority of the Franciscans who were faithful to this thinking. On the other hand, Dominic, who sought, rightly or wrongly, to develop the implications of the faith, led his movement directly into two courses of action. First, Dominicans became leaders in education, in theology, and in philosophy. Second, by developing the implications of the faith, they also developed the implications of error. Dominic became known as the "Hammer of Heretics" and his friars as the "Hounds of God." They were instrumental in the Albigensian Crusade. We may not agree with this specific instance, and may also radically disagree with Dominican philosophy (and this writer does), but the fact remains that, except when in the sentimental bondage of the concept of identification, intelligence is given to discernment, discrimination, and judgment, and the outcome is some form of conflict, whether intellectual, international, or military. For this reason intellectuals have always been prominent, both rightly and wrongly, in the role of "warmongers," to give it the worst sense, or as public defenders, to give it the intended sense.

How much more sharp, then, is the sense of discernment, discrimination, and judgment when established directly, rather than culturally, on a supernatural revelation whose implications must be developed afresh with every generation. Inescapably, there is conflict. Jesus made it very clear to all who sought to evade that harsh reality that He came, not to bring this false peace of erasure of moral and spiritual distinction and the syrup of identification, but rather to bring a sword, i.e., division even between very families, between father and son, and in terms of this faith men must be ready to lose their lives for his sake (Matt. 10:34-39).

The goal of identification thinking, however disguised, is freedom from moral responsibility. Even in Schweitzer this is apparent. Since all are guilty inescapably and without any action on their part, since all must live at the expense of other lives and were so born and reared, then, irrespective of the nature of an action, forgiveness must always be granted, for who dares insist on moral perfection? The inevitable implication of this is clear: what matters sin between men? For Schweitzer, to refuse forgiveness "would be acting as if I myself were not guilty." [15] The basic reference is thus the "I" and its attempt to escape responsibility. For the orthodox Christian, forgiveness is granted only according to God's word without any sense of personal difficulty because the believer places not only the sinner but himself also under the authority of God's word. He is not concerned with avoiding the embarrassment of judging men through courts, church sessions and consistories, and by God-appointed means, because this framework of reference is not himself but God. His concern, therefore, is to strengthen society in terms of true justice and true mercy, and he places himself and all

[15] Schweitzer, *op. cit.*, p. 252.

men under the word of God as the sole means of bringing men to true forgiveness and true freedom.

Here we come to the heart of the matter. For biblical faith, freedom is not an escape from law and responsibility, but an aspect and outcome of obedience and of responsible action. A contemporary minor celebrity has been hailed by reviewers of his autobiography as a remarkably free person, apparently because he has been married repeatedly, served time in prison, been a narcotic addict, a TV and stage celebrity, and a man involved in endless erratic and irresponsible activities, and, in various ways, shown himself incapable of a mature and consistent use of his abilities. This, apparently, is living, and this, we are to believe from author and reviewer, is freedom. Freedom is thus associated with that unpredictability and eccentricity which is the hallmark of personality breakdowns, of neurosis and psychosis. And, indeed, these "free-spirits" betray a great familiarity with the psycho-analytic couch and a singular lack of freedom in governing themselves. But, in terms of biblical faith, man only finds his freedom under God and in terms of responsible action. Instead of escape from problems and testing, he is assured their inevitability. The New Jerusalem comes, while not as a product of historical activity but eschatologically, nevertheless in direct and vital connection with the true church's struggle and triumph in history, as the Book of Revelation declares. Freedom is developed by fire and testing, and it develops with godly responsibility and is a concomitant of sanctification and has its genesis in justification.

Freedom thus develops with *creaturely* responsibility. It cannot exist where man seeks to be god and to claim powers and responsibilities that he does not possess. Man cannot be his brother's keeper, but only his brother's brother. To claim unwarranted powers and responsibilities is itself a dangerous form of irresponsibility. Man cannot identify himself as a god without damage to his humanity, nor can he assume unwarranted, unreal, and impossible burdens without forsaking his real responsibilities.

Schweitzer, in a late restatement of his position, affirmed his basic skepticism as far as any "concept of the world" is concerned. His "ethics of self-sacrifice" has no objective justification but is "thoroughly subjective." It is "the principle of self-sacrifice through compassion," and he was certain that "ethics is primarily a matter of compassion," that is, of identification, and it is a concept that "constantly forces us to attempt the impossible," in that it requires reverence, worship, and identification with all life. Commented Schweitzer, "Philosophy fears, and rightly so, that this huge enlargement of the circle of our responsibilities will take away from ethics the small hope which it still has to formulate reasonable and satisfactory commandments." We become "by necessity, guilty. We should seek forgiveness by never missing an occasion to rescue living creatures." [16] Thus, Schweitzer himself stated that critics fear the implications of his doctrine, "and rightly so," because it destroys ethics by reducing it to impossibility! An impossible ethics which makes man "by necessity, guilty," seeks atonement by unconditional and unlimited forgiveness and the rescue of every living creature is nothing more than rampant masochism and the death of ethics. It is a means of self-punishment and suicide, more politely called "self-sacrifice." It is a policy of willful destruction operating under the illusion of unlimited capacity. As applied to politics, it calls for the self-destruction of the strong in a manner designed to further weaken the weak through *planned irresponsibility*.

At one point, however, taxpayers in the United States can be grateful: while the continents and nations have been heard from and generously cared for, no application for foreign aid has as yet come from "our brother worm." But perhaps the President and Congress, with their usual foresight, will graciously remedy this oversight.

[16] Albert Schweitzer: "The Evolution of Ethics," in *The Atlantic Monthly*, November, 1958, vol. 202, no. 5, pp. 69-73.

3

THE HERESY OF LOVE AND THE NEW TYRANNY

One of the fundamental and often repeated commandments of Scripture is the love of neighbors and of enemies. In Leviticus 19:18, personal acts of vengeance, taking the law into one's own hands, are forbidden, and, as the positive aspect of the same statement, it is required that "thou shalt love thy neighbor as thyself." That this includes one's enemies is made clear in verses 33-34.[1]

There are two especially prevalent misinterpretations of the biblical law of love. The first may be called the monastic view. The love of neighbor in this perspective means the despising of one's life, of personal property, and of creation itself out of a selfless love for God and neighbor. Its logical conclusion is an other-worldly perspective, a withdrawal from the world into a cell, and the summoning of all men to share in the same conventual communism. The true love of God and neighbor means a despising of things, a superiority to considerations of rights and property as mundane, and an assumption of voluntary poverty as the truly godly life. Roman Catholicism, social gospel and liberal or modernist Protestantism, romantics and sentimentalists have been advocates of this concept of love, with variations. The popularity of Francis of Assisi has been due to his extremely sentimental and non-theological application of this same principle. A throwing away of one's life, an abandon to sacrifice, this is true love from this point of view. Numerous corporations of a secular sort have been dedicated to this faith, such as the Oneida and Kaweah colonies, with notable problems ensuing. The unwritten premise immediately appears, which is basic to every misinterpreta-

---

[1] The great treatment of the meaning of love in its biblical sense is Frederick Nymeyer: *Progressive Calvinism*, I, 1955. His "Essays Against Sanctimony and Legalized Coercion" are some of the most powerful and brilliant studies of our time.

tion of this commandment: *to love your neighbor as yourself means to hate yourself, your life and property, and hence, inevitably and ultimately, to hate your neighbor as your self. The commandment to love is made in essence a law of hate because of this unwritten premise.*

This law of hate, masquerading as a law of love, is also basic to the second common misinterpretation, best seen in Marxism, which calls for enforced sharing and enforced self-abnegation. In the first view, heaven is usually the remote reward, and, sometimes, in secular forms, a future paradise on earth. In the non-voluntary forms, the reward is more usually the future order on earth, a messianic state without God, and, in essence, without a recognizable man. This enforced love and sharing will ostensibly eliminate all sin, misery, and grief from the world and all problems of every kind. When perfect communism is attained, man will both have nothing and need nothing while theoretically possessing all things by virtue of forsaking all things. In this mysticism, an ant-hill society, not unlike the Incas, is envisioned. From this point of view, victory in war must of necessity be turned into defeat as a moral obligation, and, accordingly, the United States, having won in World War II, proceeded to conduct a radical program of sharing and self-abnegation in order to further a compulsive desire for this love-induced bankruptcy. The United Nations, the International Bank for Reconstruction and Development, and other such agencies, are monuments to this widespread faith.[2] Part and parcel of it too are the sociological and literary demands that we love the criminal, the homosexual, the insane and the depraved, the cruel and the sadistic, and it has even been suggested that the West failed to love sufficiently and hence "created" Hitler and Stalin. *Not only is this law of love in essence a law of hate, but truly personal love is viciously attacked and condemned as "charity" and hence degrading.* A direct, personal act of kindness or love towards a needy and deserving person is seen as a social affront, an attempt to evade social responsibility and a proud presumption. Indeed, in the 1960 state senatorial campaign in Cali-

[2] For one aspect of this, see J. Fred Rippy: *Globe and Hemisphere,* Latin America's Place in the Postwar Foreign Relations of the United States. Chicago: Regnery, 1958.

fornia, one politician waged a highly popular campaign in "behalf" of "our senior citizens, urging the repeal of the responsible relative law which is an undue hardship on many families." Thus, children with means are to be relieved of any responsibility for the financial welfare of their parents as an act of love and social responsibility! Christ, on the other hand, made it clear that God was not honored by any gift from one who failed to support his father or his mother (Matt. 15:1-9; Mark 7:9-13); such conduct made "the word of God of none effect," reduced it to a mockery, by this pretended and hypocritical love of God while parents were neglected. But all such private acts of responsibility are now labelled at the very least a "hardship" and are regarded as social dereliction. This new law of love is much easier: *instead of the hardship of responsibility it offers total irresponsibility to all men individually as the pathway to the responsibility of all men collectively.*

The true interpretation of the law of love, taught by Scripture itself (Lev. 19:15-18, 33-37; Matt. 22:34-40; Rom. 13:8-10) is very different from the emotional or social connotation read into it by these heresies. The second table of the law, and all related commandments, are "briefly comprehended in this saying, namely, Thou shalt love thy neighbor as thyself" (Rom. 13:9). The law of love, therefore, is a summation of these commandments: "Thou shalt not kill. Thou shalt not commit adultery. Thou shalt not steal. Thou shalt not bear false witness against thy neighbor. Thou shalt not covet. . ." (Ex. 20:13-17). Let us examine each of these more specifically:

1. "Thou shalt not kill." The state is given the right to kill in terms of God-given laws and principles, and in its defense. The individual, having the gift of life, must respect that same God-given life in others. Even as he loves and protects his own life, so he must grant that same privilege to others. He can kill only in defense of his life or property (Ex. 22:2).

2. "Thou shalt not commit adultery." The love and respect for one's own home and family means the same respect for and immunity of the homes of others, neighbors, friends, or enemies.

3. "Thou shalt not steal." Property is a God-given privilege and is to be respected both for one's own sake and for others. Neither through personal acts, through agents, or by means of governmental activities do we have the right to steal another man's property.[3]

4. "Thou shalt not bear false witness. . . ." Even as we want the protection of our own good name, so we must grant to others the immunity of reputation against false witness.

5. "Thou shalt not covet. . . ." Because another may be more privileged than we are with respect to any of these God-given aspects of life does not entitle us to that inward covetousness, in essence idolatry (Col. 3:5), whereby a man hatefully seeks to pull down all those who are better than himself.

Since this commandment so defines loving our neighbor as ourselves, it means clearly also that no man is capable of so loving his neighbor if he does not first love himself; if he has no respect for his God-given privileges of life, family, property and reputation, he is not likely to grant them to another. Thus the commandment requires that man's person, family, property, and reputation be granted this immunity from evil attack by word, thought, or deed, that we grant this immunity to others even as we expect it for ourselves. The law of love is thus not voluntary or involuntary communism, but rather liberty and the essence of any true bill of rights. If any man's immunities are attacked, we have an obligation, as the parable of the Good Samaritan states, to answer responsively and affirmatively to the question, "Who is my neighbor?" (Luke 10:25-37). The good neighbor, the Samaritan, seeing a man robbed and wounded, offers charity, assistance to help the man on his feet again, and then passes on. Three things are notable:

1. The good Samaritan shares no property but reveals rather a sense of compassion, as the law of charity requires.

2. Samaritans and Jews had religious and racial differences, and hated one another. The Samaritan did not change his opinion of

[3] The life set forth in biblical law is family-based and property-oriented. The laws protecting the family and property are many.

Jews. He showed respect for the person and needs of the Jew, whose immunities had been assaulted, and then passed on.

3. The Samaritan did not subsidize the Jew; he merely rescued him, and then went his way.

The modern heresy of love is the proclamation actually of a law of hate, and inevitably so. The will to death and the hatred of self is inescapable for unregenerate man, at war with God and man, and with himself, guilt-ridden and in flight from life, reality, and self-hood. The oblivion of Nirvana was an inescapable conclusion for the Buddha to seek, haunted by Karma as he was and hating his life as he did. Only he who loves God, fulfilling the first table of the law, can love himself and accordingly respect his neighbor's person and privileges, and enjoy life and its bounty under God.

The heresy of love takes the biblical declaration that God is love in isolation from all else whereby God defines himself, and then reverses it in meaning to conclude that love is God, and hence love is omnipotent. Accordingly, the hope of man's salvation is not the omnipotence of God but the omnipotence of human love. This in effect makes the man of love omnipotent and super-human. Gandhi, for example, tranquillized himself by chewing a drug root, avoided the humanity of sex, and espoused the pacifism of love as a means to both social victory and the attainment of oblivion from self-hood and humanity.

Not only is love omnipotent, but its omnipotence is by definition, according to Anders Nygren, in *Agape and Eros*, spontaneous, self-less, and uncaused, i.e., completely irrational. Such is God's *agape* or love, according to Nygren, thereby ruling out the eternal decree and God's predestinating counsel, and such must be man's love. Similarly, the kenotic conception of Christ in Russian theology made the entrance of communism possible in that culture, Christ ostensibly being virtuous and perfect by means of His emptying of himself of all power, a "love" of humiliation, a forsaking of prop-erty and of all prudence and common sense, and an adoption of an undiscriminating and promiscuous love.

This counsel of love, according to the heresy, requires a supine submission to evil, for anger, resistance, and conflict constitute the essence of sin, and are also separating and discriminating attitudes. In a very mild expression of this heresy, Oren Arnold has written, "There is no such thing as a church quarrel. If two factions of a congregation start quarreling, they have automatically denied the Christian fellowship." [4] In such thinking all principles other than love are gone. Paul was thus wrong in quarreling with Judaizers and legalists and denied the Christian fellowship; Athanasius was sinful in upholding the full trinitarian theology, and Luther and Calvin wicked in destroying the unity of the Church.

Here again, another aspect of this law of hate masquerading as love appears: *its concern is for unity rather than truth or liberty*. Hence, such thinking is strongly partisan to church unity and ecumenicity as in itself good, irrespective of truth. It upholds the United Nations and world peace at any price, because love, peace, and unity are more to be valued than truth or freedom. Divisiveness is thus the sin of sins in church and society, whereas truth is always divisive according to Jesus, the bearer of the discriminating sword of justice rather than the peace of compromise, surrender, and the reign of the lie (Matt. 10:34). This *heresy of love* ends finally in the new *tyranny of love*, in as rigid a compulsion as the world has yet seen. Whether he believes in "voluntary" and personal "love" or in state enforced "love," the champion of this heresy demands what not even God requires, that ultimately every last person be compelled to submit to the power of love. The God of Scripture allows to the dignity of the creature's rebellion the security of hell, but no such privilege will be allowed the enemies of this strange love. As one such theologian has stated it, "The goal of the universe is the end of all estrangement," so that not only the demonic powers but Satan himself will be finally loved into salvation.[5] This love run amuck will make a harp-plucking angel even of Satan. Man .is thus made an automaton in the name of love. Love of self is revealed to be hatred of self and hatred of the integrity of self. A universal levelling is demanded, and truth and man must be crushed under this jugger-

---

[4] Oren Arnold: "Family Man," p. 37, *Presbyterian Life*, vol. 13, no. 9, May 1, 1960.

[5] John S. Whale: *Victor and Victim, The Christian Doctrine of Redemption*, p. 41. Cambridge: University Press, 1960.

naut of hate that screams of love. This heresy of love will not permit man to love his family, property, or himself. Whether preached from pulpit or senate, or affirmed in psychiatric counselling, it is the counsel of death and despair and the foundation of a new tyranny.

The meaning of Leviticus 19:18 is thus clear-cut: "Thou shalt not take vengeance, nor bear any grudge against the children of thy people; but thou shalt love thy neighbor as thyself: I am Jehovah" (R.V.). Personal acts of vengeance, taking the law into one's own hands, are forbidden in the first part of this law. Law and justice are to be administered only through the appointed social and civil agencies. This is the negative aspect of the law of love. The positive aspect makes clear that, while justice in its penal aspects cannot be administered by the individual, justice in its positive aspect does involve the individual and rests firmly on the character of the people. A man must love and respect his God-given privileges of life, family, property, and reputation, and must respect these same privileges in others, whether friends or enemies. Thus to love one's enemy does not mean to feel an emotional attachment to him, or to share one's property with him, but, in spite of personal hatred, however well grounded, to respect his God-given immunities because of a love of God and a love of one's own self, out of a conviction that, because God is God, the truest justice begins with God and then manifests itself in the context of man's personal life.

4

THE PURPOSES OF LAW

The effect of relativism and pragmatism has been to erode the concept of law so that the idea of law, often very explicit to tribal man, is a vague and meaningless thing to secular man. But social order is impossible without law, and the decline of order is a product of the decline of law.

What, then, is the current evaluation of law? Max Radin, in *Law as Logic and Experience*, sees law as often having been in intent logic, logic here meaning the manifestation of an eternal and rational order of law and justice. But, following Oliver Wendell Holmes, who began *The Common Law* (1881) with the statement, "The life of the law has not been logic: it has been experience," Radin sees it also as experience. For Radin, however much committed to law as experience, logic is still indispensable. "We cannot state human experience except in terms of some generality which involves logic." [1] The logic Radin chooses to use is in essence humaneness: "the better kind of justice was determined by an irrational sense of human brotherhood, by a concession to humanity which in this case was the same as humaneness . . . the justice that just men who are also humane men will apply when they are judges. Just men are men who are so far Kantians that they do not think of other men as a means to their ends, not even when the others are concededly and immeasurably inferior to themselves. . . . Humanity is, after all, the business of the law." [2] We can certainly agree with the need for humaneness, but when we reduce the law to humaneness and equate justice with it, then we have replaced justice with pity and sub-

[1] Max Radin: *Law as Logic and Experience*, p. 98. New Haven: Yale University Press, 1940.
[2] *Ibid.*, pp. 162-164.

stituted sentimentality for law. The logic of Radin's system is that of autonomous man, whose only law is himself.

Thurman W. Arnold holds a related position to Radin's. "True" and "false" are by-passed as categories of thought and replaced by "scientific thinking." Indeed, Arnold is so naive as to believe that he begins without preconceived assumptions, and, as a scientist, merely produces "instead of a system, however, a series of observations, mostly concerning details." [3] However, every observation is from a point of view and in terms of a highly developed if unrecognized philosophy. Arnold attacks relentlessly the idea that law represents any eternal order of truth; rather, it is merely folklore.

> If it be true that economic, legal, and political theory is only the folklore of modern society, the reverse side of the paradox must be kept in mind. Folklore which is frankly recognized by a people to be folklore is from that moment no longer folklore. Its magic is gone, and a new folklore, which is not so recognized, must arise.[4]

What this jargon conceals is the fact that, when a society doubts the *truth* of its foundations, it seeks *truth* anew, renouncing the error, because it refuses to live in terms of a *recognized lie*. Arnold himself notes that "the law is a barometer of the spiritual contentment of a people," and the courts and law are a measure of its stability.[5] At present, Arnold sees a new philosophy emerging whose fundamental axiom may be "that man works only for his fellow man," in other words, a collectivist faith.[6] Truth, however, remains irrelevant as a test. "The world will never see a permanently valid philosophy until science discovers a method of making Time stand still." [7] In spite of all this, Arnold looks hopefully to the rise of psychiatry, the rise of a "competent, opportunistic governing class" free from "preconceived principles" so that "the practical alleviation of human distress and the distribution of available comforts" may

---

[3] Thurman W. Arnold: *The Symbols of Government*, p. 30. New Haven: Yale University Press, 1936.
[4] *Ibid.*, p. 237.
[5] *Ibid.*, p. 248.
[6] *Ibid.*, p. 263.
[7] *Ibid.*, p. 267.

be attained rather than frustrated. Thus indeed, in Arnold's own words, he "has faith" in the triumph of certain things "and to that hope this book is dedicated." [8] Humaneness and humanity are again the new principle of law in this ostensibly principle-free "science."

Modern thinkers to the contrary, law is a product of metaphysics, a cultural expression of a basically religious faith. The contemporary avoidance of metaphysics is by no means its elimination. Men do not dispense with metaphysics merely because they refuse to discuss it, any more than a polite avoidance of reference to defecation eliminates that fact. Metaphysics underlies everyday speech, thought, and action. Religious presuppositions undergird every activity of man and are the unspoken premises behind every word. Sentences are like icebergs, concealing beneath the surface the more massive world of meaning which supports them. The concealed and the unspoken are not thereby eliminated. The modern philosophic prudery regarding metaphysics is thus too often a pathetic example of magical thought-patterns, a belief that facts can be dissipated and caused to vanish by mental or verbal conjurations. Pragmatism has not banished metaphysics from its philosophy; it has only become more primitive therein. Logical analysis, by renouncing metaphysics while presupposing it in every sentence, is only demonstrating its naive lack of self-analysis and its incomprehension of the meaning of pre-reflective presuppositions.

As Bronislaw Malinowski and others have observed, all social organization, without exception, implies a series of norms, so that the whole of social life and activity are regulated by these norms. Law is one aspect of this normative living, and, like religion, of which it is a cultural manifestation, it has its creed, ritual, ceremony, and form. Indeed, Aristotle reported that the Agathyrsians of Transylvania expressed their laws in song, a not uncommon way for men to manifest their faith. Because law is important, its procedure is important, and laws are thus both substantive and adjective laws.

From the beginning, man, in trying to understand what law must be, has been seduced by the concept of natural law as against the biblical insistence on supernatural law. Between the two, despite

8 *Ibid.*, pp. 267-271.

all medieval and post-medieval attempts at synthesis, is an irreconcilable conflict. The Bible indeed speaks of the material universe as hostile to the evildoer (Judg. 5:20), but only because that world is absolutely controlled and used by the Lord of Hosts.

Long before the concept of natural law was ever formulated in its most primitive form, it was an article of faith in such legal forms as trial by fire, trial by combat, trial by sea, and other forms of trial by ordeal. Basic to the concept of the ordeal is the belief that nature, the world as it is, is normative and will reject the evildoer. The universe is law incarnate, and the outcome must inevitably reveal that law. The hostility of the Bible to this is immediately apparent; biblical faith sees the world as fallen and perverted and definitely not normative. As the psalmist observed, "I have seen the wicked in great power, and spreading himself like a green bay tree" (Ps. 37:35). The source of law therefore can in no wise be a fallen and rebellious creation, both because it is derivative and created, and because it is perverted. It can only be the sovereign and omnipotent God. The Mosaic law, given in an age dominated by the concept of the bond of heaven and earth as one, and the normative character of nature, in one startling law parodied the trial by ordeal and forced a comparison between God's law and all current law. This is the trial of jealousy in Numbers 5:11-31, given in meticulous detail.[9] Indeed, Scripture gives more attention to this principial law than to others of seemingly greater moment to modern readers. Briefly stated, the trial of jealousy was as follows: a woman suspected of adultery by her husband was given water by the priest to drink before the Lord, the water carrying the consecration either to bless or to curse. If the woman were guilty, the water would become bitter, cause her belly to swell and her thigh to rot, "and the woman shall be a curse among her people," and, if innocent, "then

[9] This passage is dealt with, uncomprehendingly, by Hans Kelsen: *What Is Justice? Justice, Law, and Politics in the Mirror of Science*, p. 28f. Berkeley: University of California Press, 1957. Kelsen dismisses it as magic and as "highly repulsive to the religious feeling as well as to the idea of due process of law prevailing among modern Christians." No attempt is made to understand this passage, which, like others, is dismissed from the lofty perspective of "science" so called.

she shall be free." By contrast, in the natural law trial of ordeal, the woman would be given poison to drink and would be guilty if natural consequences followed. The difference is a very striking one. In the Mosaic ordinance, nature is incapable of convicting; a supernatural act could alone bring judgment. In the other, nature is normative and determines the case. In the one instance, judgment is supernatural, in the other, natural, each operating on radically different premises. For natural law, justice is the nature of nature. For biblical law, justice is a divine interposition, usually through ordained human agencies, into the world of man and nature, and is the *restoration of order* to a disordered and fallen world and the *addition of growth and direction* to a decaying and directionless society. In the long history of the ordeal in Western culture, there is a close relationship between the ordeal and the prevalence of natural law theology, a faith widely held in both the Roman and Protestant churches. The ordeal gave way finally only to other expressions of the same faith in the normative character of nature, which is the basic tenet of the trial, whether in its Chinese, Teutonic, Iranian, or pseudo-Christian forms. This belief in the rejection of the evildoer by nature is hostile to a faith which holds that nature itself is in bondage (Rom. 8:15-23), and that, while indeed nature reflects the glory of God (Ps. 19:1), only "the law of the LORD is perfect" (Ps. 19:7), and God alone is the author of law. The starting point and premise of the law is "I am the LORD (Jehovah)" (Ex. 20:2). The natural law concept, whether in its form of trial by ordeal or in philosophical formulation, has inevitably given way to relativism and pragmatism, which indeed, are forms of natural law and developments thereof.

The concept of natural law profited for some centuries by its association with Christian thought and its relation to an absolute and sovereign law-giver, God. As the supernatural lost its relevancy to Western man, natural law became "naturalized" and increasingly identified with some aspect of the human order such as the majority, the general will, the state, or positive law, until it lost all meaning, until finally realists such as Holmes turned from it in disgust in favor of a concept of law as experience.[10]

For biblical faith, nature is not the source of the law, but God alone, who is the law-giver but himself free from the law, not because He is outside the law but because He is above it. In other words, the law does not govern God but is governed by Him. Law is thus the boundary between God and creation, in that the creature cannot transcend his creaturehood. The sin of man was "to be as God" (Gen. 3:5, RV), to be his own source of law and to be both his own law-giver, and yet free and outside all law. For biblical thought, as Dooyeweerd has pointed out, "the lex is recognized as originating from God's holy creative sovereignty, and as the absolute boundary between the Being of the *arche* and the meaning of everything created as 'subject,' *subjected* to a law." [11]

What are the purposes of law? In virtually every culture, whatever other purpose the law may have, its central function is *to make men good*, to bring them into conformity with the right order of things. Indeed, in some languages the words for "right" and "law" are identical. The attempts of man to attain the millennium or the golden age through law and law reform are legion, and their failures conspicuous. As Seagle has observed, "It has been said that those who live by the sword shall perish by the sword. It is equally true true that those who live by the law shall perish by the law!" [12] Certainly, whatever conceptions philosophers may hold, the popular conception of law is very simply stated: its purpose is to make men and society good. Legislation from time immemorial has been directed to this end, and moral crusades have usually ended in the statute books. The Briand-Kellogg Pact of Paris, August, 1928, outlawed war, and by August, 1932, sixty-two of the sixty-four nations of the world had signed it. Behind that pact stands a long history of ancient, medieval, and modern endeavor and legislation, and the United Nations is a monument to that continuing hope.

[10] For a study of the breakdown of natural law, see John H. Hollowell: *The Decline of Liberalism as an Ideology, with particular reference to German Politico-Legal Thought.* Berkeley: University of California Press, 1943.

[11] Herman Dooyeweerd: *A New Critique of Theoretical Thought*, Vol. I, p. 108. Philadelphia: Presbyterian and Reformed Publishing Co., 1953.

[12] William Seagle: *Law: The Science of Inefficiency*, p. 167. New York: Macmillan, 1952.

Legalistic moralism or Phariseeism seeks to legislate men into goodness, and to so order society that man will become inevitably and necessarily good as well as happy. The modern era certainly gives widespread evidence of this hope. The Roman Church, both by its penitential system and by its moralistic concept of salvation, seeks to legislate man into heaven, and, by its concept of the Christian state, strives to create an order where men must be godly. Protestant Christianity, by seeking legislation against personal vices as the means to social order on the one hand, and by its social gospel on the other, seeks to make men good by means of the state rather than by Christ. Marxism, a modern form of Phariseeism, affirms the same faith in the ability of law to recreate man, and the purpose of the state is to use legislation to reshape man and society. The welfare state in the West has a similar function. In each and every one of these forms, the law is moralism with a maximum use of the whip. No morality can forego the whip, but every morality becomes a beggarly moralism when the whip replaces religious faith as the basic impetus to action. In morality, the priority in action is a God-centered motivation; in moralism, the theocentric impetus is either gone or is secondary. And the modern era is passionately moralistic in its orientation.

Wilhelm Ropke has called attention to the moralism inherent in all modern socialists, collectivists or centrists.

> We see also that the centrist is what we have called a moralist, a moralist of the cheap rhetorical kind, who misuses big words, such as freedom, justice, rights of man, or others, to the point of empty phraseology, who poses as a paragon of virtues and stoops to use his moralism as a political weapon and to represent his more reserved adversary as morally inferior. Since, again, he looks at things from on high, well above the reality of individual people, his moralism is of an abstract, intellectual kind. It enables him to feel morally superior to others for the simple reason that he stakes his moral claims so high and makes demands on human nature without considering either the concrete conditions or the possible consequences of the fulfillment of those demands. He does not seem capable of imagining that others may not be lesser men because they make things less easy for themselves and do take account of the complications and

difficulties of a practical and concrete code of ethics within which it is not unusual to will the good and work the bad.

The "left" moralist all too often reaches the point where his big words of love and freedom and justice serve as a cover for the exact opposite. The moralist, with his lofty admonitions, becomes an intolerant hater and envier, the theoretical pacifist an imperialist when it comes to the practical test, and the advocate of abstract social justice an ambitious place-hunter.[13]

The purpose of moralists of every variety is to use both government and law as instruments in making man and his society good.

Moralism thus reveals its conception of the good life by means of its laws, but it also reveals far more, for law is an index not only to the ethics of a people but also to its religion. Law is thus not only a representation or symbol of the good life but of life itself, either as it is, in formally religious societies, or as it will be, in the secular religions of scientific evolution. Life, in Darwinian and post-Darwinian evolutionary thinking, is in process, and therefore reality is in process, but that process has a goal, the perfection of man and his society. Darwin, in the concluding two paragraphs of *The Origin of Species*, affirmed his basic faith in that goal. From a "simple" and wretched beginning, "from the war of nature, from famine and death, the most exalted object which we are capable of conceiving, namely, the production of higher animals, directly follows." Man can therefore "look with some confidence to a secure future of great length. And as natural selection works solely by and for the good of each being, all corporeal and mental endowments will tend to progress towards perfection." Several pre-scientific presuppositions are immediately discernable in these few lines:

1. The process is indeed ugly, but the goal is a glorious one and justifies the process.

2. Progress is thus a basic aspect of reality.

3. Progress is not endless but is towards perfection and is thus in terms of a realizeable and approximate goal.

4. Not only is the process towards the goal for the perfection of

13 Wilhelm Ropke: *A Humane Economy, the Social Framework of the Free Market*, p. 229f. Chicago: Henry Regnery, 1960.

the whole, but it "works solely by and for the good of each being," so that the perfection is for the whole and every part. Thus, the biblical promise of Romans 8:28 is surpassed: all things work together for good, not merely for the elect, but for every single individual as well as the totality.

5. "The most exalted object which we are capable of conceiving" is not God but "the higher animals," by implication man in particular. Thus, the goal of the universal process is by inference the apotheosis of man.

There can be no denying the fact that this indeed has been the presupposition of all political thinking oriented to the Darwinian and evolutionary theory. As a result, law has had a very simple and utilitarian or pragmatic function: to hasten man into this eschatological order of bliss. The unwilling must, for their own welfare, be legislated into this goodness. However unwilling modern thinkers may be to reveal the basic moralism of their theories of law, the basic moralism remains. Note, for example, John Dewey's definition of law: "Law is a statement of the conditions of the organizations of energies which, when unorganized, conflict and result in violence— that is, destruction or waste." [14] Certain implications stand out clearly:

1. Since, as Dewey himself pointed out, force cannot be separated from law, Dewey obviously presupposes some concept of *force* which makes it differ from *violence*.

2. Again, there is an assumption that certain energies are destructive or wasteful whereas others are both lawful and constructive, or, at least constructive and potentially lawful.

3. Law, therefore, with the support of force as the necessary fuel for law, organizes the energies of society to produce the maximum of desired "construction" as against "destruction."

4. "Energies" should not "conflict," as they will do when "unorganized," which obviously means, as Dewey so obviously intends, that planning and central direction are necessary to a society.

[14] John Dewey: *Intelligence in the Modern World*, p. 489. New York: Modern Library, 1939.

5. The result is law without transcendence in a society without transcendence, one in which the organized energy which suppresses conflict is in effect divinized and made the law behind law. As one of Dewey's most astute critics has observed, "The State can do no wrong, for right is determined by what the State does." [15]

The outcome of Dewey's thinking is no different from that of every other moralistic system. Wherever ethics takes priority over metaphysics, and morality over religion, there we have inevitably man's divinization and the reduction of law to man's will. This is as true of the ostensibly orthodox *Christian Commitment* (1957) of Edward John Carnell as it is of the works of Auguste Comte.

Again, when the Church of Rome moved from the Augustinianism of Anselm to the Aristotelianism of Abelard and Aquinas, it moved into a radically non-Christian epistemology which stressed man's autonomy and Hellenized Christian thought. The biblical contrast between sin and grace was replaced by a contrast between nature and grace, the world of nature thus being separated from God and given a separate existence. The world of grace became the cloister and the retreat, and the other-worldly note, so alien to biblical faith and so increasingly prominent in post-apostolic Christianity, became increasingly reinforced philosophically by Scholasticism, until Occam's razor implicitly shaved the supernatural out of the universe. Reason became the prerogative of philosophy and science by virtue of the divided world, and a blind and irrational faith the diminished area of religion. Sin and grace had nothing to do with nature, sin being merely a loss of supernatural grace and not a perversion of nature, so that grace had no relation to nature or to reason, merely restoring as it did the supernatural gift or appendix. This legacy of Aquinas divorced God from nature and made moralism the practical man's substitute for God. Mystical experience and the intellectual vision of God were the expert's means to salvation; for most men, the ladder of works was the practical answer. This concept of works, set in the framework of a non-Christian epistemology, was the triumph of moralism in that the whole of man's life was made to rest, not on the grace of God, but on the work of man, which

[15] Gordon H. Clark: *Dewey*, p. 33. Philadelphia: Presbyterian and Reformed Publishing Co., 1960.

governed the flow of grace. This governed flow has dominated not only the Roman faith, and some Puritan and Anabaptist concepts of the coming of the Kingdom of God, but secular revolutionary movements as well.

Moralism thus has deep roots in church history and has been the predominant temper of its thinking. In its secular form, the Enlightenment set out to re-create the earth in terms of moralism, and the French Revolution united three factors as essential to all such thinking since then, "the alliance between irreligion, utopian hope and compulsion. The outcome of this combined Secularist venture has been so far not an earthly paradise but something very different— the modern State." [16] The church has been impotent in dealing with this crisis of culture, because, whether through papal encyclicals, World Council of Churches reports, the social gospel, or fundamentalistic revivals, it has itself had only a baptized moralism to offer and thus been unable to challenge autonomous man's drift to suicide.

A forthright answer to moralism and its anthropocentric concept of law is the essence of the biblical concept of the law, summarized by Paul in Romans 3, Galatians 3, etc., and restated at the Reformation, but unfortunately too soon neglected by both Lutherans and Calvinists. John Calvin, in *The Institutes of the Christian Religion* (first draft, 1534 or 1535, final edition 1559), and the Lutheran *Formula of Concord* (1576), clearly defined the purposes of law in biblical terms. *The Formula of Concord* clearly showed the influence of Calvinism and was not given as wide an acceptance by Lutherans as were other confessions. Calvinism itself was soon infected by rationalism and became as moralistic as any of its rivals, and areas of ostensible orthodoxy, such as Scotland, were areas of a strident rationalistic moralism. Thomas Reid (1710-1796) radically rationalized the nature of Calvinism and left his mark on Scottish and American Presbyterianism, leaving only the shell of Calvinism and replacing its theocentricity with a pronounced anthropology.[17]

[16] Erich Meissner: *Confusion of Faces, The Struggle between Religion and Secularism in Europe*, p. 63. London: Faber and Faber, 1946.

[17] Lee Sydney E. Ahlstrom, "The Scottish Philosophy and American Theology" in *Church History*, XXIV, 3, September, 1955, pp. 257-272, and H. Evan Runner in *Christian Perspectives 1960*, pp. 109-158, Pella, Iowa: Pella Publishing Co., 1960.

Calvin wrote of the threefold office and use of the law in *The Institutes*, Bk. II, Ch. VII, "The Law Given, Not to Confine the Ancient People to Itself, but to Encourage Their Hope of Salvation in Christ, till the Time of His Coming." For Calvin, not only can the law make no man good, but no man can by any means observe the law, i.e., "reach the standard of true perfection."

> If we inquire from the remotest period of antiquity, I assert that there never has existed a saint, who, surrounded with a body of death, could attain such a degree of love, as to love God with all his heart, with all his soul, and with all his mind; and, moreover, that there never has been one, who was not the subject of some inordinate desire. Who can deny this? I know, indeed, what sort of saints the folly of superstition imagines to itself, such as almost excel even the angels of heaven in purity; but such an imagination is repugnant both to Scripture and to the dictates of experience.[18]

Man's hope is not moralism but the sovereign grace of God and reliance thereon.

What, then, are the purposes of law, if moralism be eliminated? The first purpose, Calvin said, of God's law in its widest sense is the condemnation of moralism. The righteousness of God "is the only righteousness which is acceptable to God." The law thus serves to reveal the righteousness of God and the moralism of self-righteousness of "man, blinded and inebriated with self-love," who is driven by the law "into a knowledge of himself, and a confession of his own imbecility and impurity." The law is thus a schoolmaster striking at the arrogance of man's moralism and pride. "As long as he is permitted to stand in his own judgment, he substitutes hypocrisy instead of of righteousness, contented with which, he rises up with I know not what pretended righteousness, in opposition to the grace of God." The law reveals man's moralism to be a facade for ethical rebellion against God. As Paul observed, "I had not known lust except the law had said, Thou shalt not covet" (Rom. 7:7).[19]

> Thus the law is like a mirror, in which we behold, first, our impotence; secondly, our iniquity, which proceeds from it; and

18 *Institutes*, II, vii, v.
19 *Ibid.*, II, vii, vi.

lastly, the consequence of both, our obnoxiousness to the curse; just as a mirror represents to us the spots on our face. For when a man is destitute of power to practice righteousness, he must necessarily fall into the habits of sin. And sin is immediately followed by the curse. Therefore the greater the transgression of which the law convicts us, the more severe is the judgment with which it condemns us. This appears from the observation of the Apostle, that "by the law is the knowledge of sin" (Rom. 3:20). For he there speaks only of the first office of the law, which is experienced in sinners not yet regenerated.[20]

This "first office of the law is not confined to the pious, but extends also to the reprobate." [21] Thus, this first office of the law is the radical condemnation of moralism wherever found, in Christian and unbeliever alike. For a Christian to hope in law as a means of making men good, whether negatively or positively, is thus to sin radically and to place a burden on the law forbidden to him. Legislation for social order is one thing, but legislation for moralistic purposes, to make men and societies good, is radically proscribed as arrogance and wickedness. This double-edged aspect of this purpose of law thus strikes not only at Marxist, socialist, and welfare economy moralisms, but equally at Roman, Anabaptist, Puritan, and modernist versions of the same arrogant pride and presumption. The faithful declaration of the righteousness and law of God is necessary that moralism be checked, and this office of the law involves that fact.

The second office of the law is social order, the protection of society from the ravages of evildoers, "to cause those who, unless constrained, feel no concern for justice and rectitude, when they hear its terrible sanctions, to be at least restrained by a fear of its penalties." [22] There is a frankly punitive aspect to this office of law; no social perfection is claimed for it, but its validity is not marred thereby. The law in this sense is *retribution*, the far-reaching significance of which will appear when justice is analyzed. No honest man can deny that the fear of consequences has not acted as a deterrent in his life. The psychopath and masochist who seek con-

[20] *Ibid.*, II, vii, vii.
[21] *Ibid.*, II, vii, viii.
[22] *Ibid.*, II, vii, x.

sequences and court punishment only testify thereby to the psychological validity of punishment. What the masochist says in effect is that, recognizing that law-breaking must be punished, he seeks a license to sin by paying, often in advance. He thereby witnesses to the efficacy of the law. The law as a barrier is thus a fence against evil. It cannot reform men or make them in any degree better men morally. It can only act as a limited brake, and Scripture is aware of the limitations of that brake on man. In and of itself, law cannot function merely as a means of social order, for it would quickly collapse if it had no basis but the desire to preserve order. Without that proclamation of the righteousness of God and the fashioning of personal and social life in dependence on that foundation, society would lose all order. For men are by virtue of their fallen nature sinners, "not disposed to fear and obey God; and the more they restrain themselves, the more violently they are inflamed within; they ferment, they boil, ready to break out into any external acts, if they were not prevented by this dread of law." [23] The measure of order gained by law is "constrained and extorted righteousness" which is "induced not by voluntary submission . . . but with reluctance and resistance, only by the violence of fear." This is "necessary to the community" and to "public tranquility." [24] Social order is necessary to create the measure of discipline needed for the birth of a godly culture. Indeed, the very word "culture" implies discipline and restraint. But that order and culture can follow only if the law rests on God's eternal order. Dostoyevsky saw the significance of this fact with telling clarity, as *Crime and Punishment*, among other works, gives witness. A prostitute who knows she is a whore, and that she is sinning against God, is thereby a greater source of social order than an intellectual, whether a probing mind as yet without crime, or a "justified" murderer, who does not recognize the fact of sin and asserts a moralistic autonomy. A Raskolnikov recognizes no ultimate principle of order other than his will, whereby all things stand or fall, while the despised prostitute affirms the validity of the law even as she sins against it. This

---

[23] *Ibid.*, II, vii, x.
[24] *Ibid.*, II, vii, x.

same recognition of law was present in Francois Villon, who could judge himself more sharply than today's moralists would, because he had the context of God's eternal law in mind, acknowledged although not obeyed. As Villon wrote of himself as pimp in the "Ballade for Fat Margot,"

> I am a lecher, and she's a lecher with me.
> Which one of us is better? We're both alike:
> the one as worthy as the other. Bad rat, bad cat.
> We both love filth, and filth pursues us;
> we flee from honor, honor flees from us,
> in this brothel where we ply our trade.[25]

If God's righteousness be not the perspective, then social order and self-evaluation disappear or collapse into meaninglessness.

The third use or office of the law, which is the declaration of God's righteousness, is "the principal one." The Law is a guide or instrument to give godly man, "from day to day, a better and more certain understanding of the divine will to which they aspire, and to confirm them in the knowledge of it." Study of the law will "excite to obedience, confirm man therein, and accordingly restrain him from transgression."[26] As a redeemed man, the law is now the principle of his life, and his new nature in Christ. This need of godly man for the law has been developed by subsequent Calvinist thinkers into a principle of great import, as the ground of man's freedom in Christ. God's law, as the ground of all life, is thus a restraint on all evil. R. B. Kuiper has used the illustration of a fish given freedom from water as destined quickly to die, being out of its law area or sphere for which it was created. H. Evan Runner, commenting on this has observed,

> And so it is also with man: he can be free to live as man only when he is in the Law-environment for which he was created. That "environment" is the full range of the divine Law for the creation, is every law-word that proceeds from the mouth of God. In this sense the Law is the condition of man's freedom. The world-order is thus an order of law, a law-order; the

[25] *The Complete Works of Francois Villon*, Anthony Bonner, ed. and translator, p. 107. New York: Bantam Books, 1960.
[26] *Institutes*, II, vii, xii.

Law holds everywhere. It holds also for man; indeed, man is embedded in it. Law is everywhere the *indispensable condition of life*, the all-encompassing context of our lives. Notice that in Romans 7:12, 14 Paul calls the Law holy, just, and spiritual. If the creation is good, so is the Law.

It is only when we are not in a right relation to the Law that we feel Law as a curse, as something that binds and limits us in a way that is undesirable, something that takes away our freedom. But then we must not condemn the Law, but convert ourselves.[27]

The law in this sense, to use Calvin's words, is to prepare us for "every good work," is "spiritual" and positive in its ultimate scope.

For men generally understand the virtue which is opposite to any vice to be an abstinence from that vice; but we affirm that it goes further, even to the actual performance of the opposite duty. Therefore in this precept, "Thou shalt not kill," the common sense of mankind will perceive nothing more than we ought to abstain from all acts of injury to others, and from all desire to commit any such acts. I maintain that it also implies, that we should do everything that we possibly can towards the preservation of the life of our neighbour.[28]

Law so considered, however, is not the *source* of life but the *condition* of life, and, as such, there is an *identity of liberty and law*. Law is thus the condition but not the source of liberty and of life itself.

At this point, the moralist assumes that he has both Scripture's and Calvin's warrant for his use of law, but a fundamental difference exists. The moralist believes that "love" for his neighbor or enemy will change that man into the desired person; the godly man is under no such illusion as to the "power" of his activity. Neither the law nor his legal activity are sources of life in himself or to other men through him. He "loves" all men, i.e., grants to them the privileges of the second table of the law, the sanctity of life, family, property, and reputation, and avoids coveting these things, not because he believes he can change men or society thereby but as his duty to God and his neighbor.

[27] H. Evan Runner: *Christian Perspectives, 1960*, p. 104.
[28] *Institutes*, II, viii, ix.

This fundamental difference is far-reaching. If I can "change" men by loving them, or by my law-keeping, then I have a very real social control over them, which, for their good and for a faster social result, I can apply through legal and coercive means. Power in the first sense as my brother's keeper should certainly obligate me to use power in the second sense to further a desired purpose. On the other hand, if I have no power to "change" men in the first and personal sense, but have only a duty under God to them, I cannot legally claim a power over them which abrogates my religious duty.

The implications of this position were not immediately seen. Indeed, it can be stated that Calvin did not always see the far-reaching implications of many aspects of his magnificent *Institutes of the Christian Religion*. However, this concept of law carried sufficient weight in Germany to be written into the Lutheran *Formula of Concord*, which reflected strong Calvinist influence:

> It is established that the Law of God was given to men for three causes: first, that certain external discipline might be preserved, and wild and intractable men might be restrained, as it were, by certain barriers; secondly, that by the Law men might be brought to an acknowledgment of their sins; thirdly, that regenerate men, to all of whom, nevertheless, much of the flesh still cleaves, for that very reason may have some certain rule after which they may and ought to shape their lives.[29]

This concept of law, however, steadily receded as scholasticism overwhelmed Protestantism from within and moralized it. The "awakening" which followed was thus an awakening of moralism in the form of Pietism, Methodism, and revivalism. The successor to this temper was modernism with its social gospel. The affinities of modernism to pietism, both a common moralism in nature, the one social and the other personal in manifestation, are seen in their common enmity to Calvinism, viewed as "immoral," as so recent a study as Leonard J. Trinterud's *The Forming of an American Tradition, A Re-Examination of Colonial Presbyterianism* (1949) gives ample witness. Law, whether in the hands of a pietist, modernist,

[29] The Formula of Concord, Art. VI, in Philip Schaff: *The Creeds of Christendom*, Vol. III, p. 130f.

Roman Catholic, Marxist, or pragmatist, is seen as a means of re-making man after a new and would-be creator's image. To re-apply Seagle's apt paraphrase, they who live by such a law, perish by that law. When man reduces the law to his own moralistic dimension, he destroys the law. Oliver Wendell Holmes, having reduced the law to man's opinion, "supported the absolute rights of the majority." [30] No other law could exist. Whenever and wherever man claims the power to re-make man, he inevitably becomes law-giver to his human creature and reduces law to man's will. But the purposes of God's law remain, and a society in rebellion against those purposes is like a fish out of water, violently active but quickly destined to die.[31]

In brief, the purpose of any law is not to make men good; this law can never do, either for man or for society, for goodness is inner rather than outward restraint, else prisons would best produce morality. Law declares the standard, and the penalty for offense, protects society, undercuts man's moralism, and is a guide to the godly. Character and righteousness must come from a source other than law. Thus, to decry law because it makes no man good is to miss the purpose of the law. In any and every culture, according to Paul, the law brings to men the same conclusions, that there is none righteous, and that all men sin and fall short of the glory of God, and to this all men must give assent (Rom. 3:10-18). Basic to most contemporary thinking is either a false hope in law, or a false pessimism because of a false expectation of law. The shadow of Aristotle, of Socrates and Plato has long clouded Western culture, with its brutal hope that laws devised by philosopher-kings could produce the good society when, in actual practice, they produced the tyrants who destroyed the culture of that day. The Cynics or dogs, uglier beatniks of that age, insisted on abandoning all law since law had failed to give them that good society once dreamed of and ac-

[30] Rene A. Wormser: *The Law*, p. 445. New York: Simon and Schuster, 1949.
[31] For a contemporary professor of law's application of the concepts of Calvin and The Formula of Concord to contemporary criminal law, see Wilber G. Katz of the University of Chicago, "Christian Morality and the Criminal Law," pp. 54-171, in A. L. Harding, ed., *Studies in Jurisprudence*: III, *Religion, Morality and Law*. Dallas: Southern Methodist University Press. 1956.

cordingly in some instances copulated publicly like dogs to affirm their contempt of all law and the futility of law. Cynicism is again becoming the order of the day as men, having erected a modern Tower of Babel, having striven to reach unto heaven, saying, go to now, let us build us a law, have, instead of uniting men into one world, only confused and scattered him further, turn now to bitter contempt of all law and add thereby to their misery. By all of this, however, the law is confirmed. Because the moralist always ends in becoming "unprofitable" in every respect (Rom. 3:12; the word means unserviceable or useless, having reference to badly soured and useless milk), so every moralistic culture and law becomes sour and is rejected. In this present age of sourness, it is imperative that both the purposes and limitations of law be made known and clearly defined. This much is certain, the sour cannot command the future, but neither can the ignorant.

And the struggle is a major one. All the impact of Hellenic culture is heavily moralistic. Aristotle defined the goal of political science as making the citizens "to be of a certain character, viz., good and capable of noble acts," [32] and stated the purpose of the law to be the training of citizens "in habits of right action—this is the aim of all legislation, and if it fails to do this, it is a failure." [33] Through Aquinas and others this moralistic infection is deeply imbedded in Western culture. This concept now circulates as ostensibly Christian, so that the godly man is compelled to wage war against an ostensible Christianity whose roots are long grown and deep. The urgency is thus all the greater.

[32] *Ethica Nicomachea*, I, 9.
[33] *Ibid.*, II, 1.

5

THE MEANING OF JUSTICE

After the fall of Rome, Marcellinus wrote to Augustine, relaying the statement of Volusianus, who accused Christianity of two things. First, the precepts of Matthew 5:39-41, as taught by Christians, contradicted the obligations of citizenship. Second, Volusianus implied that the fall of Rome was due to the Christian religion. The searching mind of Volusianus saw a contradiction between, on the one hand, the claims of justice and any and all attempts of the state to further justice, and, on the other hand, the common interpretation of Christian ethics, which, by its doctrine of love and forgiveness, subverted justice.

The question was a necessary one for Augustine to answer. His analysis of man did indeed lead to a concept of man and of love which by-passed the problem of justice. For Augustine, man lives in terms of either earthly love, *cupiditas*, directed downward and to time and self, and *caritas*, heavenly love, directed to God, eternity, and the emptying of self-hood.[1] To show the kind of love demanded by *caritas*, men should in effect live beyond justice.

Instead of coming to grips with the fundamental problem which Volusianus sensed but hesitated to express too vocally, Augustine failed to see it at all. His answer was simply an affirmation of the moralism of love, and the man who was able to see the obvious moralism of Pelagius submitted to a more subtle moralism of his own making. Augustine's answer was in essence six arguments:

1. How could this moralism be condemned in Christianity when Rome itself held to it at an earlier period, and thereby became great? Did not the great Romans affirm the need for forgiveness,

---

[1] *City of God*, XIV, 28.

clemency, pardon? Why condemn the same principle in Christian form?

2. The purpose of this moralism for Augustine was twofold, first, to produce social concord, aud, second, to save sinners by a display of forgiveness. What Augustine failed to note is that the biblical concept of forgiveness is *conditional* upon true repentance, not the *ground* of it, and is only then *unlimited* in extent. Thus, forgiveness is not a license to sin but the answer of God and man to true repentance. It is not the ground but the fruit of salvation.

3. Next, Augustine made time less real than eternity and the claims of justice less valid than a saving ethics of love and forgiveness. Eternity is to be preferred to time and justice. But the biblical position is incarnational, never *renouncing* time but *reconciling* time and eternity. Augustine thus clearly avoided the issue.

4. Augustine then came close to claiming a messianic character for suffering endured in the name of love and forgiveness, and criticized Paul for failure in this regard.

5. Augustine then defended, lest apparently he land in anarchy, the right of the magistrate to fatherly correction, asserting also that warfare must likewise be paternalistic and corrective.

6. Rome fell, finally, not because of Christian moralism but Roman immoralism. This truism did not alter the force of Volusianus' problem, however true the immorality of Rome.[2]

The verses in question, Matthew 5:39-41, were still read in a false context and seen as contrary to all else in Scripture concerning justice. What Jesus stated here had reference to personal relations, where a standing on rights would aggravate rather than right a wrong, and to cases of forced servitude by government regulations. Regarding Matthew 5:41, for example, and the word "compel," Ellicott, by no means free from Augustine's interpretation, still notes,

> The Greek word implies the special compulsion of forced servitude as courier or messenger under Government, and was imported from the Persian postal system, organized on the plan of employing men thus impressed to convey Government dis-

2 Letter CXXXVIII, A.D. 412, *The Nicene and Post-Nicene Fathers,* First Series, Vol. I, pp. 472f., 481-488. Grand Rapids: Eerdmans, 1956.

patches from stage to stage (Herod. viii 98). The use of the illustration here would seem to imply the adoption of the same system by the Roman Government under the empire. Roman soldiers and their horses were billeted on Jewish householders. Others were impressed for service of longer or shorter duration.[3]

Again, when Jesus portrayed it an act of wisdom, if sued at law for a coat, to surrender one's cloak also (Matt. 5:40), He spoke, not in terms of an idealistic pacifism, which would convert the offender, but with wisdom and grim realism. In most eras, man has been wiser by far to accede to a loss here and there in preference to the greater loss or evil of a court trial. William Seagle, who has served with both the U. S. Department of Interior and the National Labor Relations Board, has written of the inefficiency of the courts: "A study once made by the Institute for the Study of the Law at Johns Hopkins showed that in the Supreme Court of New York County less than 7% of the amount of judgments entered by the court was ever collected by the 'successful' parties." [4] We can be fairly certain that the judges collected their salaries and the attorneys their fees. In many instances, where greater efficiency appears, other factors make it even more imperative to avoid the court. Too often, in dictatorships, any encounter with a court is deadly; in democracies, too often, entry into court enriches the lawyers mostly, and can be as pleasant as a plunge into a cesspool. The Christian is called upon to be insistent for justice (Luke 18:2-8), for God honors this perseverance both with relation to human courts and himself. But there can be no illusions in such striving, nor foolish contesting over coats. The battle-line must be drawn over essentials. This grim realism must be linked to an absolute hope which acts redemptively in the name of Christ, certain of His ability to conquer or to overrule. The duty is man's, and the issue is God's. The hard reality of struggle and persecution, set forth in the very beatitudes, men turned into the theory of the omnipotence of love and its saving power. Biblical realism was thus converted into an impossible perfectionist idealism, and biblical particularity into unbending universalization. The

[3] C. J. Ellicott, *Commentary on the Whole Bible*, vol. vi, 30.
[4] Seagle, *op. cit.*, p. 3.

Bible, radically anti-idealist, has been turned into a handbook for idealists by this persistent mis-reading.

The consequences of this radical moralism were the subversion of true justice, and the confusion of justice with charity, love, and forgiveness. Such a confusion has become commonplace on all sides, as witness a declaration in 1948 by the World Council of Churches: "Justice demands that the inhabitants of Asia, and Africa, for instance, should have the benefits of more machine production." [5] It is this concept of justice that is today demanded on all sides by minority and majority groups.

But the very background of this opposition of love to justice is both antinomian and pagan and is definitely anti-biblical. It stems in part from gnostic systems which, with dualistic background, opposed a materialistic, creating God of wrath, one immersed in creation and matters of justice, with a spiritual God who was above and beyond material creation and hostile to it, and was all love and sweetness. [6] But the biblical doctrine of God sees no hostility between love and justice; the two are distinct but inseparable. For love to flourish by subverting or by-passing justice is impossible; it means then a license to evil and is in itself not love but a form of evil. [7] When Jehovah identified himself repeatedly as a "jealous God," He indicated the unity of love and justice, and that love was inevitably and inextricably an aspect of His demand for justice. The perfect illustration of this coincidence is the cross of Christ, whereby, according to biblical doctrine, the divine wrath against sin and God's

[5] *The Church and the Disorders of Society*, p. 198; cited in Ludwig Von Mises: *The Anti-Capitalistic Mentality*, p. 82. Princeton, N. J.: Van Nostrand, 1956.

[6] For an affirmation of this same Gnosticism today, see Kelsen, *op. cit.*, p. 378, note 7, where "the unsurmountable antagonism . . . between the idea of justice in the Old Testament (that is, the principle of retribution), and the justice taught by Jesus (that is, the principle of love)," is affirmed. Kelsen chooses to by-pass the fact that Jesus' stated purpose of His life and coming was "to give his life a ransom for many" (Matt. 20:28; Mk. 10:45), to satisfy the retributive justice of God and thereby manifest His love.

[7] Thus, Brunner is wrong in seeing justice as a kind of necessary but inferior morality, as compared to love, nor can justice be limited to "the ethics of systems or institutions" and love related to "personal ethics." Any personal relationship of "love" which must consistently overlook justice is either an instance of mental sickness or of compulsion. Emil Brunner: *Justice and the Social Order*, pp. 16-20. New York: Harpers, 1945.

requirement of justice were satisfied on the sin-bearer, representative and federal man, Jesus, at the one and same time that the love of God in all its startling dimensions were set forth in the same person of that God-man. The doctrine of the atonement thus forbids both the opposition of love to justice, and their confusion, for they are in unity without confusion. Thus Augustine was at this point wrong and Volusianus moving towards the right answer because of his question. *Caritas* will destroy a state, because it is a conception of heavenly love which is antinomian and subversive of justice. Inevitably *caritas* thinking must look on the cry for true justice as motivated usually by *cupiditas*, earthly love. Such thinking leads ultimately to a Francis of Assisi, to would-be saints who confuse insanity with sanctity and theft for the poor's sake with justice. Thus for Ambrose communism became Christian because it is beyond justice, beyond the realm of self-interest or earthly love. Ambrose re-defined justice in ostensibly Christian terms by excluding two "pagan" ideas from it, revenge and private possessions; the idea of power is also excluded from justice.[8]

> The just man has pity, the just man lends. The whole world of riches lies at the feet of the wise and the just. The just man regards what belongs to all as his own, and his own as common property. The just man accuses himself rather than others.[9]

Amazingly, Ambrose, by total confusion, read this conception back in "Divine justice" itself! [10] The moralism of paganism was thus heightened and intensified by the church.

Indeed, the moralism of paganism had merely been baptized and welcomed into the fold, and later Dante saw Virgil as his guide through most of purgatory (*Purgatorio* XXX); while in Paradise, he saw the spirits spell out the words of *Wisdom*, "Love righteousness ye that be judges of the earth," and then other spirits gather upon the crest of the letter and form it into an eagle, the symbol

8 Ambrose: "Duties of the Clergy," Bk. I, Ch. xxvii, *The Nicene and Post-Nicene Fathers*, Vol. x, p. 22f. See also Arthur O. Lovejoy: "The Communism of St. Ambrose," in *Essays in the History of Ideas*, pp. 296-307. New York: Braziller, 1955.
9 Ambrose, "Duties," I, xxv, 118, in *Nicene and Post-Nicene*, p. 20.
10 *Epistle* LXIII, *Nicene and Post-Nicene*, p. 469.

of Roman law and justice (*Paradiso* XVIII). It is no wonder that at this point, Dante, who saw the heaven as the triumph of Roman natural law and justice, should with anguish ask why the virtuous heathen were excluded from heaven in such clear contradiction to "God's" justice. The answer is that here is a mystery beyond human ken (*Paradiso* XIX). Dante could give no other answer: God's justice and natural law were one, and, accordingly, the Roman philosophers belonged in heaven together with the triumphant Roman symbol of law and justice. But Dante did manage to find two pagans in heaven, Ripheus the Trojan, called by Virgil "the one man amongst the Trojans most just and observant of the right" (*Aeneid*; ii), and Trajan, both, from the viewpoint of history, heathens, but, according to Dante's "information," both dying in the true faith, Ripheus in Christ to come, and Trajan in Christ come. Thus, Dante is gratified to know that predestination has saved and will save many ostensible heathen (*Paradiso*, XX). For Dante, the superiority of Christianity, which was *continuous* with noble paganism, rested in its additions to that structure which made it complete. Thus, love, added by Christianity, is ultimate and transcends justice, and the final vision is of "the Love that moves the sun and the other stars." *The Divine Comedy* was a religious and political tract, designed to lead men to true blessedness and was, without the formulation of usual terminology, still an affirmation of natural law philosophy.

Natural law was brought into the church very soon after the close of the New Testament. The early church, taking in Greek and Roman thinkers who saw the faith as a means to the renewal of the empire, saw it as the fulfilment of the old virtues and morality Rome had once honored. Thus, they were ready to welcome any moralism as an ally in spite of itself, so that each enemy was met with strong formal intolerance and yet a ready assimilation of its natural law thinking.

But, as Troeltsch has rightly pointed out, the general background of natural law thinking was pantheistic.[11] This background no de-

[11] Ernst Troeltsch, "The Idea of Natural Law and Humanity in World Politics," p. 205, in Otto Gierke: *Natural Law and the Theory of Society, 1500-1800*. Boston: Beacon Hill, 1957.

velopment of natural law theory has been able to overcome, nor is it possible to do so. Natural law presupposes a normative order as inherent in the universe or in nature, whereas biblical thought sees the universe as fallen and perverted, and the only source of law under any circumstances being neither the creature nor creation but the Creator, God, in and through His Word. Natural law is thus inescapably anti-Christian and presupposes an ultimate and autonomous order in or identical with nature or man in distinction inevitably from God.

In recent years, there has been both a revival of and renewed attack against natural law theories.[12] It may be affirmed, however, that both the exponents of natural law theory and its critics alike hold to a natural law philosophy. The triumph of natural law philosophy in many respects was the philosophy of Kant, in which the immanent law and man were firmly and inextricably united, making possible Hegel and Marx, with their historical process as the new natural law, existentialism with a highly personal version, and pragmatism, with a new and instrumental concept of that now thoroughly immanent and changing truth.

Natural law theory is ultimately relativism,[13] and more clearly so with the rise of the hypothesis of evolution. If the world of na-

[12] See Otto Gierke, *op cit.*, and *Political Theories of the Middle Ages*, Boston, Beacon Hill, 1958; Leo Strauss: *Natural Right and History*, Chicago, University of Chicago Press, 1953; Kelsen, *op. cit.*; Learned Hand: *The Bill of Rights*, Cambridge, Harvard University Press, 1950; Jacques Ellul: *The Theological Foundation of Law, A Radical Critique of Natural Law*, Garden City, Doubleday, 1960; Edwin Norman Garlan: *Legal Realism and Justice*, New York, Columbia University Press, 1941; Roscoe Pound: *What Is Justice?* New Haven, Yale University Press, 1951; Homer Cummings: *Liberty Under Law and Administration*, New York, Scribner's, 1934; Benjamin N. Cardozo: *The Paradoxes of Legal Science*, New York, Columbia University Press, 1928; Laurence Stapleton: *Justice and World Society*, Chapel Hill, University of North Carolina Press, 1944; etc.

[13] For an important study of natural law and the American Constitution, see Edward S. Corwin: *The "Higher Law" Background of American Constitutional Law*, Ithaca, New York, Cornell University Press, 1955. The higher law of nature, originally seen as expressed in government by laws, came to be, in the thinking of men like Benjamin Hichborn of Boston during the Revolution itself "a power existing in the people at large at any time, for any cause, or for no cause, but their own sovereign pleasure, to alter or annihilate both the mode and essence of any former government, and adopt a new one in its stead" (Corwin, p. 88). The natural law thus ceased to be law and man became a law unto himself.

ture is continuous process and flux, then process and flux are alone divine and true, and no final truth is possible until the process ends. For Hegel and Marx to divinize or absolutize a movement, institution, or class within that process was to contradict their very presupposition. At no point in the process is truth final or absolute but always and only relative, instrumental in terms of the process, and developing. Hence, pragmatism and relativism are the inevitable products, and the logical products of Hegel, and, accordingly, of natural law theory.[14] At all times, it carries within itself the seeds of its own destruction. It must approach a process as the source of norms with radical presuppositions it dare not acknowledge. Neither the natural law theorists nor their relativistic or positivistic critics will acknowledge that unfounded presuppositions are the essence of their thinking. What reason, for example, have they to suppose that life is more valid than death, or that death is not the goal of all process? Indeed, the will to death can be as important if not more so than the will to live, according to some. And if the wishes of society at the present time are the source of law, why any law, since the majority of society seems more bent on lawlessness? And since few citizens seem interested in jurisprudence, on what grounds is its study and practice justified? Why reason, when human indifference or rebellion against reason prevail, or when nature seems ultimately irrational? No relativist has faced this question more intensely or honestly than Hans Kelsen, who portrays the conflict dramatically in the confrontation of the "absolutist," Jesus, by the "relativist," Pilate:

> Then Pilate asked, "What is truth?" And because he, the skeptical relativist, did not know what the truth was, the absolute truth in which this man believed, Pilate—consistently—proceeded in a democratic way by putting the decision of the case to a popular vote. He went out again to the Jews, relates the Gospel, and said to them: "I find in him no fault at all. But you have a custom that I should release to you one at the Passover. Do you wish that I set free to you this king of the Jews?"

[14] For the relation of Dewey and James to Hegel, see Burleigh Taylor Wilkins, "James, Dewey, and Hegelian Idealism" in *Journal of the History of Ideas*, XVII, 3, June, 1956, pp. 332-346.

> Then cried they all again, saying: "Not this man, but Barabbas."
> The Gospel adds: "Now Barabbas was a robber."
>
> For those who believe in the son of God and king of the Jews as witness of the absolute truth, this plebiscite is certainly a strong argument against democracy. And this argument we political scientists must accept. But only under one condition: that we are sure of our political truth, to be enforced, if necessary, with blood and tears—that we are as sure of our truth as was, of his truth, the son of God.[15]

Significantly, by his passionate answer Kelsen reveals that his position is not relativism after all; relevatism is applied *only* to this supernatural Christian-theistic absolutism. He is "as sure" of *his* truth as Jesus was of His truth, and clearly believes *in the immanence that justifies and vindicates the historical moment because there is no absolute other than that immanence.*

The radical supernaturalism of biblical thought is thus rejected precisely because its truth comes without and apart from man's discovery and ordination of it, so that it is not a product of man's endeavor but of God's grace. This is an offense to the philosopher-kings of every age.

Learned Hand, speaking of the U. S. Supreme Court, has expressed his repugnance to rule "by a bevy of Platonic Guardians, even if I know how to choose them, which I assuredly do not." But why his distaste? "If they were in charge, I should miss the stimulus of living in a society where I have, at least theoretically, some part in the direction of public affairs." This is acceptable, even if it means being only "a sheep in the flock," to which charge Hand answers with Saint Francis, "My brother, the Sheep." [16] This deceptive air of humility does not eliminate the fact that an ultimate truth is reserved to man, as his product and discovery, and, as an intellectual and a judge, Hand stands high in the order of at least legal "guardians." And, when truth is discovered, some sheep will need narcotics in order to accept it. Who will administer the medicine?

> If we can find time for some other activity than forging fantastic engines of war and using them to destroy each other,

15 Kelsen, *op. cit.*, p. 207f.
16 Hand, *op. cit.*, p. 73f.

who knows but we shall acquire so intimate an acquaintance with ourselves that we shall indeed discover principles that will be as objectively valid as those that govern inanimate things; and if so, perhaps Mr. Aldous Huxley's mescaline, or Mr. Gordon Wasson's mushrooms will then help to get them generally accepted. Meanwhile, I can think of nothing better than to stake our future upon conclusions about ourselves that we must recognize as provisional, as no better than surmises which we must never weary of putting to a test.[17]

But there can be no test without an already existing measurement or standard, and Hand rejects both "the Divine Will" and natural law, as traditionally understood.[18] How can these "principles" be discovered, if skepticism itself is an absolute, so established by his Harvard teachers? "In the universe of truth they lived by the sword; they asked no quarter of absolutes and they gave none. Go ye and do likewise."[19] And if truth or "principles" be so abstruse as to have evaded countless centuries of human searching, how can it be known except by an elite of philosopher-kings, "a bevy of Platonic Guardians" like unto Learned Hand? In such a world indeed, the masses will have to be managed as in Plato's *Republic* or Huxley's *Brave New World*, and given mescaline or Wasson's mushrooms to make them amenable to the rule of "principles." The philosopher-kings always play god with a thoroughly becoming modesty! Socrates was more honest, as he openly avowed his ideal state, with its free access to women by the philosopher-kings, their fiat will by virtue of reason, and their extensive ability to play gods, to be a happy and gratifying daydream.[20]

The offense of revealed law is its radical destructiveness with regard to this aristocracy of intellect; reason is dethroned as god and compelled again to be reason. Truth is made promiscuous and granted to both Paul the learned and Peter the fisherman, to illiterate

[17] *Ibid.*, p. 74.
[18] *Ibid.*, p. 2f.
[19] *Ibid.*, p. 77.
[20] For a study of this aspect of the *Republic*, see Frederick Nymeyer. *Progressive Calvinism*, II, p. 74ff. South Holland, Illinois: Libertarian Press, 1956. As Nymeyer observed, "It is then not difficult to explain why there are *Plato Clubs* on college campuses but never *Moses Clubs*," the first making man at least the source of law, the second, Moses, placing man under God's law."

Africans and royal princes, and the wisdom of the wise is surpassed, and confounded equally with the folly of fools. Nothing is to be more distrusted or feared than the humility of the wise.

Religiously, relativism appears in the mysticism of love without or beyond justice. Love so conceived and regarded as the superlative virtue is in essence antinomian at the least and inevitably relativistic. By abandoning (although ostensibly transcending) justice, it leads to a pragmatic relief from the fixity of absolutes and is hostile to them in the name of this higher virtue, which becomes by exclusion the sole virtue. The cult of love appears together with the rise of relativism and is a sentimentalized excuse for its denial of justice and law in the name of a supposedly higher justice and law, namely, anarchic love.

Religious relativism is the ground of political absolutism. The conception and demand for an absolute just order is strongest where men are most insistent that Christianity's absolutes are without reality. Certain forms of religious absolutism, when based on the concept of continuity or the great chain of being, inevitably divinize the social order, and relativism inescapably does the same. When man denies the transcendent and ontological trinity (as both relativists and many churches do), the order of immanence prevails and becomes the inevitable absolute. Thus, however pragmatic Dewey claimed to be, the unavoidable outcome of his thinking was the absolutization of the state as the order of life, the source of morality, and the source of truth. The processes of nature were invested with an infallibility that moved with certainty to the creation of "the great community."

In all such relativizations, not only is the state made the absolute, and justice is what the state does, but man, ostensibly exalted and freed by this emancipation from God, is also emancipated from character and virtue as well.[21] Whenever law, the condition of man's life, is in the power of the state and is the creation of the state

---

[21] Ellul, *op. cit.*, p. 122, points out that Kelsen, by his relativism, reduces law to an irrelevance as far as justice is concerned. "Law is in the power of the state, whatever its basis for action and its goal may be." Such a position is in essence no different from Mussolini's interpretation, "The state as universal ethical will is the creator of law."

and without transcendental reference, then man too is the creature of the state and in its power, however ostensibly benevolent the purposes of that state. Law is the condition of life, and, in terms of biblical law, man, created in the image of God, is vice-gerent under God in Christ, and king of creation. His responsibility, the law of his being, is to exercise dominion, to subdue the earth and all creation, scientifically, agriculturally, aesthetically, politically, in every sphere of human endeavor, under God. When such a concept is held in terms of the biblical doctrine of the ontological trinity and the discontinuity of Creator and creation, the dignity of the creature is established and the divinization of man and his social orders made impossible. Justice is established firmly in God and His revealed will and preserved from becoming the creature of the would-be-gods, man, the state, church, family, school, or tribe.

Under the impact of relativism, justice, together with law, is made the creature of the state and is thus destroyed. Justice is what Stalin, Hitler, the President, Supreme Court, or people say it is, and no more. However, the relativist rejects the barrenness of this conclusion and insists that justice is in process, a development evolving together with man and his state towards a constantly higher stage or truth. The function of the jurist, in this process, becomes, as it was with Holmes and increasingly with others, the interpretation of that direction and the social mind, a rather mystical jurisprudence as a result. For the skeptical jurist, justice and positive law are inevitably the same; justice is what the state says and does, so that Holmes could feel justified in being "anti-labor" at one period and "pro-labor" at another. In every instance, he was "just" because sensitive to the "law" behind law, i.e., the social temper of his day. Holmes treated humanitarian interpretation of the law with contempt. Laws are "beliefs that have triumphed," and no more.[22] Justice is thus the will of the mob, the belief of the pack, and no more. It has no relationship to God, and makes therefore no moral

[22] Max Lerner, ed.: *The Mind and Faith of Justice Holmes, His Speeches, Essays, Letters, and Judicial Commentary*, pp. 372, 389f., 336-341. Boston: Little, Brown, 1943. See also Charles P. Curtis, Jr.: *Lions Under the Throne, A Study of the Supreme Court of the United States*, pp. 25, 281, Boston: Houghton Mifflin, 1947.

requirement of men other than conformity. A just man is not characterized accordingly as one who stands apart from men in terms of character and integrity, but as one who runs faithfully with the pack.

In the idealistic interpretation, the direction or evolution of that process is mystically known and is thus visualized and incarnated in terms of an ideal social order, such as communism, socialism, or democracy. In this ancient moralistic heresy, man must work zealously to create this ideal order which will then remove from him the necessity of being a man, the necessity for responsibility, morality, character, integrity, and the necessity for more than the barest minimum of work. Man's one function will be conformity. This dream of the ideal order is a prevalent and popular one, and most political candidates campaign as would-be messiahs. And, as de Jouvenal has observed, "The logical end of the illusions now in vogue is the quite absurd one of a society in which everything would be arranged justly and no one would have to be just." [23]

Every concept of law and justice which has its origin in time and process, whether skeptical or perfectionist in its interpretation, is a radical failure in providing any law or justice. While demanding conformity, and creating a facade of it, it fails completely in maintaining order. A police-established, concentration camp-enforced, conformity is never a substitute for order which springs from meaning. When men walk in terms of a calling and in a confidence in the proximate truth of their society, social order is the product of faith and life rather than the sullen submission to fear and bayonets. In any and every relativistic conception of law and justice, the courts inevitably become Platonic Guardians, themselves the lawmakers. The U. S. Supreme Court, operating on relativistic principles, has accordingly assumed, as the Conference of Justices declared, on August 23, 1958, "What seem to us primarily legislative powers." [24]

---

[23] Bertrand de Jouvenal: *Sovereignty, An Inquiry into the Political Good*, p. 164. Chicago: The University of Chicago Press, 1957.

[24] The chief justices of 36 states voted for this resolution, 8 opposing, 2 abstaining and 4 not present. *U. S. News and World Report*, Oct. 3, 1958, pp. 92-102. See also Hand, *op. cit.*, pp. 31-55. See Luther Curtis, *op. cit.*, 234ff, 266.

Man, having been created in the image of God, can only live in terms of God's law, the condition of life for him, so that his rebellion against God, sin, is the source of the entrance of physical death into the world. This separation from God is also the source of man's continuing inner death and his social death, so that the will-to-die is a major factor in human history in every era of unbelief and in every culture hostile to the presuppositions of biblical faith.[25]

Every immanent and relativist concept of law and justice falls under the sway of subjectivism and is thus made a contradiction to itself. The radical supernaturalism, transcendence, and discontinuity of the ontological Trinity as revealed in biblical revelation is rejected by many because it comes separate and apart from man's discovery and ordination, but this is precisely its strength and authority. Time and process are not destroyed by eternity and the eternal decree of the triune God, but, rather, derive their meaning therefrom and are rescued from meaninglessness. The ontological Trinity is the very ground and necessary premise of *all* human thought.[26] No knowledge is possible on any other premise, and man, on any other premise, is immersed in the sea of brute factuality and left without either knowledge or hope of knowledge. All knowledge gained by the unbeliever is on borrowed premises, on the unadmitted premise of the eternal decree of the ontological Trinity. Law and justice are thus theocentric. Ellul, by declaring that "Law is entirely Christocentric," [27] weakens his otherwise able exposition of *The Theological Foundation of Law*, because, if law is *entirely* Christocentric, the transcendence of God and His law are denied. God is made exhaustively present, in Barthian fashion, in His revelation, in time and process, and again there is no law beyond positive law, no law beyond the state. All such so-called Christocentric thinking is actually a denial of biblical Christology and leads back to the void

---

[25] For an important study of the urge to defeat and death in modern culture, see Samuel J. Warner: *The Urge to Mass Destruction.* New York: Grune and Stratton, 1957.

[26] For a development of this philosophy, see R. J. Rushdoony: *By What Standard?*, 1959; Cornelius Van Til: *The Defense of the Faith*, 1955; and *A Christian Theory of Knowledge*, 1969, all published by Presbyterian and Reformed Publishing Co.

[27] Ellul, *op. cit.*, p. 69.

of undifferentiated being, to the chaos of brute factuality and the blind vastness of meaningless time and process.

Law is theocentric and is a manifestation of the nature and life of the ontological Trinity. As made especially clear by Paul in Ephesians, the Trinity is the source of all life and meaning in the universe, not by participation in the divine essence but in terms of creation in and through the divine Logos. Language is thus not anthropomorphic but typical in speaking of God as Father, in that human fatherhood is a shadow or type of the substance, the Fatherhood of the Father to the Son. Fellowship, community, order, marriage, law, love, and all things have their derivation from the creative act of God and are shadows or types of the inner life of the Trinity. They have a unity in diversity by virtue of their common source in the Trinity, who is at one and the same time both the one and the many. Separation from God is thus separation from life in its every form, and sin is spoken of as a living death. No man can separate himself from God, whom he is called to glorify and enjoy, without at the same time taking leave, as it were, of himself and of life. We live, move, and have our being in the Triune God, and His law and justice are the conditions of life. Law is thus either theocentric or it is non-law and non-justice. Ellul is correct in asserting, "This Law is not a principle for organizing society. It is a condition for life imposed on man." [28] This is the Reformed faith. Again, he is emphatically right in asserting, "Jesus Christ has become the righteousness of God. There can be no justice whatsoever, even relative, outside Jesus Christ . . . there can be no study of law outside Jesus Christ; there can't even be human law, however relative, if it is not founded in Jesus Christ. Apart from Him, we shall end up with 'non-law.' " [29] But this Christ cannot be the Barthian caricature but only the Christ of Scripture, himself theocentric, who declared, as Ellul himself notes, "I can of mine own self do nothing: as I hear, I judge: and my judgment is just; because I seek not mine own will, but the will of the Father which hath sent me" (John 5:30).

This "will of the Father" Jesus came to fulfil, confirming every

28 *Ibid.*, p. 55.
29 *Ibid.*, p. 42.

"jot and tittle" of the law (Matt. 5:17f), although foolish men have insisted on seeing a rejection of Old Testament justice by Christ, an interpretation made possible only by an evolutionary presupposition which suppresses all evidence to the contrary.[30] Law is either man's condition of life or the ground of his death. In a fallen world, law functions thus in a double sense, first, to bring judgment even unto death upon the law-breaker, and, second, to be an instrument in the divine plan for the restoration and regeneration of all things. The law itself *cannot* work this regeneration, but the fulfilment of the ultimate order, the Kingdom of God *requires* retribution and restoration. Creation, by its fall, is not damned and destroyed forthwith but made the area of God's incarnation in order that a reconciliation and restoration might be effected. The restoration, however, is not to a past status, to an Eden, but to the divinely ordained community, is future in reference, and requires a fulfilment not only of all that which was potential in the original creation but a fulfilment of all the possibilities and potentialities of the process. Thus, even as truth is in order to goodness, so judgment is in order to fulfilment.

Two major declarations of the law sum up this double aspect of law. The first is God's repeated declaration, "Vengeance is mine; I will repay, saith the Lord" (Rom. 12:19; Deut. 32:35; Ps. 99:8; Isa. 34:8; Jer. 50:15; Ezek. 24:25; Nahum 1:2; II Thess. 1:8; Ps. 58:10; 94:1; Heb. 10:30; Prov. 6:34; Isa. 61:2; Jer. 51:6; Isa. 35:4; 59:17; Luke 21:22; Jude 7). The second declaration, called Mosaic, although introduced as the word of God to Moses for proclamation (Ex. 20:22), is the familiar law, "thou shalt give life for life, eye for eye, tooth for tooth, hand for hand, foot for foot, burning for burning, wound for wound, stripe for stripe" (Ex. 21:23-25; cf. Lev. 24:20; Deut. 19:21). Vengeance is defined as "the infliction of a deserved penalty; retributive punishment." Together with retribution, it is today an unpopular word. Kelsen rightly sees retribution as closely linked with the concept of causality, and, accordingly, to eliminate retribution reduces causality to probability, although later, to retain man's responsibility and freedom, he recognizes that pre-

[30] See Kelsen, *op. cit.*, p. 12, etc.

dictability "is not causality itself." For Kelsen, causality must be retained and emancipated from retribution both to undergird science and establish the freedom of the will.[31] No such verbal gymnastics are necessary to the Christian-theistic position and its happy acceptance of the principle of retribution. Despite the attempts to read a primitivism into this law, no evidence of it exists in Scripture. "Eye for eye, tooth for tooth" means bluntly and simply that the punishment must fit the crime, that neither excessive nor inadequate punishment can be called justice. Thus death was the penalty for premeditated murder (Gen. 9:6; Ex. 21:12, 14; Num. 35:16-21), but not for manslaughter (Ex. 21:13; Num. 35:15; Deut. 19:4-6), where the penalty was different (Ex. 21:18-20; Num. 6:9-15, 22-28; Deut. 19:11-13). The right of self-defense was recognized (Ex. 22:2). Where the death penalty was required in other cases, as of adultery (Lev. 20:10), it was because it constituted assault and treason against the central institution of biblical society, the family. The modern lack of punishment for adultery is not a sign of progress as much as an evidence of the collapse of the family. Treason against the state is now a capital offense, but was not under biblical law, the state having no such pre-eminence. Laws are an expression of social values, and the rigor of modern law exceeds that of Mosaic law, and functions, not to protect the family, property, and the covenant, but merely the state, leaving man defenseless before the law rather than strong and free by virtue of it.

Both the vengeance and retribution of God have reference to time and eternity. God, in reserving vengeance to himself, both honors it as essential to justice, and reserves it to non-personal and divinely ordained channels, such as courts of law, as well as to supernatural, providential activity. Both vengeance and retribution are so basic to justice that those who seek to by-pass them openly end up in by-passing justice in favor of anarchic love, psychiatric therapy, or rehabilitation. Such "justice" is oriented to the law-breaker and his welfare, whereas biblical justice has reference to the Kingdom of God and the protection and welfare of man, God's image-bearer, to the end that man might effectively serve God in his every capacity,

[31] *Ibid.*, pp. 303-349.

with the believer, gladly, and with the unbeliever, in spite of himself, in that all his law-abiding activity will but further the Kingdom.

The extent to which law has by-passed God and lawful man in favor of the law-breaker is apparent in the abandonment of *restitution*, a fundamental principle of biblical law. Prison sentences have no place in biblical law, imprisonment being only temporary until sentence was declared (Lev. 24:12; Num. 15:34). In certain types of cases, such as assault, compensation to the injured party had to be the sentence of the court, and a variety of related cases also required compensation or damages (Ex. 21:19, 32, 35, 36). Thus, the injured did not have to sue for compensation, but the sentence of the court was ordered compensation. In cases of damages to property through unpremeditated action, the equivalent of the property had to be restored plus twenty percent (Lev. 5:16; Num. 5:7). The same was true of the concealment of lost property which was regarded as theft (Lev. 6:1-6). These cases involved breach of trust and trespass primarily. Cases of deliberate theft were more serious, and the restitution proportionate:

> There was enacted an elaborate system for compensating an injured party under the sanction of Mosaism. As far as possible the restoration was identical with, or analogous to, the loss of time or power (Ex. 21:18-36; Lev. 24:18-23; Deut. 19:21). He who stole and then slew or sold a live ox had to restore fivefold; if it was a live sheep fourfold. The penalty was designed in part to be prohibitory, because sheep were more exposed in the desert, while oxen were necessary and not so easily taken.[32]

In double restitution, the thief had to restore what was stolen plus the exact amount or equivalent thereof, so that he was penalized to the extent that he hoped to profit by his theft. Where animals capable of reproducing themselves and thereby increasing their value were involved, the restitution was proportionately greater (Ex. 22:1-4). Restitution was also basic to the laws of redemption, property, debt, and inheritance. Retribution was central to Christ's teaching, as witness the parables of the unforgiving servant, the marriage feast, the wicked husbandmen, and the steward and the

[32] J. Poucher, "Crime and Punishment," pp. 520-527, in James Hastings: *A Dictionary of the Bible*, I.

servants. God repeatedly affirms that He requites every man according to his work, with exactitude and thoroughness.

On the other hand, where the criminal was guilty of crimes which broke the bond of relationship to society, excommunication, a "cutting off" from the people, followed, so that the community was protected from its deliberate enemies. The incorrigible delinquent, on report of his parents and the investigation of the authorities, was sentenced to death (Deut. 21:18-21) for the protection of the commonwealth.[33] Love, psychiatric therapy, and rehabilitation have their place, as functions of friendly persons, physicians, and religious workers, but they cannot be a substitute for justice without a radical breakdown of social order ensuing. They have validity only if made part of a total program of restitution and restoration, not as a substitute thereof. In the present situation, the person robbed is rarely if ever compensated, and restoration is by-passed, in favor increasingly of action which would place society at the service of the law-breaker if carried to its logical conclusions. Thus, Ellul is right in insisting that "the ultimate manifestation of God's justice reveals God's will to restore," and that "the idea of restoration" is "essential for the understanding of divine law." [34] The law is a manifestation of the righteousness of God and the condition of life for man. Ellul has noted this emphatic declaration by God of the significance of obedience to law. "And the Lord commanded us to do all these statutes, to fear the Lord our God, for our good always, that he might preserve us alive" (Deut. 6:24). "That which is altogether just shalt thou follow, that thou mayest live" (Deut. 16:20). Christ and Christ only is the *ground* of liberty, openly so in the New Testament, clearly so in the Old Testament as the typical sacrifice. The law, however, is to the redeemed man the *condition* of liberty.

[33] Various jurists delight in taking this and other laws out of all context and meaning and ridiculing them as objects of primitivism and savagery. Unhappily, no book is written pointing out the return to primitivism and savagery inherent in all the concepts of modern law. Again, those who like Kelsen believe that moral relativism leads to tolerance and freedom would do well to read de Jouvenal's analysis "that moral relativism cannot lead to toleration" in the man of action but rather to "pressure and violence" as modern jurisprudence and political history gives ample evidence (de Jouvenal, *op. cit.*, p. 288f.).

[34] Ellul, *op. cit.*, pp. 47, 52.

In Deuteronomy 4:8, "the words 'statutes and judgments' (as in Lev. 19:37) denote the whole of the law of the covenant in its two leading features: . . . *statutes* include the moral commandments and statutory covenant laws . . . that is to say, all that the people were bound to observe; . . . *rights*, all that was due to them, whether in relation to God or to their fellow-men" (cf. Deut. 26:16-19).[35]

Law is covenant law, and is consequent to judgment and functions then to restoration (Deut. 26:16-19). As covenant law, it establishes man, no longer an outlaw, as a person of restored status having "received from God a certain number of rights that are now his: the right to dominate creation," and other specified rights confirmed in covenant man with covenant powers.[36] Take away man's relationship to God and the divine source of law, and the rights of man disappear, together with man's power to maintain them. Even Jefferson, in 1776, wrote in his *Notes on Virginia*, "Can the liberties of a nation be thought secure when we have removed their only firm basis, a conviction in the minds of the people that these liberties are the gift of God?" In what has been termed "the most influential treatise on political science in the decades just after the Civil War, *Political Science* by Theodore Dwight Woolsey, earlier president of Yale and then professor of political science, we find it affirmed: "Judges are in no sense representatives of the people or the king, or of any will whatever, except so far as they take a place which the people or king filled before. In a higher sense, they are not representatives of the community nor of its chief magistrates, but of justice and of God. . . . They are in fact more immediately servants of God than any other men who manage the affairs of a country." [37] Men like Holmes, in ruling out God, while disclaiming any desire to play God, ultimately played that role. The consequence has been, as it always is, the exaltation of the state as the source of law and justice, so that the concern of the court becomes the welfare of the state, not the man. This is apparent in the U. S. Supreme Court, where, as Curtis among others has observed, only public and increasingly govern-

---

[35] C. F. Keil and F. Delitzsch: *The Pentateuch*, III, p. 308f.
[36] Ellul, *op. cit.*, p. 55.
[37] Vol. II, pp. 330., 1877; cited in Curtis, *op. cit.*, p. 54.

mental concerns and appeals are heard. "Disappointed litigants often say they will carry their appeal right up to the Supreme Court of the United States, if necessary. They do not get there. For the Court has all but ceased to handle ordinary private litigation." [38] When law becomes the creature of the state, man also becomes the creature of that state and has no life beyond its will. The court hearkens then, as courts do now, to the appeal of government agencies against man, as man seeks to stand in terms of ancient and now denied liberties. Such liberties as the court has chosen to grant are to admittedly guilty men in order to further their evasion of law; the ordinary citizen's immunities, on the other hand, have been rapidly eroded. The extent to which the court assumes the defense of government agencies as against the citizen was apparent in an ostensibly minor case, *U. S.* v. *Wunderlich*, 1951. The Court of Claims set aside "as arbitrary, capricious, and grossly erroneous, a decision of the Secretary of Interior upon a dispute concerning a question of fact arising upon a government contract, although a provision thereof made the decision final and conclusive upon the parties thereto." The Supreme Court, six members ruling and Minton writing the opinion, reversed the Court of Appeals. The usual Article 15 in government contracts binds the contractor and makes the government department head the only source of appeal, and a partisan one. The only exception to this plenary power which the Court had previously allowed was "fraud or such gross mistake as would necessarily imply bad faith, or a failure to exercise an honest judgment." While granting that the decision of the department head in the Wunderlich case was "arbitrary," "capricious," and "grossly erroneous," the Supreme Court narrowed its previous exception by refusing to call this fraud. In his dissent, Douglas, with Reed concurring, commented of the majority opinion:

> But the rule we announce has wide application and a devastating effect. It makes a tyrant out of every contracting officer. He is granted the power of a tyrant even though he is stubborn, perverse or captious. He is allowed the power of a tyrant though he is incompetent or negligent. He has the power of

[38] Curtis, *op. cit.*, p. 61.

life and death over a private business even though his decision is grossly erroneous. Power granted is seldom neglected.

The principle of checks and balances is a healthy one. An official who is accountable will act more prudently. . . . We should allow the Court of Claims, the agency close to these disputes, to reverse an official whose conduct is plainly out of bounds whether he is fraudulent, perverse, captious, incompetent, or just palpably wrong. The rule we announce makes government oppressive. The rule the Court of Claims espouses gives a citizen justice even against his government.

Jackson in his dissent observed, "It should not follow that one who takes a public contract puts himself wholly in the power of contracting officers and department heads." [39] But it does so follow, and no change of judges suffices, since most, whatever their politics, are swayed by the same basic relativism which inevitably makes man the creature of the state and the court "a bevy of Platonic Guardians." Justice is a religious concept, and, without its biblical foundation, it quickly loses all meaning and becomes no more than a cynically held myth and an instrument of social control. The second office of the law, the protection of society, requires the principle of retribution and restitution to be the substance of the law. Without this biblical foundation, the law decays, and judges become cynical men who skeptically ask, "What is justice?" and will not wait for an answer.

Others, indeed, refer to the demand for justice as an instance of primitivism and savagery. Henry Weihofen, Professor of Law at the University of New Mexico, denies that "a reprehensible crime" moves us to righteous indignation. Our demand for justice in such cases is rather "all our ancient tribal fears of anything that threatens the security of the group." The demand for justice or punishment is the "way we relieve our own sense of guilt without actually having to suffer the punishment—a convenient and even pleasant device for it not only relieves us of sin, but makes us feel actually virtuous." The urge to punish, as he terms the call for justice, is of "primitive and irrational nature." "Understanding and love instead of hate are enjoined upon us not only by the teachings of religion but also by the teachings

[39] *U. S. Supreme Court, Law, ed. Advance Opinions*, vol. 96, no. 3, December 17, 1951, pp. 67-71.

of psychology." Weihofen is ready to grant that some punishment "probably performs a needed function," but not for any other than psychiatric reasons; justice as such is not in view.[40]

We have thus in Weihofen, without any of Augustine's faith or brilliance, a setting forth of the same fundamental error which so greatly troubled Volusianus. Of psychiatry and law alike it may be asked, as Volusianus in effect asked of Augustine, have you not denied the reality and possibility of justice by your doctrine of understanding, love, and forgiveness? And what love or understanding is there or can remain in any order which subverts justice?

[40] Henry Weihofen: *The Urge to Punish*, pp. 130-146. New York: Farrar, Straus and Cudahy, 1956. This study was an Isaac Ray Award Book of the American Psychiatric Association.

THE RELATIONSHIP OF MAN TO LAW

According to a very popular and dangerous half-truth, "You can't legislate morality." This is true insofar as it refers to the fact that the law cannot govern a man's heart, the fountainhead of true morality, nor can law produce a change of heart. The law cannot regenerate man; it cannot make a bad man good. On the other hand, we must, and do, legislate morality, in that all law is enacted morality or procedural thereto. Laws against murder, theft, perjury, and other crimes are moral laws; they are enacted and legally demanded requirements of conformity to a moral law. This is also true of traffic laws, which require a respect for the rights of others and a recognition that no man is a law unto himself. Thus, as a *first major premise*, we can assert that all law is either enacted morality or else it is a series of legal and juridical procedures for the maintenance of that enacted morality. The morality of any culture can be readily studied and understood by an examination of its laws. Its moral decline or transformation can again be studied by an examination of the enforcement of those laws. The moral standards and caliber of a people come to light in their laws and in their enforcement of those laws.

A *second premise* is that morality, and hence law, rests upon religion. There are those today who assert that it is not a necessary relationship, and that morality can exist apart from religion.[1] It is significant, however, that such writers are actually asserting that morality can exist without God rather than without religion; they themselves ground their non-theistic morality on a humanistic religion. Their main thrust is to separate contemporary morality and

[1] See Henry H. Hazlitt: *The Foundations of Morality*. Princeton: Van Nostrand, 1964.

law from the Christian religion and attach it to the religion of humanity.[2] Very simply defined, morality is concerned with right and wrong and the application of this standard to life and character. But our conception of what constitutes right and wrong rests on a religious or metaphysical judgment concerning ultimate reality. Morality is inescapably religious in foundation. Historically, as Sir Patrick Devlin has noted, this means Christianity:

> I think it is clear that the criminal law as we know it is based upon moral principle. In a number of crimes its function is simply to enforce a moral principle and nothing else. The law, both criminal and civil, claims to be able to speak about morality and immorality generally. Where does it get its authority to do this and how does it settle the moral principles which it enforces. Undoubtedly, as a matter of history, it derived both from Christian teaching. But I think that the strict logician is right when he says that the law can no longer rely on doctrines in which citizens are entitled to disbelieve. It is necessary therefore to look for some other source.[3]

For Devlin, both criminal and civil law rest on "Christian teaching." Since we no longer teach or require that faith for citizenship, we are moving towards another religious source for law. When the faith of a people differs from its laws, and "about which the community as a whole is not deeply imbued with a sense of sin; the law sags under a weight which it is not constructed to bear and may become permanently warped." In other words, the people cannot be expected to obey a law whose religious foundations they are not taught.

> A man who concedes that morality is necessary to society must support the use of those instruments without which morality cannot be maintained. The two instruments are those of teaching, which is doctrine, and of enforcement, which is the law. If morals could be taught simply on the basis that they are necessary to society, there would be no social need for religion; it could be left as a purely personal affair. But morality cannot be taught in that way. Loyalty is not taught in that way

[2] See Rushdoony: *The Nature of the American System* on "The Religion of Humanity."

[3] Sir Patrick Devlin: *The Enforcement of Morals*, p. 9. London: Oxford University Press, 1959.

either. No society has yet solved the problem of how to teach morality without religion. So the law must base itself on Christian morals and to the limit of its ability enforce them, not simply because they are the morals of most of us, nor simply because they are the morals which are taught by the established Church—on these points the law recognizes the right to dissent—but for the compelling reason that without the help of Christian teaching the law will fail.[4]

Devlin is correct in observing that "No society has yet solved the problem of how to teach morality without religion." One could also say that no society has attempted it. The secularization of Western culture since the French Revolution has really been the separation of Western civilization from Christianity to humanism. It has been the steady disestablishment of Christianity and the establishment of humanism as the law of the state.

The *third premise* is an obvious one: the power and meaning of law is derived from an ultimate authority, and the source of a culture's law is its god. The origin and ultimate source and conclusion of a culture's law is its god. The god of a culture can be located by fixing its source of law. If the source of law is the ontological Trinity of Christain revelation, then that Trinity is the God of that culture. If the source of law rests in the people, then the voice of the people is the voice of God (vox populi, vox dei), and that voice finds expression and incarnation either in a leader, a legislative body, or a supreme court, depending on which gains the ascendancy. The highest point in the processes of law is the god of that system. If no law exists beyond man, if law is entirely man-made, the supreme court or source of that man-made system of law must of necessity assume the functions of a god, functions which are imposed upon it by the faith of that society. The supernatural God having been denied, the divine society of man must express its mind concerning true law through an instrument, a man, an assembly, or a court, and that instrument is the functioning god of that culture. Crudely put, the god-idea is inescapable; detached from the supernatural, it attaches itself to an aspect of the natural, and on no level can it be detached from law. It is the source of law and the supreme

[4] *Ibid.*, p. 25.

court of law. Where your law starts and stops, there is your god.

With these premises in mind, *first*, that all law is enacted morality or procedural thereto, *second*, that all morality rests on a religion, and *third*, that the source of a culture's law is its god, let us examine now *the relationship of man to law*.

If man is the creature of the supernatural God of Christianity, then man is both under God and under God's law. He is under obligation to obey God by obeying law in every sphere of life insofar as it is faithful to God's law: *Man is under law*. But if the ultimate source of law resides in humanity, and humanity is seen as divine, then man cannot be placed under law, because he himself is beyond law as the source of law. In a humanity possessed of divinity, man cannot be under law, but he can have two other possible relationships to law: man can be *over* law, or man can be *apart from law*. *Man over law* means, as we shall see, statism; *man apart from law* means anarchism.

Let us examine the first of these three classifications of man in relation to law: *man under law*, with God as the source of law. The first consequence of this position is that Christian order means that man is placed, together with his every institution, under law. The state, church, family, school, private associations, business, farming, science, and every other human activity are equally bound by the absolute law of God. The sovereignty of God precludes the sovereignty of man. Neither church nor state nor any other institution can claim, without departure from the faith, sovereignty for itself. A sovereign power is beyond law and is the source of law. The claim of sovereignty by kings meant absolutism, a claim to be *beyond* law. Thus, with respect to Queen Elizabeth I of England, we read:

> It was asserted that the queen inherited both an enlarging and a restraining power; by her prerogative she might set at liberty what was restrained by statute or otherwise, and by her prerogative she might restrain what was otherwise at liberty; that the royal prerogative was not to be canvassed, nor disputed, nor examined; and did not even admit of any limitation: that absolute princes such as the sovereigns of England, were a species of divinity: that it was in vain to attempt tying the queen's hands

by laws or statutes; since, by means of her dispensing power, she could loosen herself at pleasure: and that even if a clause should be annexed to a statute, excluding her dispensing power, she could first dispense with that clause and then with the statute.[5]

The ground by which the Queen was placed above and beyond the law was that she was "a species of divinity." This is basic to the claim. The divine rights of the crown, after 1688, came to be exercised by Parliament. In other countries, this divine right has passed into varying hands. In the United States, both the Supreme Court, by its legislative decisions, and the presidents, by their executive orders, are manifesting the same power. But the United States, in its War of Independence, was at war with the idea of sovereignty, and, according to Pollard, "revolted against the doctrine of the sovereignty of the State. . . . It is this denial of all sovereignty which gives its profound and permanent interest to the American Revolution." [6] The American system avoided placing sovereignty in any human order; its basic principle is the supremacy of law, and even Corwin has cited the fact that constitutional law rested on "Higher Law." [7] American liberty rested on this denial of sovereignty to any human order.

The second aspect of *man under law* is that man's relationship to law becomes *ministerial, not legislative*, that is, man does not create law, does not decree what shall be right and wrong simply in terms of his will. Instead, man seeks, in his law-making, to approximate and administer fundamental law, law in terms of God's law, absolute right and wrong. Neither majority nor minority wishes are of themselves right or wrong; both are subject to judgment in terms of the absolute law of God, and the largest majority cannot make valid and true a law contrary to the word of God. All man's law-making must be in conformity to the higher law of God, or it is false.

[5] David Hume: *The History of England, from the Invasion of Julius Caesar to the Abdication of James the Second, 1688*, vol. IV, p. 336f. New York: Harper, 1852.

[6] A. F. Pollard: *Factors in American History*, p. 336f. New York: Macmillan, 1925.

[7] Edward S. Corwin: *The "Higher Law" Background of American Constitutional Law.* (1928). Ithaca: Cornell, 1955.

A third aspect concerns the concept of liberty. For the Christian, *liberty is under law.* Liberty under law means that man finds his freedom, not apart from law, but under law, for grace fulfils the law, perfectly in Jesus Christ, and progressively in believers. The free man is the law-abiding man, and the purposes of law are not alien to man's liberty but definitely conducive to it. In verses which were important to the Puritans and basic to the Mosaic perspective, we read, "And the LORD commanded us to do all these statutes . . . that he might preserve us alive" (Deut. 6:24), and "Justice, and only justice, you shall follow, that you may live" (Deut. 16:20). God's law is not bondage to the believer but his element and basic to his liberty.

A fourth aspect of man under law is that *law means true order as justice.* The law is justice, and it is order, godly order, and there can be neither true order nor true law apart from justice, and justice is defined in terms of Scripture and its revelation of God's law and righteousness. The law cannot be made more than justice. It cannot be made into an instrument of salvation without destruction to justice. Salvation is not by law but by the grace of God through Jesus Christ.

A fifth aspect immediately becomes apparent. Since man is under law, and law is not capable of salvation, i.e., its function is not salvation but justice, *the area of civil government is restricted to justice, and government becomes broader than the state.* Since the state is restricted to justice, great areas of government are left outside the jurisdiction of the state. The basic government is man's self-government. Other governments of man include the family, the church, the school, his business, and many private associations as well as public opinion. Government is a broad concept; justice is a strict and narrow one; by restricting law to justice, and the state to the administration of law as justice, both salvation, which is left to God, and vast areas of self-government, which are left to man, are kept out of the hands of the state. If the state is not restricted to justice, it will relentlessly claim to be the only government of man, a claim made repeatedly in history.

Let us now examine a second category of man's relationship to law: *man over law.*

The first implication of this position is that man, as the autonomous and ultimate form of being, is himself the source of law, vox populi, vox dei. The state is the walking god on earth in terms of which *man, as the source of law*, expresses himself. The state is the divine expression of man's law. Man finds himself in and through the state. Statism is the consequence of this position, and man's true life is seen in terms of the state. Man is simply a political animal.

Second, *law is man's creation*, and no law of God nor any past law or constitution can bind or limit man today. Man in every age must move in terms of his present needs, not past laws, and neither the past nor the future can bind him. Only the law of his own being, as it expresses itself in the state and its will, the general will of the citizens either as a majority or in the "democratic consensus" of an elite minority, has any meaning for him. For this position, law must of necessity change. The idea of a fixed law is a contradiction, because man is not a fixed but an eternally evolving being. Since man is the source of law, all law must be pragmatic; it must serve him, or else it is invalid.

Third, if man is seen as over law, and man's law expresses itself in the state, then *man's true liberty is state law*. From ancient Egypt and Mesopotamia to our present-day welfare states and socialist empires, we find this common belief that man is free only under the total state. Stalin repeatedly affirmed the freedom of the Soviet workers precisely in and under the dictatorship of the Communist Party in its elite leaders. Aristotle defined man as essentially a political animal, deriving his meaning and liberty from the state, and Plato held that the very right to be born was subject to state approval.

Fourth, if man's liberty is in the law of the state, it also implies that *law means salvation*. Man finds salvation through political programs, through legislation, so that *salvation is an enactment of the state*. The state does not restrict itself to justice, because every area of life is its proper domain. As a saving order, the state concerns itself with cradle-to-grave security, because, as the expression of man's divinity, it must play the role of god in man's life. It becomes man's savior.

Fifth, it follows then that *government means the state*. The collective expression of man's divinity assumes all of man's governmental functions. No area of government remains outside the state. The total state takes control of man.

The third possible relationship of man to law is *man apart from law and without law*.

In analyzing this position, it is apparent, first, that this position is philosophical anarchism. Man recognizes no law except himself. No truth exists outside of man to be a law over man, and thus there can be no legitimate authority over man. The only truth or reality for man is his own being and will, and man recognizes "Neither God nor master." As one such believer wote,

> All truths *beneath* me are to my liking; a truth *above* me, a truth that I should have to *direct* myself by, I am not acquainted with. For me there is no truth, for nothing is more than I! [8]

This champion of philosophical anarchism protested against morality and law as relics of Christianity from which man must free himself:

> Take notice how a "moral man" behaves, who to-day often thinks he is through with God and throws off Christianity as a bygone thing. If you ask him whether he has ever doubted that the copulation of brother and sister is incest, that monogamy is the truth of marriage, that filial piety is a sacred duty, etc., then a moral shudder will come over him at the conception of one's being allowed to touch his sister as wife also, etc. And whence this shudder? Because he *believes* in those moral commandments. This moral *faith* is deeply rooted in his breast. Much as he rages against the *pious* Christians, he himself has nevertheless as thoroughly remained a Christian—to wit, a *moral* Christian. In the form of morality Christianity holds him a prisoner, and a prisoner under *faith*. Monogamy is to be something sacred, and he who may live in bigamy is punished as a *criminal;* he who commits incest suffers as a *criminal*. Those who are always crying that religion is not to be regarded in the *State*, and the Jew is to be a citizen equally with the Christian, show themselves in accord with this. Is not this of incest and monogamy a *dogma of faith*.[9]

[8] Max Stirner: *The Ego and His Own*, p. 374. Translated by Steven T. Byington. New York: The Modern Library, n.d. Max Stirner, whose real name was Kaspar Schmidt, lived from 1806-1856.

[9] *Ibid.*, p. 47f.

Nothing is true and nothing false, nothing good and nothing evil of itself; the only law and morality is that man fulfil himself, that man do as he pleases. Man is his own god, and no collective body can represent him or exercise his divinity for him.

Second, such a believer holds that he has a responsibility *to free himself by breaking the shackles of law*, so that *law-breaking becomes the act of freedom.* He is not a sinner under the law, but an outlaw against all law. He feels duty-bound to assert his liberty from law by waging war against the very idea of law. He challenges laws against pornography, immorality, and obscenity, laws against libel, against subversion, laws against the use of narcotics, and in every area asserts the right of man to be free from law. His studied purpose and mission is *to destroy the law in the name of human rights, and his premise is that human rights cannot be subjected to any law whatsoever*, and this means any law of God or man.

A third implication is now clearly apparent: for the anarchist, *liberty means freedom from law, antinomianism.* The Christian finds freedom under law by grace; the statist finds freedom in statist law; the anarchist finds freedom only by escaping from all law and by systematically breaking and destroying all law.

Fourth, for the anarchist, *antinomianism is salvation; man is saved by being lawless.* This means freedom from every kind of law or standard, including standards of cleanliness. Thus, Arthur Rimbaud, who practiced debauchery and homosexuality to destroy any feeling of law, wrote of himself that when he staggered into bed drunk, he on an occasion defecated all over himself, and was not troubled by it. This was for him a victory. According to Starkie, "His life of debauch was for him one long martyrdom, but a martyrdom giving him all the ecstatic joys of a religious martyrdom, and to reach this sublime condition he was willing to sacrifice dignity, health and purity." [10] The rationale of Rimbaud's position is summarized by Starkie: "Everything is good that breaks down the control of reason: everything is precious that can succeed in freeing the faculties from their normal inhibitions." [11]

[10] Enid Starkie: *Arthur Rimbaud*, p. 158. New York: New Directions, 1961.
[11] *Ibid.*, p. 122f.

Fifth, for the anarchist, *government means man alone.* Stirner ridiculed the ideas of the "liberals" of his day, pointing out that their liberty meant statism, and their revolutions, as in the French Revolution, meant greater slavery for man:

> The monarch in the person of the "royal master" had been a paltry monarch compared with this new monarch, the "sovereign-nation." This *monarchy* was a thousand times severer, stricter, and more consistent. Against the new monarch there was no longer any right, any privilege at all; how limited the "absolute king" of the *ancient regime* looks in comparison! The Revolution effected the transformation of *limited monarchy* into *absolute monarchy.* From this time on every right that is not conferred by this monarch is an "assumption"; but every prerogative that he bestows, a "right." The times demanded *absolute royalty,* absolute monarchy; therefore down fell that so-called absolute royalty which had so little understood how to become absolute that it remained limited by a thousand little lords.[12]

Liberalism in essence meant statism. "Political liberty means that the *polis,* the State, is free; freedom of religion that religion is free." [13] "It does not mean *my* liberty, but the liberty of a power that rules and subjugates me; it means that one of my *despots,* like State, religion, conscience is free." [14] "Every State is a *despotism,*" and this bondage can be broken "Only by recognizing no duty, i.e., not *binding* myself nor letting myself be bound. If I have no duty, then I know no law either." [15] World history is of no concern to the free man: "only *his* history has value, because he wants to develop only *himself,* not the mankind-idea, not God's plan, not the purposes of Providence, not liberty, and the like." Man is his own and only absolute.

> They say of God, "Names name thee not." That holds good of me: no *concept* expresses me, nothing that is designated as my essence exhausts me; they are only names. Likewise they say of God that he is perfect and has no calling to strive after perfection. That too holds good of me alone.

12 Stirner, *op. cit.,* p. 107.
13 *Ibid.,* p. 112f.
14 *Ibid.,* p. 113.
15 *Ibid.,* p. 204f.

I am *owner* of my might, and I am so when I know myself as *unique*. In the *unique one* the owner himself returns into his creative nothing, out of which he is born. Every higher essence above me, be it God, be it man, weakens the feeling of my uniqueness, and pales only before the sun of this consciousness. If I concern myself for myself, the unique one, then my concern rests on its transitory, mortal creator, who consumes himself, and I may say:

All things are nothing to me. (Ich hab' Mein' Sach' aug Nichts gestellt.)[16]

The anarchist thus opposes the limited powers of Christian civil government, and the unlimited powers of liberal and socialist statism, in favor of the unlimited powers of the individual. In terms of practical politics, however, the statist and the anarchist are in agreement in their hostility to orthodox Christianity and in their studied assault on Christian law and order.

It should be apparent now that man's concept of his relationship to law is a framework which governs his every attitude and colors his every action. The statist and anarchist will approach the Bible and will read its statements in terms of their presuppositions rather than the presuppositions of the Bible itself. To cite a specific instance: Jesus said, "Therefore all things whatsoever ye would that men should do to you, do ye even so to them: for this is the law and the prophets" (Matt. 7:12). This "Golden Rule" is also stated in another form as love to one's neighbor and to one's enemy: "Thou shalt love thy neighbour as thyself: I am the Lord," is defined by Moses as including one's enemy (Lev. 19:18, 33-37). This commandment, restated in Matthew 19:19; 22:37-40; Romans 13:8-10; 15:2; Galatians 5:14; 6:10; etc., is a summary of the second table of the law. Thus, for the Christian, this is a true charter of civil and personal liberties. To love his neighbor or enemy means to grant unto him those immunities of life God has ordained for all, of life, sanctity of home, of property, and of reputation, in word, thought, and deed. For the statist, it means socialism: to love means to share, and to obey the Golden Rule fully means communism. Anarchists vary in their interpretation between voluntary communism

[16] *Ibid.*, p. 386f.

or total abeyance from all interference, leaving all men alone to allow each to be a law unto himself. In each instance, *the perspective determines the meaning*. The Golden Rule, for example, appears in many cultures and religions, but in each instance its meaning is determined and conditioned by its framework. To assume that the same statement has the same meaning for all men is to be open to easy subversion.

Let us again apply the perspectives of these approaches to law to Matthew 5, to the Beatitudes and the ostensibly "non-resistance" passages. For the Christian, to be the blessed poor means to know one's spiritual need and to find its fulfilment in Christ and His word. The Christian is dead to the law as an indictment, a sentence of death, but alive to it now as his new nature, written on the tables of his heart (Jer. 31:31-33; Ezek. 11:19, 20, etc.). He thus lives under law by faith, and in Christ law is his new nature. His social goal is a godly order, *justice, not perfection*. He submits to evil when compelled to, and returns good for evil (Matt. 5:39-42). For him, God's law stands as long as heaven and earth stand (Matt. 5:17-19). The perfection of which the Sermon on the Mount speaks (Matt. 5:48) is in terms of God's righteousness, which for man means the fulfilling of the law in word, thought, and deed, so that murder, theft, or adultery are committed, as are other sins, if they are only in the form of intent, as covetous desires (Matt. 5:21-45). Liberty is under law; perfection is never apart from the law; "love is the fulfilling of the law" (Rom. 13:10), and a just order is the *social* goal of man, even as faith is the *personal* requirement.

For the statist, whether "liberal" or socialist, the state is the true agency of love, and perfection for man and society comes through state love, i.e., statist legislation requiring compulsory sharing, integration, association, and unity. Love is the higher law than justice, and the state acts as the social agency of love. Perfection comes through statist legislation. Justice must thus surrender to the "higher claims" of love, because justice stands on individual rights, whereas love represents social rights. Therefore, love of all persons is required as the personal and statist faith. Jesus Christ as savior and as the object of faith is replaced by this concept of love as savior and salvation.

For the anarchist, love is also a higher way, but true love means absolutely free love, so that anarchy must be introduced in order to free love from law, and perfection comes through free love. However, love cannot be made the law of man's being, because for the anarchist man cannot be placed under any law, including love as a law. Therefore, there is no necessity to love, and love, together with justice, must be regarded as a bondage to be broken. Perfection is thus to be yourself and to have faith in yourself. Free love is therefore simply the first step towards freedom; the next step can be free hatred. The basic step is man's total freedom from all claims, his assertion of total anarchy and autonomy.

Our crisis today is accentuated and aggravated by the fact that the statist and the anarchist are fully aware of the foundations of their concept of law, but the average Westerner, a product of two thousand years of Christianity, clings vaguely to the *law and order* that Christian culture has produced and hungers for a return to its safety and certainty, but he lacks the *faith and theology* which alone can sustain that order. As a result, although this culturally Christian man is generally in the great majority, he is easily manipulated and controlled by the articulate and epistemologically self-conscious minorities. Unless *the relationship of law to Christianity* is re-established, there is no future except destruction for Western culture.

The Relationship of Man to Law

I.   Law is enacted morality or procedural thereto.

II. Morality, and hence law, rests upon religion.

III. The source of a culture's law is its god.

Possible relationships of man to law:

Man Under Law	*Man Over Law*	*Man Apart from Law*
1. God is the source of law. Man and all his institutions are under law.	1. Man in the state is the source of law. The state is the divine expression of man's law.	1. Anarchism. Man recognizes no law apart from himself. Man is his own god.

2. Law is ministerial, not legislative.	2. Law is man's creation. Constitutions cannot bind man.	2. Man's responsibility is to break the shackles of law.
3. Liberty is under law. Grace fulfils law.	3. Liberty means state law.	3. Liberty means no law. Antinomianism.
4. The purpose of law is justice.	4. The purpose of law is salvation. The state is man's savior.	4. Lawlessness means salvation.
5. The state is restricted to justice, and government is more than the state.	5. Government equals the state.	5. Government equals man alone.

The Meaning of Love of Neighbor and Enemy

| Respect for God-given immunities of others; life, home, property. | True love is total sharing or socialism, communism. | The true way can be either (1) total sharing or (2) total "freedom." |

Man's Way of Life and Fulfilment

Justification by faith.	Justification by love, love seen as total sharing.	Justification by total egoism and anarchy.
Liberty is under law. Faith therefore is law-abiding.	Love is the higher way, love as statist sharing	Love, as free love, is a higher way.
Perfection is not apart from Law.	Perfection is through legislation by the state.	Perfection is to be yourself, to do as you please.
Love structured by law must be shown by the individual.	The state is the agency of love.	The individual is the agency of free or anarchistic love.
The law is fulfilled by love, a love which expresses justice.	The law is fulfilled by socialist love. Justice is too individualistic.	There is no necessity for love or justice. Man is free from all things.
Justice is the social goal.	Justice surrenders to love.	Justice and love surrender to the independent ego.
Faith is the personal requirement.	Love, socialist love, is the true faith.	Anarchism, egoism, is the true faith.

7

TRUTH AND LIBERTY

Historically, a basic premise of Western civilization has been the belief that the only valid foundation for and source of social order is truth. This truth, in the form of a religion, has been the mainspring of society and the structure of cultural order. The concept of a secular society has been alien to this tradition. The question has not been, "Shall we establish a religion as the foundation of our society?" but rather, "which religion?" The state must be grounded on truth, it was held, and religion was the vehicle of truth. Differences existed, indeed, as to the role of religion. Non-Christian states held that the function of religion, however basic, was that of social cement to the true order, the state; in this concept, the true "church" of the established religion was the state. Orthodox Christianity insisted on the independence of Church and state as institutions, and on their interdependence, together with their mutual dependence and "establishment" on the Scriptures as the infallible truth of God. This concept found sharp expression in the Form of Government of the Westminster Standards, which affirmed

> That truth is in order to goodness; and the great touchstone of truth, its tendency to promote holiness; according to our Saviour's rule, "By their fruits ye shall know them." And that no opinion can be either more pernicious or more absurd than that which brings truth and falsehood upon a level, and represents it as of no consequence what a man's opinions are. On the contrary, they are persuaded that there is an inseparable connection between faith and practice, truth and duty. Otherwise it would be of no consequence either to discover truth or to embrace it (Westminster Standards: Form of Government, Chapt. I, 4).

Beginning with the French Revolution, however, another tradition has steadily come to the surface, one denying the validity of religion and truth as the foundation for society. Instead of a doctrine concerning ultimate truth and its relationship to civil government, this movement began by asserting the importance instead of "Liberty, Fraternity, and Equality." At first, the break was primarily with revealed truth, with religion as such, but progressively it became apparent that the hostility was not merely to a particular church establishment but to truth as such in any form.

The hostility to truth came very quickly, as witness Karl Marx. Marx ridiculed not only Christianity but also the nature worship of men like G. Fr. Daumier, whose "natural religion" Marx properly called "drivel," with its sentimental hymn on Nature:

> Nature holy, Mother sweet,
> In Thy footsteps place my feet.
> My baby hand to Thy hand clings,
> Hold me as in leading strings! [1]

For Marx, "the state is not to be constituted from religion but from the reason of freedom. Only the crassest ignorance can assert that the theory of making the state-concept independent is a passing whim of modern philosophers." [2] "The reason of freedom," a freedom not bound to a doctrine of truth but only to itself, is the foundation of this "new" order. Instead of looking, with "the old materialism" to "civil society," Marx's standpoint was "*human* society, or socialized humanity." "The philosophers have only *interpreted* the world, in various ways; the point, however, is to *change* it." [3] Engels, in a eulogy of Marx, declared, "Our dialectical philosophy abolishes all the notions of absolute and definitive truth, and any absolute human conditions which correspond to them. For dialectics nothing is definitive, absolute or sacred; it reveals the relativity of all things and nothing exists for it but the uninterrupted process of

[1] Karl Marx and Frederick Engels: "Review of G. Fr. Daumier's *The Religion of the New Age*," in *K. Marx and F. Engels on Religion*, p. 95. Second Impression; Moscow: Foreign Languages Publishing House.
[2] Karl Marx: "The Leading Article of No. 179 of Kolnische Zeitung," in *ibid.*, p. 38.
[3] K. Marx, "Theses on Feuerbach," in *ibid.*, p. 72.

development and change." [4] This theoretical anarchism was rejected by Marx as a practical social goal; "the reason of freedom" could best realize itself in "socialized humanity."

This separation of liberty and the state from truth was not limited to Marxism. It was common to Fabianism, existentialism, various forms of religious modernism, and, increasingly, to liberalism. The disestablishment of liberty from truth has increasingly become the policy of the United States Supreme Court.

Associate Justice William O. Douglas has associated relativism with liberty and truth with totalitarianism:

> To say therefore that the search for "truth" is not man's mission may seem to some to be the ultimate sin. But those who construct a political system on the basis of their "truth" create totalitarianism. [5]

The struggle for liberty is for Douglas a struggle against the domination of the "truth" of some majority in power:

> The struggle of men has been to create political institutions which prevent government from putting its imprimatur on what the majority or those in power may conceive to be the "truth." In that sense the problem of our age is not to discover "truth" but to accommodate conflicting views of "truth" and the common good or conflicting needs. [6]

Men have long sought to establish society on truth. It is high time, according to Douglas, to establish it on more pragmatic foundations, ones conducive to liberty. Not truth, but liberty, is the goal for Douglas:

> Truth is not the goal, for in most areas no one knows what truth is. The search is for a way of life that offers the individual the greatest possible opportunity for fulfillment. The goal may change from age to age; or even if it remains constant, the means of achieving it may need revision as, for example, when

[4] Cited in Jean Ousset: *Marxism Leninism*, p. 39. Quebec: International Union, 1962.

[5] William O. Douglas: *Freedom of the Mind*, p. 35. Reading for an Age of Change, No. 3, Published by the American Library Association in cooperation with the Public Affairs Pamphlets, New York, 1962.

[6] *Ibid.*, p. 36.

automation produces vast unemployment or when the need to keep a critical foreign nation out of one political orbit means giving it trade preferences which have severe repercussions at home. . . .

If we are to have freedom of the mind in America, we must produce a generation of men and women who will tower above the press, as well as the crowd, and make tolerance for all ideas the symbol of virtue.[7]

This perspective is consistently applied by Douglas. For him, sovereignty, which orthodox Christianity reserved to God alone, is in the people.[8] According to Douglas, "The philosophy of the First Amendment is that man must have full freedom to search the world and the universe for the answers and puzzles of life."[9] Moreover, "In theory, government should be interested only in conduct, in overt acts."[10] The United States began "as a congeries of states with theocratic creeds, much in the fashion of Pakistan and Saudi Arabia today," and "the gradual secularization of government should be an oft-told tale" in the history of liberty.[11] Although restricting government in theory to overt acts, Douglas also defends "the right of revolution" as a part of "the right of dissent."[12] Although ready to grant that the Communist Party is an international body in affiliation, and recognized by the courts as a conspiracy, Douglas holds "that government has no concern with thoughts and beliefs."[13] "Unorthodoxy in the field of political and social ideas is no business of government."[14] The same is true of ideas in the realm of sexual morality. "Sex cannot be suppressed in life. Should it be attempted in literature?" Obscenity laws have as their "real purpose . . . to make the public live up to the censor's code of morality."[15] For Douglas,

[7] *Ibid.*, p. 36f.
[8] William O. Douglas: *The Right of the People*, p. 13 . New York: Pyramid Books, 1961 (1958).
[9] *Ibid.*, p. 20.
[10] Douglas: *Freedom of the Mind*, p. 11.
[11] *Ibid.*, p. 32.
[12] William O. Douglas: *America Challenged*, p. 14. New York: Avon Books, 1960.
[13] Douglas: *The Right of the People*, pp. 59-61.
[14] *Ibid.*, p. 73.
[15] Douglas: *Freedom of Mind*, p. 29.

Freedom in this broad sense is the ultimate aim of the good society. We have the institutions as well as the traditions that make that freedom possible. That is the one overwhelming advantage we have over the communist camps.[16]

The implication of this position is that freedom must be given to all kinds of ideas and even practices in order to ensure liberty for all. Douglas has affirmed this: "We believe that the extinction of any civilization, culture, religion, or life-ways is a loss to humanity." [17] This same position was more radically affirmed by the Marquis de Sade, who call for total toleration of all practices as equally valid because equally natural. Hence, homosexuality was natural and good. "Can we possibly imagine Nature giving us the possibility of committing a crime which would offend her." [18] A Kinsey report was critical of laws against child molestation and held that in many cases such "pre-adolescent experience had contributed favorably to their later socio-sexual development," according to the victims. The real evil, the report held, was in the repressive cultural conditioning which led the child to be "emotionally upset or frightened by their contacts with adults." [19]

This liberty means total tolerance, and, some would add, total love. It also means a hostility to law, because law rests on truth: something is illegal because it is wrong. Law is concerned with right and wrong, and with procedures to the establishment of law and order. It is not surprising to find the modernist clergy increasingly hostile to law. When a benefit ball for 600 homosexuals and their friends was arranged for January 1, 1965, by some clergymen of San Francisco, the police interfered. According to one clergyman, of the sponsoring group,

The police department wanted to deal more in theology rather than open up a dialogue. . . . They looked at the rings

[16] Douglas: *America Challenged*, p. 31.

[17] William O. Douglas: *Democracy's Manifesto*, p. 44. Garden City, New York: Doubleday, 1962.

[18] Sade in Leonard de Saint-Yves, editor: *Selected Writings of De Sade*, p. 258. New York: British Book Centre, 1954.

[19] Alfred C. Kinsey, Wardell B. Pomeroy, Clyde E. Martin, Paul Gebhard, etc.: *Sexual Behavior in the Human Female*, pp. 115, 327f., 330, 121f. Philadelphia: W. B. Saunders, 1953.

on our fingers and said, "We see you're married—how do your wives accept this?" . . . They said, "We believe in the Ten Commandments—what do you believe in?" They wanted to know what theological concepts we had. I believe their theological jargon and beliefs are somewhat outdated.[20]

A conservative writer called for a changed attitude towards laws governing homosexuality among adults:

More importantly, if less tangibly, adoption of the New York commission's proposal would tend to reaffirm one of the most ancient principles of the law, which is that men should be free to pursue their widely varying concepts of happiness so long as they do not encroach upon the rights of their neighbors.[21]

Kilpatrick did not say what law it was whose ancient principle he was affirming.

In terms of this same liberty, a midwestern professor of political science, who refused to answer under oath a question as to membership in the Communist Party, has called for the existence on the college campus of Communist clubs, an atheistic organization, a society for the promotion of free love, a league for revolution by "Jeffersonian violence," an anti-automation league, "and perhaps a nudist club."[22] This concept of liberty has led to Communist speakers on college campuses, and to speakers advocating free love.[23]

Certainly, the faculty members at the University of California who defended the Free Speech Movement at Berkeley were advocates of the free society Douglas spoke of. They defended the students as "neither nihilistic nor anarchistic." "Theirs is instead a deeply moral indignation, aroused by the confrontation with palpable injustice and inequality."[24] The liberty desired, according to

20 "Incidents at a Homosexual Benefit: Angry Ministers Rip Police," by Donovan Bess, San Francisco *Chronicle*, January 3, 1965, cited in *The Dan Smoot Report*, Vol. 11, no. 16, April 19, 1965, p. 125

21 James J. Kilpatrick, "Homosexuals and the Law," Palo Alto *Times*, Calif., p. 23, Tuesday, December 15, 1964.

22 *The Canadian Intelligence Digest*, vol. 15, no. 4, April, 1965, p. 1.

23 Palo Alto, Calif., *Times*, p. 10. Monday, April 19, 1965, "Read This Before You Vote!" adv. reprinting editorials from the San Mateo *Times*.

24 *The People of the State of Calif.*, plaintiff, vs. *Mario Savio et al.*, defendant, Before: Honorable Rupert Crittenden, Judge, *A Suggestion for Dismissal*, Submitted by: Certain Faculty Members of the University of California, Berkeley, January, 1965, p. 16.

a critical faculty member who described the events at Berkeley somewhat later, was freedom to evade military service, freedom for Communist speakers, the defense of marijuana, of "group sexual intercourse and homosexuality," and the suggestion that "students should have the same sexual freedom on campus as the dogs." [25]

It is apparent from the foregoing that the champions of this new concept of liberty detached from truth have a very broad range of tolerance. Their tolerance is not unlimited: it does not extend to orthodox Christianity, the obvious champion of truth. The hostility to orthodox Christianity is very real. The implication of total liberty for all positions and a total equality for all is that the one crime is to deny this total liberty and equality as orthodox Christianity does.[26] The new liberty must wage war against orthodox Christianity as the epitome of heresy. Having become the established religion of the Supreme Court, the new liberty, the religion of humanity, will work, as it has begun, to uproot every trace of orthodox Christianity from the governmental structures of these United States and to limit its freedom of action. Relativism has become the harsh and fanatical "new truth" of American life, a religion on the march, with its screaming dervishes marching and parading in the cities and on the campuses of America.

As long as civil government exists, it will have a rationale, a law of its being, and that law is its truth. Relativism is clearly the established religion of the "new liberty."

But let us analyze more closely Douglas' thesis that truth is totalitarian and the "new liberty" alone makes for freedom and growth in any social order. Civil government is, supremely, the coercive aspect of society as it seeks to establish justice. Remove *truth* from civil government, and the remaining aspect of civil government is simply *power, coercion.* In 1936, when the "conservatives" on the U. S. Supreme Court were themselves imbued with relativism, one of them, Justice Stone, declared that "the only check upon our own

[25] Alexander Grendon, in "Editor's Mail Box," San Francisco *Examiner*, p. 32, Tuesday, March 30, 1965.
[26] For this hostility and its implications, see Rushdoony: *The Nature of the American System*, on The Religion of Humanity. Nutley, N. J.: Craig Press, 1965.

exercise of power is our own sense of self-restraint." [27]   This self-restraint has grown steadily weaker, and Douglas certainly has not been on the side of judicial restraint. As a result, the individual, in this "new liberty," has increasingly lost his liberty to the growing "new liberty" of the majority to do as it pleases and to fulfil its will. This is increasingly the interpretation of democratic rights.

Without the restraint of truth, the naked and unfettered power of the state has grown rapidly. The "new liberty" has steadily and relentlessly become the liberty for the state to assert its claim to total power. Moral anarchy and totalitarian statism are the results of the new liberty.

In Marxism, the state becomes simply coercion. According to Plamenatze,

> Stalin quotes with approval the dictum of Lenin: "First we must convince and then coerce. We must at all cost first convince and then coerce." [28]

By declaring religion to be the opium of the masses, Marx was ruling out all truth as opinion. Liberty meant liberation from truth, religious or metaphysical, into the proletarian state, naked coercion. Lenin made clear that the withering away of the state meant the withering away of democracy or consent and the total sway of the state as coercion,

> The bourgeois State does not "wither away," according to Engels, but is "put an end to" by the proletariat in the course of the revolution. What "withers away" after the revolution is the proletarian State or semi-State.
>
> Secondly, the State is a "special regressive force." This splendid and extremely profound definition of Engels' is given by him here with complete lucidity. It follows from this that the "special repressive force" of the bourgeoisie for the suppression of the proletariat, of the millions of workers by the handful of the rich, must be replaced by a "special repressive force" of the proletariat for the suppression of the bourgeoisie

[27] In *United States* v. *Butler*, 297 U.S. 1, p. 79, 1936, in Martin Glasser, "The Judicial Philosophy of Felix Frankfurter," in *New Individualist Review*, Winter, 1962, vol. 1, no. 4, p. 28. Glasser himself is an old liberal who "acknowledges no laws of history," p. 34.

[28] John Plamenatze: *German Marxism and Russian Communism*, p. 271. London, New York: Longmans Green, 1954.

(the dictatorship of the proletariat). It is just this that constitutes the destruction of "the State as the State." It is just this that constitutes the "act" of "the seizure of the means of production in the name of society." And it is obvious that such a substitution of one (proletarian) "special repressive force" for another (bourgeois) "special repressive force" can in no way take place in the form of a "withering away."

Thirdly, as to the "withering away" or, more expressively and colorfully, as to the State "becoming dormant," Engels refers quite clearly and definitely to the period *after* "the seizure of the means of production (by the State) in the name of society," that is, *after* the socialist revolution. We all know that the political form of the State at that time is complete democracy. But it never enters the head of any of the opportunists who shamelessly distort Marx that when Engels speaks here of the State "withering away," or "becoming dormant," he speaks of democracy. At first sight this seems very strange. But it is "unintelligible" only to one who has not reflected on the fact that democracy is *also* a State, and that consequently democracy will also disappear when the State disappears. The bourgeois State can only be "put an end to" by revolution. The State in general, i.e., most complete democracy, can only "wither away." [29]

George Orwell made clear, in *1984*, that the socialist state becomes concerned only with power, and "the object of power is power." [30] In 1964, the chief negotiator of a union, in explaining union demands to members, quoted Golden and Ruttenberg on coercion:

Of course, its coercion. That's what all the argument is about, the right to force someone against his will. Coercion is the fundamental basis of organized society. Civilization can be said to have attained maturity when men become intelligent enough to order their affairs and compel the recalcitrant, the ignorant man to submit to certain compulsory rules for the common good of all men. [31]

[29] Vladimir I. Lenin, "State and Revolution: Marxist Teaching about the Theory of the State and the Tasks of the Proletariat in the Revolution," written in 1917 and first published in 1918; later included in Volume XXI of Lenin's collected works as part of "Toward the Seizure of Power." Cited from Waldo R. Browne, editor: *Leviathan in Crisis, An International Symposium on the State, Its Past, Present, and Future*, p. 70f. New York: The Viking Press, 1946.
[30] George Orwell: *1984*, p. 200. New York: Signet Books, 1950.
[31] Clinton S. Golden and Harold J. Ruttenberg, *Labor Law Journal*, 1952, cited by W. C. Davis, Chairman, United Air Lines, MEC, in ALPA, October 12, 1964, p. 8.

Because of the secularization of the state, its separation, from truth in the name of liberty, the state has assumed an amoral character. According to Huizenga,

> As State it claims absolute autonomy and independence in respect to all moral standards. In so far as it allows the Church and religion, with their explicit and binding moral code, to carry on an existence of their own, their position is no longer one of freedom and equality but of subjugation and compulsory allegiance to the doctrine of the State itself. It is clear that only those devoid of all religion will be able to embrace an ethical system of such glaring ambiguity.[32]

The separation of the state from truth has simply meant liberty for the state to claim total and unlimited power while promising unlimited freedom from truth to its citizenry. For the people, this means a season of license to immorality as a facade to a steady loss of liberty to the state. *Unlimited power* for the state and *unlimited liberty* for the people are mutually exclusive concepts. The premise of John Cotton with respect to all human earthly institutions, church, state, school, and all others, was mindful of this: "It is necessary . . . that all power on earth be limited." [33] On the premise of the sovereignty of God and the authority of His infallible word, all earthly powers and liberties are strictly limited. Unlimited power and unlimited liberty are absolute concepts applicable only to God. Man as a creature is of necessity under law, and his human condition can only be one of *limited power* and *limited liberty*. Power is under law, and liberty is under law, God's law. Only by placing power (or coercion) and liberty alike under God's law and truth can man live in any freedom and power.

To "liberate" the state from God's truth is to surrender man to the state's "truth." *God and truth are always to be found in the source of law: if the state is itself the source of law, then it is truth and God incarnate.* As courts deny the concept of a higher law in

[32] J. Huizinga: *In the Shadow of Tomorrow*, p. 155. New York: Norton, 1936. Translated by J. H. Huizinga.
[33] John Cotton: *An Exposition upon the Thirteenth Chapter of the Revelation*, p. 72. London: 1655. On Cotton, see Rushdoony: *This Independent Republic*, pp. 28f., 152-155. Nutley, N. J.: Craig Press, 1964.

their jurisprudence, they thereby claim to be that highest law itself. Government rests on authority, and authority in its ultimate form is certain and infallible authority. If God's infallible word is denied, the concept of infallibility is not denied. It is instead transferred to the historical process as it incarnates itself in the dictatorship of the proletariat, or it is transferred to the scientific method in its ultimate forms. For Benedetto Croce, the aesthetic experience became, in a sense, sacred, blameless, and uncensurable, and the bearer of inerrancy and inspiration. Infallibility is ascribed either to God or to the mind or activity of autonomous man.[34]

In pursuing the myth of unlimited power, and in offering to the people a mythical unlimited liberty, the modern state posits its own god-like and infallible power to control history and to mold it to its intended decrees. But this is to live in terms of a suicidal delusion. Man can, as God's creature, live only in terms of limited power and limited liberty as exercised under God's sovereignty and word. To assume more is to live in terms of an impossibility. The fact that for a time it seems to "work" is itself a delusion. The man who believes that he can flap his arms and fly will certainly find it a fast and simple flight, as he leaves the Empire State Building, until he meets the hard earth. No less a destiny faces modern man and his state.

[34] Calvin G. Seerveld: *Benedetto Croce's Earlier Aesthetic Theories and Literary Criticism*, pp. 83, 78, 98; J. H. Kok, Kampen, 1958. See also Rushdoony review of the Seerveld study of Croce, in *Torch and Trumpet*. December, 1960, vol. X, no. 7, p. 22.

8

LIBERTY AND PROPERTY

When Theodore Roosevelt, speaking at the Sorbonne on April 23, 1910 separated the concept of human rights from property rights, he brought to public attention an approach which was clearly alien to the American system. "Liberty and Property" was a battle-cry of resistance to Parliament's encroachment in the events leading to the War of Independence. The belief that "a man's house is his castle" rested on the assumption that liberty and property not only go hand in hand but are inseparable. The increasing separation of property from liberty, and the idea that "human rights" can exist to the detriment of or in opposition to property rights, clearly means the end of the historic American system, if it be continued. To understand the relationship of liberty and property, it is necessary to survey real property in American history.

The hostility of most historians and economists to orthodox Christianity has led to neglect of the major impact of biblical thought on the concept of real property. Most treatments of the subject of property are anthropological, in that the property arrangements of "primitive" tribes and of ancient cultures are studied in an evolutionary sense in order to trace a pattern of growth and development towards scientific analyses of the subject. Humanistic conservatives have responded by calling attention to the strong sense of territoriality or of property in animals. Territoriality and status, i.e., property and social rank or order, are the basic aspects of animal life, it is pointed out.[1]

[1] See Robert Ardrey: *African Genesis, A Personal Investigation into the Animal Origins and Nature of Man.* New York: Atheneum, 1961. See also Sir Arthur Keith, "Ownership of Territory as a Factor in Human Evolution," in *Western Destiny*, March, 1965, pp. 15-17, vol. x, no. 3.

Such approaches neglect the elementary fact that America was colonized by people to whom the Bible was the authoritative word of God and hence binding. They were, moreover, feudal in their outlook, which meant that they were *economically land-based* and *politically dedicated to localism*.[2] The Old Testament laws on land were taken seriously by them, as were all the biblical laws generally. Thus gleaning was practiced and regulated by law in Europe. In America, it was also a part of rural practice.[3] It continued to be practiced in the United States well into the 20th century.[4] It was held that biblical law was God's law and had to be obeyed.

In biblical law, land could not be sold in perpetuity. The earth is the Lord's and men cannot alienate their inheritance: "the land shall not be sold for ever; for the land is mine; for ye are strangers and sojourners with me" (Lev. 25:23; cf. Lev. 23-28; Gen. 23:7-20; Jer. 32:42-44. The Genesis passage makes clear that land sales were common among the Canaanites.). Lands could only be mortgaged for a limited number of years, and in effect leased by the lender, but they reverted to the owner on the jubilee. The rural population was thus established as an area of conservatism, with the possession of land remaining in the family or being restored to it each half century. An area of unchanging tradition and stability was thus erected. The concentration of land was prevented, and an open society maintained.

In the towns and cities, the situation was different (Lev. 25:29-31).

> In the cases of houses in a walled city only one year was allowed for redemption, after which if not redeemed the land was held by the purchaser in perpetuity. The theory seems to have been that houses represented an accumulation of personal property rather than real property.[5]

[2] See R. J. Rushdoony: *This Independent Republic*, 1964, and *The Nature of the American System*, chap. 1, 1965, both Nutley, N. J.: Craig Press.

[3] Eric Sloane: *The Seasons of America Past*, p. 82. New York: Wilfred Funk, 1958.

[4] The Rev. Jefferson G. Duckett has described to this writer its prevalence in rural South Carolina during his youth.

[5] Roger Sherman Galer: *Old Testament Law for Bible Students, Classified and Arranged as in Modern Legal Systems*, p. 98. New York: Macmillan, 1922.

Taxes were not levied against the land, but rather against "the increase from that land," so that men could not be dispossessed.[6] In a later era, during Persian rule, Nehemiah reported changed conditions: men had "borrowed money for the king's tribute, upon our fields and our vineyards," with the end result that "other men have our fields and our vineyards" (Neh. 5:2-5). It was clearly recognized that the power to tax is the power to confiscate and to destroy.

There is evidence that the American colonists held real property to be immune to taxation. According to Dietze, at the Continental Congress, in 1774, "As to property, the delegates felt it should be free from seizure and taxation," [7] although it is not entirely clear in what sense this was intended. Certainly, the Continental Congress denied that Parliament had any jurisdiction over the Colonies within their limits and with respect to their property, as the Resolutions of Friday, October 14, 1774, in Sullivan's first-draft of the sub-committee's report and the formal resolutions make clear:

Sullivan's Draught

1. That the power of making laws for ordering or regulating the internal polity of these Colonies, is, within the limits of each Colony, respectively and exclusively vested in the Provincial Legislature of such Colony; and that all statutes for ordering or regulating the internal polity of the said Colonies, or any of them, in any manner or in any case whatsoever, are illegal and void.

Resolved, N.C.D. 1. That they are entitled to life, liberty, & property, and they have never ceded to any sovereign power whatever, a right to dispose of either without their consent.

2. That all statutes, for taxing the people of the said colonies, are illegal and void.

Resolved, N.C.D. 2. That our ancestors, who first settled these colonies, were at the time of their emigration from the mother country, entitled

[6] Howard B. Rand: *Digest of the Divine Law*, p. 111. Merrimac, Mass.: Destiny, 1943.

[7] Gottfried Dietze: *The Federalist, A Classic on Federalism and Free Government*, p. 58n. Baltimore: The Johns Hopkins Press, 1960.

3. That all the statutes before mentioned, for the purpose of raising a revenue, by imposing 'rates and duties' payable in these Colonies, establishing a Board of Commissioners, and extending the jurisdiction of Courts of Admiralty, for the collection of such 'rates and duties' are illegal and void.[8]

to all the rights, liberties, and immunities of free and natural-born subjects, within the realm of England.

Resolved, N.C.D. 3. That by such emigration they by no means forfeited, surrendered, or lost any of those rights, but that they were, and their descendants now are, entitled to the exercise and enjoyment of all such of them, as their local and other circumstances enable them to exercise and enjoy.

Clearly, the jurisdiction of Parliament over American property was sharply denied. In an address by Congress "to the people of Great Britain" on Friday, October 21, 1774, it was denied that the colonists had ever granted to anyone jurisdiction over "our lives and property." Notice was served on Britain:

> *Know then*, That we consider ourselves, and do insist, that we are and ought to be, as free as our fellow-subjects in Britain, and that no power on earth has a right to take our property from us without our consent.[9]

Questions of life and property were local concerns. They were, moreover, subject to "the inestimable right of trial by jury."[10] The Americans had no intention of submitting to or "confessing the omnipotence of Parliament, and acquiescing in whatever disposition they might think proper to make of their lives and property."[11] In appealing to Quebec to stand also against Great Britain, the Wednesday, October 26, 1774, statement asked, "What can protect your property from taxing edicts, and the rapacity of necessitous and cruel masters?"[12]

For the Americans, liberty to a large degree included and meant

[8] Worthington Chauncey Ford: *Journals of the Continental Congress, 1774-1789*, vol. I, 1774, p. 67f. Washington: Government Printing Office, 1904.
[9] *Ibid.*, p. 82.
[10] *Ibid.*, p. 85; cf. 107.
[11] *Ibid.*, p. 86.
[12] *Ibid.*, p. 111.

real property. A major function of civil government, it was held, is the protection of property.[13] Massachusetts was ready to introduce, as early as 1646, an income tax,[14] a tax on "increase," but not a tax on real property. The early New England tax was a "poll tax: a tax on the gross produce of the land, which was finally developed into a general property tax." The Southern colonies were slower in turning to a property tax. "The property tax developed in the 17th century in New England and then spread to the Middle colonies. It never took root in the Southern colonies, which used it for a few years during the fiscal crises of the war."[15] The right to impose a direct tax on persons and on property was not granted to the Federal Union nor attempted with respect to inheritance or income until the Civil War.

The property tax came to be, in the American system, the province of the county. Because of the close correlation in American thought of liberty and property, and the feudal context of both, the property tax was not trusted to any but local authorities. The property tax has become the foundation of the county government, in that it is the county's central source of income, and the major function of the county is the administration of local law and order, and the protection of life and property. Despite assaults against it, the county still retains extensive vitality and power in most states, although least of all in New England. Connecticut abolished counties by legislative action in 1959; Alaska avoided, in 1956, establishing counties in writing its constitution. Counties exist in Rhode Island, but not as units of local government.[16] The centrality of the counties to the American system is basic. To the framers of the Constitution, "the principle of local rule" was their central concern, according to James M. Beck, former Solicitor-General of the United States.[17]

[13] Gottfried Dietze: *The Defense of Property*, p. 84ff. Chicago: Henry Regnery, 1963.
[14] George Lee Haskins: *Law and Authority in Early Massachusetts*, p. 251. New York: Macmillan, 1960.
[15] Wayne Andrews and Thomas C. Cochran, editors: *Concise Dictionary of American History*, p. 921. New York: Charles Scribner's Sons, 1962.
[16] *Ibid.*, p. 257.
[17] James M. Beck: *The Constitution of the United States, Yesterday, Today — and Tomorrow?* p. 238. New York: George H. Doran, 1922.

With this centrality of the county in mind, let us examine the relationship of the county to property.

First, the basic tax, the property tax, is reserved to the county. It is thus subject to local control. It is a tax by real property owners upon themselves for the maintainence of their local self-government. A basic surrender of that self-government comes about when the power to tax property is surrendered to a more distant and less easily controlled governmental body.

Second, the police power rests on a local foundation, the county and the property tax. The police are supported by the local property owners by means of a tax on property. This is their sole means of support, and their framework of reference is the protection of local life and property. They have no national or political reference or responsibility. Moreover, the police are a non-military and civilian body of men, although in uniform, who simply exercise for the local citizenry the citizens' police rights. *The police power, according to the American system, is not a state power nor a county power; it is a citizens' power, delegated by the citizens without surrender to a locally created and controlled agency supported by a local tax on property.* Without this, there is no true police, only a statist or totalitarian power over a local area. The citizen does not lose his right of citizen's arrest by having a police force; he delegates but does not surrender his power. His police power, like that of his delegate or officer, *is under law*, but it is nonetheless *his power. The police power is the citizen's right of self-defense, and every attempt to destroy the entirely local nature of the police is an attempt to take away from the citizenry their right of self-defense against a central state and against criminals.* Present-day trends towards a national police force are thus aimed at disarming and capturing the citizenry for totalitarian purposes.[18]

Third, citizenship in the United States is impossible without citizenship in a state and county. It is in a very real sense a triple citizenship. There can be and are differing voting regulations for each area of citizenship, although there is a studied assault on these regu-

[18] See Rushdoony: *The Nature of the American System*, Appendix 1, "Localism and the Police Power," for an extended study of this subject.

lations in the name of a uniform federal law. The county has historically been the key to acceptance into citizenship; the basic power has been *locally* oriented. The present trend is towards "*national*" or federal orientation.

Fourth, suffrage has historically been subject to three sets of regulations. From the beginning, property requirements for suffrage have been lacking on the federal level, state requirements have been a minor factor. However, on the county level, since the county votes the property tax, county property requirements for suffrage were originally the rule and continued in many areas into the 20th century. It was held that only those who owned property had any right to vote where voting affected property and the voter could vote taxes on property. Karl Marx agreed with the logic of this position, stating,

> man proclaims politically that private property is abolished as soon as he abolishes the property qualification for the vote. . . . Is not private property as an idea abolished when the non-owner becomes legislator for the owner? The property qualification for the vote is the ultimate political form of the recognition of private property.[19]

County government has been historically the self-government of property-owners by means of a tax on their property. The introduction of voters without real property into county voting has meant the steady exploitation of property and the use of county government against property owners.[20]

Fifth, the basic law order of the county, and indeed of the country, its civil and criminal law, is *county law*, and the financial support of this law rests on property. Any attack on the county system and on property is thus an attack on the political cornerstone of the American system and is destructive of law and order. The political aspect of the decline of law and order is the steady drift of local self-government away from property, and of the county government towards state and federal interventionism.

[19] Karl Marx: *A World Without Jews*, p. 11. New York: Philosophical Library, 1960.
[20] See Rushdoony: *This Independent Republic*, pp. 52-64.

Sixth, liberty and property are closely linked to each other and together to Christian faith. From its origins, America was characterized by a dedication to Christian faith and to real property. "Land-hunger" was an important motive in the immigrants who came to America, and its basis was not only economic but religious. Bishop Sheen has noted the relationship of faith and property to liberty:

> There are several reasons why there is no place for God in communism. One is because of its concept of freedom. Suppose I correlate the problem of religion and the problem of freedom in answering your question, and let me begin with freedom and then go to religion.
>
> A man is free on the inside because he has a soul that he can call his own. Wherever you have the spirit you have freedom. A pencil has no freedom, ice has no freedom to be warm, fire has no freedom to be cold. You begin to have freedom only when you have something immaterial or spiritual.
>
> Now, freedom must have some external guaranty of itself. The external guaranty of human freedom is property. A man is free on the inside because he can call his soul his own; he is free on the outside because he can call something he has his own. Therefore private property is the economic guaranty of human freedom.
>
> Suppose now you concoct a system in which you want to possess man totally. On what conditions can you erect a totalitarian system so that man belongs to you completely? One, you have got to deny spirit; two, you have got to deny property.
>
> That is why the existence of God and private property are both denied simultaneously by communism. If a man has no soul, he cannot allege that he has any relationships with anyone outside of the state. If he has no property, he is dependent upon the state even for his physical existence. Therefore the denial of God and the denial of freedom are both conditions of slavery.[21]

Reference was made earlier to the biblical laws concerning real property. The purpose of these laws was both religious and political.

[21] *The Ideological Fallacies of Communism*, Staff Consultations with Rabbi S. Andhil Fineberg, Bishop Fulton J. Sheen, Dr. Daniel A. Poling, p. 11. September 4, 25, October 18, 1957. Committee on Un-American Activities, House of Representatives, Eighty-fifth Congress. Washington: G.P.O., 1958.

The principle is, as before, that as the land is God's land, not man's, so the Israelites were the slaves of God, not of man, and that if the position in which God placed them was allowed to be interfered with for a time, it was to be recovered every seventh year, or at furthest every fiftieth year.[22]

Man will be the servant either of God or of the state. The purpose of the biblical land law is *the preservation of man from the attempts of the state to become god over man, and to assert instead the total dominion of God over society*. The logical concomitant of state control over a man's property is the loss of a man's liberty, and both will arise with a lose of faith. The state, to affirm its lordship over man, must seek to control both Christianity and private real property and to negate the meaning of both.

A seventh important point is the independence of the local police and of private real property from other jurisdictions, state, federal, and international. This independence has been under studied attack for some time, but this independence is basic to the American system. By the doctrine of express powers, it was left entirely to the local governments and to the people. So strongly did the people feel about their independence from the centralist powers of the Federal Union that the Bill of Rights had to be added to the Constitution to reinforce these immunities. The federal government was subordinated to the citizenry and their local self-governments. In Amendment I, the Federal Union was barred from interfering with any establishment or settlement of religion, or creating its own establishment. Freedom of speech, press, and assembly was assured, not as grants from the Constitution, but as prohibitions against federal interference in the liberties of the people. "The right of the people to keep and bear arms," an aspect of their police power and right of self-defense, was admitted by Amendment II. The security of person, property, "papers, and effects, against unreasonable searches and seizures" was emphasized in Amendment III, and the right to trial by jury and to due process of law, to fair trial and defense, were stated in Amendments V - VIII. Moreover, except for powers

[22] Rev. F. Meyrickin, H.D.M. Spence, and Joseph S. Excell: *The Pulpit Commentary, Leviticus*, p. 393, Commentary on ch. xxv. New York: Funk & Wagnalls, n.d.

specifically delegated to the United States by the Constitution, all other powers were reserved to the people and the states (Amendments IX, X).

The function of these prohibitions was to restrict the powers of remote governmental agencies and to retain control over life and property to the individual and his local self-government. Although the Constitution placed severe restrictions on the powers of the federal government, there were still many who feared even those limited powers, as witness Patrick Henry. Luther Martin of Maryland bitterly opposed it as "the cup of poison" and as "chains" for America.[23] The distrust of any central power as a potential threat to liberty was a major aspect of the thinking of most of those who either favored or opposed the Constitution, and with good reason. As the powers of centralism have increased, the immunities of person, life, and property have decreased. And, most ironically, contemporary "liberals" and radicals have separated the concept of liberty from Christianity and from property. To Americans of an earlier era, this division would have appeared as utterly fantastic, and, quite rightly, as an instrument of intended enslavement. By the division of liberty from orthodox Christianity and from property, that enslavement is in process.

[23] Luther Martin, "Letter to Thomas Cockey Deye," in *Secret Proceedings and Debates of the Convention Assembled at Philadelphia in the Year 1787, for the Purpose of Forming the Constitution of the United States of America,* p. 96f. Warner Guy, 1838.

9

CHRISTIAN SOCIAL ETHICS: LOVE, JUSTICE, AND COERCION

A deeply rooted tradition and faith in Western civilization has long insisted that love and justice are incompatible. True social order, according to this tradition, must be based on love; all men are brothers, humanity is one family, and mankind must be brought together. In the name of this doctrine of love, and for the unity of mankind, coercion must be applied to unite and integrate men. This coercion is justified as necessary to the welfare of men and a necessity towards ending the ostensibly more dangerous coerciveness of a justice which insists on property rights, on the right to privacy, and on personal liberty.

The roots of this concept need to be examined in order to understand the nature and purpose of this ethics of love. This doctrine of love has two major philosophical origins. First of all, it is rooted in monism, a metaphysical concept which holds that there is but one fundamental reality or being, of which all particular aspects of reality are but modes or expressions. In ancient times, Parmenides of Elea was the classical example of monism; the monism of Parmenides was so thorough-going that he held the particularity of individual things to be mere appearance or illusion. The only reality for Parmenides is the one, unchangeable and homogeneous being. Benedict Spinoza, in the modern era, also a monist, held to the doctrine of one substantial reality, all inclusive in nature, of whom finite beings are simply modes. More recently, Christian Science has held to monism, reducing reality to all-inclusive mind. A modified monism appears in many philosophers such as Josiah Royce.

For monism, the goal of being is unity, the absorption of the many into the one, the all, the Great Being. Because we are all one being, all men are brothers metaphysically and in their common destiny. Men are regarded as members one of another and hence obligated to unite in love. Justice is seen as divisive, because its emphasis is on the individual and the particular rather than on the collective and on the unity of being. Justice, by calling for an emphasis on individual rights and liberties as against union in the great oneness of being, is in this perspective a limitation upon man and his destiny, a frustration of the goal of being.

The second source of this doctrine of love is dualism, a metaphysical doctrine holding that there are two independent, hostile, and mutually irreducible substances in the universe. Various forms of dualism prominent in history include Zoroastrianism, Manichaeanism, the Messalians, Bogomiles, Albigensians, and others, including many gnostic cults and their descendants. In this perspective, there are two gods or beings, two creators, two sources or fountains of reality. The universe is at present a scrambled mixture of these two beings, and man's task is to unscramble the universe. From one being comes love, spirit, and unity. From the other being comes hate, matter, and justice. Between the two there can be no reconciliation: love and justice are mutually exclusive concepts. The gnostic cults held that the Old Testament and most of the New Testament represented the religion of Jehovah, the God of hate and justice, whereas they represented the God of love, who appeared here and there in the New Testament and was the good God, whereas Jehovah was equated with the devil, except that He was seen as an *ultimate* evil being. Love therefore was the only true way of salvation, and justice belonged to the evil being whose religion was one of wrath, hatred, division, and disunity.

Both of these doctrines, therefore, see justice as divisive and love as unitive. Salvation is by and through love. Justice is anathema, in its Christian sense, because love represents a higher way, a true justice, as it were. These doctrines of love require coercion, in that unity and brotherhood must be enforced if society is to avoid the demonic powers of divisive justice, of a social order in which men live in terms of individual liberties rather than in collective love and unity. Both monism and dualism have left deep marks on the church, and the modern religious devotees of salvation by love echo ancient monistic and gnostic doctrines of redemption in their demands for civil rights, world brotherhood and government, and the universal triumph of love.

Christianity is theistic, not monistic or dualistic; it is of necessity hostile to these two faiths as destructive of theology. Moreover, monism and dualism are metaphysical doctrines which hold that man's problem is not ethical but metaphysical, not sin but finitude. Christianity asserts that man's basic problem is moral, i.e., man's apostasy or rebellion from God and his desire to be as God (Gen. 3:5). All men are not brothers except in sin, in Adam, and sin leaves them in disunity and enmity. The purpose of Christ's coming is divisive, an ethical or moral division or separation in terms of Christ. As Jesus declared, very early in His ministry, "Think not that I am come to send peace on earth: I came not to send peace, but a sword. For I am come to set a man at variance against his father, and the daughter against her mother, and the daughter in law against her mother in law" (Matt. 10:34, 35). This division is an ethical and religious separation in terms of Jesus Christ.

In this biblical perspective, there is no tension between love and justice. They are neither hostile and irreconcilable, as in dualism, nor are they reduced to one, to the destruction of either love or justice, as in some forms of monism. Love and justice, law and liberty, have a common origin in God, and they are therefore not in conflict. The supreme example of their common purpose is the cross of Christ, whereby the absolute justice of God is demonstrated in the death penalty upon sin; and at the same time, the cross reveals also the love of God, whose justice requires atonement and whose love provides it in the person of His only begotten Son. We have thus in the cross the perfect coincidence of love and justice.

Love is neither antinomian nor is it merely sentimental and emotional; moving with justice in terms of a common will, the will of God, love and justice, law and liberty, cannot be artificially separated. Love is at all times structured by justice, and liberty by law, and vice versa. The command to love our neighbor includes our enemy, and it is defined as the fulfilment of the second table of the law (Lev. 19:18, 33-37; Matt. 19:16-19; Rom. 13:8-10). If we respect our neighbor's or our enemy's right to life, the sanctity of his home, property, and reputation, in thought as well as word and deed, we act justly and with love, irrespective of our personal emotions, and we fulfil the law. We have moved in obedience to the law: Thou shalt not kill, commit adultery, steal, bear false witness, or covet.[1] The non-resistance spoken of in Matthew 5:38-48 is set in this context together with the reality of a situation wherein an alien state has control of the law, can "compel" forced service for a mile, can "smite" with impunity, and can confiscate coat and money at will. In such a situation, realism is godliness, and it must be united with a return of good for evil, and love and justice for injustice. The normal situation of justice, or restitution ("an eye for an eye") does not prevail in law but it must prevail in the form of a response of righteous forbearance and love.

The biblical principle of love and justice is not man-centered but God-centered. Its primary concern is not the love of man and human rights but the righteousness of God, and His holy justice and love as revealed in the cross of Christ. The requirement of God's justice is restitution, and the criminal law of the Bible has as its goal, not the punishment of the criminal but restitution to the injured party, and, supremely, the restoration of godly order. Humanistic criminology has usually had, not the restoration of order and restitution, but the salvation of the criminal in mind. Aulus Gellius, in line with Greek and Roman thought, saw "three reasons for punishing crime." First, "for the purpose of correction and reformation," second, for "the preservation of honour," i.e., to save the face of the offended man, and third, "for the sake of example, in order that others through fear of a recognized penalty may be kept from similar sins."[2] The criminal is to be saved by coercion, by imprisonment, by punishment. The biblical principle does not look

[1] See Frederick Nymeyer: *Progressive Calvinism*, vol. I, 1955, "*Essays Against Sanctimony and Legalized Coercion*." South Holland, Illinois: Libertarian Press.
[2] John C. Rolfe, translator: *Attic Nights of Aulus Gellius*, vol. II, p. 127ff. London: William Heinenann, 1928.

for salvation by coercion but by the grace of God; the function of legal coercion is not to save but to effect a restoration of property, and, in cases of murder, restitution by forfeiture of life. But, basic to the religions of love is the concept of *salvation by legal coercion.* Man must be made good, not by God but by man, and this means coercion by law, the compulsory obligation to share with one's fellow men.

Coercion in some form is inescapable to any philosophy, however much some attempt to deny it. Coercion of a kind is also basic to the biblical position, since it is God-centered, and man must conform to God's law. Coercion is inescapable. The basic question concerning coercion is twofold: What is its ultimate source? And to what purpose?

Let us examine the nature of coercion through a simple illustration. There is coercion involved in the established custom of eating at morning, noon, and night. The routine of school life and of employment coerces us into conformity to these hours, whatever our personal wishes. We can normally eat only at the times allocated by the routine of institutional or industrial life. This is coercive. We cannot each demand a freedom in this respect and continue working. But the purpose of this coercion is social order, not the government or control of us individually but the establishment of a common ground of operation for all. This is *just* order. This is a coercive order designed to further the maximum liberty under law. This is the nature of biblical law in part, to create an orderly society in terms of God's order and for the continuing welfare of its members. If, however, a group of managers decide that our salvation requires eating certain foods in stated amounts only, and, in the name of our health and of love, coerce us to that end, we can then call their purpose *not justice but salvation.* The root meaning of the word "salvation" is health, and salvation in its fullest sense means the physical and spiritual health of man. Its Christian goal is not only the salvation of the soul but the resurrection of the body and the glorification of redeemed man. *In replacing justice as a social goal with salvation by man-made laws, man is guilty of the great and central sin, of playing god. Salvation is the province and work of God, not man, and the saving society is the Great Society of Anti-Christ.*

When law becomes salvationist, it becomes hostile to justice and to liberty. In the Christian view, *liberty and law* are different as-aspects of the same thing. Predestination, or total law, is not fatalism but rather total liberty. The predictable person is the free person; discipline is liberty, and predestination and liberty are one because the biblical concept of liberty is not antinomian. Liberty is under law and in law. The unpredictable person is insane; he lacks law in his being, is without discipline or order in his actions and thoughts. And, without law, anarchy results. Man is not the ultimate source of order: God is, therefore God predestines man. When man makes himself ultimate, he makes himself also, in the form of the state, the ultimate source of order: the state is ultimate, therefore the state predestinates man. The source of law and of order, of social and personal control, i.e., predestination, is *either God or the social planners.*

Whenever man's law gains control, tyranny results. Civil rights become the cornerstone of civil wrongs, because man's "rights" are made more basic than justice and law. In a lecture at the Sorbonne, April 23, 1910, Theodore Roosevelt contrasted human rights to property rights:

> In every civilized society, property rights must be carefully safeguarded. Ordinarily and in the great majority of cases, human rights and property rights are fundamentally and in the long run, identical; but when it clearly appears that there is a real conflict between them, human rights must have the upper hand; for property belongs to man and not man to property.[3]

More honestly stated, Roosevelt's antithesis should read: man's wishes and demands must have the upper hand; if this can be attained with justice, well and good, but, if not, man must prevail over justice. Theodore Roosevelt, of course, felt that this exaltation of man over justice represented true morality, i.e., love of man, and, in terms of the religion of love, he was right, but it clearly did not represent any

[3] Racine, Wisconsin, *Daily Journal*, Saturday, April 23, 1910, vol. LVI, no. 97, p. 1, "Roosevelt's Address on Citizenship."

respect for justice. Assuming that the situation is one of injustice, as Roosevelt believed, the answer to injustice is not injustice. The religion of love, however, believes in salvation by man's love, not by God's justice nor by God's grace, and thus it turns to coercion in order to predestinate man and society into salvation.

The goal of this coercive love is brotherhood, human solidarity, unity, and corporateness. Corporateness and community are attainable in two ways: first, by imposition from above as a coerced and enforced requirement by a total state. Corporateness is gained but liberty is lost and tyranny prevails. Second, the Christian corporateness and community is from above in that it is derived from God's saving grace, but its human manifestation is in free associations. It requires liberty; it runs the risk of tensions, schisms, and divisions, but it is true community and corporateness in its development.[4] It is personal and societal rather than statist. Wherever corporateness by statist action is introduced, individual and societal corporateness and freedom are destroyed.

This religion of love, being, like all religions, concerned with salvation, is a religion of salvation by man's works, by man's love, and by the coercive laws of that humanistic love. Statist action is thus *mandatory*. Churches which hold to this doctrine are deeply concerned with social action, with civil rights, lobbying, and every kind of legislation which will compel men to be loving. Thus, the Rev. Paul Beeman, a Methodist minister in Seattle and acting as a Council of Churches legislative representative during the Washington State legislative session, has declared: "If the church doesn't take an interest in the corporate lives of men, who will? If Jesus were alive in America today, he might very well have run for the legislature."[5] The biblical Jesus refused to be king when men tried to force him into kingship (John 6:15) because His kingdom, while *over* this world, was not *of* this world (John 18:36). The mythical Jesus of Paul Beeman would run for the legislature because his only

[4] See R. J. Rushdoony: *This Independent Republic*, pp. 84-89. Nutley, N. J.: Craig Press, 1964.
[5] Oakland *Tribune*, Friday, January 29, 1965, p. 13, "Unusual Lobbyist Seeks 22 Point Church Program."

power over men is of this world through coercive and political love, a very limited Jesus, indeed.

This doctrine of salvation by love, or by coercive political action to enforce this required love, is simply a manifestation of what the Reformers called the religion of salvation by works. Works salvation is salvation by man, and its coercion is the coercion of state law. The coercion of a works salvation doctrine moves inevitably to total statism, to man-made total planning or predestination.

Biblical religion holds to the doctrine of salvation by God's sovereign grace as manifested in Jesus Christ and His atoning death and His resurrection, and man's acceptance of this by faith. It is justification or salvation through faith, not works. Salvation by faith also has its doctrine of coercion, but it is coercion by God, by the action of the Holy Spirit in man's heart whereby regenerating faith is born. This is supernatural coercion, but it is a coercion which operates within the framework and total context of the individual's person and personality. This is total control, but it is a total control towards the total moral liberty of man. Civil law and religious law are delivered from the totalitarian claims of saving man. The function of civil law is restricted to the restraint of the evil-doer, the imposition of restitution upon the law-breaker, and the provision of that liberty which a just social order makes possible. The purpose of coercion, being separation from salvation, becomes closely linked to the assurance of liberty.

A religion of love as the means of salvation means that man's work leads to salvation, and this faith makes flagrant and unjust coercion its law and practice because, being unable to work internally upon man's heart, as God is able to do, it must therefore work upon his body. It will attempt, through education and through mental health programs, to enter man's soul, but these methods, however heavily used, are secondary to the basic thrust, salvation by coercive and total law.

The biblical social ethics provides a slower but surer means of social order. It ensures order, it provides for community of a vital rather than juridical nature. It is creative of social order and individual liberty. It rejects monism and dualism and sees love and justice as in harmony, and it regards law and liberty as closely inter-related concepts. It limits human coercion because it limits human powers, and, to the extent that any religious doctrine departs from the biblical doctrine of the sovereignty of God to affirm the sovereignty and self-saving power of man, to that extent it will introduce coercion into the social order. A measure of coercion is inescapable in any social order. The question is, will that coercion be used to ensure justice and make possible human liberty and the exercise of love, or will that coercion, in the name of love and of saving man, destroy love, justice, and social order? The Christian answer is clear-cut: we must reserve unto God the sole power of salvation.

THREE PHILOSOPHICAL AND RELIGIOUS APPROACHES TO SOCIAL ETHICS

MONISM	DUALISM	CHRISTIAN THEISM
The Ultimacy of the One, i.e., ultimacy of Unity	Equal Ultimacy of Good and Evil	Equal Ultimacy of Love and Justice, Law and Liberty, in a common source, the triune God, in whom the one and the many and all these attributes and aspects are equally important.
† † †	*Good* *Evil* † † † † † †	† † † † † † † † † †
Love as the Higher Way † † †	Love Justice Spirit Matter Unity Individuality	Love and Love and Justice Liberty
Justice as the Lower Way	Hostility between two equally ultimate realms of ethics. Life Force Death Force	

Champions
Parmenides of Elea
Spinoza
Mary Baker Eddy etc.

Champions
Zoroastrians
Gnostics
Bogomiles
Albigensians
Illuminists, etc.

Champions
Biblical religion
Augustine
Leo the Great
Calvin, etc.

10

THE UNITED NATIONS: A RELIGIOUS DREAM

The poet Tennyson, while striving earnestly to maintain a Christian perspective, found nonetheless that Darwin's evolutionary theory had made the old certainties difficult for him. Thus, despite certain pious affirmations from time to time, his basic perspective was doubt, doubt of God and of God's existence or goodness. He saw

> . . . this Earth, a stage so gloom'd with woe
> You all but sicken at the shifting scenes. (*The Play*)

The one reality of life and man is mutability, change and decay. On all sides, the eloquent testimony of earth is the relentless ruin of time, the unceasing prevalence of death and decay over life and man, for all things are in perpetual flux. For Tennyson, the central problem is this ever-flowing stream of change:

> The hills are shadows, and they flow
> From form to form, and nothing stands;
> They melt like mists, the solid lands,
> Like clouds they shape themselves and go.
> (*In Memoriam*, CXXIII, 2)

"Nothing stands," Tennyson said, but something should stand. Man can accept mutability and flux when the ceaseless flow and change has as its counterbalance a factor for permanency, eternity, and certainty, an unchanging factor as the agency of control over change. The answer of men to this problem of perpetual flux has in the main been twofold: first, either to accept the transcendental and supernatural Creator God as the agency of origin and control, or, second, denying God, to see in nature an agency, such as evolution, which man can now control and guide to create a human order as the agency of control. In terms of this, the builders of Babel declared, Go to, let us build us a city and a tower. In terms of this, John Dewey, denying God as the answer and ridiculing the quest for certainty from God, offered certainty in and through the Great Society. The quest for certainty is inescapable, unless meaning is rejected and suicide is affirmed; the problem has been the *source* of certainty and control over change, God or man? Tennyson looked for a world state to provide that control and a world where

> . . . the war-drum throbb'd no longer, and the battle-flags were furl'd
>
> In the Parliament of man, the Federation of the world.
>
> There the common sense of most shall hold a fretful realm in awe,
>
> And the kindly earth shall slumber, lapt in universal law.
>   (*Locksley Hall*)

Tennyson was not being perverse or anti-British in affirming this hope. It was simply a logical necessity. Man needs a source of certainty and an agency of control: if he denies this function to God, he will ascribe it to man and to a man-made order. This order will, like God, be man's source of salvation: it will be a *saving* order. The Charter of the United Nations, in its Preamble, begins by declaring that "We the people of the United Nations determined to save . . . have resolved to combine our efforts to accomplish these aims." [1] The phrase "determined to save" is expressive of the high religious resolution of the United Nations. The United Nations is, by its own Charter, clearly a humanistic organization, dedicated, as a special report of the Unified Command on the Armistice in Korea, August 7, 1953, stated, to "humanitarian principles." [2] We will either fail to understand the U.N. or to cope with it unless we

---

[1] See R. J. Rushdoony: *The Nature of the American System*, chapter VII, "The United Nations," on the salvationist or soteriological nature of that body. Our concern here is with its theological nature, its parallels to the doctrine of God. Nutley, N. J.: Craig Press, 1965.

[2] *Review of the United Nations Charter, A Collection of Documents*, p. 602. Subcommittee on the United Nations Charter, Pursuant to S. Res. 126, 83rd Congress, 1st Session, Presented by Mr. Alexander Wiley, January 7, 1954, 83rd Congress, 2nd Session, Senate Document no. 87. Washington: GPO, 1954. On the man-centered faith associated with the U.N., see also Robert Keith Spenser: *The Cult of the All-Seeing Eye*, New York: Monte Cristo Press, 1964.

recognize that it is religious in inspiration and a religious necessity for humanism, for the religion of humanity. *First*, man needs an agency of certainty and control in order to meet this world of change and decay and give it meaning, and, *second*, man will make of that agency a substitute god. The necessary attributes of the godhead are inescapable needs to man in order to sustain meaningful life and thought. Wherever there is no theology of God, there will be a theology of the state, or of the world super-state. The attributes of God are the inescapable substrata of human existence and thought, the necessary categories of meaning and order.

The first and basic requirement of a theology is the unity of the godhead. A divided or disunited god, or a schizoid god, is useless to man and to himself. The deity, in order to exercise the control which is required of him, and in order to be an assured source of certainty, must be united; he must be one god. When humanity and a human order takes on the role of a god, the same basic requirement must prevail. The unity of every godhead is a theological necessity. Accordingly, for the religion of humanity, as represented in the United Nations, the unity of mankind, without discrimination or subordination, is a necessity. The central sin becomes, not rebellion against God and His law, but everything that hinders the union and peace of the new god, humanity. President Lyndon B. Johnson, in speaking of "The Quest for Peace," declared, "On a world-wide basis, we place much hope in the United Nations." Not sin but war, poverty and ignorance, misery and disease, are seen by Johnson as man's basic problems, and it is the uprooting of these evils which will make possible the desired world order:

> We believe the most plausible solution to war is simply for each nation to leave its neighbors in peace. This would free us all to attack those ancient enemies of all mankind that for centuries have warred on man and his hope—poverty and ignorance, misery and disease. If we will join together to destroy them, we will destroy the roots of war.[3]

[3] Lyndon B. Johnson: *My Hope for America*, pp. 105, 109. New York: Random House, 1964. During World War II, Carl Becker wrote, "War is, then, the first and worst thing that is wrong with our world. The second thing that is wrong is best known as 'unemployment'"; *How New Will the Better World Be?* p. 6. New York: Knopf, 1944.

"The roots of war" thus are seen to be "poverty and ignorance, misery and disease," not sin. The solution to man's basic problem is thus not the God of Scripture but statist action against social conditions.

Johnson, in his State of the Union address, declared, "We are entering the third century of the pursuit of American union." This is a curious reading of American history. The War of Independence was fought, not in pursuit of union, but to gain freedom from statist invasion and power. But for Johnson the key concept is union, the closer union of the United States to the central government, and "now, in 1965, we begin a new quest for union. We seek the unity of man with the world he has built." This means the Great Society and the welfare state. It means also, this growing union, "the community of nations," and a new immigration policy, as well as civil rights at home. This idealistic message concluded with a religious doxology:

So it was in the beginning.
So it shall always be, while God is willing, and we are strong enough to keep the faith.

This faith we are to keep is not in God but in ourselves, in "the state of the union: Free, restless, growing and full of hope." [4]

The United Nations Charter, in its Preamble, asserts that its purpose is "to save succeeding generations from the scourge of war," and, according to Chapter I, Article 1, 3, to gain "fundamental freedom for all without distinction as to race, sex, language or religion."

Such a purpose requires the unity of man and sees disunity, and war, a product of disunity, as the greatest evil. Increasingly, in many legislative acts, such as the Rumford Act in California, discrimination with respect to race, color, or creed is seen as evil and criminal. It divides mankind, and the godhead must be united.

The goal of all humanists, all advocates of the religion of humanity, is the unity and oneness of all men. It is a mistake to see the forces

[4] "This Is the State of the Union," Oakland *Tribune*, Tuesday, January 5, 1965, pp. 3, 4.

for world unity and government primarily in terms of the United Nations. The United Nations organization is dedicated to a wide variety of projects which recognize no territorial boundaries: community organization and development, migration, the prevention of crime and the treatment of offenders, housing and planning, children, education, money, and a wide variety of other causes. While ostensibly limiting itself to international rather than domestic issues, its definition of what is of international concern is all-inclusive. This has been demonstrated repeatedly, as witness its concern over apartheid and the treatment of people of Indian origin in the Union of South Africa.[5] All the same, the zeal for world unity displayed by various United Nations agencies is clearly surpassed by some national agencies and especially by private groups, citizens, and by clergymen of the humanistic faith. These persons and agencies religiously dream and work for the great redeeming order, the one-world state, the unity of man, believing, like Tennyson, that in this order the battle-flags of the world will be furled and the whole world "lapt in universal law." The 1965 demands for immigration law changes in the United States reflected this hope.

The United Nations has asserted that "It has long been recognized that migration constitutes a problem requiring international action." [6] In a United Nations population study, which calls attention to the "over-population" of Asia, we are told:

> On the other hand, if emigration were to have any great effect on the trend of population in some of the largest, most densely populated under-developed countries, like India, China and Java, it would not only have to equal, but to surpass by a wide margin the highest emigration rates ever experienced in European countries during the era of the great transatlantic movement. Such a feat appears to be entirely out of the question under the conditions that exist in the world today.
> Within the limits of what is possible, emigration may nevertheless be of some help in relieving the economic pressures due to excessive density of agricultural population and too rapid growth of numbers, particularly the smaller under-developed

[5] *Everyman's United Nations, 1945-1955*, pp. 124-129. Fifth edition. United Nations Department of Public Information, New York, 1956.
[6] *Ibid.*, p. 237.

countries. Its possible effectiveness in favourable circumstances, at least in the short run, is shown by the recent experience of Puerto Rico. Puerto Rico, of course, is a special case, since its citizens have unrestricted access to the United States and the cost of their transportation and relocation in that country is minimal.[7]

Like most United Nations studies, this raises great questions but gives only vague answers. Possibilities are considered, such as a major migration from Asia (to America?), but the possibility "appears to be entirely out of the question," a curious statement. It *appears* to be so, but is it necessarily so?

We are reminded of the difference between Europe and Asia: "Early in the century, there was one European for every two Asians; by the end of the century, this ratio may have become one to four." [8] We are told, with respect to the future of world population, that

A new process is about to begin, or has perhaps already started, and the first signs of that "socialization" of the world which appear on the horizon may be significant in this connexion.[9]

What is this new process of world socialization which is about to begin, with respect to population? There are indications of this in a study of the *Elements of Immigration Policy*, prepared by the U.N. Department of Social Affairs, Population Division, with help

[7] ST/SOA/Ser. A/20, *Population Growth and the Standard of Living in Under-Developed Countries*, p. 9. Population Studies, no. 20. United Nations, New York, 1954.

[8] ST/SOA/Ser. A/28, *The Future Growth of World Population*, p. 24, Population Studies no. 28. U.N. Department of Economic and Social Affairs, New York, 1958. On the other hand, the *National Security Seminar, Presentation Outlines and Reading List* (Industrial College of the Armed Forces, Washington, D.C., 1964-1965), p. 165, gives the following ratios of world population by races: White 31%, Yellow 31%, Brown 28% Negro 8%, Red 2%. The religious ratios, p. 166, is: Christian 32%, Buddhist and Confucism 16%, Islamic 16%, Hindu 11%, Tribal 4%, Judaism 0.5%, Unknown 18%. The nature of the U.N. gives power to the lowest common denominator. Thus, "the 35 members of the Organization of African Unity, a powerful U.N. bloc, pay exactly 1.7% of the annual U.N. budget (when they pay)" in "For the Record," *National Review*, January 26, 1965, vol. XVII, no. 4, p. 80. On the U.N. and the lowest common denominator policy see R. J. Rushdoony, *op. cit.*

[9] *The Future Growth of World Population*, p. v, preface.

from the International Labour Office, the Food and Agricultural Organization, UNESCO (United Nations Educational, Scientific and Cultural Organization) WHO (World Health Organization), the Division of Economic Stability and Development of the Department of Economic Affairs of the U.N., and the International Bank for Reconstruction and Development. We are assured, in the Introduction, that "No attempt is made to propose solutions for the problems stated." Moreover, "The present study is not to be regarded as an argument in favour of immigration or against it." [10] The title indicates the purpose of the paper: to provide the "elements" of immigration policy without specifying the policy. Some very curious "elements," however, quickly appear:

> A point which may count in favour of immigration, when the cost of settlement is considered, lies in the avoidance of duplication of overhead capital. In the case of transfer of local population to developing areas, the services and housing already provided in the areas of out-migration, might be left unutilized or under-utilized, thus causing wasteful duplication. In the case of immigration, such waste is avoided since the local population will continue to utilize the services provided for them. Equally, of course, waste could be avoided if, at the same time that the local population was transferred, immigrants were moved in to take the place of the transferred population without undue cost of settlement. Where the receiving country is underdeveloped, however, the provision of general services in the areas of out-migration will often be insufficient to begin with.[11]

This is a startling passage, especially when we recognize the legal care and precision of all these documents. Notice that the people or "local population" as well as the "immigrants" do not move: they are moved. The verbs are passive, not active. People are moved from a developed area to "developing areas," and other peoples are "moved in" to avoid waste of the homes and facilities. Both emigrants and immigrants are passive: they are moved. Since these are the "elements of immigration policy" presented by the United Nations, the contemplated policy is total control by a world state which

10 ST/SOA/19, *Elements of Immigration Policy*, p. 1, United Nations, New York, 1954.
11 *Ibid.*, p. 7.

feels free to reshuffle populations at will. This re-shuffling of world populations would not be a new policy. Assyria and Babylon used it, forcibly breaking up various nations and moving them in an effort to internationalize and unify their great empires into a united world order.

We are also given a picture, in this study of the "elements" of policy, of the transfer of functioning farms to new farmers, the immigrants:

> A distinction must be made between the settlement of new lands and the placing of new farmers on lands already cultivated. Where agricultural immigration is encouraged as a part of a programme for reorganization or diversification of agriculture, involving the transfer of lands already under cultivation to the hands of immigrant farmers, the methods of effecting the change need to be planned in such a way as to produce the least possible disruption of agricultural operations as well as a minimum of social disturbance and hardships. Schemes may have to be devised to enable the population formerly engaged in the discontinued types of agricultural activity to be absorbed in the new forms of agriculture in conjunction with the immigrants.[12]

Farmers are to be moved, farms transferred to immigrants, and new types of farming started, all with the population passive. In free migration, successful farmers, in a free and profitable situation, are not the migrants, but, according to these planners,

> . . . virtually all plans for agricultural settlement will inevitably call for the immigration of expert farmers, fully proficient in their occupation.[13]

Does this mean that "all plans" for world agrarian reform "will inevitably call" for the forced migration of American farmers, the world's most expert and proficient agriculturalists, to various parts of the world?

We are further told that mixed marriages will facilitate resettlement.

> The children in immigrant families are an extremely important factor in social and cultural integration. The first generation is not easily adapted; it is hard for adults to remake their lives, and

[12] *Ibid.*, p. 16.
[13] *Ibid.*

learning the language thoroughly is a difficult task for them. The children, on the other hand, adapt themselves much more readily to the new environment, and exert a strong influence toward conformity of their parents. It is through the children that the school, that great agent of social and cultural integration, makes its influence felt throughout the immigrant population.[14]

Of the "institutions assisting integration," we are told, "most important are the schools." [15]

These are the "elements of immigration policy": do we see any signs of the policy itself taking shape?

On October 2, 1964, President Johnson, in Proclamation 3620, declared 1965 to be "International Cooperation Year" and dedicated it to "strengthening world organization" and "international cooperation." [16] As a major step towards this goal in 1965, the Kennedy-Johnson Immigration Bill was promoted as the replacement for the McCarran-Walter Immigration and Nationality Act of 1952, a summary and codification by McCarran, Walter, and others, of existing immigration policy. The Kennedy-Johnson Bill, S. 1932 in the Senate, was introduced by Senator Hart of Michigan, and in the House by Congressman Celler of New York as H.R. 7700. Senator Strom Thurmond observed that

> Both bills seek to establish immigration as an alien right instead of a privilege, putting foreign interests above our own. Senator Javits of New York has even referred to the bills as being "civil rights legislation for the world." [17]

It was charged, by champions of the Kennedy-Johnson Bill, that the McCarran-Walter Act "discriminates against southern Europe, Asia and Africa." The quota system, however, has had, not race as much as cultural compatability in mind. As an editorial stated,

> It cannot be emphasized too strongly that the ethnic question has nothing to do with racial characteristics. It is based, rather, on cultural compatibility.

14 *Ibid.*, p. 19.
15 *Ibid.*, p. 21.
16 See Theodore Jackman: *The Great Society*. Greenville, S. C., 1954.
17 *Strom Thurmond Reports to the People*, Vol. X, No. 32, August 24, 1964.

Generally, existing law favors immigration from nations whose cultures are closest to our western ideals and traditions. It is also weighted in favor of those whose skills and training can be put to use here. Selection on these bases minimizes the problems of assimilation.[18]

Others, however, accused defenders of the McCarran-Walter Act of "xenophobia" and held such laws to be "bigoted and stupid." [19]

Three central aspects of the Kennedy-Johnson Bill can be briefly cited. First, as Senator Javits stated, it was intended to be "civil rights legislation for the world." The idea of an American heritage and existence in separation and distinction from other cultures is implicitly held to be wrong. A world culture requires an open world with respect to immigration, and therefore restrictive immigration to preserve cultural identity is of necessity evil. In an earlier era, free trade was held to be the substitute for immigration; the free flow of goods and ideas resulted in world-wide progress which brought growth to the backward areas without the necessary movement of peoples. Now, the movement of populations is a "right" and the visualized means of growth. A world culture requires population movements and blendings and the elimination of differences. The new godhead, humanity, must be *one*, it must be united.

Second, the Bill transfers control of immigration from the legislative to the administrative department. Not only does the Bill create a new pattern of immigration, but it establishes an Immigration Advisory Board with power to "implement" the legislation.[20]

Third, administrative powers enable the President to by-pass the law, overcome quota limitations, and, by waiver of existing restrictions, permit entry to persons whose presence is not in the national interest. The principle of selectivity would be by-passed as prejudicial to the immigrant and his "rights." In effect, it would be a major step towards a surrender of effective control over immigration.

[18] The *Sunday Tribune*, Oakland, California, Sunday, January 3, 1965, p. 40, "Toward an Equitable Immigration Act."
[19] Rabbi Magnin, "Restless," in Los Angeles *Herald-Examiner*, Comment and Opinion, p. B3m, Wednesday, February 10, 1965.
[20] *Our Immigration System*, p. 5. The American Committee on Immigration Policies, Washington, D. C., 1964.

Such a step has already been taken, as in 1963, when the State Department agreed to Castro's demand "that he designate fifty percent of all persons migrating to this Country." [21]

Immigration changes in the Year of International Cooperation were a necessary step towards the unity of the godhead, humanity, under its federal head, the one world state. The basic premise of immigration policy is not economic but rather the religious goal of unity. These immigration changes, although basic, are being introduced with Fabian strategy, the strategy of the inevitability of gradualism.

A second basic requirement of an effective theology is the omnipotence of the godhead. Sovereignty and creative power must reside in the source of certainty and agency of control or there will be neither certainty nor control. Accordingly, as the new faith has taken over steadily, and Christianity has been by-passed, omnipotence has been transferred from God to the state. The democracy of God was asserted by early champions of the social gospel even as they began to dream of the omnicompetence of the state. The various national states have become progressively more nearly total in their powers over their citizenry, in their claims over religion and education, and in their messianic pretensions. Meanwhile, these states, like quarrelling gods of the modern Olympus, have taken counsel together towards the creation of a new hierarchy and a world government of gods. The United Nations is the humanistic Mount Olympus and Tower of Babel, a dream of reason whereby man becomes his own god and totally governs the earth and his destiny. The developing omnipotence of the state and of the world order of states can only be undercut as men submit to the total sovereignty of God.

A third basic aspect of the godhead is omniscience. Total sovereignty and total government require total knowledge. How can God govern man totally if He has no knowledge of man's every fiber and thought? Omniscience is a necessary concommitant to total government, and even to effectual government. If the mind of man is a free and separate realm and outside God's knowledge and

[21] *Closer-Up*, Year 21, no. 1, January 1, 1965.

control, outside God's determination, then man's inner life is completely free of God and is a world without any God other than man. It is impossible, therefore, for any god to be god without a control over and in man's mind. Don Bell has described "The Hateful Parallel":

Followers of Christ know one thing (though we try to turn our backs to the fact): God knows our every thought, our every action, He knows all about us, past, present, and future—though He looks no more on the past which has been erased by the Blood, we have an Intermediary to plead our transgressions of the present, and He is able to keep His own for all future; the Seed within you cannot sin, and He is able to forgive His children.

But He is our Creator, we are His slaves, and He knows our very thoughts before we even think them. And we cannot hide from God. "I know that thou canst do every thing and that no thought can be withholden from thee," said Job. "Shall not God search this out? for he knoweth the secrets of the heart," sang David. "The eyes of the Lord are in every place, beholding the evil and the good. Hell and destruction are before the Lord: how much more then the hearts of the children of men?" asked Solomon. The Lord told Jeremiah: "I the Lord search the heart. I try the reins, even to give every man according to his ways, and according to the fruit of his doings." And Paul was very definite: "For the word of God is quick, and powerful, and sharper than any two-edged sword, piercing even to the dividing asunder of soul and spirit, and of the joints and marrow, and is a discerner of the thoughts and intents of the heart."

If we look to Christ Jesus as our Saviour and Redeemer, then we know—and accept—the truth that we are slaves of Christ, and that He knows all and everything about us. This is His right.

Now, let's reverse the coin: If we look to State as our keeper, then State has every right to know all there is to know about us. We cannot serve two masters; and if we accept gifts or aid from State, then we must serve State by letting State become the discerner of our very thoughts! We must allow State to substitute the IBM Card for the Book of Life. And we must confess to State all our sins and shortcomings, our strengths and our weaknesses, the thoughts and intents of our heart. We cannot have it two ways: either we must accept Christ or State as master; we must answer to God or the IBM Card; we must have a name written in heaven, or a number punched on a card at a data processing center. We can have one of two Big Brothers: Jesus Christ or IBM. We cannot serve both, else we will hate one.[22]

The state seeks to gain this total knowledge of us, first, by controlling our education, second, by controlling our minds through its program of mental health, and, third, by controls invading our privacy. The United Nations Draft Resolution Against Discrimination in Education, is designed for the eventual control of all education, "public," private, and parochial.[23] The mind of man must be a necessary area of control for any effective god. The choice before man is which god shall he turn himself over to, the state, a world state in its final form, or the God of Scripture?

Every god requires worship and sacrifice, and what men sacrifice for, and what men sacrifice to, is properly their god. It is significant that the modern tithe is to the state in the form of taxes. Again, it is significant that John F. Kennedy's death was seen by some poets as an atoning sacrifice for the new world order. For Lewis Turco, Kennedy was "a man, but more: you were an idea dreamt in a sweet hour while the spider slept." [24] David Ignatow made much of the fact that "The man is gone on a Friday." [25] For G. S. Fraser, he was an Apollo and a Caesar,[26] and Robert Hazel saw him going to Dallas as a "young god without wound," [27] to be killed there, in this "Post-Christian Era," by the old, impotent "Sacred emblems of religious awe, of tribal arrogance." [28] For John Tagliabue, Kennedy was an incarnation of democracy,[29] while Barbara Guest wrote that Kennedy "lived to be consecrated to *Demos*." [30] X. J. Kennedy saw him "nailed . . . on the cross of a rifle sight." [31] All this is quite natural: the state is the area now of salvation, and the saving

[22] *Don Bell Reports*, Year 11, no. 51. December 25, 1964. In reporting on the federal civil defense program, William Beecher wrote, "One wrinkle has been added: A survey of private homes will be made to determine which residences offer some fallout protection," in "Johnson Plans to Cut Defense Cost $300 Million in Year Starting July 1," *The Wall Street Journal*, Tuesday, January 19, 1965, p. 3.

[23] See I. E. Howard, "Will the UN Control the Little Red Schoolhouse?" in *Christian Economics*, vol. XIV, no. 2, January 23, 1962, p. 4. See also the editorial, "Is UNESCO's Design Subversive?" in *Christian Home and School*, February, 1962.

state and leader is the world statesman, dedicated, as was Kennedy, not to national independence but to world interdependence. Significantly, however, the poets saw no cleansing in the blood of this "god." According to Barbara Howes, "We are stained by its stain." [32]

A sovereign God is not under law; He is law, and He is the source of law. The economists of the new world order do not feel themselves bound by economic laws because, as members of the godhead, they are themselves the source of law. An economics in which man is a creature, and God is Creator, is an economics of scarcity, because man is limited to whatever God makes his portion. An economics resting on the divinity of man and his world order is an economics of abundance, because the world state, as god, is able to create ex nihilo, out of nothing. Its basic problem is not supply but distribution. It believes itself to be able to create wealth: it has only to gain control and proceed to the distribution of its abundance.

A necessary aspect of the godhead is its transcendence, whereby the deity, although knowable, is still incomprehensible since he so greatly transcends man. Wherever statism develops, the complexity and divine incomprehensibility of the king, ruler, or head of state is emphasized. This terminology, as George N. Crocker has pointed out, has become the language of state. Robert E. Sherwood, in *Roosevelt and Hopkins*, spoke of Roosevelt's "incomprehensible power." Eric Sevareid compared L. B. Johnson to Julius Caesar and saw in him a "complex" nature, while other "worshippers" have hinted of his "incomprehensibility." [33]   To the activities of the

[24] Erwin A. Glikes and Paul Schwaber, editors: *Of Poetry and Power, Poems Occasioned by the Presidency and by the Death of John F. Kennedy*, p. 21. Foreword by Arthur Schlesinger, Jr. New York: Basic Books, 1964.
[25] *Ibid.*, p. 23.   [29] *Ibid.*, p. 93.
[26] *Ibid.*, p. 31.   [30] *Ibid.*, p. 106.
[27] *Ibid.*, p. 64.   [31] *Ibid.*, p. 127.
[28] *Ibid.*, p. 67.   [32] *Ibid.*, p. 61.

[33] See George N. Crocker, "Incense for LBJ," in the San Francisco *Examiner*, Sunday, January 31, 1965, Sec. II, p. 3; for evidence of this, see on the same page Eric Sevareid, "The Way of LBJ," which calls for an aloofness by Johnson, who "is going to have to shut himself off to a considerable degree as Harry Hopkins testified Mr. Roosevelt had to do, even from his closest friends." See also William F. Buckley, "The State of LBJ," in *National Review*, January 26, 1965, vol. XVII, no. 4, p. 56.

United Nations, the same inscrutable wisdom is ascribed increasingly.

This, then, is a religious faith. Its origin is in the apostasy of Western men from Christianity, and it is the steady creation of another god, a golden calf, being steadily fashioned by covenant-breaking man. The United Nations is the product of this religious quest, and its basic source is not primarily in plotting internationalists but in men who, like Tennyson, have sought to find a certainty and an agency of control in a world where "nothing stands" and the very "hills are shadows and they flow from form to form." Man is a religious creature: he will either worship God, or he will make himself a god. And the United Nations is that new god appearing on man's questing horizon.

It is easy to point out its absurdities. Thus, a U.N.O. delegate, travelling through New Guinea, in an area completely backward and primitive and "only recently weaned from head-hunting," is said to have "enquired critically why no university had yet been put up." [34]

Again, the Institute for Defense Analysis (IDA) can be cited. In *Information and Strategy Stability*, this private agency, "which has done millions of dollars worth of 'peace' studies for the government," declared that intelligence-gathering is a hostile act which can lead to war. Intelligence, therefore, should be shared on occasion with the Soviets to indicate friendliness and to reassure them that we are peaceful in our intentions. "One proposed solution is for the Soviets to be able to demand that a few submarines, of their choosing, surface and make their positions known." [35]

Such things are easily ridiculed, but these religious attitudes are not so easily changed. If men will not find their security in God, they will find it in a world order, and they are more consistent and logical than those who reject both God and the state and are caught then in the futility of sterile protest.

The United Nations is a religious dream, and a very logical one.

[34] Robert E. Kuttner, in a review of Tambaran: *An Encounter With Cultures in Decline in New Guinea*, in *The Mankind Quarterly*, vol. V, no. 2, October-December, 1964, p. 119.

[35] Oakland, California, *Tribune*, Wednesday, January 27, 1965, p. 22, editorial, "Giving Secrets Away."

Its basic source is in the inescapably religious nature of man. Order and meaning are a necessity to man, who cannot live by bread alone. The rapid development of free economics in the 19th century gave to man, as he entered the 20th century, a life of remarkable material wealth and promise, but, by its secularism, this industrialism left man open to the command of new and demonic religious forces. We can, indeed, chart the conspiracies and the revolutionary cabals in all this, but we must remember that the alpha and the omega of man's being is his creation in the image of God and his inescapably religious nature. The majority of men are demanding more and more of the state, and their demands are religious demands, demands for salvation. The basic source of the United Nations is this apostate religious hunger of man, and it will not abate until man surrenders himself and his every hope, his every institution and order, to the sovereignty of the triune and only true God.

III. THE POLITICS OF MONEY

1

MONEY AND POWER

A young couple, the husband a soil conservation expert, were living, immediately after World War II, on an isolated Western Indian reservation, one hundred miles from the nearest town. When they learned that a movie was being shown in the Indian school building, the couple, eager for entertainment, attended. They were the only non-Indians present, apart from the projectionist. The film was an old "cowboy and Indian" story, and the young couple, sitting to the front in the crowded hall, found to their horror that the Indians delighted in the attack on and massacre of the white settlers' wagon train. The hall resounded with excited shouts and whoops, and the terrified couple wondered if the scalping fever would extend to them. Later, as the cavalry forced the Indians into flight and defeat, groans and moans arose on all sides. For these Indians, the "good guys" were the Indians, and the "bad guys" were the white settlers.

Much of man's thinking and writing rests on this kind of simple identification. Whether it be a Communist, a Democrat, Republican, or a clergyman, a road to easy success is to identify one's listeners or followers with the "good guys" and their enemies with the "bad guys." The "bad guys" are thus capitalists, workers, Communists,

Republicans, Democrats, or what have you, depending on the circumstances. There is often a real measure of truth in such identifications, but there is also a serious error, in that evil is projected onto the enemy, and thus an easy morality is gained by way of contrast. It *is* true that communism is an evil system and that Communists as a rule are evil and guilty men, but it is definitely not true that an anti-communist is thereby offering a good system or that he is a good man. Virtue is not gained merely by opposition to an evil, but rather by positive adherence to righteousness, and, more than that, by Christian faith and its consequent character. A moralistic approach can lead to real complications and a legalistic, Pharisaic reckoning of virtues. Thus, the Communists can claim as their virtues an opposition to intemperance, indolence, complacency, and a variety of other peripheral virtues. Such an approach evades the central issue: what is the main thrust and essential nature of a man's life, or of a system's purpose?

Thus, the definition of an enemy as evil, if correct, is merely an elementary fact. It must be followed by an examination of one's own position: is my position evil also? Unhappily, in the area of economics, most conservatives and Christians pursue a course which is implicitly evil, and they claim virtue only by identifying their enemies as evil, not by any positive righteousness.

One of the most common means of gaining this pseudo-righteousness is by identifying and attacking a hidden money power. That a monetary establishment exists, like other establishments, is clearly true. That such families as the Rothschilds have exerted a powerful influence on men and nations is also true.[1]

A variety of books, however, first point the finger at the "hidden money power," of whom they have often accurate and very often very inaccurate information. Second, they ascribe to these bankers a vast power, the power to manipulate and control the world economy, and, third, they propose an answer, fiat money, a state-issued

[1] See Count Egon Caesar Corti: *The Rise of the House of Rothschild, 1770-1830* and *The Reign of the House of Rothschild, 1830-1871*, New York: Cosmopolitan, 1928.

unbacked circulating media, paper money without a gold and silver backing.[2]

The first two points can be answered together. These critics of the "hidden money power" are, at the very least, Manichaean in their thinking, and, more accurately, they are Satan worshipers. They actually believe that evil can successfully rule the world. They ascribe the power to determine the world's economy and history to a small group of evil men rather than to the triune God, His eternal decree, and the unchanging laws of the economic order. Economic law is a part of God's order, and it cannot be set aside by men. The penalty for the violation of economic law by anyone is economic death. The fact that international banking and world states are today off the gold standard to varying degrees is not a means whereby they will rule the world but a means whereby a short-term socialist power is gained at the price of economic suicide. The world is under God's law, not under man's law. Significantly, these critics not only believe that the world is under the law of men, of "the hidden money powers," but they propose to place it under the law of another set of men, themselves. Their answer is more deadly than the disease. To assume that man's law can set aside God's economic laws is the essence of Satanism, of the temptation to be one's own god, establish law out of one's own being, and determine good and evil out of one's own existential realities (Gen. 3:5). The critics thus are often even more dedicated to Satanism than their enemy, because their belief in this conspiratorial power is without restraint.

It is possible for men to conspire to rule the world, politically, economically, or religiously, but whether it can be done is an-

2 The following are a few examples of such books: Wickliffe B. Vennard, Sr.: *What's Wrong in Washington?* Boston: Forum, 1959. W. B. Vennard, Sr.: *The Federal Reserve Hoax*, Boston: Forum. W. B. Vennard, Sr.: *Conquest or Consent*, Boston: Forum. Silas Walter Adams: *The Legalized Crime of Banking and A Constitutional Remedy*, Boston: Forum, 1958. John R. Elsom: *Lightning Over the Treasury Building*, Boston: Forum. Anon.: *Money Made Mysterious*, New York: American Mercury Magazine, 1958. A. N. Field: *The Truth About the Slump*, Lynwood, Calif.: Lynwood, 1931, 1962. A. N. Field: *All These Things*, Lynwood, Calif.: Lynwood, 1936, 1963. Frederick Soddy: *Wealth, Virtual Wealth and Debt*, Hawthorne, Calif.: Omni, 1933, 1961. Ove M. Nelson: *Our Legalized Monetary Swindles*, New York: Vintage, 1960.

other question. Certainly, it has been attempted through the ages and is being attempted today. It is possible too for a group of men to conspire against death, to resolve to destroy death and live forever. It is further possible that, in the course of their activity, they may, by research or by health care, succeed in postponing death and lengthening the life span. Certainly, the effort to destroy death is being attempted. But life and death are in God's hands, and for man to attempt to become god is an exercise in futility, an invitation to judgment, and a high road to hell and damnation. Every attempt to set aside economic law is as futile as man's attempt to conspire against death, and even more so, for the man who conspires against death will at least be careful of his health, but the men who conspire against economic law thereby destroy their economic health and finally life itself.

With respect to the third point, the answer of these critics is total socialism. Thus, Nelson, milder than most, still asserts that "Furnishing the nation with a sufficient supply of money—a medium of exchange—is a function of government and should not be considered in the category of freedom of enterprise, for it is not an enterprise in the sense of that term." [3] But money is more than a medium of exchange: it is a form of wealth, and it can serve as a medium of exchange of wealth only because it is itself wealth. And the first premise of interventionism and communism is money management, and money management produces communism, so that Nelson's answer is ultimately communism. And yet Coogan assures us that a turn "right" towards gold, instead of being "conservative," is a "direct step backward into the clutches of the financial backers of Bolshevism." [4] Supposedly, the adoption of communism's monetary policy will deliver us from communism! Moreover, as Gary Kilgore North has noted, Coogan would have a paper currency which would be "demand claims." [5] This would mean that anyone possessing a stack of paper money, whether the state or a person,

[3] Nelson: *Our Legalized Monetary Swindle*, p. 91f.

[4] Gertrude Coogan: *Money Creators*, p. 289. Hawthorne, California: Omni, 1935, 1963.

[5] *Ibid.*, p. 256. Coogan seems unaware of the implications of her statement, or of its threat to the liberty she desires to see furthered.

could compel a man to sell his home or properties because he bore a legal demand in his hand! The "hidden money power" has not yet asked anything resembling such a power! Can we call this deliverance?

A curious aspect of these critics is their often strange ideas and associations. Thus, the Forum Publications, catalog of Forum Publishing Company, lists a novel by Ronald G. Garver, *The Saucer People* (1957), in which various ideas are propounded in fictional form. Stan Layne's *I Doubted Flying Saucers* (1958), another novel, has as its purpose for the reader "to convince him of another, greater pattern of life." *The Advancing Ego* (1959), by "The Scribe," is a "compilation covering the universe's most colorful, powerful and important phenomena—man's continuous advancement toward God!" Moreover, "this book contains the irrevocable truths released by all the Brotherhoods for your enlightenment and understanding." Among the "Religion" books are such items as John Driskill's *Truth at Any Price* (1951), which "purports to state the relatively absolute truth for earthbound humanity and to prove that mankind is headed towards an inevitable organization of a single religion, existing within the framework of a world-wide political and economic system." And yet these peoples would present themselves to us as champions of conservative Christian constitutionalism as they promote such literature!

The strength of the "money power" rests on an open and obvious fact, *debt*. Debt and interest *are* legal, according to the Bible, and banking is a legitimate business. Christians are to avoid debt as a moral principle, but this does not mean that debt or interest is forbidden to all (Deut. 15:11; 23:19, 20; 28:12, 44; Ex. 22:25; Lev. 25:36f., Rom. 13:8, 9). The basic principle is clearly stated in Proverbs 22:7b, "the borrower is a servant (or slave) to the lender." Slavery is a way of life to many. The basic bondage and slavery is to sin (John 8:31-36), and political and economic slavery is only the outer manifestation of an inward fact. The immorality is not in the acceptance of a man's status: it is in the man's own spiritual surrender to sin. No monetary or political "reform" can alter this inward fact. It is not the money-lender who creates the debtor-slave, but the debtor-slave who creates the money-lender because his way of life requires this kind of office and a deficit financing of public and private economies. Moreover, as debt increases, quality declines, because the debtor commands, not quality goods, but cheaply available goods. Cheaply available goods are cheaply produced goods, goods produced to sell quickly in terms of debt, whereas cash sales, sales without debt, require quality as well as money-value. A debtor-class thus creates a shoddy producer and destroys the quality producer, but it meanwhile grumbles about the decline of quality.

Debt is for the Christian a violation of the commandment, "Owe no man anything save to love one another" (Rom. 13:8). Debt rests on covetousness, a desire to possess what our neighbor has, even though we lack his means. As a result of covetousness, the slave desires to possess a home, car, furnishings, and clothing which he sees the wealthy possessing, and his means of securing these things is *debt*. St. Paul declared, "But godliness with contentment is great gain. For we brought nothing into this world, and it is also certain that we can carry nothing out. But having food and clothing, let us therewith be content" (I Tim. 6:6, 7).

The covetous man or nation goes into debt to gain added power, purchasing power, prestige, resources, and other forms of visible might. The result is indeed an increase of power, but it is short-term power purchased at the price of long-term disaster. The debtor sees perpetually additional goals, new increases of power possible through debt, and as a result plunges ever more deeply into slavery. Debt is a way of life, a covetous way of life and a form of slavery. The eventual outcome of a debt-economy, for men and nations, is bankruptcy.

The short-term power, however, is impressive. The debtors themselves are profoundly impressed by this power, and hence they ascribe to the greatest debtors the greatest power. They believe, moreover, whenever they become aware of the pinch of debt, that the evil is in the money-lender, not in themselves for having lived covetously. As a result, they begin to rant against "the hidden money power," and often amass data concerning it. The grains of truth concerning the money establishment obscures the grim reality that debtors create this money-establishment, and the real evil is covetous living, not banking, erroneous though modern principles of banking are.

But, meanwhile, another force is operative. As "public" and "private" debt accumulates, there is a steady flight of gold from the various civil governments and their treasuries, and from the various bankers. The civil treasuries borrow gold from the international bankers, only to have this borrowed gold flow outward also, outward and downward. The thrifty people of the world begin to hoard gold and silver at an accelerated and desperate pace. They bury it, store it, search it out eagerly, because they recognize that disaster is rapidly nearing for the prodigal debtor men and nations. The money-lenders are pledged to continuing the debt-economy; their own prosperity and power depend upon it. The debt-economy is theirs to manipulate to ever greater power ostensibly, but the gold needed to maintain the security of states and treasuries drains steadily away from the banks and treasuries into the buried treasuries of provident people. The result is not only a flight of gold and silver downward, but a hidden flight of power downward, until finally, after a period of anarchy, with the old establishments broken, a new power group gradually emerges.

The perspective of those who concern themselves about the "money-trust" is thus a very faulty one. They believe in the triumph of evil, and they fail to see the basic evil as debt, as covetousness. Such people would outlaw banking, a legitimate activity, instead of forsaking covetousness. Money-lending is not a sin; slavery is a fact of life, and the debt-slave cannot blame a man who honestly and legitimately lends him money. The Bible recognizes such a transaction as legitimate; the slave is not outlawed by God, but is merely regarded as a person whose way of life is a very limited one. The biblical law makes provision for the slave who wants slavery; it simply insists that he publicly acknowledge what his way of life is, an act of will (Ex. 21:1-6).

The believer who avoids debt declares thereby that he refuses to be a slave, refuses to be covetous, acknowledges that the earth is the

Lord's and man also, and, therefore, that life can be lived *only* in terms of God's law. The Christian cannot mortgage himself or his future: it is God's, not his own. In terms of this faith, and this way of life, power returns to the Christian man, whose loss of freedom and of power began with a loss of faith and that covetous mind which is the mainspring of debt-slavery. *The beginning of true power is always obedience to God.*

2

MONEY AND CENTRALIZATION OF POWER

One of the most dangerous fallacies which today plagues conservatism, is Satanism as a philosophy of history. It is one thing to believe in the reality of conspiracies, but it is entirely a different proposition to assert that conspiracies govern and destine history. Only an impersonalistic view of history will logically deny the reality of conspiracies.[1] But to hand over the determination of history to conspiracies is to posit the ultimacy of evil and its omnipotence. History is not determined by international bankers but by the sovereign and triune God. History moves, not in terms of the plans, plots, and wills of men, but in terms of the absolute laws of God. And one sphere of such laws is economics. To deny the supremacy of God and His law over the world of money is to assert the power and ultimacy of evil and to be guilty of Satanism.

Because the world is under God's law, certain consequences pursue every attempt by men to control money in order to centralize power. It is true, *first* of all, that, since money is the life-blood of economics, a managed money means a managed economy. Its consequence is always socialism. Whenever and wherever men strive to centralize power in order to control it, they will then seek a managed money. This men have constantly sought to do, to gain power, and there is no likelihood that sinful man will cease to do so. Any realistic appraisal of man's nature will compel the conviction that few things are more conducive to the destruction of liberty than managed money. A sound money policy is a prerequisite of liberty. As Rist observed, "We shall save sound money, or we shall cease to be free." [2]

Second, this fact requires that we see the alternatives clearly and

[1] See R. J. Rushdoony: *The Nature of the American System*, Chapter VIII, "The Conspiracy View of History." Nutley, New Jersey: The Craig Press, 1965.
[2] Charles Rist: *The Triumph of Gold*, p. 2. Philip Cortney, translator. New York: Philosophical Library, 1961.

without illusion: the alternative is *hard money or a hard dictatorship*. Gold and silver, hard money, are conducive to economic stability and prosperity; managed money spells controls leading to dictatorships and to economic chaos and collapse. Managed money means a progressive loss of liberty. The thesis of the socialists is that scientific management and controls produce far more benefits for man than does liberty. The welfare of man is seen as the purpose of money management. But the pseudo-conservatives who call for social credit money, government-issued paper notes, hold to an identical belief: they want benevolent money-managers, guided by law, to manage money, and therefore all men; since all men are economically governed by money, to manage money is to manage or control men in the name of the general welfare of all. Between the two systems, there is only a difference of managers. Both systems are totalitarian and are hostile to economic liberty. A dictator who does not manage money, who retains free gold and silver coinage and rejects a paper media, is unavoidably a man of exceedingly limited powers. Apart from the vote, the subjects have vast areas of liberty. Because the state, lacking a managed money, remains small, the political power of such a dictator would remain very small. Accordingly, the management of money becomes the necessary ingredient of totalitarian power and control. Money, of course, is managed in a variety of ways other than debasing or counterfeiting coinage or circulating media.

As the central government progressively debauches and inflates the currency, it gains more power. As the source of the newly printed money, the central government is always in the market with the most and the cheapest money. It can outbid and outbuy private citizens and corporations as well as being able to control their activities. As the inflation becomes dangerous, the central government increases its expenditures both to increase its power and to continue the inflationary boom that passes for prosperity. On the other hand, it decries inflation and seeks to limit by controls and taxation the purchasing power of the people. It turns "to the fatal course of repressing inflation instead of removing its causes." [3] The state

[3] Walter E. Spahr: *Monetary Notes*, April 1, 1966, vol. XXVI, no. 4, p. 1, quoted from Wilhelm Roepke.

then begins to abuse the people, who are the victims, instead of admitting its own guilt as the money manager.[4] The people are assured that the dollar is strong, but they are warned that their spending can weaken it.[5] Reassurances are issued concerning the national debt by agencies of the state, and the harsh realities are "sicklied oe'r with the pale cast of thought" (*Hamlet*, III, i.).[6] Ostensibly to remedy the situation, taxes are increased to "prevent" further inflation, although the additional taxes only further the centralizing power of the state. The idea of curbing inflation by taxation has been termed "childish" by Boardman, who writes:

> One law maker put it this way. The cost of living will go up about 5 per cent this year, either in taxes or inflation so taxes will be hiked to block inflation in the public interest.
> If you can stand it, I hope you will examine that statement closely since it ignores the fact that every increase in taxes is finally added to the cost of goods and services. The truth of the matter is that every increase in taxes doubles the inflationary cycle.[7]

In the United States in 1960, the total money (including time deposits) was $250 billions; in 1966, it was $317 billions. The total gold in the United States in 1960 was $25 billions; in 1966 it was $13 billions. This tells the story of inflation, and the responsibility for this situation is with the central government and its money management.

Like it or not, when a people choose or accept money management, they have thereby chosen, in the place of hard money, a hard dictatorship, although it may take some years for their choice to come home to them. Moreover, money managers become possible and thrive when there are people who are ready and willing to be managed in exchange for a subsidy from the public treasury. The subsidy can be a federal contract, loan, subsidy, or welfare grant, but, in every form, it is a control, and its end result is socialism.

[4] See Lyle Wilson, "'Hot air' Scattered by President's Inflation Explosions," Santa Ana, California, The *Register*, Thursday (m), April 7, 1966, p. B 14.
[5] U.S. Department of Commerce, Office of Public Affairs: *Keeping the American Dollar Strong*. 1965.
[6] For an example of this, see a publication of the Federal Reserve Bank of Philadelphia: *The National Debt*, December 1965.
[7] George Boardman, "Childish Capers. 'Taxation to Curb Inflation,'" Santa Ana, California, The *Register*, Tuesday (m), April 5, 1966, p. B9.

Since irredeemable currency is a tool of socialists, communists, and government dictators of other varieties, the gates have been open since 1933 to such a form of government in this country. The power of the ballot becomes the power of those who seek sustenance from the public treasury.[8]

Third, debased and counterfeit money leads not only to centralization of power and money but of all forms of wealth. The power to manage money is also the power to confiscate wealth. A progressive consequence of money management is the concentration and centralization of wealth. Socialism does not eliminate millionaires; it creates a new kind of millionaire, one whose money comes from manipulation of statist power. There are more millionaires in the U.S.S.R. today than under the tsars, but there is no real middle class, and the lower classes are radically poorer. Moreover, none of the Soviet millionaires has any independent wealth; it is always subject to confiscation by the state whose favors made it possible. Money management is confiscation of private wealth by the state; the excuses given are the public welfare, human need, democracy, and equality, but the reality is always confiscation, and the one real beneficiary is the state. Money management, moreover, involves not only the confiscation of wealth and of economic liberty, but of political liberty as well. The state grows in power and is beyond the control of the people. As Spahr has noted,

We should not fail to understand that spending by our national government is out of control—out of control of Congress and of our people. The most serious aspect of this state of affairs is that the people of this nation have lost it because they were deprived of it when an irredeemable currency was thrust upon them in 1933. When a people lose control of the public purse, they lose control of their central government.[9]

As the consequences of money management begin to develop into the threat of a runaway inflation, the central government only

[8] Walter E. Spahr, "Sound Money and Integrity," *The Commercial and Financial Chronicle,* Thursday, August 5, 1965, reprinted by Economists' National Committee on Monetary Policy, New York.
[9] Walter E. Spahr, "Loss of Control of the Public Purse," reprinted from *The Commercial and Financial Chronicle*, Thursday, July 11, 1963, by Economists' National Committee on Monetary Policy, New York.

212 POLITICS OF GUILT AND PITY

increases its spending and confiscation while now trying to halt the easy money policy it had earlier fostered for the citizenry. A "tighter money" policy becomes necessary for the people.[10] Controls begin to appear, first of prices for heavy industry and then of other areas. Appeals are made to labor for voluntary wages controls, "a brake on wage demands," as Johnson did in early May, 1966.[11] The voluntary controls, of course, are futile, because inflation and its root cause, managed money, not only rob the people of their economic liberties but also create in them an appetite for more of the spurious prosperity of inflation. The reaction of Walter Reuther to the economic crisis was a further demand: "Walter Reuther yesterday spurred his 1.4 million member United Auto Workers union to strive for a society of both 'bread and roses.' "[12]

All the same, the federal government, by mid-1966, was beginning to think seriously of controls. Federal Reserve Board chairman William M. Martin favored controls in addressing a congressional hearing.[13] The administration was also considering using the Viet Nam War "escalation" as a reason for war-time controls.[14] The federal government, in awareness of the dangers of dictatorship, is at times both hesitant and ready for such controls, with the political administration fearful usually, and the bureaucracy ready. But the pressure for controls comes also from the people, who believe that the answer to a state-created crisis is more statist action. Thus, savings and loan men, and builders, were by June, 1966, also demanding controls to save their own areas of activity.[15]

The threat of further inflation creates crises for businessmen and investors. Because of money management, their wealth and property

[10] See *Newsweek*, December 13, 1965, "The Fed's Surprise: Tighter Money," p. 75ff.
[11] Victor Riesel, "Inside Labor: Labor Leaders Get LBJ 'No-Show,' " Los Angeles *Herald-Examiner*, Sunday, May 15, 1966, p. C-6.
[12] Dan Swinton, " 'We Want Bread and Roses,' Says Reuther," Los Angeles *Herald-Examiner*, Sunday, May 15, 1966, p. B1, Second Front Page.
[13] Oakland, California, *Tribune*, June 8, 1966, p. 45.
[14] Allen-Scott Report, Robert S. Allen and Paul Scott, "Wartime Controls Ready to Be Set by LBJ," in The Santa Ana, California, *Register*, Monday (m), May 16, 1966, p. A12.
[15] Kirk Wels, " 'Businessmen' Ask Control in Battle for Home Monies," Santa Ana, California, *Register*, June 7, 1966, Tuesday (m), p. A16.

is increasingly insecure. Interest rates rise and credit tightens as people begin to look around desperately for a safe refuge for their money. The effect on the stock market is immediate: it reflects the uncertainty of the people and the insecurity of money.[16] The central government seeks, meanwhile, to continue its self-justification by speaking of high-sounding welfare causes. Ostensibly, wealth is to be redistributed. According to President L. B. Johnson, January 15, 1964, "We are going to try to take all of the money that we think is unnecessarily being spent and take it from the 'haves' and give it to the 'have nots' that need it so much." [17] The actual result of such a program is not the redistribution of wealth to the poor but the confiscation of it by the state. Every proposed corrective to the growing economic crisis is a form of further money management, and both devaluation and inflation are hidden taxes on the people and further methods of confiscation. By devaluation, the state increases the value of its gold and silver holdings but decreases the value of the paper money holdings of the people. By inflation, the value of the paper money is also decreased. Irrespective of the device used, money management produces centralization and confiscation of money and wealth.

Fourth, there is, however, another factor at work as centralization increases, and this is economic fragmentation. Money management produces progressively worthless money together with concentration of power. Concentration breeds further concentration, as the power structure strives steadily for a consolidation of power. Money management leads to political internationalism, therefore, but it also creates economic nationalism and fragmentation. Weak money does not flow easily across borders, and the more it is debased, the weaker its flow. The result is a collapse of the economic internationalism which gold and silver foster. The professed political internationalism progressively fumbles and falls over the harsh realities of economic fragmentation and nationalism.

But this is not all. As power and money management pass to the

---

[16] Ed Morse, "Today's Mart: 'It's Got to Snap Back or Else Country Is Bankrupt,'" Santa Ana, The *Register*, Tuesday (m), May 10, 1966, p. A 18.

[17] M. Stanton Evans: *The Liberal Establishment*, p. 59. New York: Devin-Adair, 1965.

central government, *hard money flows downward*. The reaction of people to the progressive confiscation is to hoard gold and silver. Palyi has commented on Greek hoarding:

> The average Greek views this (real estate and housing) boom as part and parcel of the over-all inflation trend and tries to protect himself—by hoarding gold. The private gold holdings of the Greek people are estimated at some 500 million dollars— that is, at more than $45 on the average for every man, woman, and child.[18]

Hoarding, which simply means saving, is even more marked in Western Europe, and is in growing evidence in the United States. The hunger for gold in Asia, notably India, is very great. Gold coins sell in every time of growing money management at an increasing premium over their gold content. A shaky stock market adds to this trend. "One result of all this is that many European investors have taken their money out of the market and invest it in gold instead." As a result, the stock market declines further. "All across the Continent, when a bank customer seeks to cash traveler's checks he frequently finds himself in a line of gold-buying citizens." [19] In many parts of the world, the age-old reaction to money management is to hoard and bury gold for the time of freedom. From time to time, such long-buried hoards come to light. Another current consequence is a renewal of interest in mining shares.[20]

In the U.S., the reaction has been varied, including renewed interest in mining and the private accumulation of gold. Significantly,

A long list of foreign countries drained gold from the U.S. in

[18] Melchior Palyi, "Greeks Hoard Gold as Inflation Hedge," The Chicago *Tribune*, January 4, 1966, cited in Walter E. Spahr, *Monetary Notes*, vol. XXVI, no. 3, March 1, 1966, p. 2.

[19] See Ray Vicker, "An Old Familiar Tale: Tight Money, Labor Pinch Hurt Stocks," The *Wall Street Journal*, pp. 1, 19, Thurs., May 19, 1966.

[20] Anthony A. Gentle, "A New Interest in Mining Shares," Los Angeles *Herald-Examiner*, Sunday, April 17, 1966, p. F-6. For another kind of interest in hard money, the criminal hijacking of silver bullion shipments, see "Ring of Crime Cracked by FBI," Arcadia, California, *Daily News-Post*, Wednesday, April 20, 1966, Second Front Page; the rise in thefts of gold and silver coins is a good index to their rapidly increasing value.

the first quarter, the Treasury announced, but it said sales to domestic users slightly exceeded the outflow to foreigners.[21]

All over the world new gold was flowing into private channels rather than into state hands:

> Private demand for gold last year reached an unprecedented total of $1,585,000,000, up $465,000,000 from 1964, while the total available for governmental use dropped by $325,000,000 to $400,000,000.[22]

As a result of these and other factors, centralization is self-defeating ultimately. The increased power which money management breeds is fraudulent power, in that it cannot stand the test of freedom and competition. The economy created by managed money leads to a progressive distrust which causes hard money to flow downward and to be hoarded. The paper money is spent more readily, and the hard money held. With the growing political and economic concentration of power in Washington, gold and silver have moved away from the U. S. Treasury. The IMF (International Monetary Fund) has seen a similar flow outward and downward:

> Over its whole history, the Fund has had gold receipts of $4.2 Billion from subscription payments, repurchases, and charges. The Fund has used $1.1 Billion of gold to replenish its holdings of currencies, of which $500 million was used for this purpose in 1961, leaving $3.1 billion. Of this, the Fund has invested $800 million, the remainder of $2.3 Billion being the Fund's present gold holdings.[23]

Although the United States, faced with a growing loss of confidence in the dollar, is ready to go into a world currency, the resistance to this is very great. The one consequence would be to pass on the weakness of such currencies as the dollar and the pound to all other countries, and other countries are only ready to profit by the strength, not share in the decline or collapse, of a foreign

[21] "Gold Sales in 1st Period to Domestic Users Led Outflow to Foreigners," *Wall Street Journal*, June 9, 1966.
[22] "New Gold Supplies' Value Leaped to Record in 1965," *Wall Street Journal*, June 14, 1966.
[23] Robert V. Roosa: *Monetary Reform for the World Economy*, p. 156. Published for the Council on Foreign Relations, by Harper & Row, New York, 1965.

currency. Whether a world currency is adopted or not, the process of economic fragmentation is under way.[24] Hoarding is a vote of "no confidence" in the prevailing official currency, and the votes of "no confidence" by nations for other currencies, and by citizens for their own, is everywhere on the increase.

The decline of currencies has in most cases passed the point of no return. The central states and their money managers are not about to surrender their vast powers but seek rather to increase them. But because the world is under God's law, the nemesis of this power is that its concentration speeds its own destruction. We are supposedly on the threshold of a great era of internationalism when in actuality we are witnessing an era of economic nationalism and fragmentation, and the real breakdown is yet to come. The crisis will be severe, but the world will remain, as always, *under God's law*.

[24] The efforts of the U.S.S.R. are particularly of note. State conducted raffles are being used to drain money from the people; Vincent J. Burke, "Soviet to Raffle 4,000 Autos," Los Angeles *Times*, Monday (m), June 6, 1966, pp. 1, 17. Gold mining increased in the U.S.S.R. in order to meet the necessities of foreign trade. The ruble had to be slightly gold-backed, $100 million worth of rubles, to meet the demand of captive countries, Poland in particular, for some return for their goods taken by the U.S.S.R.; see Henry S. Bradshur, "Russian Ruble Bids for World Status," San Francisco *Examiner*, June 8, 1966. Gold hoarding was not absent in the U.S.S.R. At least one miner was shot for stealing gold; *The Review of the News*, vol. 2, no. 24, June 22, 1966, p. 16.

3

THE MORAL FOUNDATIONS OF MONEY

Throughout history, every era which has witnessed a crisis due to man's moral and religious failure has seen also the coincidence of certain phenomena. James Laver has cited some of these:

> Post-crisis epochs always have certain things in common; dance mania, an inflated currency, a wave of female emancipation, and general promiscuity. All these we find in marked degree in the period following the French Revolution and in the period following the first world war, and they are reflected, with an astonishing faithfulness, in the clothes women wore.[1]

This list, however, omits one of the most important aspects of every such era, *gambling*. Gambling comes to have a religious prominence and passion in the minds of men, so that it is more than a mere pastime: it is a hope for life. A 1964 documentary film, narrated by Terry-Thomas, "Everybody's Got a System," brought out clearly this religious presupposition in gambling. The gambler denies implicitly that the universe is under law; he insists that "all life is a gamble," and a falling brick can kill you, and totally meaningless events always surround you, because chance, not God, is ultimate. Since chance, not God, rules the universe, causality does not prevail. It is therefore possible to get something for nothing, and the gambler, knowing what the odds are, nevertheless expects chance to overrule law and enrich him.

People who believe in chance rather than God and law will inevitably call for and establish a civil government and a monetary policy to conform to their faith. The result is the Gambler State, a civil government which operates on the premise that it can create some-

[1] James Laver: *Women's Dress in the Jazz Age*, p. 6. A Hamish Hamilton Monograph. London: Hamish Hamilton, Ltd., 1964.

thing out of nothing and, by using fraudulent money, get something for nothing. God's creative activity is premised on His own being, which is law. The Gambler State's creative activity is premised on ultimate chance and a denial of economic law. The history, therefore, of every Gambler State is one of eventual disaster after a period of seeming success.

Every interventionist state, whatever it is called, whether the welfare state, the Great Society, or any other name, exists by manipulating money and by a progressive substitution of fraudulent money, in the form of a paper currency and baser metals, for gold and silver. The outcome is socialism and disaster. The purposes are ostensibly well intentioned. The state manipulates money for one or another of certain purposes:

1. More equitable distribution of purchasing power.
2. Relief of debtors.
3. Stimulation of trade.[2]

Before analyzing this manipulation of money, it is important that money be defined. Two common definitions are, first, that money is a medium of exchange, and, second, that it is a representation of wealth. Both are dangerously inaccurate. An excellent definition, from 1833, is that of William Gouge, an able associate of President Andrew Jackson:

> Money is not, as was asserted by a late Secretary of the Treasury (Mr. I) "merely the representation of property." Money of gold and silver is property—is *wealth*. A hundred dollars in silver can no more be considered as the representative of a hundred dollars' worth of flour, than a hundred dollars' worth of flour can be considered as the representative of a hundred dollars' worth of iron. Each is the equivalent of the other; but each is *real* wealth—not a mere symbol or representative.[3]

[2] Frank Parker Stockbridge: *Hedging Against Inflation*, p. 14. New York: Barron's Publishing Company, 1939.

[3] William Gouge: *A Short History of Paper Money and Banking in the United States*, p. 7f. Philadelphia: T. W. Ustick, 1833. The Mr. I. referred to was Samuel D. Ingham, who was a paper manufacturer and congressman, and Secretary of the Treasury under Andrew Jackson, 1829-1831, when he resigned.

This point is extremely important: true money is real wealth, and only because it is real wealth does true money successfully function as a medium of exchange. Gold and silver money is real wealth which is readily transferable, enduring, relatively stable in value, easily divisible, and easily transportable. No sensible person wants to exchange real wealth, a landed estate, goods, or valued services, for something worthless, something which is not wealth but is passed off as a representation of wealth or a medium of exchange. Such counterfeit money drives good money out of circulation, since people refuse to exchange good money for bad money, and it forces upward the prices of land, goods, labor, and all other commodities because people are increasingly unwilling to exchange them for fraudulent money and because that inflated paper currency has progressively less value.

But the Gambler State still hopes to hit the jackpot and bring in a bonanza, usher in paradise on earth for its people, stimulate trade, increase purchasing power, and relieve debtors. It has begun by manipulating money, i.e., by progressively destroying true money and replacing it with legalized counterfeit money. The basic methods used in this program of making money, or inflation, are three:

1. Debasement or devaluation of the basic metallic unit of money.
2. The issuance of paper or token money in amounts materially in excess of the resources of the government in metallic reserves and assured tax revenues.
3. The creation of new bank credits on the basis of an increasing public debt.[4]

As a result of these policies, the paper currency becomes progressively worth less and less, and the public and private debt increases. Because the state has cheapened money, and borrows heavily to finance deficit spending, promising to pay with what will be worthless money, the people are encouraged to go into debt also, expecting to pay off good debts with bad money. Basic to inflation, therefore, is larceny: the state and the citizenry want something for nothing, and they hope to pyramid larceny into a

[4] Stockbridge: *Hedging Against Inflation*, p. 15.

better life for everyone. This larcenous hope rests on a denial of economic law and a trust in chance. St. Paul described this mentality as sinning to make grace abound (Rom. 6:1). Tilden described ably, in 1936, the two great facts which make inflation and monetary manipulation possible.

> 1. The vital prerequisite of an effective inflation, which will result disastrously to the creditor position, *is the intent to falsify the true economic position· of a nation, or to relieve the debtor at the expense of the creditor.* Where there is no such intent, there may be a temporary inflation, not harmful, possibly beneficial—and it will contract itself when its work is done.
>
> 2. Inflation, whether of bank credit or of paper currency, cannot be effective, until *the larcenous purpose is generally comprehended.*[5]

When the larcenous mentality prevails, debt becomes sound business, and *credit*, which means normally the ability to be trusted, reliability, integrity, comes to mean instead the ability to contract debt. Moral values are thus turned upside down, and the larcenous debtor, whether a nation or an individual, becomes the "person" of credit. Debt or "credit" is an important means of inflation, and, like all inflation, it destroys those who, in terms of old-fashioned virtues, save money. A "credit" economy makes thrift foolishness, and it progressively destroys the middle and lower classes. The Gambler State gains the support of the lower classes by offering them some form of "welfare" subsidies, some share-the-wealth program. But, ultimately, these lower classes are themselves the victims also, together with the middle classes, as the cost of socialism steadily lowers the standard of living. Interventionism—socialism—makes the rich richer, the poor poorer. Since its essence is larceny, the thieves with the greatest power are able to rob not only all the victims but the other thieves as well. The petty thief who imagines that he can gain by the alliance of big government, big business, and big labor is destined to suffer. Fresh victims are continually needed, and the little man is one of the first victims. *Power always allies itself with power, not*

[5] Freeman Tilden: *A World in Debt*, p. 279. New York: Funk & Wagnalls, 1936

with weakness, and when a power allies itself briefly with some weaker power, it is not with any altruistic purpose but simply to increase its own power. This is true in the political realm; Poland, in the 1930's, foolishly believed that an alliance with Britain would enrich her at the war's end, only to be sold out by Britain (and the United States) to a more powerful ally, the U.S.S.R. This is true in the economic realm also: when the state allies itself with the worker, its purpose is to increase the powers of the state, not the powers of the worker. The worker finds eventually that his labor leaders, the big industrialists, and the politicians are in closer collaboration with each other than with him. Ultimately, the cannibalistic nature of socialism leads to the destruction of labor leaders and industrialists, and then of the politicians, as sacrificial victims, and to the death of the state itself.

There are those who, concerned about the debt-money involved in Federal Reserve notes, believe that the "conservative" answer is debt-free money printed by the Treasury Department. Various groups are ardent advocates of this hope and advance it in the name of "Humanity." Thus, the Greenback Party, in advocating government-controlled and issued printing press money, has declared, "We demand the abolition of special privilege." [6] Its program, like that of every party today which holds to paper currency in any such form, involves special privileges for the state. Private individuals are barred by law from debt-free money; they cannot print and circulate paper dollars and thereby "enrich" themselves. But the federal government, under such a plan, would have precisely that privilege: it could avoid borrowing money and incurring debt by the simple expedient of printing money. It can use its coercive power to compel people to accept this money and thus can exchange its counterfeit money for the real wealth of the people. The result in every such attempt is rapid anarchy and collapse. Advocates of fiat paper money are socialists, whether they know it or not.

A departure to any degree from gold and silver is a step in the same direction. *Every departure from real money, from gold and*

[6] *Greenback Party History in Brief, 1875-1952*, p. 30. The Greenback Party, Seattle, Washington, 1952.

silver, is a step into the planned society. Money manipulation, whether debasing the metal coinage, issuing some unbacked paper currency, or extending public and private "credit" or debt, is a form of planning. It is planning for larceny and for the avoidance of economic law or consequences. It is planning *in the name* of sound economic goals, such as the adjustment of supply and demand, the creation of incentives to produce and to produce usefully, and the production of honest standards for goods. Planning, in other words, claims for its purposes exactly the same goals as the free market does, as, specifically, the price mechanism does. However, as Jacques Rueff has noted, with reference to Germany, "And yet the price mechanism achieved in a few hours what planning—although reinforced with unprecedented powers—had failed to achieve in several years." [7] The free market is more productive than the planned market. The great age of industrial growth and expansion in the United States has been assumed to be the post-Civil War era. But that era saw interventionism and money manipulation introduced, and industrialism was instead retarded, although textbooks give a contrary impression.[8] The free market functions in terms of planning, but the planning is by millions of producers, whose desire is to produce a commodity of the highest standard to command the best price. Failure to do so will eventually put them out of the market, which means an individual failure rather than a social collapse. Private planning is realistic: the more complex a society, the more it requires specialization and therefore decentralization. Central planning calls for centralization, which is a return to economic primitivism and, in a complex industrial society, an assurance of progressive confusion and ultimate collapse. Central planning seeks to avoid the personal failures but ensures the social collapse. And its means of seeking to avoid the personal failures is twofold: *first,* it declares that personal planning is no longer necessary; the

---

[7] Jacques Rueff: *The Age of Inflation,* p. 93. Chicago: Regnery, 1964; Rueff refers to events of 1948.

[8] See Thomas C. Cochran: *The Inner Revolution* (New York: Harper Torchbook, 1964), especially chapter III, "Did the Civil War Retard Industrialism?" pp. 39-54, first published in the *Mississippi Valley Historical Review,* XLVIII, September, 1961.

state will assure the citizens of social security in every form; *second*, central planning seeks to ensure security by continual larceny; it offers impossible promises and it delivers for a limited number of years by stealing from one class of citizens to deliver to another. The Social Security program is itself a fitting symbol and administration for the Gambler State: it violates all sound economics, and its basic structure is similar if not identical to the chain-letter scheme. Those who are the earlier members of the scheme can profit by it; for the rest, it is a total loss as the inexorable reality of economic law overtakes the chain-letter, social-security scheme.

The larceny of central planning schemes is closely linked to its anti-Christian scheme of morality. St. Paul declared, "if any would not work, neither should he eat" (II Thess. 3:10). The welfare state planners are so full of love, they want the whole world to eat. They substitute coercive political action for charity to do this, and they substitute welfare politics for economics. Thus, economic law is denied. The welfare state is a Gambler State: it does not believe in economic law. *As a result, it defies economics in order to produce welfare, in order to ensure plenty for all.* Instead, it creates scarcity by its destruction of true economic planning, private planning for the free market. The result is hunger. The four basic causes of famine in human history must be noted:

1. The prevention of cultivation or the willful destruction of crops;
2. Defective agriculture caused by communistic control of land;
3. Governmental interference by regulation or taxation;
4. Currency restrictions, including debasing the coin.[9]

As Montesquieu observed long ago, "Countries are not cultivated in proportion to their fertility, but to their liberty." [10] Famine is thus the outcome of money manipulation and statist controls, whether exercised frankly in the name of larceny or done in the name of

[9] E. Parmalee Prentice: *Farming for Famine*, p. 6. Garden City, New York: Doubleday, Doran, 1936. See also Prentice's *Food, War, and the Future*. New York: Harper, 1944; and especially Prentice's *Hunger and History*, Caxton Printers, Caldwell, Idaho, 1951 (1939).
[10] Montesquieu: *Spirit of Laws*, Book XVIII, Chap. 3.

human welfare. As Tilden noted, "*Primarily, public debt is a device intended to beguile the taxpayer into thinking he is getting something for nothing.*"[11] As he noted, it would be more honest to call the Secretary of the Treasury instead the Secretary for Debt. It might be even more honest to call him the Secretary for Larceny, because deficit spending can be financed only by legalized larceny in one form or another, a stealing from the industrious and thrifty members of the population.

> For, a nation lacking saving individuals would have no surplus; without a surplus there would be no creditors; without creditors there would be nobody for government and private debtors to plunder. In order for *anyone* to be prodigal, *someone* must be thrifty.[12]

Thus, this Gambler State, a larcenous state, is parasitic. Every socialist state is a parasite. After destroying its own wealth, it must feed on another nation's wealth, and thus socialism is by nature driven to imperialism. It offers paradise on earth to other countries by means of socialism and seizes them to enable itself to survive. When the host body dies, the parasite dies. Today, the United States is the host body for the parasitic socialism of the world, and the United States, because of its interventionism, is rapidly becoming a fearful parasite, draining the wealth of the American people. When, however achieved, the host body is captured and destroyed, it will destroy the parasite also. The result will be a world-wide economic collapse of unrivalled dimensions and hardships. Out of this wreckage, a free order will emerge.

Meanwhile, the politicians of the Gambler State march forward proudly in all their ignorance. When House Majority Leader Carl Albert was asked in January, 1966, "Mr. Albert, do you see any signs of inflation today?" he answered:

> Well, I hope not. I think our real dollars have remained pretty stable.
> I think one of the concerns that the President had in the aluminum and copper matters was that this might point to inflationary

[11] Tilden: *A World in Debt*, p. 230.
[12] *Ibid.*, p. 228, footnote.

trends if the companies went through with what they had suggested they might do.

I'm not an economist. I really don't want to give a definitive answer on the subject.[13]

President Lyndon B. Johnson, after taking every kind of inflationary step as President, refused to allow the aluminum and copper industries to recognize the fact of inflation by a price adjustment. His action was a state control of industry. Monetary manipulation is eventually the substitution of state control for self-control, and it can lead only to ever-increasing controls. The more the state controls the people, the freer it is from any control over itself. The state, and the increasingly controlled banks in the state, are in the business of "making money" in order to solve all the problems of the world—personal social, and political. New wealth will be made out of nothing by the trick of manipulating money and "creating" new capital. "So long, therefore, as there are persons wanting capital, we may expect there will not be wanting applicants for the power to create capital. The evil will be cured by itself, as a natural disease is ended by terminating in death." [14] There will be no real resistance from aluminum and copper, or from the bulk of the citizenry. Each may dislike a particular control whereby its own ox is gored, but all are alike engaged in furthering an economy based on larceny and alike hope to get rich thereby. They share in a common dedication to immorality, and they shall share in a common death.

The certainty of the present order is its death. The wise will prepare for liberty.

[13] "What New Laws Congress Will Pass," interviews with House Majority Leader Carl Albert and House Minority Leader Gerald R. Ford, in *Nation's Business*, January, 1966, p. 68.

[14] Gouge: *Paper Money and Banking*, Pt. 2, p. 231.

4

THE SOVIET VIEW OF MONEY

On October 7-14, 1917, Lenin wrote an important article for the magazine, *Prosveshcheniye* (*Education*, no. 1, October, 1917), on the subject, "Will the Bolsheviks Retain State Power?" In the course of his analysis, Lenin turned his attention to the machinery of banking and finance, and declared:

> This machinery cannot and must not be broken up. It must be forcibly freed from subjection to the capitalists; the latter must be cut off, broken, chopped away from it with the threads transmitting their influence; it must be *subjected* to the proletarian Soviets; it must be made wider, more all-embracing, more popular. And this *can* be done by relying on the achievements already attained by large-scale capital (as, indeed, the proletarian revolution in general can only attain its aim by taking these achievements as its basis).
>
> Capitalism created the *apparatus* for accounting: the banks, syndicates, post office, consumers' societies, unions of employees. *Without the big banks Socialism could not be realized.*
>
> The big banks are the "state apparatus" which we *need* for the realisation of Socialism and which we *take ready-made* from capitalism. Our problem here is only to *chop off* that which capitalistically disfigures this otherwise excellent apparatus and to make it even *larger*, more democratic, more all-embracing. Quantity will change into quality. One state bank as huge as possible, with branches in every *township*, in every factory— this is already nine-tenths of the *Socialist* apparatus. This is general state *accounting*, general state accounting of production and distribution of goods, this is, so to speak, something in the nature of the *skeleton* of Socialist society.[1]

[1] V. I. Lenin, "Will the Bolsheviks Retain State Power," in Collected Works, vol. XXI, *Toward the Seizure of Power*, Bk. II, p. 29. New York: International Publishers, 1932.

For Lenin, state control of money and banking was thus the necessary precondition for socialism. As he said candidly, "Without the big banks Socialism could not be realised." By "big banks," Lenin meant a state-controlled central banking system issuing a paper currency and controlling and extending credit: "this is already nine-tenths of the *Socialist* apparatus." The key to socialization of private wealth and the total control of an economy is a state-controlled monetary system with the substitution of a paper currency for gold and silver.

Lenin's hostility to a hard money policy and his realization that power rests in a state controlled banking system appears in many of his writings, and he returns to the theme repeatedly.[2]

If the state controls money and banking, it can levy an income tax and every kind of tax without any special apparatus.[3] The state then has total economic power. By its manufacture of paper money, the state has the power to confiscate all wealth and nullify whatever wages it pays to the workers. Hard money is resistant to socialism: it provides the owners with independence. Hard money must be abolished when socialism conquers the world. As Lenin said,

> When we conquer on a world scale I think we shall use gold for the purpose of building public lavatories in the streets of several of the large cities of the world. This would be the most "just" and educational way of utilising gold for the benefit of those generations which have not forgotten how, for the sake of gold, ten million men were killed and thirty million were maimed in the "great war for freedom," in the war of 1914-1918, in the war that was waged to decide the great question of which peace was the worst, the Brest Peace or the Versailles Peace, and how, for the sake of this gold, preparations are certainly being made to kill twenty million men and to maim sixty million in a war, say, about 1925, or about 1928, between, say, Japan and America, or between England and America, or something like that.
>
> But however "just," useful or humane it would be to utilise

[2] See Lenin's *To the Rural Poor* (1903), *Imperialism, the Highest State of Capitalism* (1916), *The Threatening Catastrophe and How to Fight It* (1917), etc.

[3] V. I. Lenin, "The Threatening Catastrophe and How to Fight It," in *Works* XXI, Bk. I, p. 186.

> gold for this purpose, we nevertheless say: Let us work for an-
> other decade or so with the same intensity and with the same
> success as we have been working in 1917-21, only on a wider
> field, in order to reach the stage where we can put gold to this
> use. Meanwhile, we must save gold in the R.S.F.S.R., sell it at
> the highest price, buy goods with it at the lowest price. "When
> living among wolves, howl like the wolves." As for exterminat-
> ing all the wolves, as would be done in a sensible human so-
> ciety, we shall act up to the wise Russian proverb: "Don't boast
> when going to war, boast when returning from war." [4]

Gold was necessary for the Soviet Union in order to do business
with the free world. Worthless, irredeemable paper would nowhere
be accepted by free men, and, therefore, gold would have to be
retained for international use as long as freedom survived. When
the whole world is conquered, there will then be no area of freedom
where men can demand hard money, real wealth, in exchange for
their wealth in the form of labor and goods. With total world control, gold, the symbol of wealth and liberty, would then become obsolete, and it could be used to build public lavatories. There would
then be a public defiling of the very symbol of ancient wealth and
freedom.

Lenin emphasized the necessity of a central banking system as the
necessary precondition of socialism. Any country embarking on a
paper money course and a central banking system is therefore developing towards socialism to the degree that it continues in this
course of action. It is of importance therefore to analyze modern
economic policy, with particular reference to the United States, in
terms of its movement towards Lenin's conclusions.

The price of any item of goods has in it *five* aspects which govern
the cost of production. *First*, there is the cost of the materials in it.
Second, there is the cost of the labor required to produce it. *Third*,
there is the cost of taxes, and *fourth*, there is the wages or profit of
the capital, in money, machinery, land, etc., required to produce
the goods, *fifth*, there are often interest charges.

Taxation strikes at four aspects: the worker is taxed, the raw

[4] V. I. Lenin, "The Importance of Gold," (1921), in *Selected Works*, vol.
IX, p. 299f. New York: International Publishers, 1943.

materials are taxed, and the profits are taxed, in addition to the direct taxes on the item of goods. Taxation robs both the worker and the owner, so that both must realize more wages in order to maintain the same purchasing power.

When a state begins to control the monetary system, it has the power to out-buy the people because, with an irredeemable currency, it is the manufacturer of money. When its money is debt money, created by deficit financing and bonded indebtedness, it again both limits the purchasing power of the people ultimately and inflates the currency. Whatever temporary benefits accrue to debtors as a result of inflation are finally nullified, because monetary inflation is the power of confiscation. The debtor confiscates the creditor's wealth by paying off in worthless money for valuable goods or properties. Then the state confiscates the goods accumulated by these exploiters of inflation and debt by further inflation or by direct confiscatory taxation.

The great depression which began in 1929 was not caused by any failure of free enterprise. It was a product of state intervention in the economy and in money and banking. There was an inflationary expansion of money and credit in the preceding years, and the consequence was collapse.[5]

But the root causes of the depression were never corrected by the New Deal; on the contrary, the answer of Franklin Delano Roosevelt and his advisors was to intensify the very policies which created the depression, i.e., an inflationary expansion of money and credit. The advent of World War II aided this expansion, and, after the war, the military policy, and foreign policy, of interventionism was maintained on a world-wide scale to further the expansion of money and credit. A vast program of foreign aid and domestic welfare also aided in furthering this expansion. The increase of debt money gave an appearance of prosperity, but the reality remained that the depression was never solved. The depression was only covered or

[5] Murray N. Rothbard: *America's Great Depression*. Princeton, New Jersey: Van Nostrand, 1963. See also Benjamin McAlester Anderson: *Economics and the Public Welfare*. Princeton: Van Nostrand, 1949, 1963. A brief summary is provided by Hans Sennholz, "The Great Depression," *The Freeman*, October, 1969.

suppressed by a vast program of public spending; as a result, steady decapitalization set in. Public and private debt increased, and capital decreased, and more and more enterprises were capitalized by debt, heavy debt which was calculated to destroy them with any recession. The depression was there, growing steadily more virulent under the surface, and the slightest pause in government spending brought on a serious recession. The pace of spending and inflation increased, and there remained no way off the inflationary treadmill except to revert to the underlying and *repressed depression.*

The situation, then, of the United States as well as the other countries which have taken the same course, is one of *repressed depression.* The longer the suppression continues, the more aggravated the economic crisis becomes, because the central ingredients of a repressed depression are, *first, progressive inflation* to mask the crisis, and, *second, progressive controls* as the economy is increasingly dominated by the state's controlled money and growing confiscatory power. The state by these means grows progressivesly stronger and money grows weaker. As a market analyst has noted, "there are only 2 types of govt: money and man. When money is strong (sound) then govt need *not* be. . . . When money is weak (unsound) govt has to be strong." [6] Schultz has also added, "Big govt makes small people." [7]

A country with *repressed depression* may not have any intention of turning socialist, but it will inevitably socialize as long as it continues to inflate. It is not a question therefore of inflation versus depression which then confronts the state as a matter of choice. The choice was made in the 1930s, and the choice was inflation. With every deficit, with every welfare and foreign aid program, the same choice has been re-established as the basic economic policy. With the disappearance of gold and silver as the monetary media, the choice has been riveted into a hard policy. If a depression results, it will be a product of unforeseen circumstances, the loss of public confidence, too heavy a control of and braking on the private sector, and like conditions.

[6] *The International Harry Schultz Letter,* January 27, 1967, no. 107, p. 2.
[7] *The International Harry Schultz Letter,* March 9, 1967, no. 112, p. 2.

The fifth point of the *Communist Manifesto* declared that one of the necessary measures was the "centralization of credit in the hands of the State, by means of a national bank with State capital and an exclusive monopoly." This centralization the United States accomplished in large degree by creating the Federal Reserve System, an agency of the Federal Government. The control was furthered by the abandonment first of gold and then of silver in favor of an irredeemable currency as the alternatives to an *open depression*. The result has been a *repressed depression* with increasing controls.

In the Soviet Union, the economy has remained in a state of permanently suppressed depression since the Bolshevik Revolution. Instead of any relaxing of controls, there has been a steady intensification of controls, so that a decapitalized country has been further crippled. Agriculture and industry have steadily declined in productivity, despite claims to the contrary. The Soviet economy has maintained itself and has recapitalized only by means of, *first*, credit extended to it, largely by the United States, and, *second*, by imperialism, by the seizure of capital in conquered and satellite areas. The extensive assistance from the United States, however much the terminology speaks of it as credit or a loan, is nonetheless basically free capital for the U.S.S.R. Moreover, by means of the continuing imperialism of the Soviet Union, new capital is incorporated into the communist economy. The economy of Marxism is thus of necessity parasitic and imperialistic as its means of survival. Because socialism leads to decapitalization, it can capitalize only by parasitism and imperialism.

The radical collapse of the Soviet economy is apparent in its money, which is totally worthless. Before World War I, when the tsarist ruble was badly inflated, a Russian counterfeiter added in tiny letters this statement on the back of his bills: "My money is no worse than yours." [8] The tsarist ruble had some value, however; it was potentially redeemable. The Soviet ruble has no relationship to real money. There is in reality no exchange rate between the dollar and the ruble. According to Jones, "the ruble is primarily a political fact rather than an economic one, and . . . a rational relation between

[8] Ned Seidler: *The Story of Money*, p. 40f. New York: Odyssey Press, 1965.

the ruble and the monetary unit of a free market is impossible." [9] In the Soviet Union, prices are political; they have no relationship to the cost of production, i.e., the cost of materials, of labor, of taxes, and of the wages of capital. Prices in the Soviet Union are fixed by the decree of officials. Taxation takes two basic forms, a reduction in wages, and an enormous sales tax, since there is no land, property, or income tax (although a nominal income tax exists). With the total controls, cost is almost impossible to ascertain. Price is also determined by social direction and planning; that which the state wishes to discourage from wide use is priced out of reach. Moreover, since price determination is influenced by the national income and outgo factor, this means that the total picture of the economy enters into the price of a single item, not merely the cost of that single item.[10]

The Soviet money is thus purely political paper, not an economic yardstick or a form of wealth. Yet the desire for pure paper is increasingly in evidence among Western liberals.[11]

The purpose of the Marxist economy is to produce a workers' paradise, but its money, because it is what d'Andrade has called "costless money," has made life "easier for governments," not for the workers. Costless money brings forth two new concepts as a way of life. "First: work is not the only way to earn a living. Secondly: work can receive a value independent of the worth society attributes to the services rendered." [12] In semi-socialist states, welfarism becomes a way of life for many people. Under full-scale socialism welfarism is only for the state, which now restricts welfare mainly to itself and its servants. Money is no longer related to work, nor price to cost, because "money is taken today as an abstraction, as an instrument that can be used to right any wrong, or to bring

[9] Robert V. Jones, "Understanding the Ruble," in *Modern Age*, Winter 1960-1961, vol. 5, no. 1, p. 70.

[10] *Ibid.*, pp. 62-68.

[11] See David T. Bazelon, "The Paper Economy," in Norman Podkoretz, editor: *The Commentary Reader*, pp. 489-506. (From *Commentary*, September, 1962.) New York: Atheneum, 1966.

[12] J. Freire d'Andrade: *Freedom Chooses Slavery*, p. 61. New York: Coward-McCann, 1959.

into life humanitarian ideals." [13] The conclusion under Marxist socialism is that people do not work for money, because it is largely worthless, but for the avoidance of force, because savage penalties are attached to failure to work. The quality of work rapidly declines. In the Soviet economy, money is related entirely to politics and only incidentally to economics.

In the Western interventionist economics, welfarism destroys the will to work even as it weakens the money by its inflationary pressure. As Von Mises noted, "Social insurance has thus made the neurosis of the insured a dangerous public disease. Should the institution be extended and developed, the disease will spread. No reform can be of any assistance. We cannot weaken or destroy the will to health without producing illness." [14] The erosion of man and of money goes hand in hand. As men become worthless, their economy becomes worthless also, because they are both spiritually and materially decapitalized.

The heir of such exhaustion is a totalitarian regime which climaxes the decapitalization by attacking Christianity and by issuing fiat money, purely political money. Capital is the product of work and thrift, i.e., of character of some degree, of the ability to work productively and by thrift to accumulate capital in order to increase productivity. The basic decapitalization is the decapitalization of character. It is followed by the decapitalization of material wealth. The cry of the people then is for a return to the slavery of Egypt. This return can be forestalled only by a Christian recapitalization.

[13] *Ibid.*
[14] Ludwig von Mises: *Socialism*, p. 478. New Haven: Yale University Press, 1951.

5

MONEY AND PROGRESS

A minister, when asked his opinion of the gold crisis, stated emphatically that gold was an arbitrary and meaningless symbol and that, if men agreed to make wooden tokens the legal tender of a nation, it would do as well or better than gold. This minister, a moderately conservative man, was, without intending to be one, implicitly an atheist. He was denying that there is any fundamental law order in economics or any other sphere, any God-given framework of law that governs every aspect of creation. When pushed to his theological foundations, he denied the validity of law in favor of grace. But grace without law is not only antinomian, it is anti-God. God is either totally God, or He is not God at all. God either governs absolutely in every sphere of creation, or He governs in none, because the creation is then an independent existence and its own savior. The question, are there valid laws of economics, or is economics an area of pragmatic practice and social convention, is then a question with reference to the existence of God. And the biblical position is that every sphere, economic, political, educational, social, marital, scientific, and all others are governed by the absolute laws of God and are set within a context of law.

But this minister is not alone in his opinion. On December 5, 1967, Federal Reserve Board Chairman W. M. Martin condemned gold as a "barbarous metal" and said that the United States "must not bow down to the idol of gold again. Somewhere you are going to learn to trust the Government for you cannot go on indefinitely relying on gold." [1] Martin's dramatic statement, trust in gold versus trust in civil government, in a measure both disguises the issue and

[1] *Myers' Financial Review*, December 19, 1967, no. 24a, p. 3, 304 Lancaster Bldg., Calgary, Alberta, Canada.

also states it baldly. The implication is that trust in man and a man-made order is superior to a trust in God and a God-given order. The plain choice offered is gold versus the state. The rapid outflow of gold into the hands of private persons all over the world is an indication of the choice which men are making.

The state, however, is making its choice also. Because the various central governments deny God and law, they deny the validity of economics. And, however protectively they may act with reference to foreign currencies, they are basically committed to the principle that there is no God and that man is his own law-maker in every realm, including economics.

This basic lack of faith reveals itself even in ostensibly conservative periodicals. Their conservatism is based on the same premise as is the state's monetary radicalism, namely, a denial of fundamental law. This appeared clearly in *U. S. News & World Report*:

> The dollar's future is uncertain. But there are two things that are certain:
> *The dollar is weak.
> *Yet the rest of the world is afraid to try anything except the dollar as the basis for world business. So industrial countries are ready to do practically anything to protect the dollar. They don't want today's world monetary system to collapse. . . .
> The U. S. must take action itself. What does the U. S. have to do?
> First, the U. S. must hold down prices. This means higher taxes and tighter credit. It also means a rise in unemployment to above 4 per cent of the labor force.
> Second, restrictions may be necessary on the flow of private capital overseas. . . .
> Legally, there is no reason why the U. S. must sell gold to anybody for any purpose. Our policy of selling gold is just that—a policy.
> We didn't attempt to hold the price of gold at $35 an ounce on the free market until 1960. We started then only because somebody thought it looked bad for the market price to get too high.[2]

[2] "An Authority Tells: What to Do to Strengthen the Dollar," in *U. S. News and World Report*, January 1, 1968, vol. LXIV, no. 1, p. 53. The "authority" is not named in this article.

A week later, this same periodical stated the case even more plainly:

> Why not just forget about gold as a measure of the value of the U. S. dollar?
> That's a good question. If gold no longer were considered a "money" metal—supported in price by the U. S.—some experts think it would be less than $10 an ounce, not $35 an ounce. The lower price, it is said, would be the value of gold to jewellers and industry.[3]

In essence, the thesis implicit in these statements is simply this:

1. Value is basically conferred by state action. A monetary system is what the state makes it. Wealth is a fiat creation of the state, as is money also.
2. There is therefore no market value that can sustain a currency or some form of wealth apart from state action.
3. The fault for inflation lies essentially in labor and in capital, rather than in the state. As a result, wage and price controls must be instituted to limit the spending capacities of the people, while freeing the state for more inflationary activity. Freedom is the sickness, controls the answer to the problem from this perspective.

An atheist cannot be expected to trust in God; an atheist state cannot be expected to believe very long in objective economic law. The blindness of the United States and of other nations in the silver crisis and in the gold crisis has been because of their denial of objective law. These statists believe, not in *objective* law, but in *positive* law, statist law. As a result, in every monetary crisis their answer is to search for the right combination of statist controls as the solution to problems. Since they deny objective law, the standpoint of objective economics is to them simply a call to anarchy, because for them there is no reality to economic law.

Social progress comes with the accumulation and development of *wealth*. Wealth comes, in a free economy, as a product of *work and thrift*—in short, of character. Capital is often accumulated by inheritance, a God-given right which is strongly stressed in the Bible.

[3] "If the Dollar Were Devalued—," in *U.S. News and World Report*, January 8, 1968, vol. LXIV, no. 2, p. 48.

According to Proverbs 13:22, "A good man leaveth an inheritance to his children's children: and the wealth of the sinner is laid up for the just." Inheritance makes possible the accumulation not only of wealth within a family but of social power. Power is inescapable in any social order: it can either be concentrated in the state, or it can be allowed to flourish wherever ability makes it possible among the people. This decentralized wealth means also decentralized and independent power. Instead of a concentration of power in the state, there is instead a decentralization of power which moves in terms of varying and independent goals.

Again, in a free economy, *property* is freed from the restrictions of the state because it is under the restrictions of the family and of a religiously oriented community. In biblical law, there is no property tax, which means a basic and inalienable social security in the family and in property. The security of a man in his property, and in his inheritance, means a stability in the social order which is productive of progress.

Moreover, in a free economy, the monetary basis, the currency, is gold and silver. The value of gold and silver coinage is a value independent of state action; the Austro-Hungarian order is gone, but the gold coins of that realm are still valuable, as is the gold coinage of tsarist Russia and imperial Germany. The result is an independent wealth which can function on a variety of fronts to effect social progress.

These three factors then are basic to social progress in a free economy: inheritance, freedom of property, and hard money, i.e., gold and silver.

The state, however, is no less concerned with progress than the people. Indeed, the state concerns itself more directly with progress than does a free economy, where it is a by-product in some respects of a variety of independent goals. The state *plans* for progress, and the state requires *wealth* to institute its plans for progress. The state as a result must be able to create wealth in order to fulfil its social goals, because wealth is its *fuel*.

The state creates wealth for itself, in order to further its social goals and its plan for progress in a number of ways. *First* of all, the state *taxes*. The more ambitious the plans for progress, the heavier the tax, because funds must be forthcoming in order to further the plan. The scope of taxation as a result increases: property, income, production, sales, inheritance, investments, all things become subject to a progressively confiscatory tax.

A *second* central means of gaining wealth which the state employs is *borrowing*. A national debt becomes a symbol of progress, and it is not a matter of concern to the planners because it represents the plan in progress, and it means ultimate wealth for the state and its people, it is believed. In order to borrow more easily, the state enters into the control of banking and creates its own controlling bank, such as the earlier Bank of the U. S., and the present more powerful Federal Reserve System. By means of this control, the state has access to the bank savings and deposits of all its people, and it can issue bonds and replace the bank deposits with bonds. The interest on the bonds, as well as the principal, is secured by taxing the same people, and by inflationary policies.

Third, the state creates wealth, for example by printing more money progressively, which, with borrowings, is also an inflationary policy, and a more drastic one. It also debases the coinage, and creates wealth by circulating a low value coin at a high value, a 25¢ piece worth 2 - 3¢ for 25¢.

There are thus two contrasting approaches to social progress. The complaint against the free economy is that it penalizes the less capable and the less provident and the lazy in favor of men of ability, industry, and foresight. This is clearly true. *Every social order exacts a penalty;* the only difference is in the parties penalized. In the statist social order, it is precisely the men who are hard-working, provident, and thrifty who are penalized in favor of the state and its welfare recipients. Another penalty of the statist economy is its corruption of the people. Debt becomes a way of life, and it infects the once-conservative areas of society.

Most conservatives are today socialists without knowing it. Such men favor federal economy but not personal economy, and they are head over heels in debt. Their ideas of personal progress involves debt. Their personal economy is therefore geared to inflation, to more and more cheap money. They live in terms of inflation and demand it when their work is threatened. They go into debt to cash in on the inflation and then scream if the inflationary credit crunch cycles hurt them. Men who are in debt and who live in terms of debt favor inflation and socialism: for them, wealth is living off another man's providence and profit.

As a result, a *free economy produces, and a statist economy consumes*: wealth for the one means production, for the other, consumption. The free economy protects capital, wealth, by eliminating bad risks for capital, by subjecting bad risks to the elimination process of profit and loss and the market economy. The statist economy creates wealth by burning up capital to produce a consumption geared to planned goals. Thus, atomic power is produced, not because a market economy has tested it and found it profitable, but because a welfare economy has subsidized atomic power as a goal. Atomic power may prove to be valid from the standpoint of a free economy, but, *as produced by a statist economy*, it has consumed wealth by taxation in order to produce a consumer-orientated goal.

It is inescapable, therefore, that the statist economy sooner or later finds itself in trouble. It shows its wealth by burning up capital. Like the man who burned $100 bills to demonstrate his wealth, the welfare economy consumes capital to prove its wealth. But, before the statist economy can appear, the free economy itself has begun to wither, in that the faith and character which produces work and thrift leading to economic growth gives way to conspicuous consumption. The result is an era of "big spenders," men of wealth who consume capital in conspicuous display." [4] The private "big spenders" are followed by the federal and statist "big spenders"; conspicuous display is now a part of the national character, and both statist and private economies are in serious trouble.

In such a situation, the blame is placed at once upon some foreign power, upon speculators, hoarders, upon a variety of causes other than the essential one. Walter W. Heller, economist, has declared

[4] See Lucius Beebe: *The Big Spenders*. New York: Pocket Books, 1967 (1965).

that the United States should invite the whole world to get all its gold at $35 an ounce:

> Perhaps also, he said, the United States should "invite the world to 'come and get it' as a demonstration that the dollar is not only as good as, but better than gold."
>
> "Perhaps we also need to expose gold speculators, both official and unofficial, to down-side risk. One approach would remove our pledge to buy gold at $35 an ounce, while maintaining our pledge to sell at that price.
>
> "Finally, we need to think about the unthinkable—our dollar devaluation—if only to show why it is unworkable, even if not unthinkable. Even if we wanted to devalue, which we clearly don't, who would let us?
>
> "As country after country matched our devaluation, the up-shot would be simply to raise the price of gold, to the delight of gold hoarders and gold producers. How much more rational and equitable it would be to activate and expand our new reserve asset, the SDRs, and at last free the world economy from its gold bondage."
>
> (The SDRs are the "supplementary drawing rights" approved in principle in September by member nations of the International Monetary Fund as an additional source of foreign exchange for the settlement of international obligations—in effect, a new international currency.)[5]

There are more errors in this statement than we have time to analyze, but one in particular is our concern, the SDRs. Heller called this "our new reserve asset." The SDRs are simply another form of loan available to member nations, i.e., an additional area of credit for bad credit risks who cannot borrow money elsewhere. The problem faced by the various nations is too much debt. The answer proposed is more debt. This is a cure as sensible as liquor to cure an alcoholic; but this is precisely the rationale of a statist economy: wealth is consumption, wealth is living on borrowed money, taxed and confiscated wealth, and on counterfeit currency.

This credit or wealth which is consumed is the capital of Christian civilization. The Christian West has been replaced by a new pseudo-

[5] "Heller Proposes Bold Moves to Fortify Dollar," in the Los Angeles *Times*, Wednesday, January 3, 1968, Part I, p. 19. In March, 1968, the two-bier so-called "free market" in gold was inaugurated.

international culture for which consumption is an ultimate human value. The humanism of the new order sees no value beyond man, and man's desires. Therefore, his consumption is an ultimate value in such a culture. Amery has, without condemnation, but simply as a reporter, remarked of this new civilization:

> In contrast to this, in the art of our contemporary mass civilization, *everything, as a matter of principle, is permitted.* Art is free. Valuations of it can no longer be derived from any basic principles. It is pledged to no idea, to no ideology. Its boundaries are determined solely by the market, which during prosperous times has a powerful capacity for absorption, and (to a lesser degree) by a few communities of taste whose members declare themselves to be experts.[6]

The new civilization has "only one point of reference—consumption."[7] In defense of this, Amery observed, "Consumption . . . can certainly also be an ultimate value."[8] Indeed it can, but consumption as an ultimate value is erosive and destructive of civilization, in that it eats up the heritage of the past while becoming progressively unproductive.

We began by stating that the issue with respect to gold is an issue more centrally with respect to God. Is there an ultimate and absolute order, and does God's sovereign law establish an inescapable order with respect to every sphere, so that transgression of that law brings social penalties and decay? Or is humanism true, and the only value is man and his desires, his pleasure in consumption, display, and expression? The monetary crisis reflects a cultural crisis.

Those opposing welfare economics must of necessity have a sound monetary policy. But a sound monetary policy rests in the framework of absolute law, in the basic premise of the sovereign and absolute God whose law-order governs all reality. Without this faith, the conservative's economics lacks the consistency of the statist's. The monetary policies of socialism reflect, after all, a consistent faith in the ultimacy and sovereignty of man and man's ability to

[6] Jean Amery: *Preface to the Future, Culture in a Consumer Society*, p. 275. London: Constable, 1964.
[7] *Ibid.*, p. 298.
[8] *Ibid.*, p. 299.

create his own law, money, and world at will. Here as elsewhere the question is simply this: who is God? If the Lord be God, then follow Him. But if Baal be god, then Baal must be followed. Not without significance, the U. S. coinage, from the days of the Civil War, bore the imprint, "In God We Trust." Chairman Martin has another answer: "Trust the Government." Of the outcome of such a course, there can be no doubt.

Unsound monetary practices are the state's practical denial of God and a declaration that the state is god. Of the dislike of sound money by the new economists, Rist wrote:

> In reality, those theoreticians dislike monetary stability because they dislike the fact that by means of money the individual may escape the arbitrariness of the government. Stable money is one of the last arms that remains at the disposal of the individual to direct his own affairs, whether it be an enterprise or a simple household. It is certain that nothing so facilitates the seizure of all activities by the government as its liberty of action in monetary matters.[9]

Their hatred of gold is more than a matter of economics. Similarly, our hatred of unsound economics must involve more than economics. It must be grounded not only in a love of freedom, but, above all, in a religious faith, in biblical Christianity.

[9] Charles Rist: *The Triumph of Gold*, p. 139. New York: Philosophical Library, 1961.

6

A BIBLICAL VIEW OF THE PROBLEM OF INTEREST

Because of the influence of Pietism, in recent centuries the church has withdrawn from many of the problems which once deeply concerned the Christian world. One of these problems is the question of interest or usury. Originally, and in the Bible, the two words were identical in meaning; they have come, in recent modern times, to be differentiated, *interest* being legitimate rent for money, and *usury* a high or an illegitimate rent for money. The Bible makes no such distinction; where interest or usury is legitimate, it is governed by the market-place, not by legislation; where it is not legitimate, any rate is immoral.

The early church adhered here as elsewhere strictly to the Mosaic law *as it interpreted it*, and interest was accordingly banned, a prohibition which endured in various forms for centuries. In part, the church's prohibition was based on the hope of a totally Christian society, in which all men, as brothers in Christ, ministered to each other's needs. The biblical law is more realistic.

Howard B. Rand, in his *Digest of Biblical Law*, declared that the Bible forbad interest, a statement which Scripture contradicts. H. B. Clark's *Biblical Law* gives a better report of the pertinent legislation and commentary.

The biblical law sees believers as brethren, with mutual obligations one to another. In time of need, believers are to seek the relief of their brethren's need and this charity is administered personally and through religious channels, the deacons' fund in the New Testament (Acts 6:1-6). This relief was never a subsidy for laziness: "if any would not work, neither should he eat" (II Thess. 3:10). Where financial help was needed, loans could be made. These loans, an aspect of brotherly love and charity, had certain requirements. First, they had to be without interest: "Thou shalt not lend upon usury to thy brother: usury of money, usury of victuals, usury of any thing that is lent upon usury" (Deut. 23:19). *Second*, borrowing by the poor is permitted for emergency reasons, but it is discouraged, for "the borrower is a servant (or slave) to the lender" (Prov. 22:7). The believer must seek to avoid debt as far as possible: "Owe no man any thing, but to love one another" (Rom. 13:8; the word owe, opheilo, appears also in Matt. 18:28; Luke 7:41; 16:5, 7; Philem. 18, always with reference to money. Other non-monetary uses of the verb appear in John 13:14; 19:7; Acts 17:29, etc.; the monetary meaning was at least the primary sense of opheilo). The believer is by nature a free man, and hence debt is an abnormal even though sometimes necessary way of life for him. *Third*, while works of mercy towards unbelievers are emphatically stressed by the Mosaic law, the difference between believer and unbeliever is also stressed, and a separation required. The unbeliever is not a free man; he is a slave to sin. It is therefore foolish charity to assume that he is free. The very law which speaks of charity in the form of a non-interest bearing loan to a believer declares that such charity is not for the unbeliever: "Unto a stranger thou mayest lend upon usury . . ." (Deut. 23:20). For the unbeliever, debt is a way of life, because his unregenerate nature makes him a slave. There is no point in useless charity. *Fourth*, even charity must be business-like, in that, while a gift is a gift, and the foregoing of interest is a gift, a loan must be protected. The ability to lend is a privilege and a power (Deut. 15:6). Security was required usually, and the requirement of a security prevented the borrower from making more than one loan on his property (Ex. 22:25-27). The maximum life of a debt was six years (Deut. 15:1-6, 12-18). No believer has the right to mortgage his future indefinitely, nor does a godly nation have any such right. St. Paul, despite some trying situations when he "wanted," i.e., was in need, prided himself that "I was chargeable to no man" (II Cor. 11:9). As a servant of the Lord, he avoided becoming the servant of man (I Cor. 7:23). *Fifth*, it is clear from the foregoing that the biblical law with respect to interest had reference to charity, to help extended to a brother in the faith. In such a case, the law took care lest the borrower and lender exploit each other, and the law protected the act from abuse. The failure of a society of believers to maintain God's moral law, and charity one towards another, means death for that society or community (Ezek. 18). But the reference in these things is to the personal relations of believers, not to their business activities. Unbelievers could be and must be the object of acts of godly mercy, as the Parable of the Good Samaritan makes clear (Luke 10:30-37), but the inner life of the redeemed community has special laws for special needs in terms of the greater responsibility of redeemed men. Apart from this realm of charity, interest has a legitimate sphere. Jesus spoke of it in Matthew 25:27. If such an investment of money at interest had been immoral, the whole point of the parable would have been destroyed in the minds of the hearers. To suggest an immoral act as a necessary one would have given the Pharisees a major weapon against Jesus.

This biblical pattern long influenced colonial and early America. The six-year debt span is still reflected in bankruptcy laws. Clark, in *Biblical Law*, noted that "Modern statutes of limitation and bankruptcy acts fulfill the purpose of the ancient law of sabbatical release—the former by forbidding the bringing of an action upon a debt after a certain number of years and the latter enabling a debtor to turn over his property in satisfaction of his debts." The spirit of these laws, however, is greatly abused.

Prior to World War I, the United States normally saw no personal debts except for homes and land. Installment buying was an alien concept. Debt living has since then become the normal situation, both for persons and businesses. The medieval hostility to interest was not biblical, although its intent was religious. The modern debt-living is alien to biblical law in intent as well as execution.

7

USURY AND COSMIC IMPERSONALISM

The modern system of commercial credit has been traced back to Babylon, the great source of modern financial enterprise. As against this system and history, another concept early made its appearance in man's records, the biblical law. The biblical concept was subverted steadily after the Babylonian Captivity, revived by the Christian Church, and is now again in eclipse.

There was a developed system of commercial credit in Babylon, but no such system in ancient Israel.[1] In normative biblical culture, it was always the poor who borrowed.[2] These were then debts of emergency and hence speedily repaid[3] when the emergency ended. The "emergency" might be, as with Judah, not a valid one, but only a temporary exigency normally led to debt. More usually, debts in Israel were the products of failures of crops and heavy foreign tribute.[4] Borrower and lender were cited by Isaiah as types in the nation,[5] but it is significant that the Hebrew had no clear-cut word for *debtor*, which fact appears in I Samuel 22:2. The reading here for *debtor* is "everyone that was in debt," or, as the marginal reading gives it, "every one that had a creditor." This would indicate that a debtor class did not exist, no word existing for it. Emergency situations, famines, wars, such things led to debt, and tragedy as well,[6] but normal times were relatively debt-free times.

To borrow meant tragedy, and hence the necessity of graciousness

[1] See W. H. Bennett, "Debt," in James Hastings, ed., *A Dictionary of the Bible*, vol. I, p. 579f. New York: Charles Scribner's Sons, 1919.
[2] Exodus 22:25.
[3] Genesis 38:18.
[4] Nehemiah 5:3, 4.
[5] Isaiah 24:2.
[6] II Kings 4:1-7.

on the part of the lender.[7] The blessing of God meant a debt-free economy.[8] Mercy toward the needy was to be exercised even when the jubilee year was nigh, loans being made despite the nearness of cancellation time.[9]

Debts were limited by the sabbatical year and jubilee. Debts of money, if not repaid, were cancelled on the seventh year, not of issue but in cycles of forty-nine. The fiftieth year, the jubilee, led to a restoration of foreclosed lands, so that foreclosures were valid to the middle and end of each century (when this law was observed). The land was to rest, to lie fallow, on each seventh year, this being the *release* of the land as well as of debts.[10] The Babylonian Captivity lasted seventy years because seventy sabbath years were due to the land,[11] the captivity coming "To fulfill the word of the LORD by the mouth of Jeremiah, until the land had enjoyed her sabbaths: for as long as she lay desolate she kept the sabbath, to fulfil threescore and ten years." [12] The release of debts every seventh year[13] did not apply to foreigners, nor did the jubilee, foreigners here meaning unbelieving foreigners.

At this point, the biblical law is often severely criticized as being partial. The criticism is unjust. The law required *justice to all men*, Leviticus 19 making clear that our neighbor is every foreigner. To all such, the second table of the law is strictly applied. We must expect all men to keep it, and we must abide by it ourselves. To love our neighbor or enemy means to keep the second table of the law.[14] To love in the biblical sense here used is not an emotional attitude but a keeping of the law in relation to our neighbor. This means respecting his right to life (Thou shalt not kill), the sanctity of his home (Thou shalt not commit adultery), and of his property (Thou shalt not steal), and of his reputation (Thou shalt not bear

[7] Deut. 15:7-11.
[8] Deut. 15:6; 28:12, 44.
[9] Ps. 37:26; 112:5; Prov. 19:17; Ex. 22:25; Deut. 23:19, 20; Lev. 25:36, 37; Ps. 15:5; Prov. 28:8; Ezek. 18:8-17; 22:12; Neh. 5.
[10] See Ex. 23:10ff; Lev. 25:1ff.
[11] Jer. 25:9, 12; 26:6, 7.
[12] II Chron. 36:21.
[13] Deut. 15:1-6.
[14] Matt. 19:18, 19; Rom. 13:8, 9.

false witness), and finally, respecting these things in thought (Thou shalt not covet) as well as in deed.

This is the general law of justice. Beyond that, our conduct is to be regulated by relationship. We must render honor and justice to all men wherever due, but we have a particular responsibility to care for our own. This means first of all our families, for the man who fails to care for his own is worse than an infidel.[15] No special gift could be dedicated to God and accounted acceptable if a man meanwhile failed to provide for his parents.[16] Next in order of concern are fellow believers, true believers. Here, however, no false charity was allowed to prevail.[17] The biblical laws forbad false charity. But, to the deserving, in addition to gleaning permission, and emergency relief, non-interest loans were made. There was a duty of lending and of paying.[18] Pledges or security could be required to protect the lender, but the law restricted the type of security which could be exacted.[19] The creditor could not enter the home to remove the security but had to wait outside.[20] Some pious men required no pledge[21] or else would promptly restore it.[22]

Biblical conduct is regulated by relationship, and to subvert this is to lead directly into welfare economics and socialism. If a man must exercise towards all men the same care, oversight, and charity he does towards his own family, then an impossible burden is placed on him. Statist foreign policy places this burden on men, a form of enslavement. Biblical ethics, by calling for justice to all men, brotherly love among believers, and full care for one's own, is an ethics of freedom and responsibility. Every system of "universal" ethics is at one and the same time a system of universal slavery. A man's relationship to his wife is ethically different from his relationship to all other women, and the same applies to his children, parents, and relatives. To universalize the relationship is to communize man

15 I Timothy 5:8.
16 Matt. 15:4,5,6; Mark 7:11,12.
17 II Thess. 3:10,11.
18 Luke 6:34,35; Rom. 13:8; cf. Matt. 6:12.
19 Deut. 24:17; 24:6; Job 24:3.
20 Deut. 24:10-13.
21 Job 22:6; 24:9.
22 Ezek. 18:7-16; 33:15.

and the family and to destroy the church. And today the family is weak, and the church very fragile, because of this unbiblical universalism.

Usury to the believer is forbidden,[23] first, because this poor man belongs to the people of God and has lost a measure of freedom through troubles and needs help, and second, usury adds to his burden. The believer is to avoid debt, because, as God's servant, he cannot be men's servant. Leviticus 25:36, 37 held to no interest on loans to a believer, and no limitation on interest to an unbeliever. This is restated in Deuteronomy 23:19, 20 with reference to foreigners, i.e., unbelievers.

Thus, years 7, 14, 21, 28, 35, 42, 49, and 50 of each fifty-year cycle called for sabbaths of the land and of debts. Two very important principles are clearly apparent here:

1. The believer cannot mortgage his future. His life belongs to God, and he cannot sell out his tomorrows to men, nor bind his family's or country's future. This means that long-term personal loans, deficit financing, and national debts involve paganism. What we cannot do to ourselves we cannot permit either our families or our fellow believers to do to themselves. A country which is Christian is similarly to be governed. But we cannot expect unbelievers to live by our faith or by God's law; and to allow them the liberty of their way is no sin, providing we deal justly with them.

2. The land also belongs to God. As Scripture repeatedly affirms, "The earth is the Lord's." The land therefore must be used in conformity to His law.

The believer lives in a world of unbelievers, and commercial credit is the order of the day. Interest is not condemned in the New Testament,[24] but debt on the part of believers is to be avoided.[25] However, the intrusion of Babylonian practices into the temple met with Christ's whip.[26] The believer must be in the world but not of the world.[27]

---

23 Ex. 22:25.
24 Luke 7:41, 42; 19:11-27; Matt. 18:23-35; 25:14-30; Luke 16:1-13.
25 Rom. 13:8, 9.
26 Matt. 21:12f; Mark. 11:15-18; Luke 19:45-48; John 2:12-17.
27 John 17:14, 15.

The modern system of commercial credit is, like the Babylonian, a form of *slavery*. The Civil War saw the abolition of limited *private* slavery, involving three million people, and the imposition of slavery to the state and the furtherance of slavery to financial interests. Some people are by nature slaves, demanding total security of a master, employer, or of the state. But to impose slavery on our children is no less a sin.[28]

The Sabbath and Jubilee Years again are central. These were types, as was the weekly Sabbath, of the restoration of paradise and the work of Christ. Man ceases from working because he knows it is God's work of grace that saves him. All days of rest in other religions are imitations of biblical faith. No day of rest existed otherwise. Other religions, Babylonian and Pharisaic, are in essence and practice *works* religions. Christianity, as was true Old Testament faith, is not; hence, it rests in worship to indicate that salvation is not man's work. The rest of the land involved confidence that God's bounty would more than replenish what was lost by man's inactivity. DeTocqueville commented on the importance of the Christian Sabbath in the American republic. The decline of that day of rest has gone hand in hand with the rise of a works religion and a credit economy which mortgages man's future. The deeper significance of this external parallel is that civil slavery is the analogue of spiritual blindness and bondage. But, "If my people, which are called by my name, shall humble themselves, and pray, and seek may face, and turn from their wicked ways; then will I hear from heaven, and will forgive their sin, and will heal their land." [29]

The difference between the Babylonian and biblical outlooks has been cited; it remains now to develop it briefly. Economic man had high authority in Babylonian culture. War was seen in essentially economic terms and as a means to economic power. To the Babylonians of Nebuchadnezzar's day, "What mattered to them, so far as the king's victories were concerned, was not the glory of battle so much as the fact that it was a means of consolidating their economic supremacy." [30]

28 Ex. 21:16; Deut. 24:7.
29 II Chron. 7:14.
30 Albert Champdor: *Babylon*, p. 114. New York: J. P. Putnam's Sons, 1958.

The roots, however, lie deeper, back into the Old Babylonian period of Hammurabi and earlier. There was a class known as *tamkaru* (singular *tamkarum*). The word *tamkarum* can be translated as merchant, broker, merchant banker, money-lender, and government agent.[31] Fulfilling all these functions, he was an able instrument of imperial power, in that, long before any armies marched, he had bound foreign powers to himself both hand and foot. This same policy characterized Assyria, and Nahum cited as a central sin of Assyria before God that it had "multiplied merchants above the stars of heaven," [32] i.e., exercised economic slavery in one area after another. The Babylonians were money-lenders not only out of dedicated policy but with fervor, zest, and relish. One of their proverbs expresses this outlook clearly: "The giving of a loan is like making love; the returning of a loan is like having a son born." [33] They were thus a breed of proud and happy Shylocks. Their whole world of business moved in terms of credit financing, and their whole concept of social control and of imperialism rested on usury. It is not surprising that Babylon the Great, the harlot, is the type in Revelation of the one-world order which shall seduce all nations.

For biblical economy, loans are not the basis of normal operation as with Babylon, but of abnormal circumstances. As such, and definitely as such, they have their place, but they operate in terms of implicit as well as explicit restrictions. Two kinds of loans were recognized: to the believer without usury but with security, and to the unbeliever, with usury and security. But in both instances the presupposition is that something *real*, in goods or in money, is transferred, a tangible asset involving only the two parties to the contract. Modern banking, however, is radically different. Banks "create" money by fiat and by the unilateral action of simply recording a loan and a deposit on their books. The consequence is, not the personal and limited action of a biblical loan, but inflation, the dilution of the prior relationship of money units to total goods and services. As a

[31] H. W. F. Saggs: *The Greatness that Was Babylon*, p. 287f. New York: Hawthorn, 1962.
[32] Nahum 3:16.
[33] Saggs, p. 290.

result, there is a dilution of all money, and such "loans" mean an element of robbery in that they reduce the value of all other money units previously in existence. Fractional reserves and modern central banking (i.e., the Federal Reserve System) are modern applications of the old Babylonian principles and are equally conducive to the dream of empire.

Prior to the introduction of central banking, the ability to create fiat money was relatively limited, and it depended in large measure on the confidence of individuals in the local bank. Today, the instrument of control has passed to the larger units, and the Federal Reserve System, its directors and stockholders, the Treasury Department, the Federal Deposit Insurance Corporation, and other agencies are engaged in manipulating the money supply. In 1959, "Federal Reserve notes comprised 90% of paper money in circulation and 84% of total money in circulation." [34]

Biblical law is hostile to this pyramiding of credit. It is premised on immediate responsibility, whereas the Babylonian and modern systems evade immediate responsibility. Today, the law penalizes the individual with almost unlimited liabilities, so that every kind of insurance is necessary for the individual as homeowner, driver, and parent (in the event that his child blackens a bully's eyes). On the other hand, corporate irresponsibility is fostered by limited liability laws which, over a period of time, separate property from control, ownership from management, and management from responsibility. Social irresponsibility is thus furthered, and the responsible man hamstrung. Biblical faith declares that a personal God created every fact in the universe, so that every fact is a personal fact. Impersonality is thus ruled out of the universe. As we deal with ourselves and everything under the sun, we deal also with our very personal Creator. Any attempt to introduce impersonality into the universe is to that degree an attempt to separate the universe from the government of God.[35] The impersonal economics of Babylon and of today are

34 Thomas C. Cochrane, Wayne Andrews, eds.: *Concise Dictionary of American History*, p. 711. New York: Charles Scribner's Sons, 1962.
35 In 1664, Thomas Mun, in *England's Treasure By Forraign Trade*, espoused usury in terms of its purely impersonal values to England. This scientism and impersonalism were commended without any attempt to deal sys-

thus anti-biblical and are attempts to substitute fiat "creations" of man for the absolute government of God. As such, they incur the wrath of God, whose advance judgment Scripture proclaims: "Babylon the great is fallen, is fallen. . . . And the merchants of the earth shall weep and mourn over her. . . ." [36] In terms of this comes the summons, "Come out of her, my people, that ye be not partakers of her sins, and that ye receive not of her plagues." [37]

In conclusion, in Scripture interest was legal for loans which were not charity loans. Debt was not to be a normal thing or a way of life. Debt was an emergency, or "need," matter, not normally a consumption loan, and only a severely conservative production loan.

tematically with the Christian issues involved. Mun was republished in 1949 by Basil Blackwell, Oxford, and is an excellent example of good, non-theistic economic thought.

[36] Rev. 18:2, 11.
[37] Rev. 18:4.

LIMITED LIABILITY AND UNLIMITED MONEY

In the middle of the 19th century, liberal regimes in England passed legislation which was designed to suit the convenience of various elements of the commercial community: joint-stock companies were given the privilege of limited liability. Arthur Bryant has called attention to the implications of this step:

> Up to this time a man's power to make money by transferring his credit and freedom of commercial action to others was restrained by his liability for the obligations they might incur. This check on irresponsible delegation was now removed. A man could grow rich in security and even innocence from business practices which would have outraged his conscience as an individual. He could avoid both the risks and stigma of transactions done by others in pursuit of profits which he shared.[1]

At first, Bryant points out, the investing public was slow in taking advantage of the act. After the failure of the City of Glasgow Bank in 1879, many shareholders were required to meet financial obligations "hundreds of times greater than the value of their shares." This started a trend to limited liability concerns, which became marked in the last eight years of the century. As Bryant observed,

> The consequences of the Companies Act of 1862 were perhaps greater than that of any single measure in English parliamentary history. They completed the divorce between the Christian conscience and the economic practice of everyday life. They paganised the commercial community. Henceforward an astute man by adherence to legal rules which had nothing to do with morality could grow immensely rich by virtue of shuffling off

[1] Arthur Bryant: *English Saga (1840-1940)*, p. 215. London: Collins with Eyre & Spottiswoode, 1940.

his most elementary obligations to his fellows He could not only grow rich by such means. He could grow immensely rich.[2]

The rise of limited liability companies created a new, managerial aristocracy. It also established a sharp and hard division between employer and employee. Again, Bryant's discerning analysis needs citing:

> . . . by directing money into enterprises designed not so much for stable long-term production as for quick capital appreciation the new financier tended to make industrial employment even more precarious than it had been before. Mushroom companies sprang up in all directions to initiate or develop industrial processes which could have little or no enduring future. This directly affected the working man and his social background. More than ever his job and home became dependent on circumstances beyond his control. As an individual he became more and more helpless.
> The stimulus to joint stock manufacturing and trading afforded by the principle of limited liability had another fatal consequence on the life of the working man. Under *laissez-faire* individualism it at least paid to be efficient. The workman who by his skill and industry furthered the interests of his employer had a reasonable chance of promotion, for he was too valuable to lose. But when the control of business passed out of the hands of the private employer using his own capital into that of the financial company representing an intangible mass of absentee shareholders without active knowledge of its affairs, the industrious workman found it increasingly difficult to better himself. His efficiency and steadfastness had no value to directors whose only aim was to sell the concern that employed him at an inflated value. In any case he was less likely to be noticed by managers whose stake in the business was confined to salaries paid them by the shareholders and who were not personally interested in its successes. Thus the conscientious workman was increasingly discouraged. The man with ambition and intelligence, instead of identifying himself with the industrial system of which he was a part, was driven to rebel against it. Instead of becoming a small capitalist, he became a socialist.

Adam Smith had always maintained that manufacturing by joint-stock companies must prove injurious to the public interest. He argued that efficiency and consequently wealth resulted

[2] *Ibid.*, p. 215f.

from every man attending scrupulously to his own self-interest. Such attention could not be successfully delegated.[3]

Very early in the history of the United States, some states made legal the limited liability company, but such concerns were not too commonly established. They were regarded as essentially irresponsible, and they failed to attract capital. After the Civil War, the moral and industrial climate changed, and, as in England, such concerns began to succeed.

Limited liability did not become legal without extensive opposition. The opponents of limited liability believed that it would in the end destroy capitalism. They believed, in fact, that a principle of responsibility which is basic to free enterprise was at stake in the issue. To understand the nature of their opposition to limited liabiliy, it is important to analyse their arguments. George Sweet, writing in England in 1855, and in part answering John Stuart Mill's objection to the English law which then prohibited partnerships with limited liability to creditors, pointed out that to expect the state to limit liability for trade debts, without limiting profits, was hardly a valid premise. The prohibition of limited liability placed responsibility where it belonged, both morally and commercially:

> He who transacts any business on behalf of another, whether avowedly or not, binds his employer by all that he does while acting in the business confided to him; so that a merchant is answerable even for the fraud of his factor in selling one kind of goods for another. And Lord Chief Justice Holt gives a sound reason for this:—"Seeing that some one must be a loser by the deceit, it is more reason that he that employs and puts a trust and confidence in the deceiver should be loser than a stranger." [4]

Liability is inescapable; by limiting the liability of the company which contracts a debt, or permits a fraud, the liability is then passed on to innocent parties. Limited liability thus shifts responsibility away from the responsible to society at large. A partner or shareholder in a company will exercise cautious and conscien-

[3] *Ibid.*, p. 217.
[4] George Sweet: *Limited Liability, Observations on the Existing and the Proposed Rules for Ascertaining the Debtor in Mercantile Dealings*, p. 9. London: H. Sweet, 1855.

tious control over his company, if his liability for the debts and frauds of that company are not limited to the extent of his investment. The result is sound, moral, and careful management of a company by the actual owners. But, with limited liability, a premium is placed on profit irrespective of responsibility. The shareholder is less concerned with buying responsible ownership and more concerned with buying a share in profits. And then, as the state further protects the shareholder against liabilities in his irresponsible pursuit of profits, the shareholder becomes less and less concerned with the responsible and moral management of his company.

As Sweet noted, with respect to the "prohibition" of limited liability, "what is here called a prohibition is nothing more than a rule of evidence for ascertaining the real debtor, and a rule which solves the problem in the way most satisfactory to the common sense." [5] Sweet, as a barrister at law, at the Inner Temple, was especially concerned with the legal and moral anarchy implicit in limited liability. We might add too that, since limited liability was in effect a state subsidy to commercial firms at the expense of the public, it was inescapable that, what the state subsidized, the state would eventually also control.

Bramwell and others, in denying that the state had the right to prohibit limited liability, argued on the principle of non-interference, of laissez faire, certainly a strange application of the idea. Sweet answered that "What is called the principle of non-interference, when correctly stated, amounts to no more than this, that unnecessary and mischievous interference with the free agency of subjects is the besetting sin of governments, and should always be held in fear when the propriety of any particular interference is under discussion." [6] A legal requirement of moral responsibility was not wrong. The proponents of limited liability were for a laissez faire attitude regarding moral issues. A Gresham's law factor enters in with their laissez faire immoralism: morally bad concerns drive out good ones.

So when a mercantile undertaking is started with a large

[5] *Ibid.*, p. 11.
[6] *Ibid.*, p. 14.

capital and limited liability, those to whom it offers custom are
under duress to deal with it, however much they may dislike
the limit of liability. They would prefer the English common
law; but finding that limited partnerships obtain credit, they
must either go with the stream or retire from business in favour
of others more adventurous. The reckless debtor thus creates
the reckless trader.[7]

The limited liability company has an advantage over the company
without such protection. Having limited responsibility for its
debts, it is free to take chances which a fully responsibile company
will not take: the limited liability has state protection in its risk-
taking which the other companies do not have. It is not surprising,
therefore, that Sweet's expectations have been fulfilled. Limited
liability is now the routine and standard status of business companies.

The consequences have been twofold. Previously, the fact of
unlimited liability made investors wary of too speculative a company, or unwilling to risk too great a debt. True, Hunt reports on
the fact that some banks were more ready to extend credit rashly
to companies with unlimited liability, thus leading to some over-
extension.[8] But the problems created by the rashness of some unlimited liability companies were few in contrast to those later
created by limited liability companies. The evidence is also strong
that both investors and the public, especially in the United States,
were usually wary of limited liability companies.[9] The *first* effect
of limited liability was the progressive separation of ownership from
responsibility, of management from property. Burnham called it
the "managerial revolution," without analyzing its origins in limited
liability.[10] Berle has also described it as a revolution, one in which
a group of executives control a corporation whose owners have
retained little power over their property: "the historic field of
responsibility—a group of financially interested stockholders to

[7] *Ibid.*, p. 14f.
[8] Bishop Carleton Hunt: *The Development of the Business Corporation in
England 1800-1867.* Cambridge, Massachusetts: Harvard University Press, 1936.
[9] See A. B. Levy: *Private Corporations and Their Control*, vol. I, pp. 109ff.,
113ff., 374, etc. London: Routledge & Kegan Paul, Ltd., 1950.
[10] James Burnham: *The Managerial Revolution.* New York: The John
Day Company, 1941.

which each corporate management must account—is progressively being eliminated." [11] Moreover,

> The rise of the corporate system, with attendant separation of ownership from management due to concentration of industry in the corporate form, was the first great twentieth-century change. In three decades it led to the rise of autonomous corporation management. The second tendency, pooling of savings, voluntary or forced, in fiduciary institutions now is steadily separating the owner (if the stockholder can properly be called an "owner") from his residual ultimate power—that of voting for management. In effect this is gradually removing power of selecting boards of directors and managements from these managements themselves as self-perpetuating oligarchies, to a different and rising group of interests—pension trustees, mutual fund managers and (less importantly) insurance company managements.
>
> These emerging groups are themselves self-perpetuating. Though allied to corporate managements, they are on the margin of that world, closer to the world of bankers than to the world of production and sales executives.[12]

There is a divorce of individuals from economic initiative; there is now "power without property," i.e., without responsible individual ownership; persons and organizations other than owners control or manage property. The stockholders, technically owners, "have the right to receive only. The condition of their being is that they do not interfere in management." [13]

The average "conservative," not liking Berle, tends to reject his argument and call attention to some broad generalizations. Preferring perhaps Roger Blough, they tend to accept his defense of corporations as the more "conservative" position.[14] But the fact still remains that Adam Smith would not call the present order capitalistic. And it can be argued that the limited liability company destroyed capitalism. Free enterprise requires risk, and the risk is taken by the capi-

11 Adolf A. Berle, Jr.: *Power Without Property*, p. 56. New York: Harcourt, Brace, 1959.

12 *Ibid.*, p. 59.

13 *Ibid.*, p. 74.

14 Roger M. Blough: *Free Man and the Corporation*. New York: McGraw-Hill, 1959.

talist, by the entrepreneur. If there is protection from risk, there is protection from freedom, and if the risk is passed on to others at state instigation, it logically follows that the farmer and the working man can claim some form of limited liability from risk, some protection from consequences. *Risk* is inescapable in any and every society; in a free society, full responsibility is assumed by individuals or associations. It is their duty to protect themselves by prudent measures, and, failing that, to assume the consequences. When the risk is assumed by the state and by society at large, the ultimate failure of the entire order is assured, in that the irresponsibility of all the people is encouraged. Capitalism and limited liability are alien concepts.

Second, limited liability has, in the long run, assured a greater readiness by corporations to assume debt. After all, the homes and incomes of those involved are not at stake, but only their limited investment. The effect of this has been to replace a hard money economy with an inflationary credit economy. It is interesting to note that both paper money and limited liability became entrenched in the United States after the Civil War.

Paper money is limited liability money. Gold and silver, and 100% reserve banking and currency, place a state and banking under unlimited liability. (Significantly, banks in the U. S. were among the first to make use of limited liability.) The justification for the Lincoln greenbacks was quite an honest one:

> In his report of December, 1861, Chase laid down his favorite principle, that a paper circulation was a loan without interest made by the people, and that the government was fairly entitled to the profitable privilege. He followed this up by a clear statement, from which he never wavered, "that Congress under its constitutional power to lay taxes, to regulate Commerce, and to regulate the issue of coins possesses ample authority to control the credit circulation." [15]

This is plain speaking, but not quite plain enough. Chase could have added that, not only is paper money a loan without interest made by the people to the state, but it was also ultimately a loan

[15] Albert Bushnell Hart: *Salmon Portland Chase*, p. 276. Boston: Houghton Mifflin, 1899.

without repayment. The issue of the Lincoln greenbacks produced a rise in the price of gold, and a decline in the value of the greenbacks. On June 16, 1864, Chase wrote to Horace Greeley, "The price of gold must and shall come down, or I'll quit and let somebody else try." The next step by the Lincoln administration was to abolish the gold market altogether, having failed to control it. The bill prohibiting all contracts for the sale of gold for future delivery and the sale of gold by a gold broker outside his office, had to be repealed as a failure almost at once.[16]

It is commonplace to blame the federal government for the inflationary policies of the twentieth centuries. The radical change in purchasing power scarcely needs documenting. In 1905, an excellent house of half-timbered construction cost only $1,000; the same home in 1968 would cost perhaps $40,000 - 60,000.[17] But has this change been entirely, or even mainly, the fault of the federal government? Have not the people steadily voted in those who inflated most?

When a business atmosphere is geared to limited liability, the business world competes to accumulate debt as a means of advantage for rapid expansion. In 1968, one major and somewhat conservative business corporation required an annual increase of $600,000,000 in new credit or debt. And how is this kind of liability to be paid off? The answer is clearly by more inflation, by paying off good debts with bad money. On the whole, the commercial world is not conservative: it is geared to inflationary policies: its expansion, growth, *and survival* require continuous inflation. Having felt secure by means of limited liability to contract debt irresponsibly, limited liability companies are therefore prone to take the next step: to secure their limited liability from debt and responsibility by pushing for an unlimited money supply. In the process, business competes with state in a race towards an astronomical debt, to be repaid with unlimited printing press money. The corporations, as they

[16] Wesby Clair Mitchell: *A History of the Greenbacks, With Special Reference to the Economic Consequences of their Issue, 1862-65*, pp. 220-235. Chicago: University of Chicago Press, 1903, 1960.
[17] For an illustration of the house, see Russell Lynes: *The Taste-Makers*, illus. after p. 210. New York: Harper, 1955.

accumulate their debts, still cry "socialism" at the mounting federal debt. But socialism begins at home, and the significant and neglected step towards socialism was limited liability. The end of limited liability is unlimited money—and unlimited disaster. Before there can be a hard money policy, there must be a hard and fast responsibility. The alternative to hard money is finally a hard dictator, and disaster.

IV. THE SOCIOLOGY OF JUSTIFICATION

1

CALVIN IN GENEVA:
THE SOCIOLOGY OF JUSTIFICATION BY FAITH

To the average historian, the significance of John Calvin is limited to the fact that he loomed large in his era. He dominated the scene briefly, thinks the historian, and then disappeared, together with his influence, before the march of reason and tolerance, and his place in history is like that of a bare mountain which bulks large at a particular point in the horizon but has no significance or value other than prominence.

Such an approach is devoid of any understanding of the central significance of Calvin, and, in like manner, of Luther. The Protestant revolt was significant primarily, not for its rupture of the medieval church, but for its proclamation of the radical doctrine of justification by faith, which abolished not only the priesthood and the Church but the Holy Roman Empire and the whole social order which depended on the soteriology of mediating institutions. The full implications of the sociology of justification by faith were never realized by the Reformation, but in John Calvin there began a rigorous re-orientation of all theology and all society in terms of that concept, the development of which constitutes the most urgent responsibility today of Calvinist thinkers.

In order to understand the significance of this sociology of justifi-

cation by faith, it is rewarding to review the relationship of John
Calvin to Geneva and to understand why that city, which found
itself in sympathy frequently with theologians who opposed Calvin,
and showed actual disinterest in the theological divergencies of
Servetus, still found Calvin a social necessity and executed Servetus.
And that same city council, despite its sympathy with Calvin's
enemies and its distaste for Calvin, found it necessary to insist on an
"intolerant" Calvinism.

No society can be tolerant of an assault on its fundamentals. It
can extend tolerance to opinions, actions, and beliefs peripheral to
its foundation without harm to itself, and, in times of great peace
and security, may temporarily countenance a measure of questioning
with regard to its central dogmas. But let that probing grow to more
than a trivial degree, and a tightening of defense follows, and the
dogmas are enforced rigidly. The greater the threat or crisis in a
society, the more rigid is the defense of the dogmas. The essence
of Nazi Germany was not totalitarianism but rather a new racial
foundation to society. Had the Nazi regime attained its ideal and
made its dogma the common assumption of its era, the totalitarian
methodology could have been relaxed, for its dogma would have
become the "self-evident" truth of the age, even as in India, ages
ago, the outcasts came to accept the caste system as self-evident
truth. Similarly, Soviet Russia is not dishonest in maintaining that
its totalitarian "dictatorship of the proletariat" is an interim regime,
to be discarded when the workers' paradise is established and the
world-wide plotting against the workers' state destroyed. For the
present, to the vast majority of the world's peoples and countless
numbers of its own, the Marxist dogmas are not self-evident truths.
To Russia, this attitude constitutes treason to history, and, on the
part of the proletariat, is a disloyalty to their future, and must
be dealt with accordingly. Every society has its own definitions of
treason and loyalty, and defines them in terms of its faith.

The medieval Inquisition was the totalitarian defense of the
Roman Catholic culture of its age, and it became a reality only when
the seeds of decline began, even amidst the greatness of the culture,
to give promise of an alien world. The declining culture was now

intolerant of much that had been previously permissible. The growing insecurity of the central dogma led to a growing severity in its
defense. It is not at all surprising that the first three chapters of a
study of the Inquisition deal with the "Growth of Nonconformity"
and the rise of the intolerance of it.[1] The fundamental dogma of
medieval culture was the belief that society was ordained to be God-
centered, and its interpretation of that God was Graeco-Christian
and hierarchical. God had established one true Church and His will
and word were expressed through that institution, which as the
extension of the incarnation, as the body of the Lord, was God
manifest in this world. Three forces challenged this God-centered
culture. The first was the rise of the modern state, which, borrowing
Greek thought from the church, established the state in natural
law rather than the revealed will of God, thereby undercutting its
earlier theocentric foundation. The second was the revival of the
undercurrent of pre-Christian paganism, which, although ruthlessly
dealt with in the "witchcraft" trials, grew only stronger. Recent
scholarship has clearly shown that the "witches" and "devils" of the
medieval trials were abusive terms applied to the leaders of this
persisting and now reviving paganism.[2] The third was the rise of
the burghers, who supplanted the supremacy of saint and bishop
with merchant and banker and developed an economic-centered
world. Their growth was the central element in the new humanism
of which the Renaissance (a term too often used narrowly for art
and literature) was a cultural product.

Because the foundation of medieval culture was God-centered,
it was of necessity committed to the suppression of all that challenged
it. Because the humanistic era dating from the seventeenth century
to the First World War was politico-economic in its axis, it could
tolerate religious diversity but not a political or an economic heresy.
Citizens of the United States do not trouble their consciences about
those Nazi sympathizers and agents who were executed by the
Allies for treason during the Second World War because, even

[1] G. G. Coulton: *Inquisition and Liberty*. London: Heinemann, 1938.
[2] M. A. Murray: *The God of the Witches*. London: Sampson Low, n.d.,
and *The Witch Cult in Western Europe*. Oxford: Clarendon, 1921.

though they died for their faith, it was a wrong and treasonable faith. The Middle Ages could make the same defense with regard to its heresy trials and executions: they only killed the treasonable enemies of the just social order. The same is true of the Servetus case in Geneva. What people really object to nowadays in the death of Servetus is that a man should be executed for so trivial a thing as religion—heretical religion, of course, but still religion, a thing peripheral to life and this world. The United States loyalty purges of 1947 and later pointed to a growing rigorism because the source of present danger to its dogma is from Soviet Russia. If the danger abates, the rigorism will also, but if it does not, the rigorism will increase accordingly. Since monarchy is no longer a threat to American security, a man could hold monarchist ideas in 1952 which would have been a source of trouble to him in 1776. No society can allow its central dogma to be threatened. Because communism was not a threat to the Middle Ages, since it did not challenge its theo-centricity, it was an opinion that could be tolerated: it was not heresy. Today the opposition of Roman Catholicism to Soviet Russia is not based on its communism but on its "Godless material-ism." Soviet Russia, having made a man-centered, this-worldly order ultimate, could not reconcile itself to Roman Catholicism with any economic order. But, if Soviet Russia were to grant the claims of the Roman Church to represent the truly ultimate and supernatural or-der, its economics could be tolerated through countless vagaries.

Liberal, humanistic society is profoundly shocked by the in-tolerance of Catholicism and Calvinism, because they exacted so heavy a legal penalty in matters of religious aberration, which liber-alism regards as the realm of the purely personal. But religion is the realm of purely personal faith only to modern man: it was not so to the Council of Chalcedon. That Council would have regarded economics as a private, or at best secular and peripheral, matter and, for its time, accurately so, for the civilization of the day hung on the correct definition of the nature of Christ. From 1933 to 1939, the common cause for concern and discussion in the Western world was, "What will Hitler do?" and, in the United States, another common question was the success or failure of the Roosevelt economic policies. But, according to Gregory of Nyssa, the barber-shop conversation towards the end of the fourth century was different:

> Constantinople is full of mechanics and slaves, who are all of them profound theologians, preaching in the shops and the streets. If you want a man to change a piece of silver, he informs you wherein the Son differs from the Father; if you ask the price of a loaf, you are told by way of reply that the Son is inferior to the Father; and, if you enquire whether the bath is ready, the answer is that the Son was made out of nothing.[3]

Modern man does not recall the grievous errors of the Lincoln assassination trials with the celerity that he does the trial of Servetus. Few are troubled by the *ex post facto* laws used to convict Nazi war criminals: they were, almost all agree, guilty men. The attitude of the Middle Ages toward the heretic was similar: he was a man who had wilfully sinned against God and society, and mercy and pity were displaced sentiments if applied to him. True mercy required the rigorous protection of the greater body, but he was always given the opportunity to recant and share in the salvation to come.

This is, certainly, no justification of heresy trial brutality, but simply an attempt to render them understandable in terms of their culture. The vices of a man are apt to be closely akin to his virtues, gaining thereby protective coloration. Similarly, the blind spots of a society are likely to be closely related to its central dogma. The conclusion of psychosomatic medicine that "the mind is the body" is true of society: its mind, or central dogma, or belief, is likely to be its total world as well. Even in philosophy, when Descartes began with the autonomous self in his dictum, *Cogito, ergo sum*, "I think, therefore I am," he reduced the world to that autonomous self, as Kant and subsequent philosophy made clear. The self supplanted God and the world, and ended by absorbing and becoming God and the world. As Spengler has shown, each civilization has created a new world, even to the mathematics thereof. Christianity, by outrunning several civilizations, has given Western man a limited and

[3] J. S. Whale: *Christian Doctrine*. New York: Macmillan, 1942, p. 111, from Migne: *Patr. Gr.*, xlvi, 557.

tenuous detachment which makes criticism possible, but it has not always been operative. Liberal man can see clearly the weaknesses of the medieval scene, and his protest finally ended civil punishment in heresy trials, but it was earnest Christians, possessing a new detachment in the liberal era which they lacked previously, who inaugurated, for example, almost all the prison reforms of the humanistic Western world.

The change from a God-centered foundation to a man-centered politico-economic orientation created a new world with its own peculiar problems and rendered obsolete the concerns of the previous era. The most dramatic instance of the contemporaneous existence and struggle of the two worlds was Calvin's Geneva. The country of Geneva had become the possession of the house of Savoy in the fifteenth century, when in 1401 Amadeus VIII, Count of Savoy, purchased it from Eude de Villars. Within the city of Geneva itself, Amadeus had no right save to appoint the chief executive officer, the vidomme; otherwise, the city was relatively independent under its bishop. Although not a priest, Amadeus became Pope Felix V in 1440 and secured in 1444 the bishopric of Geneva for himself. The result for Geneva was poor and inefficient government, which the burghers resented greatly. In the next century, a treaty of *Combourgeoisie* with Freiburg sought to destroy the power of Savoy but was unsuccessful. In 1533, after a long period of dissension and dissatisfaction, the Bishop of Geneva, unwilling to face the reviving storm, left the city, returning in 1534 with an army. The conduct of the Bishop gave the reformers a chance to make Protestantism popular in Geneva, and it speedily became so. The Council therefore was faced with the task of reorganizing the life of the state, deprived now of its Roman Catholic basis.

The burghers, however, were the conservative element in the European ferment in that they had no thought of social revolt and offered no conscious challenge to the medieval synthesis. Their primary concern was the profitably ordered society rather than revolution. They proved, nevertheless, to be new wine to the old skins of Europe. The Roman Church had long looked for the threat in terms of itself and hence visualized opposition of an analogous character. It could produce a Counter-Reformation to deal with Protestantism, but it had no answer to the burghers. It was unprepared for the new order, which came finally from a totally unexpected area and dealt, not with the familiar problems of medieval culture, but with, and in, radically alien categories. The Renaissance scholars were at the time readily absorbed, the ecclesiastical power of the emperor curtailed, and a Council of Trent was called to deal with the Reformation, but the Roman Church had no conception of the existence of the greater threat from the burghers, who with their daily humdrum efforts were creating a new man-centered economic order. The society of the burghers was non-religious, but not irreligious. The burghers themselves were scarcely aware of this revolution they were creating: they were concerned primarily with a free and stable social order which would make profitable commerce possible. The only society they knew was the theocentric one of the medieval Church: they had favored now the Church and then the rising monarchies in their interpretations of that order in an effort to find stability. They could visualize no other society than the fundamentally Christian one, and therefore the Geneva Council turned to the reformer Farel to act as the trained technician of that order. And Farel commanded the assistance of John Calvin.

Neither John Calvin nor the Geneva experiment can be understood in terms of the contemporary picture of a grim, ruthless, inhuman, and autocratic Calvin. The picture has no reality whatsoever. Calvin was primarily a scholar, summoned unwillingly from his studies to apply his theories regarding the social order to a concrete situation. When Calvin first went to Geneva, the scholar was "a young man, nervous, sensitive and distrustful of his powers." [4] He had pleaded a preference for scholastic research, but Farel had finally won him over with the blunt assertion: "I speak in the name of Almighty God. You make the excuse of your studies. But if you refuse to give yourself with us to this work of the Lord, God will curse you, for you are seeking yourself rather than Christ." Calvin felt the force of this description of his desires and as a devout

[4] R. N. Carew Hunt: *Calvin*. London: Centenary Press, 1933, p. 56.

man yielded in terror. In his Strassburg exile, after his first experiment in Geneva, Calvin turned happily to his pastoral work, his studies, and teaching. He showed little concern over local church and state issues, but returned happily to his preferred destiny. When he was asked to return to Geneva, the news left him trembling with horror. It was a distasteful and revolting prospect, and he resisted it earnestly. Only when faced again with Farel's ultimatum that by shunning this clear call to duty he would be fighting against God did Calvin reluctantly accede to the Council's call.[5] For Calvin to the last was primarily a scholar and so described himself even in his death-bed speech to the ministers of Geneva:

> I have lived through some extraordinary battles here. At night before my door I have been saluted in mockery with the shots of fifty or sixty arquebusses. You can imagine how that must have terrified a poor, timid scholar as I am, and as I confess have always been. Then I was hunted out and went to Strassburg; but when I was recalled, I found it as difficult as ever to fulfil my office. They would call out "Scoundrel," and set their dogs at me.[6]

Calvin's nature was well revealed in these lines. And the myth of his Genevan dictatorship is also answered: no dictator ever has had the opposition's dogs set on him, or shots, designed to frighten him out of the state, fired under his window. Calvin was a quiet, rigorous scholar, given to a gentle but lively sense of humor all his days. He relished intelligent and thoughtful friends, and remembered his favorite teachers and classmates with gratitude and real assistance in later years. As a student he had been shy and timid but with a real gift for making friends. He was generally charitably inclined towards his enemies (and in Geneva often naive in being too ready to forgive and assume all was forgotten), but towards foolish and irresponsible thinkers he was curt and contemptuous. Thus his pupil Castellio, over-ambitious and unstable, was praised for his work as a rector by Calvin but dismissed for his heresy. When Castellio developed a persecution complex and a virulent hatred of Calvin, who had discouraged his inaccurate attempts at a French

[5] *Ibid.*, pp. 55, 105-113.
[6] *Ibid.*, p. 309.

translation of the Bible, and then drifted on into social and moral atomism, Calvin could only speak of him with contempt. He had a scholar's scorn for the muddle-headed thinker. As a youth he had risked his life with a return to Paris in an attempt to convert Servetus, but when Servetus' irresponsible thinking became more apparent in later years, Calvin could only dismiss him with a pitying and scornful contempt. He came to differ sharply with Laelius Socinus in his letters but regarded that scholar as worthy of communication and never quite broke off his correspondence. But of Luther Calvin declared that, even if Luther called him a devil, he would still believe him "an eminent servant of God."

Calvin, the scholar, was called in as a technical expert to help the Geneva Council, re-establish and maintain the Christocentric foundation of society. He functioned as the ruling bishop in a state which had abolished that office but required its function. Before Calvin entered Geneva for the first time in 1536, the Council had sought to function as both bishop and vidomme, assuming such ecclesiastical powers as to give absolution to excommunicated parishioners. A rigid control of morals was attempted in order to give stability to a social order that had grown corrupt and slovenly under bishop and vidomme. Although the Council consulted its preachers on such details as a bride's head dress, and more important matters as well, it functioned as both church and state and treated the clergy as its civil servants. The Council established dogmas, gave absolution and appointed ministers, and the church had no independent existence. The four principles of the Genevan Protestant State, according to Foster, as it existed between 1528 and 1536, were:

1. The Civil government was dominant over the church. (The same situation prevailed throughout Protestant Switzerland.)
2. Papal abuses were rejected.
3. The Word of God was adopted as the standard.
4. Universal primary education, free to the poor, was established.

According to Foster, the changes and additions made by Calvin were:

1. Establishment of the church as a distinct organism with

co-ordinate and constitutional rights with the state (1541), thus limiting the latter's ecclesiastical power and preventing absorption of church by state (caesaropapism).
2. Definite organization of creed and religious training including catechism (1537); discipline and supervision of morals (1541), including substitution of new marriage laws for old canon law (1561).
3. Unflinching enforcement of the "Word of God" in all matters of daily life—moral and social, private and public, and upon all inhabitants (1555).
4. University education, to train for church and state (1559).
5. A different temper and fibre—conscientious, unyielding, unflinching, austere (1555).[7]

The burghers were not interested in Calvin's *Institutes* or in his doctrine of the church. They wanted stable Christocentric government and, inexperienced in the technicalities of dogma, entrusted the matter to an expert, and unofficial bishop. Calvin's place in Geneva is not understandable except in terms of the central role in the state of the Bishop of Geneva, and the continuing sociological necessity for that office. The state was still far from simply civil: it was still extensively ecclesiastical. Calvin proved to be obnoxious to the burghers in his high doctrine of the church and in his theology as well, but they had no other recourse, for he alone impressed the majority as the one man capable of providing the required leadership. When Bolsec was summoned before the Council, that body found itself in the embarrassing position of sympathizing with the theology of a man who disturbed the social order. Bolsec's rejection of predestination seemed much more logical than Calvin's strange dogma. But the Council backed Calvin and a doctrine that made no sense to them, even after correspondence with various scholars, simply because the stability of the social order required it. They were the fathers of liberal, economic man, and Chalcedon was as incomprehensible to them as to Edward Gibbon; but no man lives in the future, and most men live in the past. The only conceivable society was the Christian one: Calvin alone could provide them with a stable Christian order: hence Calvin must be

[7] H. D. Foster: *Collected Papers*, Hanover, N. H., 1929, "Geneva before Calvin," p. 23, and "Calvin's Programme for a Puritan State," pp. 31ff.

supported even if incomprehensible. On the other hand, nothing would have suited the burghers better than to control Calvin's implementation of the moral society of his scholarly vision, but to control it without losing Calvin and his vitality. More than once Calvin's wings were clipped. In 1545, for example, the Council returned to its pre-Calvinian caesaropapism and promised to appoint Jean Trolliet to the next vacant pastorate. Later, in the midst of the Servetus case, the Council sought to undermine Calvin's authority by removing the ban of excommunication on Berthelier, and when Calvin preached on the following Sunday, he told the people it might be his last sermon. Calvin faced then the double threat of caesaropapist burghers and Servetus, suspected of being in league with his enemies, challenging the Christocentric foundation of society. There had, moreover, been constant conflict over the state's attempt to control the Church by appointing a syndic, an officer of the state, to be the president of the Consistory, the court of the Church. Similarly, the state had early insisted on full authority in selecting the Church elders, although later it was compelled to submit such names to the congregation for approval. The state neither understood fully nor accepted, other than politically, Calvin's doctrines. What it did understand was that under Calvin's orderly structuralization of society, trade had revived and the population increased. Geneva faced not a choice between Calvin and Bolsec, or Calvin and Servetus, but between Calvin and a once-again disordered society, declining trade, religious rupture, and civic decline. Thus the Council backed down rather than Calvin. Calvin could dispense with Geneva, but Geneva could not dispense with its Calvin. Calvin had to be retained and the Calvinistic interpretation of Christocentric society defended as the only stable order. Thus when Servetus was arrested, the early hearings were bewildering, unintelligible, and tiresome to the Council and judges. Such theological discussions as Calvin and Servetus waged over the term "hypostasis" were irrelevant. The man was a heretic, likely to disseminate dangerous ideas, and a threat to the social order. The case was therefore turned over to the public prosecutor, Claude Rigot, who *assumed the heresy* and "Servetus was now called upon to show that his views did not subvert the bases of religion and the welfare of society." [8] In 1535 Geneva had abandoned the Roman Catholic laws against heresy, and so the sentence was illegal in condemning his heresy, but to the Council the heart of the matter was the fact that it constituted treason to the state at a time when Geneva could not trust Swiss aid, when the Roman Catholic reaction was gaining power, and across the border in France Protestants were being executed in increasing numbers. Servetus' doctrines were, like Calvin's, incomprehensible, but the man was a menace to society and his ideas treason, while Calvin was its guiding engineer. Calvin himself, in defending the execution of Servetus, recognized that certain errors in dogma must be tolerated and that rigid conformity is impossible. Servetus, however, was going further than non-conformity: he attacked the very foundations and thereby rendered toleration impossible. A trinitarian Servetus could have preached democracy, oligarchy, or monarchy in Geneva and been tolerated, but he could not be suffered to attack the central dogma of Genevan society, and his presence on Genevan soil brought swift arrest.

At that time, Calvin faced a Council whose four new members were against him, and whose chief Syndic was his leading opponent. These men encouraged Servetus with false hopes simply to strike at Calvin, and gave rise to the erroneous idea of a common plot. Meanwhile, the rights of citizens of alien origin, Calvin's allies, were abridged, and Calvin virtually ready to concede defeat.[9] The Council could have ousted Calvin, but it had no real alternative to him.

In the trial of Servetus, Calvin was aware of two conflicting demands, the social danger he felt Servetus represented (social because society was theological in basis), and his own antagonism to a state trial of a church offense. He resolved the matter in action but not in thought. Calvin was aware of a necessity for keeping the two spheres faithful to their task, but society had not changed sufficiently

[8] Hunt: *op. cit.*, p. 211.
[9] For a fair and Unitarian review of the case, see Earl Morse Wilbur: *A History of Unitarianism: Socinianism and Its Antecedents.* Cambridge: Harvard, 1946, pp. 150-185.

for any such distinction to be real. It was Calvin's still young sociology rather than his integrity that proved inadequate.

What was it in John Calvin's thinking which made him indispensable to Geneva, and, for a hundred years, the ferment of European revolt? Rome furthered the Counter-Reformation with the aid of the powerful monarchs. Lutheranism depended on German and Scandinavian princes. Anglicanism could extend its influence only to the limits of the king's permission and authority. But Calvinism berated monarchs and overturned thrones, and it was not carried by princes and rulers, but carried them.

Calvinism's power rested in its radical re-thinking of Christian faith, and its biblical re-ordering of all society. The essence of the new sociology which made Calvin the architect of Genevan society is to be found in two concepts: the kingdom of God and justification.

The kingdom of God, according to Roman theology, is closely identified with the church. All godly society must by its very nature be in and of Christ, whose visible manifestation in this world is the Church of Rome. The church is the kingdom in this world and holds within its power and jurisdiction every aspect and domain of life. Augustine and Ambrose had held that "the empire is in the church" as against current views that "the church is in the Empire," and their view, later, in the Middle Ages, came to prevail. The church as the voice on earth of the kingdom, the extension of the incarnation and headed by the vicar of Christ, mediates the divine purpose to the world. No other institution has the right of interpretation. The church determined the nature of the Word of God, established a just price in economics, crowned monarchs in the state, decreed in some measure in literature and press what was permissible for publication, assessed and judged philosophy and science, and, in every area, claimed and sought to exercise power and jurisdiction as the ultimate authority by nature of its divine prerogative. The Roman Church was not without challengers. The Roman emperors sought to establish the state as the mediating institution and the manifest kingdom, and thereby precipitated the fourth century controversies on church and state so well analyzed by Williams. Ambrose stated the Nicene faith with clarity when he insisted:

"The City of God is the Church and the Church is the Body of Christ; whosoever despises the laws of the Celestial City, sins against heaven and violates the sanctity of the immaculate Body by the filth of their vices." [10] The victory, for a few centuries, went to the state in both east and west. The Roman Empire, as refounded by Otto I in 962, was the true Jerusalem, and, for many years, was so recognized by the Church. This Holy Roman Empire, as it was subsequently called, was, as Bryce has pointed out, "but another name for the Visible Church," and the emperor was called "Lord of the World"; claiming Pauline as against Petrine authority, Otto III signed himself *servu Jesu Christi*. Rome claimed to be no more than *prima sedes*, and the first among many sees, and never *una sancta* in this era, and the "universal" title was disclaimed. From 800 to 1056, the Empire reformed the Church as it saw fit, and assumed the decision in forms of mass, ceremonial, ritual, and creed. Under Otto III, the emperor became the locale and voice of the Holy Ghost. [11] The medieval Roman Church subsequently assumed this role and placed the Empire under and in the Church and ruled as the true City and Kingdom. The sole possible challenge to its claims, the university, failed to develop a full and sustained argument, but its progress is significant. The first step came when the university claimed for its members the right of trial, on violation of secular law, in church rather than civil courts. The university thus declared itself a part of the kingdom and an arm thereof. The next step came when the university sought the same autonomy from the Church. This was never fully gained, although German universities eventually gained their own jails, English universities their own representatives in Parliament, and Paris briefly dared to correct the papacy, as with John XXII, speaking as the authentic interpreter of Christian faith.

The German universities came into their own as the voice of the kingdom with the Lutheran revolt, apart from which the German uni-

---

[10] George Huntston Williams: *Church History*, XX, 3, pp. 3-33 and XX, 4, pp. 3-26, "Christology and Church-State Relations in the Fourth Century," citing Ambrose: *Expositio in psalmum* cxviii, *sermo* xv, 35.

[11] Eugen Rosenstock-Huessy: *Out of Revolution.* New York: Morrow, 1938, pp. 485-515.

versities cannot be understood. As Rosenstock-Huessy has pointed out, "the universities became the heirs of the bishop's chair, the cathedra. The professor's chair was called 'Katheder.' " [12] The university became the representative of the Holy Ghost in the German nation, and princes were only "God's hangmen and jailers." "This salvation-character of scholarship, utterly foreign to the rest of the world, is the religious key to the political building erected by the Reformation" in Germany.[13] Petrine authority over the visible life of the Church was given to the prince, but Pauline authority, over the spirit, and the right of inspiration, interpretation, and instruction belonged to the university. The university determined the nature of the law, and the prince assumed its operation. Unlike Calvin, Professor Luther believed in a just price: he subscribed to the old concept of a manifest kingdom whose voice carried jurisdiction in every realm, and that voice was now the Christian conscience and reason as revealed in the free university. The redeemed image of God in man re-opened Scripture, and as prophet, priest, and king in Him, found its clearest voice in the free Lutheran university. But, with the decline of Protestantism in Germany, the restraining hand as well as the divine authority of the university disappeared, and the pre-Reformation man reappeared in Hitler.

In John Calvin, these concepts of the kingdom of God were swept aside by a rigorous biblical theology which made impossible the presumption of mediating institutions and voices. The Word interprets the Word, and Christ is the universal mediator. In his (*Institutes*, III, xlii), he discusses the meaning of the kingdom of God in terms of the second petition of the Lord's Prayer, and thus establishes the kingdom of God as eschatological, not historical: it is to come, but it is not here in the form of an institution, such as church, state, or university. It is present in part where men's hearts in obedience yearn for the fullness of His reign, but it has no mediatorial institutions. In its earthly manifestation, this "kingdom consists of two parts; the one, God's correcting by the power of his Spirit all our carnal and depraved appetites, which oppose him in

[12] *Ibid.*, p. 390; see pp. 359-450.
[13] *Ibid.*, p. 399.

great numbers; the other, his forming all our powers to an obedience to his commands." Because of Calvin's belief in total depravity and his antagonism to perfectionism, he ruled out the possibility of redeemed man claiming to be the kingdom manifest. For him, man is never the kingdom. A favorite passage of Calvin, however, was Romans 14:17, 18, and in his *Commentaries on Romans*, he stated concerning the man who fulfilled these conditions "the kingodm of God fully prevails and flourishes in him. . . . Wherever there is righteousness and peace and spiritual joy, there the kingdom of God is complete in all its parts: it does not then consist of material things." This, his boldest statement on the kingdom, needs this important observation: Calvin is here emphasizing the total lack of dependence of the kingdom on any material form, on meats or drinks, on any human activity. The kingdom of God is thus the presence or activity of God wherever found, and that presence or activity is pure grace, totally unrelated to the works or will of man, and eternity is its origin and its motive. Thus when Calvin seems to assert the human form of the kingdom, he is most rigorously separating it from the will of man. It is a kingdom of pure grace, wholly eschatological and never institutional and historical. Because it is eschatalogical, Calvin tended to distrust some human activities, such as art, which did not seem to bear directly on the framework of human daily life under the expectation, Thy Kingdom Come. But Calvin in part, and later Calvinists in full, by emphasizing Thy Will be Done, in relation to its implications for all of life, brought art into the circle of the kingdom. Kuyper is thus right in defending (in *Calvinism*) Calvinism's relation to art. Medieval theology gave art a relationship to God through the mediation and government of the kingdom, i.e., the church. Calvin, despite his distrust, opened the door to a direct and non-mediated relationship between the artist and the kingdom and gave art its charter of independence from man and its mandate from God. And that commission can gain its full significance only if the artist realizes that justification by faith places him under the direct sovereignty of God and within the eschatological sustentation. His concern therefore is neither realism, impressionism, expressionism, nor any other school of art

as such but an exercise of the creation command to exercise dominion
in obedience, under the framework of redemptive hope. Calvin's
position, despite his distrust, was the more significant to art than
Rome's patronage. The Roman Church can be the patron of art;
the Reformed church is a co-laborer with art. Berkhof has summarized the Calvinist position on the kingdom by denying that
Christian schools, labor unions, political organizations, and the like
are manifestations of the church as an organism. "The Kingdom
may be said to be a broader concept than the Church, because it
aims at nothing less than the complete control of all the manifestations of life. It represents the dominion of God in every sphere of
human endeavor." [14] More bluntly stated, Calvinism denies that the
church can be equated with the kingdom: it is not *the* kingdom, but
it is *in* the kingdom. Thus Calvin, because he saw economics, not
as an aspect of the life of the church but of the kingdom, implicitly
denied the jurisdiction of church, state, or university over econ-
nomics. To him, the just price made no sense whatsoever, imposing
as it did an alien category over economics. As Tawney himself
recognized, Calvin "throws on the conscience of the individual" the
question of a fair rate of interest. It was not, as Tawney thought,
because Luther's eyes "were on the past" and Calvin alert to the
future, but because Calvin's conception of the kingdom eliminated
the church as the manifest kingdom and made the individual Christian, in his activity, the citizen of that eternal order by virtue of
divine grace. The individual was thus the primary area of responsibility. If the conscience of the individual made justice impossible,
the state could not supply what the individual lacked. The state has
its jurisdiction, the church its realm, art, economics, the university,
the family, all have their respective jurisdictions, and the key to the
life of each is the Word of God in the heart of man. The church's
place in the kingdom does not depend on a Petrine or apostolic succession, nor on any human conditions. In the Scottish Confession of
Faith of 1560 (Arts. 18, 19, 20) it was insisted, after Calvin, that
neither historical primacy, a majority rule, the rule of the elect,

[14] Louis Berkhof: *Systematic Theology*. Grand Rapids: Eerdmans, 1946,
p. 570.

apostolic succession, nor any other authority carried any weight, but only the Word of God, the church existing within the kingdom of God rather than the kingdom of Satan only where there prevailed a faithful preaching of the Word, proper administration of the sacraments, and correct ecclesiastical discipline. The individual Christian is subordinate, whatever his position, to the Word of God, and the kingdom shows itself in the fruits of the Spirit in the man obedient to the Word. Thus no institution can claim jurisdiction where none is granted, and Calvin accordingly refused to recognize what Scripture had refused to confirm.

Closely related to Calvin's concept of the kingdom is his interpretation of justification. His rigorous biblical exposition of justification needs no reviewing. For Calvin, justification was not by works, intelligence, or institution, nor *in* faith, but of God by faith. Because God ultimately and immediately justifies, predestination is, as Scripture affirms, the corollary of justification. Salvation is thus wholly the work of God. This, of course, is offensive to man, who insists on finding the grounds of salvation in his own activity, thinking, or faith and credits God with assistance at best. To this Calvin replied, striking at autonomous man's insistence on his own standard of justice: "On this hinge turns the whole question: Is there no justice of God, but that which is conceived by us?" God as the Creator can be held to no standard of justice but His own, and "the great and essential end of man's creation" is "for his own glory." [15] Because justification and salvation are thus totally dependent on God, human activity and mediation are rendered irrelevant. The church and the saints in heaven have no mediatorial role left them. As Calvin pointed out, "the papists acknowledge Jesus Christ to be the only mediator of redemption; that it is He alone that redeemed the world: but as touching intercession, that He is not alone, that the Saints who are dead have this office as well as He." [16] The Roman and Reformed theologies have their distinctive sociologies of justification. The sociology of Roman justification involves a hierarchy of mediatorial

[15] Calvin: "The Eternal Predestination of God," in *Calvin's Calvinism.* Grand Rapids: Eerdmans, 1950, pp. 32, 85.
[16] Calvin: *The Mystery of Godliness,* sermon on "The Only Mediator." Grand Rapids: Eerdmans, 1950, p. 203.

institutions under the rule and supervision of the manifest kingdom of God, the Church. The functions of state, school, art, literature, and economics are mediatorial: they guide man to salvation and act as instruments of the Church, the City of God, in the great task of justification. The duty of each is to be, to use a modern Roman category, Christophers, Christ-bearers to man. Thus none of these activities has any sovereignty in its own sphere: as instruments in the process of justification, they were and are subordinate to the jurisdiction, law, and principles of the Church, and to its hierarchy. Thus Roman sociology sees man in at least a life-long process of justification (with purgatory also involved in the process) and orients all society in terms of this process. Society is tutorial and mediatorial.

Reformed sociology, on the other hand, sees no such process. Man is either redeemed or reprobate by the sovereign act of God, and thus no mediatorial institutions exist. No social distinction between redeemed and reprobate is possible, because the separation of the tares and the wheat is the prerogative of God, who sends His rain on the just and the unjust. Society is a mixed field, and even the church is a netful of mixed fish, good and bad. Thus neither man nor his institutions, his reason, emotions, or activities are to be trusted. Society has no mediatorial function: its role is not priestly but ministerial. The priest of the Jewish dispensation was not a priest in his own right: he was only a substitute whose dress, drink, food, marriage, and his very steps within the sanctuary were minutely prescribed, because he had no authority in his own right: he was merely a temporal and temporary priest, a substitute awaiting the coming of the eternal high priest, Jesus Christ, who fulfilled and ended the ritual. Likewise, Christian society, whose members are kings, prophets, and priests in Christ, has only a ministerial role: it discharges an assigned task without any independent authority. Its purpose is not to justify—God has done that before the foundation of the world—but to assert the coming of the eschatological kingdom and attempt in limited form to exercise the duties of the redeemed image of God in man: to exercise dominion, to ascertain knowledge, establish righteousness, and live in holiness in family, church, state, economics, education, art, and every other sphere of human activity. Like the priests of the Old Testament, its actions are prescribed by Scripture, and it awaits the general resurrection and the coming of Him who shall usher in the true and full kingdom, with all its redeemed activity. Calvin's conception of justification led inevitably to the concept of sphere sovereignty. No other theology has been able to develop the soteriology of justification by faith because none other is willing to accept the full meaning of that doctrine, namely, predestination. And unless this is accepted, the freedom under God of justification sociology is denied society.

Calvin, of course, was not always consistent in the details of application, nor are modern Calvinists who maintain church colleges, official church magazines, and medical missions, all functions of free Christian society rather than of the church. But the main outlines of his adherence to justification sociology are clearly seen in Geneva.

Of central importance to the new sociology was Calvin's view of holy days, the Jewish Sabbath, and Sunday. Commenting on Galatians 4:10, he points out that while no condemnation of "the observance of dates in the arrangement of civil society" is involved, Paul condemns "that which would bind the conscience, by religious considerations, as if it were necessary to the worship of God . . . we do not reckon one day to be more holy than another." Although, in its early years, the Reformation saw daily preaching, its purpose was instructional. Roman sociology requires a constantly open church: since man's justification is in process, there is a constant dependence on the church, and the supreme penalty on erring man and society is a closed church. For Calvinist sociology, the locked church on week-days is inevitable. When the church closes its doors, the day does not become secular and unredeemed, because man is justified by God, and without the necessity of human mediation. Redeemed man, not the church, redeems the day, and this gives rise to the important Calvinist concept of the Christian calling. "Redeeming the time" (Eph. 5:16ff.) is the task of man for Calvin, and involves, not the monastery, but circumspect living, sobriety, inner joy in and worship of God, and social order, which involves submission. "God has bound us so strongly to each other, that no man ought to endeavour to avoid subjection; and where love reigns, mutual services will be rendered. I do not except even kings and governors, whose very authority is held for the *service* of the community." Redeeming the time thus involves obedience to God and "this mutual subjection" of men, and "we may not refuse the yoke . . . of serving our neighbours." [17] Sunday worship is not a necessity for justification, but the celebration of the justified. The redeemed rejoice in redemption, and gather to give thanks and to learn more of the Word of God, so that in their daily life and activity they may more fully redeem the time. Thus Calvin freed the Christian from not only institutions but from days and seasons. Christian man and not the church redeems the time, and the church can lock its doors in the assurance that the kingdom of God consists of righteousness, peace, and joy in the Holy Ghost. The locked church, a tragedy for the Roman, is the triumph of the Reformed believer and an assertion of the free and non-mediated activity of the Holy Ghost, who forgives, remits sins, and blesses man in his home and business.

Calvin, of course, did not thereby dismiss the need for observance of the seventh day. Sabbath observance is for him a necessary part of redeemed activity rather than a necessary part of the redeeming process. While insisting on the observance of the Lord's Day, Calvin pointedly stated, "the Lord's Day is not observed by us upon the principles of Judaism; because in this respect the difference between us and the Jews is very great. For we celebrate it not with scrupulous rigour, as a ceremony which we conceive to be a figure of some spiritual mystery, but only use it as a remedy necessary to the preservation of order in the Church" (*Inst.* II, viii, 33). For him, the Sabbath was abrogated and fulfilled in Christ, and he cited Colossians 2:16, 17, the Sabbath was "a shadow of things to come; but the body is of Christ." This true Sabbath, wherein "we must rest altogether, that God may operate within us," is still binding on us in its moral sanction, and hence the necessity for its observance to permit the preaching of the Word, the sacraments, and physical rest for ourselves and servants. But the true Sabbath "is contained not in one day, but in the whole course

[17] Calvin, *Commentaries on Galatians and Ephesians*. Grand Rapids: Eerdmans, 1948, pp. 314-333.

of our life, till, being wholly dead to ourselves, we be filled with the life of God. Christians therefore ought to depart from all superstitious observance of days" (*Inst.* II, viii, 29, 31, 32, 34). In this world, the moral necessity of the Lord's Day was perpetual for Calvin, but only in terms of this true Sabbath, which he called the "substance" of the Christian man's true observance. The Christian thus lives all his life in the eternal Sabbath, the heavenly rest of the redeemed Body of Christ. His participation in this remains fragmentary or partial in this world, but nonetheless real. He cannot be in Christ and outside the eternal Sabbath. Thus the chief end of man, as stated in the beginning of the Genevan Catechism by Calvin, is "to know God and enjoy Him forever," a Sabbath activity which finds fulfillment in the eternal Sabbath.

Calvin, in his interpretation of the Fourth Commandment, avoided mysticism, and he definitely placed the day under grace. This has, in a sense, fostered secularism with regard to the Sabbath. In Roman Catholic and pagan holy days, all observance is redeeming and the day is "open" to all men. Rome condones much on the Sabbath because its people are sinners in the process of redemption. The Christian Sabbath in Calvin is for redeemed saints and thus has higher standards and automatically excludes as secular much of what the world previously condoned. It thereby makes secularism more self-conscious, and the tare begins to be seen as a tare.

Calvin in Geneva tried steadily to free the church in its realm from the jurisdiction of the state. For him, the church was "founded on the election of God" and thus not discernible to any but God alone. The visible church, containing both elect and reprobate, is our spiritual mother, and "out of her bosom there can be no hope of remission of sins, or any salvation" because through her the gospel is proclaimed and the sacraments administered. Calvin's description of the church frequently suggests Roman theology in its high doctrine of the church, but with this significant difference: for Calvin the church was always the net, never the Fisherman (Matt. 13: 47-50), whereas for Rome the Church was the Fisherman (*Inst.* IV, i). The church is Christ's mystical body, but never Christ. The true church is present where the Word is faithfully preached and the two sacraments properly administered. In dealing with the sacrament of the Lord's Supper, Calvin's interpretation is generally misunderstood in that it is judged from the standpoint of Roman and Lutheran thought. He asserts unmistakably Christ's real presence in this sacrament in which "we are incorporated into one body with Christ" and in which "we may confidently consider . . . Christ himself . . . presented to our eyes, and touched by our hands. For there can be no falsehood or illusion in this word, 'Take, eat, drink; this is my body . . . this is my blood.' . . . Though it appears incredible for the flesh of Christ, from such an immense local distance, to reach us, so as to become our food, we should remember how much the secret power of the Holy Spirit transcends all our senses, and what folly it is to apply any measure of ours to his immensity." While asserting the real presence, Calvin specifically denies transubstantiation and consubstantiation, because "the bread is called *the body* in a sacramental sense." To fall into the Lutheran or Roman error is to misunderstand the meaning of the sacraments, for a sacrament is a *channel of grace*, not an *incarnation*. To make it the latter is to pervert its meaning and attempt a false visibility that "while remaining on the earth, they might attain a proximity to Christ without any need of ascending to heaven." The sacrament is not the incarnation itself but its ordained channel: thus it gives us the real *presence*, but not the *incarnation* itself (*Inst.* IV, xvii). Even as the kingdom is present in the world, but not incarnate in it, so Christ is present in the sacrament but not incarnate in it. The Holy Spirit has been given to the church and is present within her, but the church is not the incarnation of the Holy Ghost. Thus for Calvin the church can never extend its sway over all of life as Rome did. Hers is a ministry, not a priesthood, and it is a ministry of Word and sacrament.

Likewise, the state is not a priesthood nor the kingdom but the ministry of justice. As with all institutions and activities, Calvin places the state directly under God and His Word. He frees it from the church's jurisdiction, and thus gives it more than Rome conceded; but Calvin limits its area, and thus gives less. "They are responsible to God and to man in the exercise of their power," he comments on Romans 13:4. The magistrate is the sword-bearer, entrusted with the responsibility of waging war and maintaining justice. "They are constituted the protectors and vindicators of the public innocence, modesty, probity, and tranquillity, whose sole object it ought to be to promote the common peace and security of all" (*Inst.* IV, xx). Thus the limited state, a minister of the kingdom and not the kingdom, was the Calvinist concept. Calvinists could boldly reprimand kings, as fellow subjects of God, and correct rulers when they interfered in the realm of the church. For their sovereignty was not derived from the church, state, or people, but from God, and the sovereignty was exercised in a world tainted by an original sin pervasive in the realm of the state as well as elsewhere.

Concerning the family, Calvin, like all the Reformers, expressed indignation over the "petulant reproaches" of men like Jerome "by which he attempts to render hallowed wedlock both hateful and infamous. . . . God . . . ordains the conjugal life for man, not to his destruction, but to his salvation" (*ad* Gen. 2:18). For the Roman, marriage is tutorial and under the jurisdiction of the Church. For the Calvinist, marriage is the blessed union of the redeemed and a type of the union of Christ and His church, the mother as a type of the church and the father of Christ. As such, the father assumed a priestly role in the family, with the household as his congregation, and that essential Protestant ritual was born, family worship. As the sociologist Rosenstock-Huessy has observed, "Here lay the socio-economic *reality* of the Reformation, a field in which the Christian's inward freedom could incarnate itself in daily life, in which living faith became works." The Reformed family, "by transplanting the sacrament of the Word into every household," "Christianized what had previously been simply a part of the natural world." [18] By way of answer, the Church of Rome developed the cult of the Holy Family and of St. Joseph, but Rome subordinates this area to the Church, while the Reformation saw in the family, man's first and last school, church, state, and society, directly under God and free of the jurisdiction of church and state.

[18] Eugen Rosenstock-Huessy: *The Christian Future*. New York: Scribners, 1946, pp. 34-42.

Tawney has written with great learning but less insight on the relationship of Calvinism to a free economy in his *Religion and the Rise of Capitalism*. He has sensed the emphasis of Calvinism on "personal responsibility" and the significance of the Christian calling, but without any awareness of its theological foundations. He had delineated the failure of other reformers, including Calvin's associates and successors, to show the same concept of freedom from ecclesiastical and magisterial control, but erred in seeing Calvin as a representative of urban modernity. Calvin was as limited in his outlook as were the men of his day: he showed a general conservatism towards change and new ideas, even to following the implications of some of his own. The importance of Calvin to the rise of capitalism has no connection with the man's personal nature or background. It was rather Calvin's rigorous biblical theology which gave economics an independent role under God, freeing it from the jurisdiction of a kingdom on earth and placing it within the framework of the redemption of time. Calvin's theology created a sociology of justification the implications of which, though only fragmentarily realized at that time, were revolutionary and are basic to an understanding of the Reformation and modern eras.

In terms of this program, Calvin's horror of Servetus is more understandable. Having defeated the concept of an incarnate and manifest kingdom on earth, Calvin saw in Servetus' theology not only the return of a divine institution but a divinized humanity, Christ blasphemously reduced and humanity exalted. Such a society is the antithesis of Christian society and is the restatement of the demonic offer, "Ye shall be as God," and, accordingly, constituted a fearful threat to Geneva, where Calvin's program was at best a frail success.

In many aspects of his program, Calvin fell short of achievement. Even within the church, his primary concern, the goal was never reached. His desire for weekly communion, tempered to a request for monthly communion, was resisted successfully. Geneva had no desire to see high church Calvinism flourish: it was sufficiently overpowering in its limited status. In many respects, church government was always kept under state control, despite Calvin's unrelenting struggle. On the other hand, the moralistic regime was on the whole approved of heartily, despite minor irritations. It provided the stable social order the burghers desired. Most of the objections came when the moral laws were applied against themselves: it was a desirable law for other people primarily. These "puritanical" laws were in fact common to Roman Catholic Geneva but had not been enforced, and serious moral laxity prevailed. Pre-Calvinist Protestant Geneva had made an attempt to enforce them, but it remained to Calvinism to create the power to do so. The rationale of the moralistic regime can be seen by examining that classic line of clandestine lovers, "We are married in the eyes of God." This is nonsense to the Calvinist, because the eyes of God see man not in isolation but simply in terms of church, state, and family. Marital vows according to the rites of church and state are therefore not purely legal requirements: they are moral categories. No act of man is a solitary act: it is at all times a social act as well. This latter concept is especially stressed by Calvinism and hence its circumspection of all life. What a man thinks and does in the privacy of his home or in a solitary, closeted place, is a thread in the weave and pattern of human society. Allow a single thread to unravel, and the whole cloth is endangered. Society is thus a maze of interlocking responsibilities, none independent and none subordinated to the other. Calvinism from the beginning has often been tempted to make church or state the key to this maze, but its basic answer has become redeemed man under the Word of God.

Calvin's achievement was a great one: a scholar entrusted with the engineering of a social order, he had in the main succeeded, and after eighteen years of service, the Council finally admitted this foreign expert, its unofficial bishop, into the rights of bourgeoisie, of citizenship. The aging Calvin counselled Knox to undertake his experiment with more moderation of spirit and charity. Certainly ex-priests, even though unworthy, should be treated humanely and allowed to draw pensions, and surely the children of the excommunicated as well as the illegitimate should certainly be accepted for baptism. And episcopacy could be retained if it were not sacramental. When the great scholar died, his new ordering of Christian society seemed an enduring one, destined to be a pattern for Protestant civilization, but he had not reckoned with the order being created by the burghers who understood neither predestination nor hypostasis. The plain citizens of Constantinople understood the significance of hypostasis, but the burghers of Geneva, although their Council required weekly church attendance of itself to set an example for the people, remained hopeless outsiders to the problems of theology. Those were matters for John Calvin to deal with as painlessly as possible and with the least disturbance to their social order. They were finally grateful for his work, but they never understood it.

Calvin understood them much more clearly. A thoughtful realist, he knew that a new economy prevailed and had, in fact, been in existence for some time. Unlike Roman Catholic and Lutheran thinkers, he made no attempt to force the principles of scholastic thought onto capitalism. As Tawney has pointed out, Calvin frankly recognized "the necessity of capital, credit and banking, large-scale commerce and finance, and the other practical facts of business life." [19] As such, Calvin was the successful social engineer of his day, and his appeal to the bourgeoisie was a powerful one. Calvinism thus won its victories in commercial and urban areas. It finally failed because neither Calvin nor Calvinism could visualize capitalism as anything more than the new economy whereas it was in fact the new culture. The early Renaissance movement had derived considerable backing from the burghers, from the rising capitalists of Europe. It appealed to them with its neo-Platonist emphasis on the integrity and essentiality of the individual soul. Society was reduced to simple, "elemental" terms. But the Renaissance lacked the moral virility and the economic awareness the burghers needed: this Calvinism supplied, and carried the day. Giannozzo Manetti, the Florentine humanist, wrote On the Excellency and Dignity of Man, before the middle of the 15th century, as a counterpart to Innocent III's On the Misery of Man. Marsilio Ficino glorified man's universality and his cosmic centrality: man became the measure, and his liberty the esssence of true culture and society. Yet none of these humanists had any grasp of the real revo-

[19] Tawney: Religion and the Rise of Capitalism.

lution of their time, nor did Erasmus, who simply repeated the conventional criticism more ably. Luther provided the religious catalyst but viewed the social revolution with horror and incomprehension, in traditional Roman Catholic categories mainly. Calvinism recognized the new economy as *part* of a new order and had a sociology to meet it and thus briefly commanded the situation. But because Calvinism by its very nature was all or nothing, it was soon discarded; the pilot was dropped, and capitalism continued to develop along its earlier Renaissance lines, with the benefit of Calvinist rigorism and morality, into the civilization of liberalism or humanism, of politico-economic man.

Today, the sociology of justification is all but forgotten, and the free society it created in part disappearing. Man has become the visible deity, whose general will is manifest in the state. As the visible kingdom, the state concerns itself with all areas of human life: church, school, family, economics, literature, art, all things live and move and have their being within the state. What Rome was in the thirteenth century, the state has become in our era, even to the dream of one universal see in the United Nations. Against this, Rome proclaims her ancient creed, while many Protestants, under the influence of the social gospel, declare that the kingdom of God is and is becoming in that order known as the state. Calvinism, whose main activity has often been limited to a defense of Scripture, needs anew to launch forth the fullness of Scripture. The proclamation of the eschatological kingdom and of predestination means the responsibility to develop the sociology of justification and to destroy all human idols set up as images of the kingdom whose builder and maker is God.

2

THE MODERN PRIESTLY STATE:
THE SOCIOLOGY OF JUSTIFICATION BY LAW

Culture and society are, as Henry Van Til has pointed out in *The Calvinistic Concept of Culture*, simply religion externalized and made explicit. The concept of justification by faith leads inevitably to a radical reconstruction of society in terms of that faith, which has broad implications for all of life.

Common to all cultures of antiquity is the *priestly character* of the state, ruler, or central office of the particular society, so that the works of mediation, remission of sins, intercession, and other priestly duties have been central aspects of the life of the body politic. Such a state of things has not been the product of usurpation by the state or merely of confusion, but a healthy recognition of the fundamental nature of law and order. In any healthy society, the *courts* and all other administrators of law serve to preserve social order and well being, and any serious breakdown of the integrity, validity, and enforcement of law leads to the progressive collapse of society. Social sin must be atoned for, and the arms of the law function to effect restitution, punishment, and, by removal, the purgation and purification of society. The law in itself is therefore inevitably a manifestation of religion and in essence, even in the "secular" state, religious. The black and clerical robes of modern jurists are an evidence and continuing witness to its medieval claim to priestly status, a claim from which the church was unable to separate the schools of law. Thus, a functioning society requires a functioning law, effective purgation of the sinner, intercession for the oppressed, and justification for the wrongly oppressed. It is no accident of theology that the language of salvation is juridical language, and salvation a legal transaction, forgiveness itself a legal term declaring that the charges are dropped, satisfaction having been rendered (or, charges deferred for the time being).

The language of salvation, of soteriology, is juridical language because the nature of sin is an offense against the law and covenant of God. Not only is law again involved, but this time fundamental law, law which must be basic to state law. The state, together with all creation, is set in the context of this higher law, however the law be construed. Again, the life of the state is inseparable from this basic environment of higher and absolute law. If social health requires the proper administration of law by the state, then how much more basic is the proper regard for the higher law? If disregard of state law leads to anarchy and chaos, how much more so the disregard of higher law? It is accordingly of fundamental concern to the state and to its continued life. To avoid punishment, with its radical consequences for the state, purgation and priestly intercession are basic to the higher offices of state. Health must be maintained both in terms of internal law and in terms of cosmic law, and hence the state has seen itself as a priestly order, called to be the great intermediary between man and the divine, the means and vehicle to the good life and the true society. The consistently relativistic society has never existed. In some societies, the higher law has been seen in supernatural or in theistic and deistic terms, as in the early and formative history of the United States.[1] Higher law still prevails where supernaturalism is eroded. Dewey's higher law was democracy, as it is for most Americans today. Phillips Payson's election sermon at Boston, May 27, 1778, gave evidence of the early rise of an immanent higher law which was to crowd out God: "The voice of reason and the voice of God both teach us that the great object or end of government is the public good." [2] Reason early became an independent power and then a judge over God, and itself the

[1] See Edward S. Corwin: *The "Higher Law" Background of American Constitutional Law*. Ithaca, New York: Cornell University Press, 1955, a study of major importance. See also V. M. Hall and J. A. Montgomery: *Christian History of the Constitution of the United States of America*, Vol. I, San Francisco: American Constitution Press, 1960, a valuable collection of primary and secondary sources, the first of three volumes, and dedicated to a restudy and revival of Christian principles of state and society.

[2] Hall and Montgomery, *op. cit.*, p. 376.

higher law.[3] Social health requires in all instances conformity to the higher law, democracy, reason, or God, lest society collapse into anarchy, and this conformity is a priestly function.

The Hebrew commonwealth of the Old Testament stood alone in divorcing priesthood and kingship, but the dominance of the kings over priests was not infrequent, the claim to priesthood by Uzziah only miraculously forestalled, and the syncretistic and apostate rulers openly priestly. The prophetic office was able to protect the integrity of the priest and sanctuary by its radically independent character, and to prevent the natural coalescence of the two offices. By virtue of Christ's atonement, His assumption of an eternal and all-sufficient high priesthood, the human office of priest was forever abolished, as Hebrews declared, and priesthood and kingship joined in Christ, after the order of Melchizedek. Not only were the implications of Hebrews radical religiously, but politically as well, as Rome quickly discovered in dealing with the church, which refused to recognize the priestly kingship of the emperors, while praying for them as kings and governors.[4] Apart from the atonement, the state remained *priestly*; under the atonement, the state became ministerial, or more accurately, a diaconate (Rom. 13:1-7, the word in v. 4 being *diakonos*). In terms of the Kingdom of God, the offices of priest and king are united in the person of Christ. Since the basic unity of the Kingdom is supernatural and messianic, the purpose of biblical history was thus to point to the ultimate and transcendental unity, while preventing an immanent and man-centered unity. Such an earthly unity of the two offices would transform the realm into the Kingdom of Man and make it a messianic order.

How has the modern state become priestly? To understand this, it will be necessary to examine both the nature and function of law in the state.

Although the reformers, by virtue of their war against the Church of Rome, distrusted the church while too often lacking a similar

[3] For Locke, "The Law, that was to govern *Adam*, was the same that was to govern all his Posterity, the *Law of Reason*." *Civil-Government*, III, 57. The text of Locke's work is included in Hall and Montgomery, pp. 57-125.

[4] See Ethelbert Stauffer: *Christ and the Caesars*. Philadelphia: The Westminster Press, 1955.

distrust of the state, they nevertheless undercut the state by their sociology of justification by faith and their ministerial conception of all authority. Only as the Enlightenment advanced, and the Reformation, with some ebb and flow, receded, did the state once again become priestly and itself the order of salvation. Since the modern state is clearly messianic, and is in its own opinion the vehicle of the good life and the true kingdom, it is clearly priestly. It is, whether democratic or Marxist, the great high priest of the order of salvation, and this is as true of the local politician as of the United Nations. *The law is thus the means of salvation*, the means to creation of the good and true society. This legalistic principle, against which Romans, and all Scripture, is directed, is as invalid politically as religiously. In modern thought, the contrast and parallelism with reference to salvation between legalistic thinking and biblical thinking is especially striking.

Man, his fourfold estate	*Law, its fourfold function*
1. The State of original righteousness.	1. The law as the means of serving God and acknowledging His sovereignty.
2. The State of sin, total depravity.	2. The law as an indictment, as a schoolmaster to reveal to man his radical impotence, and as a "terror," a means of restraining the total outbreak of sin.
3. The State of grace or regeneration.	3. The law as man's new nature, written on his heart, a guide to his conduct, and a restraint to the motions of sin; the means of sanctification.
4. The State of glory.	4. Law as totally man's new nature in total sanctification. Man's true and full freedom in and under law.

When we turn to the two forms of natural law common to modern statism, we find a different significance for law. Radically simplified, the two can be distinguished by their treatment of the state of nature. In the one, the state of nature is one of primitive innocence, as Dryden's Indians,

Guiltless men, that danced away their time,
Fresh as their groves and happy as their clime—.

Nature is normative, and the state of nature is that of innocence.[5]
In the other view, the state of nature is that out of which man must
evolve. The pattern of the first can be briefly summarized as follows:

1. The state of nature, primitive inno-cence.	1. Law as man's unconscious state. Man, being guiltless, is in full conformity to nature.
2. The fall of man into "unnatural" society and civilization.	2. "Unnatural" society is violent disregard for the laws of being, and of nature. Salvation is by a return to nature. This return is by law: the general will is the unconscious will at times but always true law for man.
3. Nature began as a primitive unity and culminates in a complex unity.	3. The general will, natural law, rules through either democracy or dictatorship and saves men and society. If need be, men, Rousseau said, are "forced to be free." [6]

Law in this conception is clearly redemptive, and the state priestly
as the mediator of this salvation. Modern democracies and Marxist
states are thus avowedly given to a program of salvation by legislation.

In the second pattern of natural law, another interpretation
emerges. The first offers us "scientific socialism," but the second is
no less "scientific":

1. The state of nature is primeval chaos or being.	1. Law is progress, development, entelechy, natural selection, or evolution.
2. Nature develops upward.	2. Law develops also, and man's salvation depends on the laws of na-

[5] See Hoxie Neale Fairchild: *The Noble Savage, A Study in Romantic Naturalism.* New York: Columbia University Press, 1928. See also Arthur O. Lovejoy: *Essays in the History of Ideas.* New York: Braziller, 1955.
[6] See *Contract Social*, Ch. 7 me. Cited in Felix Morely: *Freedom and Federalism*, p. 28. Chicago: Regnery, 1959.

ture. The discovery of natural law becomes not only a scientific but statist concern as instrumental to power and salvation.

3. Nature began as a primitive unity, and culminates in a complex unity.

3. Law works to the unity of all men in terms of that basic continuity of being which is the ground of life.

A third, and somewhat earlier, version of the law of nature appeared in markedly Christian terminology at times, in ostensibly close connection with the doctrine of total depravity, and presented a syncretistic sociology. Stated simply, its basic premises were as follows:

1. Man is a self-centered being.

1. The true law is self-interest.

2. Man seeks self-interest because of self-love.

2. Self-interest is that natural law which leads to man's real happiness and therefore social salvation.

3. Man fulfils his being and nature by self-interest.

3. The free society and true society is created by this natural law of self-interest.

This concept was early formulated. It appeared in Blackstone's jurisprudence, for example, as a guiding principle: "He (the Creator) has been pleased so to contrive the constitution and frame of humanity, that we should want no other prompter than to inquire after and pursue the rule of right, but only our own self-love, that universal principle of action." [7] The fundamental error of this position was twofold: *First*, sin and self-interest cannot be equated, as was so often done, for self-interest is not necessarily sin. *Second*, man the sinner is rarely capable of genuine self-interest but is rather destructive, perverse and perverted, as well as suicidal in his course, as Romans 1 makes clear. The "entelechy" of sin is to "burn" (Rom. 1:27) or more accurately, *to burn out* itself rather than to be intelligently capable of self-interest. In any case, in this philosophy as

[7] Blackstone's *Commentaries*, cited in Hall and Montgomery, p. 142. Blackstone's ambivalence of view was apparent in his insistence that "upon these two foundations, the law of nature and the law of revelation, depend all human laws; that is to say, no human laws should be suffered to contradict these," *ibid.*, p. 143.

well, law was redemptive, although the state, so strongly governed
by a mixture of Christian and non-Christian principles, did not
become as openly soteriological and priestly. During the early
years of the United States, this philosophy and Christian faith were
both influential among other forces. There were more than a few
ready to assert redemptive ideas during the American Revolution,
and there were many who held that the spirit actuating the colonies
"was as much from God as the descent of the Holy Ghost on the
day of Pentecost, and was introductory to something great and
good to mankind." [8] But the strong elements of the sociology of
justification by faith were clearly present in the founding of many of
the American colonies, theocratic in nature, and experiments in Christian church society and state, although the rebellion against this concept and its development was constant and marked. The tension
between the two principles is basic to the history of the colonies
and the United States. In Massachusetts, magistrates and ministers
began on the premise that the Scriptures were the *common law* of
the land, and, when pressed to a formulation of the Body of Liberties
in 1641, drawn up by Rev. Nathaniel Ward of Ipswich, stated those
statutes in biblical terms as far as possible. The natural law which
John Winthrop recognized in his "Little Speech on Liberty" in
1645, meant that "our nature is now corrupt." This "natural liberty"
is "common to man with beasts and other creatures. By this, man
as he stands in relation to man simply, hath liberty to do what he
lists: it is a liberty to evil as well as to good. This liberty is incompatible and inconsistent with authority, and cannot endure the
least restraint of the most just authority. . . . This is that great
enemy of truth and peace, that wild beast, which all the ordinances
of God are bent against, to restrain and subdue it." Law therefore
does not *convert* evil or redeem it, but is only a means of *restraint*.
For Winthrop, civil, federal, or moral liberty has its foundation under
law and "in reference to the covenant between God and Man."
"This libterty is maintained and exercised in a way of subjection to

---

[8] Hall and Montgomery, p. 352. For the various religious concepts of the
founding fathers, see Norman Cousins: *"In God We Trust," The Religious
Beliefs and Ideas of the American Founding Fathers.* Harpers: New York,
1958.

authority; it is the same kind of liberty wherewith Christ hath made us free." [9]

In this faith, *Christ* is the instrument of salvation and therefore both the principle of liberty and the great high priest. Law becomes, then, not a work of salvation, but a restraint upon evil, a guide to the godly, and the condition of true liberty.

But, in the absence of this faith, or in rebellion against it, the modern state has returned to the religion of natural man and of Phariseeism, to salvation by law. The modern state is thus inevitably a priestly state and a soteriological state, dedicated to the radically anti-Christian religion of works-salvation, salvation by law. The proliferation of legislation is impelled by this messianic urge, and every political campaign presents its program as a kind of true second advent. Only the right combination of laws is needed to create the good, true and saving society!

But law, on any other foundation than God's terms and His law, becomes anti-law, destructive of law, order, and society. This is exactly what such legislation has become, as witness the National Labor Relations Board and its administrative law. An excellent study of the breakdown of law, the rise of favoritism and violence, and the substitution of "kangaroo courts" for courts of law is Sylvester Petro's *The Kohler Strike, Union Violence and Administrative Law*.[10] The state becomes, for capital, labor, agriculture, education, for every man and institution, the saving power by means of law and the unlimited source of all bounty and blessing. The state has become the priestly mediator of the good life, at whose hands all citizens, schools, institutions, and causes must seek salvation and preservation, the great high priest after the ancient order of Babel. The lines of division are, doctrinally, as sharply drawn as in the days of Rome and of emperor-worship, which involved essentially the recognition of the soteriological and priestly role of the state as the divine-human messianic order. The lines of division, humanly and ecclesiastically, are, unfortunately, scarcely drawn as yet. But

[9] Hall and Montgomery, p. 262.
[10] Chicago: Regnery, 1961. Dr. Petro, now Professor of Law at New York University, was formerly a union leader for the steel workers.

men cannot seek justification *socially* by law and works of law, and long retain a conception of *individual* salvation through justification by faith. The presence of the former is due to the erosion of the latter. Men who have Christ as their all-sufficient priest cannot create or tolerate a priestly and soteriological state.

3

THE ROYAL STATE:
THE MODERN STATE AS DIVINE MONARCHY

Historically, monarchy has been associated with divinity, and, theologically, the association has always been both a necessary and inevitable one. The king was, in antiquity, a sacred person, by virtue of either his office, family, or function. His role was spiritual and temporal, so that "church" and state were in essence combined in his office or person. He was both a divine king and a human god; the eternal and the temporal interpenetrated and mingled in him by virtue of his office, and he set forth, by this status, the fundamental belief in the continuity of the two realms. Salvation was essentially deification for the Egyptians, who asserted the continuity very clearly, and the monarch represented the point at which humanity met divinity and the powers and impulses of the two worlds were in exchange. In India, a king was a present god; the Battak of Sumatra held the king to be a god; in Tahiti, the ruler was one of the gods, and so on. The Siamese language lacked any word "by which any creature of higher rank or greater dignity than a monarch can be described; and the missionaries, when they speak of God, are forced to use the native word for 'king.' "[1] The king's claim upon the people often rested on his "ability" to manipulate the eternal order, the divine gods, to bring victory, rain, and prosperity to his people. The sanctity of the king was great, and it could communicate itself to those whom he clothed, or to his own regalia.[2] "It would seem that the Roman king personated no less a

[1] Cited from E. Young: *The Kingdom of the Yellow Robe*. London, 1898, p. 142, in James Hastings, editor: *Encyclopaedia of Religion and Ethics*, vol. VII, p. 709, A. E. Crawley, "King."

[2] Ernest Crawley: *The Mystic Rose*, p. 115. Revised, enlarged by Theodore Besterman. New York: Meridian, 1960.

deity than Jupiter himself." [3]

The realm of this divine king was the kingdom of God on earth. The monarch personally represented God on earth. Buckler has described the role of "the Oriental monarch" in this respect:

> His face is the face of God. He is the shadow of God on earth, and, when he is seated on his throne, he is known as the threshold of the divine bounty. All this is in virtue of his possession of the divine Glory of the king, which "cannot be forcibly seized" but is the gift of God, to whom it must be ascribed, otherwise it will depart. In order to render apparent the Glory— or Grace, the alternative translation—to the eyes of the uninitiated, the king retains a long beard, avails himself copiously of cosmetics, wears magnificent robes and sits beneath a resplendent crown, suspended so as to appear to be worn, on a throne studded with precious stones. He is in this way the revelation of the Glory, if he possesses the Glory or the Grace; if not, all this paraphernalia is but empty glory—vain glory (Phil. ii. 3). The form of the court of the king is preserved in the shape of our churches. The altar is the throne of the Grace, the threshold of the Grace, and the sanctuary "within the rayle," the place reserved for the circle of the "friends" of the king.
>
> But, however divine is his person, in virtue of the divine epiphany inherent in his kingship, he is human in his limitations by virtue of his being a son of man. [4]

This divine-human king thus represented in his office and person the union and mixture of heaven and earth, the eternal and the temporal, a continuity and a commingling of God and man. There was thus, first, the unity of God and man in the king. Second, the king, through a number of rites, set forth the unity between himself and his people, whereby, through their allegiance, they became the people of the kingdom. In particular, those who entered the service of the state became "*friends*—not servants," through two rites whereby they entered the kingdom in a particular way and a third aspect of kingship which became their privilege. According to Buckler, "First, the robe of honour is the central symbol of

[3] Sir James George Frazer: *The New Golden Bough*, p. 98. New Abridgment, edited with notes by Theodore H. Gaster. New York: Criterion Books, 1959.

[4] F. W. Buckler: *The Epiphany of the Cross*, p. 4f. Cambridge: W. Heffer & Sons, 1938.

incorporation into the body royal." This was a garment belonging
to the monarch, worn by him, taken off or cast off and then given
to another to set forth his participation by succession or delegation
in the royal power. Its acceptance "denoted an act of allegiance,
while its rejection constituted an overt act of defiance, independence
and treason." In the parable of the wedding feast (Matt. 22:14),
there is a significant use of this fact. The guest who came in his own
righteousness "refused to acknowledge his allegiance to his king,
even in the presence of the king himself. His treason was aggravated
by his contumacy." [5]

Second, "The element of the embodiment of the king or incorporation into the body of the king by 'the robe of honour' receives
additional emphasis from the second institution—the royal feast."
The members or friends of the kingdom share in the king's meal.
"The element of common food, common drink and common salt
constitutes the foundation of a common body." To share in the
king's table is to become a part of his kingship and to share in the
responsibility of enforcing the royal law.

> The common meal with the king constitutes in itself not
> merely an oath of allegiance, but a vow to represent the king
> himself, to be the king himself, in any situation which demands
> his presence; to act as if he was the king in order to ensure the
> king's will being carried into effect. . . . To partake of the
> royal feast is to pledge one's self to be a "member" of the king's
> body.[6]

Third, the purpose of these two rites was to set forth "the royal
righteousness." "Servile righteousness" was the righteousness or
law-keeping of the subject. "Royal righteousness" is "the righteousness of the king *and the members of the kingship.*" Between the
two, a great difference exists.

> The royal righteousness is the *source* from which flow the
> law, which the subject must obey, justice, honour, victory, pros-
> perity, peace, life itself. These banish oppression, want, injustice,
> disorder and all that is opposed to the fruits of righteousness.
> It is a gift of God, and Sa'di informed monarchs that their king-

[5] *Ibid.*, p. 6f.
[6] *Ibid.*, p. 8f.

dom would be established if righteousness—the royal righteousness—came to their aid. The difference between the two forms can be seen if it is realized that royal righteousness is the source of action; servile righteousness is the result of limitation of action. They differ as royal majesty differs from servility. It is this difference which underlies the statement of our Lord: "Except your righteousness shall exceed *the righteousness* of the scribes and Pharisees, ye shall in no wise enter into the kingdom of heaven" (Matt. v. 20), and if that fact is borne in mind the invalidity of the pietistic interpretation of the rest of the Sermon on the Mount will be apparent.[7]

This concept of royal divinity marked both ancient and modern kingship. Akbar's infallibility decree of 1579 established that monarch as the divine king, one directly inspired of God, and the "rightful heir" of the kingdom.[8] It was declared of Queen Elizabeth of England "that absolute princes, such as the sovereigns of England, were a species of divinity." [9]

It should be noted that, not only was divinity claimed by kings, but kingship was a divine prerogative It was an assertion of sovereignty, a divine prerogative, and a claim to be the manifestation of the principle of order. When Israel was constituted as a civil government, kingship was therefore reserved to God, whose throne was the mercy seat, His sanctuary the Holy of Holies, because God was the sovereign over Israel and the principle of order, the source of law. The demand of Israel for an earthly king was seen by God, not as a rejection of Samuel but of himself: "for they have not rejected thee, but they have rejected me, that I should not reign over them" (I Sam. 8:5-8). It was declared by God to be the culmination of the apostasy which marked their entire history, from Egypt to Samuel's day.

The kingship established was used by God as a type of the kingship of His Son, but, even then, set forth severe limitations, in that the prophetic and priestly offices were kept separate, and the king

[7] *Ibid.*, p. 10f.

[8] F. W. Buckler, "A New Interpretation of Akbar's Infallibility Decree of 1579," in *Journal of the Royal Asiatic Society*, October, 1924, pp. 591-608.

[9] David Hume: *The History of England, from the Invasion of Julius Caesar to the Abdication of James the Second, 1688*, vol. IV, p. 336f. New York: Harper, 1852.

was, as the law provided, to be only the Lord's choice and totally subject to the Word of God (Deut. 17:14-20). The royal office was providentially done away with before the coming of Christ, and the attempt of Herod to seize the messianic kingship was met with immediate judgment (Acts 12:21-24).

The true kingship was openly set forth in the person of Jesus Christ, in whom God and man were in union, but without commingling or confusion. Christ, by openly setting forth His kingship to His disciples in the Last Supper, made them His "friends" in terms of their obedience (John 15:14, 15), but their participation was not in His divinity but in His perfect, law-keeping and law-fulfilling humanity. His cross and righteousness constituted their robe of glory. The members of His body enter into the glory or grace of the Kingdom of God, not by deification but by grace, not by participation in His divinity but by membership in His perfect humanity.

The Church of King Jesus faced, however, a major threat from the divine kings of imperial Rome. The Roman emperors met the challenge of Jesus Christ and His Church in several ways, by attempting syncretism, by striving to exterminate the faith, and by denaturization. The empire was ready to grant "religious freedom" to the church *provided* the church recognized the right of the state to grant that freedom, which meant a recognition of the state as the principle of order. But it was precisely this which the church fought in pagan Rome in refusing to participate in "emperor worship." The Christians were never asked to worship Rome's pagan gods; they were simply asked to recognize the religious primacy of the state and the emperor as the divine-human order.

> The officials of the Roman Empire in time of persecution sought to force the Christians to sacrifice, not to any of the heathen gods, but to the Genius of the Emperor and the Fortune of the City of Rome; and at all times the Chrisitans' refusal was looked upon not as a religious but as a political offence.[10]

All religions and all gods could have their place in Rome, as long as

[10] Francis Legge: *Forerunners and Rivals of Christianity, From 330 B.C. to 330 A.D.*, vol. I, p. xxiv. New Hyde Park, N. Y.: University Books, 1964 (1915).

the Roman state and its emperor were recognized as the link between the human and the divine orders, the link by whom all others held their continuity and linkage. The issue was this: should the emperor's law, state law, govern both the state and the church, or were both state and church, emperor and bishop alike, under God's law, and under the kingship of Jesus Christ? The orthodox Christians, before and after Constantine the Great, insisted on the supremacy of Christ and His infallible Word over state and church, and emperors and bishops were alike rebuked in terms of it. For them, the church was free from the state, and both church and state were alike under God and His word. The religious freedom which pagan and ostensibly Christian Rome granted was very much like the religious freedom of the modern era, freedom of worship, but not freedom from the state. Satan had promised Christ "all the kingdoms of the world, and the glory of them," on one condition, "If thou wilt fall down and worship me" (Matt. 4:8, 9), that is, if He would recognize the rightness of Satan's position and Satan's supremacy. The emperors of Rome, and the modern states as well, offered "religious liberty," limited to freedom of worship only; in both Rome and the states of the 20th century, the terms are the same. The early church, whatever its other faults, would not have recognized the modern situation as religious liberty: it would have seen it as a form of emperor worship.

Syncretism, and more specifically, absorption of Christ into the imperial union between God and man, was also attempted. According to Tertullian, the Emperor Tiberius proposed the apotheosis of Jesus to the senate, but the measure was rejected.[11]

Hadrian is said to have built temples in his honour. Alexander Severus had in his private chapel statues of Christ, Abraham, and Orpheus; and a similar association of Homer, Pythagoras, Christ, and S. Paul is noted by S. Augustine.[12]

The Christians could plead that they were law-abiding and honest

[11] Tertullian: *Apologeticus*, 5, in *Ante-Nicene Fathers*, vol. XI, *Writings of Tertullian*, vol. I, p. 63f. Edinburgh: T. & T. Clark, 1872.
[12] John Cuthbert Lawson: *Modern Greek Folklore and Ancient Greek Religion, A Study in Survivals*, p. 41. New Hyde Park, N. Y.: University Books, 1964 (1910).

subjects of the emperor, but, for the emperor and the state, they were outlaws of a most dangerous sort, in that they denied that the divine-human link and principle of order was the emperor and the state. All Roman law, the Roman state in its entirety, rested on this presupposition: the imperial order was the Christ, the order of man's salvation. Virgil had declared of Augustus' "advent" that, in Stauffer's summary, "Augustus is the world's saviour who was to come." [13] The emperors all sought to fulfil that role: it was the essence of their office.

When Christianity was finally tolerated and then made the religion of the empire, it was made the state cult and very quickly denatured theologically into Arianism, a faith in which again the state was the vehicle of the divine-human link and order. The persecution of orthodoxy continued.

The biblical doctrine of the state, or of civil government, has as its basic premise the establishment of godly order by means of justice. "The beginning of government" in terms of biblical mandate is often ascribed to Genesis 9:6, "Whoso sheddeth man's blood, by man shall his blood be shed." [14] Calvin accepted this ancient interpretation, but refused to limit its application to the state. The state's province is justice, but justice is a broader concept.

> Truly I do not deny that the punishments which the laws ordain, and which the judges execute, are founded on this divine sentence; but I say the words are more comprehensive. It is written, "Men of blood shall not live out half their days" (Ps. iv. 25). And we see some die in highways, some in stews, and many in wars. Therefore, however magistrates may connive at the crime, God sends executioners from other quarters, who shall render unto sanguinary men their reward. God so threatens and denounces vengeance against the murderer, that he even arms the magistrate with the sword for the avenging of slaughter, in order that the blood of men may not be shed with impunity. [15]

For Calvin, the major function of the civil magistrate was the second

---

13 Ethelbert Stauffer: *Christ and the Caesars*, p. 83.
14 Howard B. Rand: *Digest of the Divine Law*, p. 121. Merrimac, Mass.: Destiny Publishers, 1943.
15 John Calvin: *Commentaries on Genesis*, vol. I, p. 295. Grand Rapids: Eerdmans, 1948.

table of the law, justice, but, because moral order rests on theological order, the office of magistracy "extends to both tables of the law." His premise was "that no government can be happily constituted, unless its first object be the promotion of piety and that all laws are preposterous which neglect the claims of God, and merely provide for the interests of men." The state is not the church, but its existence requires not merely "the administration of justice among men" but also the protection of "the pure worship of himself according to the rule of his law." [16] This double aspect of the state's responsibility should be remembered in considering Calvin's attitude towards civil obedience: the state Christians are duty bound to obey is a state which required of men obedience to the first table of the law, and, with respect to the second table of the law, protects men's lives, the sanctity of marriage, the immunities of property and of reputation, and forbids the violation of these things by word and deed, as the case may apply. Thus, what Calvin had in mind was clearly neither the modern "secular" state nor the socialist state. Neither of these states would have met his definition of civil government.

In commenting on Romans 13:1, Calvin noted, "He calls them the *higher powers*, not the supreme." With respect to Romans 13:3, Calvin said:

> Now, the utility is this,—that the Lord has designed in this way to provide for the tranquillity of the good, and to restrain the waywardness of the wicked; by which two things the safety of mankind is secured: for except the fury of the wicked be resisted, and the innocent be protected from their violence, all things would come to an entire confusion. Since then this is the only remedy by which mankind can be preserved from destruction, it ought to be carefully observed by us, unless we wish to avow ourselves as the public enemies of the human race.[17]

In his comment on Romans 13:4, Calvin stated that civil magistrates "are responsible to God and to men in the exercise of their

[16] John Calvin: *Institutes of the Christian Religion*, Bk. IV, ch. XX, ix; vol. II, p. 779f. of the Presbyterian Board of Christian Education edition, 1936, John Allen translation.
[17] John Calvin: *Commentaries on Romans*, pp. 478, 480. Grand Rapids: Eerdmans, 1948.

power." Men should remember that "the divine goodness" established civil government to protect men "against injuries done by the wicked." [18] The protection of theological order, and the maintenance of moral order as defined by the second table of the law, is thus the duty and the area of jurisdiction of the state.

As a result of Enlightenment faith, the state increasingly denied Christian theological order and religiously restricted the realm of reality to the material. "Where the spiritual is destroyed, all that remains is the material." [19] In this material realm, the state has claimed increasingly a total jurisdiction. As Jan Huizinga observed,

> The position which the State professing its own amoral character arrogates to itself to-day is a very different one. As State it claims absolute autonomy and independence in respect to all moral standards. In so far as it allows the Church and religion, with their explicit and binding moral code, to carry on an existence of their own, their position is no longer one of freedom and equality but of subjugation and compulsory allegiance to the doctrine of the State itself, it is clear that only those devoid of all religion will be able to embrace an ethical system of such glaring ambiguity.[20]

Nock called attention to the growing powers and claims of the state, its increasing "aim being the complete extinction of social power through absorption by the State." [21] To increase power, the state has worked for "the erection of poverty and mendicancy into a permanent political asset."[22] According to Bourne, "The ideal of the State is that within its territory its power and influence should be universal." [23] Martin declared that "The State is rapidly becoming a New Church."

[18] *Ibid.*, p. 481.
[19] Vick Knight: *What Happened to the Bees, A Political Parable*, p. 5. Los Angeles: Key Records, 1964.
[20] Jan Huizinga: *In the Shadow of Tomorrow*, p. 155. New York: W. W. Norton, 1936.
[21] Albert Jay Nock: *Our Enemy, the State*, p. 21. Caldwell, Idaho: Caxton Printers, 1959 (1935).
[22] *Ibid.*, p. 14.
[23] Randolph Bourne, "Herd Impulses and the State," in Waldo R. Browne, editor: *Leviathan in Crisis*, p. 100. New York: Viking Press, 1946.

I have called the modern State a new Church; in a sense I think I have shown that it is. But I fear that such a comparison is very unfair to the medieval Church. For what a church this new one is—a soulless mechanism to which men look for the redemption of the world and salvation from themselves; its creed the teachings of Rousseau; its priesthood the professional politician; its acolyte the policemen; its offering the income tax; its litany the party campaign; its communion the exercise of the vote; its sacrament the baptism of war; its Heaven business prosperity passed around; its dreaded Hell its own logical end in the dictatorship of the proletariat; and its God the self-idolatry of "the People" as mass! [24]

The royal divinity of the ancient state was viewed as the link between the temporal and the divine. The state represented divinity on earth by its union and commingling of the two orders, but it did not exhaust the divine, and it did not deny that the divine, while best represented on earth by the state, and most real in that union, still existed in a measure apart from the state. In the modern state, a new form of royal divinity is exhaustively present. For the modern state, there is no reality beyond the material; theological order is on every hand increasingly limited or denied. A new theology of the state is instead in evidence. The state is that order in which man is truly human, in terms of this new view. In the state and its cradle-to-grave security man will find his salvation. The state has unlimited jurisdiction, because it is that order in which man realizes himself, the order in which man expresses his collective divinity: vox populi, vox dei, the voice of the people is the voice of God in this collective or democratic consensus.

Religiously, this new emperor worship is not without its champions. The modern religious Arians find their gospel in social action. Even among ostensibly orthodox Christians, these new devotees of the royal divinity of the state are not lacking. Thus, one such man denies the concept that "labor relations, education, mental and physical health, agriculture, and housing" are "forbidden areas" to the state. Marsden cannot accept the fact that "political liberalism

[24] Everett Dean Martin, in "The Religion of the State," in Browne, pp. 214, 219.

stems from theological liberalism." He wants to join an ostensible theological orthodoxy to a political liberalism.[25]

The erosion that has occured in the concept of government in the Enlightenment Era is a very extensive one. To the American Puritan, unlike the man of the 20th century, the word *government* suggested not the state, which he called *civil government*, but the self-government of the Christian man. This to him was the basic government, and it was inseparable from the Word of God, Scripture, as man's infallible guide to self-government. Again, there was the family, man's basic social institution and government, man's first church, state, and school, in a very real sense. The family, ordained by God, was under the government of God and governed by His Word. The church was also a basic government, with extensive power over Christian man and grave responsibilities in terms of the preaching of the word, the administration of the sacraments, and godly discipline and order. The school was also a government, as was man's vocation or business, for man was subject to the rules and procedures governing his calling. Social conventions, community expectations, friends and neighbors also exercised a government over Christian man. The area of civil government was thus a restricted one, the protection of theological order, and the establishment and maintenance of justice. By restricting the state to this area under God, the rest of life was reserved to the various God-ordained institutions and activities of Christian man.

The modern state, however by denying these older restrictions, has made *salvation* its function. Man is to be saved from poverty, sickness, death, ignorance, sin, war, superstition, and all things else by the saving state, which works steadily to create its divine order, the saving society. Every area the state wishes to invade and possess in the name of the welfare of man becomes its legitimate jurisdiction. A total sovereignty is asserted in the name of man. The state steadily denies the need of Christian theological order as it claims jurisdiction over every area in terms of its royal divinity.

[25] George M. Marsden, in a review of C. Gregg Singer: *A Theological Interpretation of American History*, in *The Westminster Theological Review*, vol. XXVII, no. 2, May, 1965, pp. 195-199.

The early church fought against the prospect of "religious liberty" in a Roman Empire whose claims were far more modest than those of the modern state. It yielded an obedience where obedience was due without surrender. It refused to accept freedom under Caesar by sacrificing to Caesar; it insisted on its freedom under God.

The church today has almost universally accepted the messianic state, except for a few who, like St. Athanasius the Great, resist in their desert retreats. The church is content to have freedom under the new caesars, within the new divine monarchies, and to become its servile subject. Kantorowicz wrote, of Frederick II, that

> The Emperor taught that the State herself daily begets afresh the only true and valid Law of God; that the living law of the temporal world is the Living God himself. That the Eternal and Absolute must themselves adapt and change with time if they are to remain living. This was a decisive break with the past.[26]

That "living God," the state, is now the omnipresent reality of the modern world and its Enlightenment culture. A decisive break with this present and past is needed in terms of the truly living God.

[26] Ernst Kantorowicz: *Frederick the Second 1194-1250*, p. 244. New York: Ungar, 1957 (1931).

4

DEMOCRACY AND DIVINITY

Aristotle described, in his *Politics*, the great political leader as "a God among men" and stated that "for men of pre-eminent virtue there is no law—they are themselves a law. Anyone would be ridiculous who attempted to make a law for them." Democratic states, Aristotle added, aim at equality and hence ostracize and banish such men.[1]

Aristotle to the contrary, however, such "god-like" men often more commonly arise in democratic movements than outside of them. In Rome, it was Julius Caesar, the democratic champion, who assumed divinity and was honored by the Greeks of Asia as "a revealed god, offspring of Mars and Venus, and universal saviour of the human race."[2] Roman coins, which throughout the Republic's history had on them images of the gods, now for the first time bore the image of a man, Julius Caesar. It was not Caesar's claim to divinity which offended Rome and led to his death, but the claim, grounded on his divinity, to the monarchy. Although he rejected the title of king, Caesar, in receiving the title *dictator perpetuus*, had greeted the senators on a golden throne in front of the temple of Venus Genetrix seated as a monarch.[3] Octavian grounded his power on his claim to be *divi filius*, the son of God.[4]

The policy of Octavian was to revive and strengthen the old republican forms while preparing for his own apotheosis at death. As the years passed, the emphasis on democratization kept pace with

[1] Aristotle: *Politics*, 1284a; in the Benjamin Jowett translation, introduction by Max Lerner, Modern Library edition, New York, 1943, Bk. III, ch. 13; p. 153f.

[2] Lily Ross Taylor: *The Divinity of the Roman Emperor*, p. 61. Middletown, Conn.: American Philological Association, 1931.

[3] *Ibid.*, pp. 66, 72f.

[4] *Ibid.*, p. 99.

the growth of the divinization of the emperor. The emperor became, in the most extravagant terms, god and savior on earth, and the people gained on the one hand the empty honor of virtually universal citizenship, and, on the other, the growing religious faith in the divinity of the individual soul. Technical democratization, the actual divinization of the emperor and the deification of man's soul, went hand in hand with totalitarian statism.

This relationship is a necessary one. Because man is a religious creature, the god-concept is inescapable to his thinking. Man will either serve the true God or create a false one. If man removes his gods or God from heaven, he will speedily create a new god on earth. In any system of thought lacking in transcendence, and, ultimately, only biblical Christianity has a true doctrine of transcendence, power and omnipotence become immanent concepts. As a result, *the highest point of power in any system becomes the god of that system.* As a result, statism, the most logical expression of that immanent power, becomes the manifest expression of divinity on earth. Thus, as religious unbelief increases, statism increases. To the extent that, in Christian circles, the doctrine of creation, which declares the fiat power of the triune God to create all things by sovereign acts in six days and then to sustain that creation, is denied, to that extent power is transferred from God to the universe, from the supernatural act to natural processes. Political liberalism is thus a logical development of theological liberalism, in that both involve a transfer of sovereignty from God to man; both rest on a concept of the independence of time from eternity, implicitly or explicitly. Both are indifferent, cool, or rebellious towards the sovereign decree and favor a democratization of authority as the true ground of civil order.

To analyze the relationship between political liberalism and theological liberalism, let us first examine what Hallowell has called "Integral Liberalism," the conservative, classical liberalism stemming from Hugo Grotius and John Locke, and characterized by the following beliefs:

(1) A belief in the absolute value of human personality and the spiritual equality of all individuals.

(2) A belief in the autonomy of individual will.

(3) A belief in the essential rationality and goodness of man.

(4) A belief in the existence of certain inalienable rights peculiar to individuals by virtue of their humanity. They are commonly spoken of as the natural rights to "life, liberty, and property."

(5) A belief that the state comes into existence by mutual consent for the sole purpose of preserving and protecting these rights.

(6) A belief that the relationship between the state and individuals is a contractual one and that when the terms of the contract are violated individuals have not only the right but the responsibility to revolt and establish a new government.

(7) A belief that social control is best secured by law rather than by command. The law is conceived as being at once the product of individual will and the embodiment of reason. The law alone cannot command and restrain the individual and "government under the law" is the liberal ideal.

(8) A belief that "the government which governs least governs best." The government is conceived as having primarily negative functions, the protection of the individual in his rights and freedom in order that he may be free to follow the "dictates of conscience," and the laws of nature.

(9) A belief in individual freedom in all spheres of life (political, economic, social, intellectual and religious). Freedom is conceived as freedom from all authority that is capable of acting capriciously or arbitrarily, freedom to act in accordance with the dictates of "right reason," i.e., with the dictates of natural law as it is revealed to men through natural reason.

(10) A belief in the existence of a transcendental order of truth which is accessible to man's natural reason and capable of evoking a moral response. It is an order requiring both individual thought and will for its realization, i.e., it is a potential order requiring individual thought and will for its translation into actuality. Through his autonomous reason and in the light of his conscience the individual avoids anarchy by translating the principles of this natural order into practice. The choice between order and anarchy devolves upon the individual, and more particularly, upon individual conscience. Thus conscience is the keystone of the liberal doctrine.[5]

[5] John H. Hallowell: *Main Currents in Modern Political Thought*, p. 110f. New York: Henry Holt and Company, 1959.

In this classical liberalism, the divine order and God are in the remote background as the insurance agency for man and society, but the real power has been transferred to autonomous man and to nature. Autonomous reason is lord of creation, and autonomous reason finds its liberal law written into the very being of Nature. God may be in the background as creator, but He is no longer the sustainer of the universe: natural law prevails. The universe is a self-sufficient law-realm, and the divine decree and predestination give way steadily to a natural decree and materialistic determinism. Classical liberalism is still prevalent as the political philosophy of non-Christian conservatism or libertarianism. But, with Darwin's hypothesis accepted, this position has become an anachronism.

The evolutionary, post-Darwinian view of the universe robs Nature of its deified or semi-deified status. Nature is seen instead as a lawless, blindly struggling energy in motion, creating or developing various forms of life which may or may not survive. If law is to exist in the universe, it must be man-made or statist law. Nature has shown no law-making intelligence apart from man. The high point of social evolution is thus the state.

In classical liberalism, because Nature's law governed man, laissez faire prevailed. Nature's law provided the necessary conditions for liberty, and for man to interfere was to endanger his liberty and welfare. Under the post-Darwinian view of nature, for man not to interfere in the blind processes of nature is to endanger his liberty and welfare. Man must guide and control his own evolution, socially and biologically, and the surest means to this is the scientific socialistic state. Quite logically, Karl Marx saw Darwin's work as the necessary hypothesis for socialistic theory.

The foundation of orthodox Christian political theory is the divine decree and the authority of the infallible Scripture. The foundation of classical, liberal political thought is natural law and the authority of the autonomous reason of man. The foundation of post-Darwinian liberalism is the necessity of statist law as the new predestination and decree and the authority of the scientific socialist elite of the state. Liberty under God was the concept of the Christian state; liberty under Nature was the thesis of classical liberalism; liberty under the state is the assumption of the scientific socialist state.

Political liberalism of both varieties stems from theological liberalism. Theological liberalism divorces the state from the necessity of upholding theological order as the necessary premise of true moral order and true law. It accepts either the autonomous reason of man or the autonomous state as its basic political center and principle, and it calls a state "Christian" insofar as it ministers to human needs and "human rights," not in terms of any theocentric standard. In terms of theological liberalism, to be "Christian" is to be humanitarian, and, in terms of this, the Merriam-Webster Second International Dictionary has defined "humanitarianism" as "The doctrine that man's obligations are limited to, and dependent alone on, men and human relations." This aptly summarizes the perspective of contemporary politics and of liberal "Christian" ethics. A. J. Bahm has defined humanitarianism as "any view in which interest in human values is central." [6] This is the framework in terms of which theological liberalism has championed statist action as "Christian" morality. In terms of this context, many church-going farmers placed pictures of Franklin Delano Roosevelt next to pictures of Jesus Christ: for them Roosevelt represented the epitome of "Christian" humanitarianism and social action.

As has been noted, the highest point of power in any system becomes the god of that system. Post-Darwinian liberalism has been, in varying degrees, positivistic. In legal philosophy, positivism has meant the denial of any higher law, either the law of God or the law of nature. This recurring theory, as old at least as the Greek Sophists, is always the cornerstone of statism and tyranny. It denies any appeal beyond the state to a justice that stands over and judges the law of the state. Justice becomes what the state does legally. The scientific, socialistic state is the only possible order in which evolving, developing law and justice can manifest themselves, and there can be no appeal beyond that development, since it represents the high point of being. The most one can hope for is a "leap in being," to use Voegelin's deadly philosophy, but one cannot predict

---

[6] A. J. Bahm, "Humanitarianism," in Dagobert D. Runes, editor: *Dictionary of Philosophy*, p. 132. New York: Philosophical Library, 1960, 15th edition, revised.

what that "leap in being" or new development will be. Until it comes, the present order of being is total truth. Hallowell has ably described the impasse of positivism:

> With the rejection of metaphysics the positivist rejects at the same time any possibility of evaluating the acts of the sovereign in terms of justice or injustice for justice is a metaphysical concept. Since for the positivist the only rights of individuals are those secured by the positive law, he cannot evaluate the acts of the sovereign in terms of the observance or violation of individual rights. All basis of obligation as a matter of fact disappears. Compulsion is substituted for obligation and the coercive force behind the law becomes the distinguishing characteristic of legality. Thus, ultimately, the liberal who accepts the positivistic perspective has no choice but to make either the sovereign or the individual absolute and his own logic forces him, whether explicitly or not, to an espousal either of tyranny or of unbridled subjectivism.[7]

This then is the choice that the logic of positivism inevitably confronts man with: either anarchism or statism, either the totalitarian individual or the totalitarian state. In a sense, this is only briefly and seemingly a choice, since the highest point of power in the system quickly becomes the state, and the state thus becomes the god of the system.

Post-Darwinian liberalism, having become consistently evolutionary, has been positivistic. In this development, "Justice, being a metaphysical concept, was discarded as being empirically worthless." Law had no criterion save legality or state enactment.

> Freedom under the law was retained by the positivist liberal as an article of his liberal faith but it came to mean something quite different from what it had meant originally. Originally it meant that a man could not be compelled to do anything contrary to reason or conscience, that the test of a law was its justness. Under the influence of positivism, the concept came to mean that a man could not be compelled to do anything except by a law enacted in accordance with a prescribed procedure (any prescribed procedure) with sufficient force behind it to compel obedience. Now there is a great difference between

[7] Hallowell: *Main Currents in Modern Political Thought*, p. 115.

freedom from *unjust* compulsion and freedom from *illegal* compulsion. When the test of legality, moreover, is ultimately conceived as the force behind the law, freedom from illegal compulsion amounts to no more than freedom to do whatever the state does not forbid. This is a conception of freedom much more congenial to tyranny than to the preservation of the inalienable rights of man.

But the conception of the inalienable rights of man no more survived the scrutiny of positivism than did the concept of justice. Viewed from the perspective of positivism the rights of man were conceived no longer as natural rights but as legal rights. Properly speaking, according to the positivist view, man has no rights at all; what the liberals have traditionally called rights are actually only concessions granted by the state or society. Whatever rights men have are those guaranteed by the law and since the rights are the product of the law they are not, properly speaking, rights at all but concessions to claims which the individual makes and the state recognizes. As concessions, it follows, of course, that they can be withdrawn to the extent that the state deems such withdrawal of its recognition compatible with the interests of the "general welfare." [8]

Justice thus becomes what the state does, and true law becomes what the state legally enacts, because the state, as the highest point of power, is the god of the system. In any consistent doctrine of God, law is not above God, nor is there a law by which God can be judged, because God is law himself. The modern state has thus become its own god: it is its own source of law. The modern state must therefore become "secular"; it must uproot within its structure every trace of Christian law, because it cannot permit within itself a higher law as a critique of its being. This destruction of Christian law is done commonly in the name of "human rights." It is ostensibly an extension of the autonomous man's powers, an illusory hope, as will be seen. In the process, the old law is treated with ridicule and with transparent contempt. Thus, in two San Francisco trials which struck down legislation against nude shows,

> The courts cited almost opposite reasons.
> Municipal Judge Leo R. Friedman refused to admit the photos because they were taken after police had decided to arrest the

8 *Ibid.,* p. 325f.

girls. Hence the photos were self-incriminating, the judge said.
   Municipal Judge Leland Lazarus ruled the photos submitted
in his court were inadmissible because they were taken before the
girls were arrested. Hence the photos failed to document the
alleged offense at time of commission, he said.[9]

In decisions which overturned existing legislation, the judges directed the juries to give acquittal verdicts. According to Judge
Friedman, "This is a free country. . . . I think we have the right
to pick and choose what we want to read and see. No one's pulling
anyone's arms to drag them into those places in North Beach." [10]
Ostensibly this decision was a verdict for "human rights," but "human rights" and democracy have usually been the banner by which
tyranny has come to power. Certainly, the decision did give individuals the "right" to stage or attend such performances, but the
state gained far greater "rights" in the process. *First*, the state struck
down, through its courts, the idea that any higher moral law can
have jurisdiction in either the private or the public lives of men.
If the Christian God has any law or standard in such matters, obedience thereto is purely optional and esthetic with men. For the state,
God and His law, if they exist, are purely private affairs and matters
of personal taste and choice. *Second*, while the individual is given
such additional "rights," the "rights" or powers gained by the state
are far greater. The state has ruled God and His moral law out of
the picture. The claims of God upon man and his society are not
legally admissible in this structure. The state supplants God in
determining what is right and wrong. The state as the source of law
and of "right" has conferred a "right" on the individual *but at the
price of admitting the claim of the state to be moral arbiter or god.*
Thus, the state has gained far more in this situation than the individual, because the "right" which the state grants to the individual
the state can also take away. *Third*, as a result of the priority of the
state's "moral law" to God's moral law, what follows is that *every
liberty* of the individual has been endangered and reduced to state
toleration, since the state is thus the origin and source of law. If

[9] "Bosom Pics Out at Trial," Palo Alto *Times*, Thursday, May 6, 1965, p. 33.
[10] "Topless Shows Ruled Public's Right," Oakland, California, *Tribune*, Saturday, May 8, 1965, p. 1.

there is no higher law which the state recognizes, and the state itself determines "human rights," then the state itself can nullify all "human rights" and liberties in the name of "general welfare," as Hallowell has noted. By such decisions, with their steady whittling away at the doctrine of God's moral law, the doctrine of all higher law is being rapidly eroded and being replaced with statist law, positive law. Law is what the state decrees, and liberty is what the state defines as liberty.

Judge Friedman insisted on the "right" of the individual, by implication, at least, an assertion that democratic "rights" are more important than the law of God and the claims of God concerning moral order. As has been noted, the democratization of society goes hand in hand with the divinization of the state. Power and right are withdrawn from God and given to the people. When the people become the locale of right and power, that right and power express themselves in the form of the state, the high point of power and the god of the system.

The freedom of the individual in a democracy is only a transitional freedom, existing briefly as the source of law moves from God to the state. It is impossible for the individual to maintain his liberty very long in a democracy, because power is delegated to the state, to the general will of the democratic mass as it expresses itself in the state. A fundamental axiom of political life is this, that *power allies itself with power*. A power group is not interested in charity; it is not in existence to subsidize weak and struggling groups who need but cannot give help. Unless firmly restrained, *power always grasps for more power*, and hence it allies itself with other powers, and a struggle for power between cooperating yet competing power groups follows. Thus, as a democracy develops the powers of the state, and the powers of big business, big finance, big labor, criminal syndicates, big pressure groups, powerful minority groups, all now unchecked by the higher law of God, these powers all prosper at the expense of the individual. These powers come into being in the name of "human rights" and ostensibly to further the welfare of the individual, but they then operate in terms of their purely power-hungry drives for total power. This interlocking of power groups against the individual and against God's moral order is called "The System." Franklin Hichborn in 1915 documented carefully the operations of such a power structure in his study, *"The System" as Uncovered by The San Francisco Graft Prosecution*. Any System, as it operates, seeks continual power, so that a local System allies itself with a state or provincial System, the state or provincial System with a national or federal System, and this national System readily allies itself with or creates an international System in order to increase its power. This leads either to irresponsible warfare as a result of meddling in foreign affairs, or to irresponsible alliances. Citizens are bewildered when they see "their state" ally itself with the states of an international communist conspiracy, and they regard it as an unwise or foolish act on the part of the state. It is, however, the citizens who are foolish in assuming that the state is "their state." By being divorced from God, the state has been divorced from responsibility: it is now a law unto itself, a power seeking more power, a *System*. The citizen is no more than a short-term ally to power: the real ally is another power group, and *the state increasingly knows no politics except power*. As a result, it is more congenial to a communist state than to its own people, and the "communist state" is in turn ready to consider alliances with "capitalist states," however dishonestly, in a way that it will never consider alliances with its own citizenry. Because power allies itself with power, the people, in whose name the power was seized, are, as the powerless ones, always the most expendable. The "principles" of the power state, whether Marxist, Fabian, Keynesian, or anything else, are always expendable, because no law or principle can transcend or govern the new god, the state. As a result, whenever convenient, a "New-Economic Policy" can be adopted, although a clear-cut violation of professed principle, because *power is the goal and there is no principle beyond power for the "secular state."* The classification of states therefore in terms of their economic policies and political philosophies is a classification in terms of secondary differences. The primary classification is in terms of power.

Democracy is thus totalitarian. It makes the "rights" of the people "divine right" in order to destroy the moral order based on God's revelation, and also to destroy the family and the true church as free and divinely instituted orders. All "right" and power become statist as a result, and totalitarian democracy results.

But if God be God, then man has no rights apart from God, who is the only true source of all right and of all authority. Destroy the authority of God in human society, and the only right which remains is the right of power, the assertion of sheer force, so that might makes right. Only insofar as God's transcendental law, revealed in His infallible Word, asserts that man has God-given immunities of life, family, property, reputation, and worship can man withstand the claims of the state to be the divine source of all power and right. And the only "right" the state can confer is a changing and uncertain legal right which is a tentative right, since it is always subject to cancellation in the name of the "general welfare."

Political liberalism is, even in its most conservative form, *the transference of right and power from God to man. Instead of asserting the autonomy of God, it asserts the autonomy of man.* The relationship of even this simplest form of political liberalism to religious liberalism is an obvious one. Political liberalism presupposes religious liberalism; it requires for its existence a surrender in some measure of the sovereignty and autonomy of God to the implicit or explicit sovereignty and autonomy of man. In the very introduction to *Christianity and Liberalism* (1923), J. Gresham Machen made it clear that he saw political and theological liberalism as essentially one. It is ironic that in the very movement Machen began the voice of political liberalism is occasionally heard, and, in *The Presbyterian Guardian*, expresses itself, and it represents no small impudence. The connection between political liberalism and theological liberalism is a vital one. Wherever the one is seen, the other is sure to follow. The history of *The Reformed Journal* is illustrative of this: its espousal of liberal politics has been followed by a standing attack on the confessional faith of the Christian Reformed Church and a steady liberal re-interpretation of the doctrines of that church.

In the more professedly liberal churches, the erosion is far gone. There is no infallible word, nor has there been for some time. Increasingly, there is no objective moral law. The only "law" in sexual relations is the response of "love" by the individual. This is increasingly asserted in literature aimed by the churches at college youth.[11] This "new morality" has extensive support in almost all churches. One of its premises is that a personal relationship, an I-Thou relationship, is loving and hence holy, whether adulterous, homosexual, or marital, whereas an I-It relationship, wherein the other person is treated as a thing, is by definition immoral wherever it occurs. In this perspective, morality is not God's objective law structure but simply man's subjective experience of himself and his world. Morality is not law but experience in this philosophy, which rests clearly on positivism and on anarchism.

Reference was made earlier to the San Francisco trials under Judges Friedman and Lazarus. The clergy of San Francisco have been vocal, both Protestant and Catholic, in advocating "fair" housing, "civil rights," defending the liberties of homosexuals, attacking the House Un-American Activities Committee in its investigation of subversion, and in other related social action causes. San Francisco today is seeing the way paved legally for a wide-open city which can surpass the old Barbary Coast, and all this with scarcely a murmur from the clergy. This is not surprising. The new god of the churches is the state, and the only moral law which fans the fanatical zeal of these churchmen is statist welfare legislation, "civil rights" legislation, and similar attempts by the state to usurp all government into itself and to become the source of all law, power, and beneficence.

The roots of modern statism run deeply into Arminianism and scholasticism, into religious liberalism of every kind. Wherever there is a transference of autonomy from the triune God to the new sovereign, man, political liberalism ensues, and its end product is the totalitarian state, the state as man's new divinity. The highest point of power in any system is the god of that system, and the lonely and

11 See William Graham Cole: *Called to Responsible Freedom: The Meaning of Sex in the Christian Life*, United Christian Youth Movement, National Council of Churches, New York, 1961; see also Robert C. Buckle, "Love Without Fear, A Personal View of Being Physical," in *Campus Encounter*, vol. e, no. 4, published by the United Campus Christian Fellowship.

helpless individual cannot compete with his god, the state, nor can he hope to be free from it, unless he turn, as a repentant sinner, to the only true God, who alone can deliver man and by whose law the deified state is doomed to perish, together with all who live in terms of that order. They who live by the state shall perish by the state, for the state's pretension to total power is first of all an attack upon a triune God who is jealous of His honor.

5

EMINENT DOMAIN

The doctrine of eminent domain is a basic but unexamined concept of civilization, an idea assumed without question by most people as a necessary evil. A simple definition is in order by way of introduction, and the Second Edition of the Merriam-Webster dictionary provides a convenient one:

> *eminent* domain. Law. That superior dominion of the sovereign power over all the property within the state which authorizes it to appropriate all or any part thereof to a necessary public use, reasonable compensation being made. The obligation to give compensation is considered by the best authorities as being incident to the right of eminent domain, and not an imposed limitation. The right of *eminent domain* is usually carefully distinguished from that of *taxation* and the *police power*. In Great Britain the compulsory acquisition of land for public or semipublic purposes is governed by statute, and is called *compulsory purchase* in England; in Scotland the transaction is called a *compulsory surrender*. Some consider an analogous right, wider than angary, to exist in international law for one nation to appropriate the territory or property of another as a necessary measure of self-protection.

Eminent domain is thus an attribute of ultimate sovereignty, and therefore it is an attribute of divinity. According to the Bible, "the earth is the Lord's" (Ps. 24:1), and He therefore has total dominion over it. Because "the earth is the Lord's" God requires the whole world to submit to His law and regards all things as subject to total control, confiscation, or regulation by His sovereign power and word (Ex. 9:29; 19:5; Deut. 10:14; Ps. 50:12; I Cor. 10:26, 28). As God declared to Job, "Who hath prevented me, that I should repay him? whatsoever is under the whole heaven is mine" (Job 41:11). The premise of the Bible is God's assertion of total sovereignty over all creation and all men. The Mosaic law claimed total sovereignty for God, and the jurisdiction of His law over all persons, Israelite and foreigner, within the boundaries of the nation (Deut. 31:12), but those outside the law of the covenant were not thereby outside God's jurisdiction. The judgment of *all* the nations is repeatedly proclaimed precisely because God's sovereignty extends over all nations. "Under Scriptural law, all property—the whole earth—belongs to God, who is the only owner of property"[1] in any ultimate and sovereign sense. Man holds title under God.

In the biblical law, the state has no right of eminent domain, and no right to tax the land. "It was impossible to dispossess men of their inheritance under the law of the Lord as no taxes were levied against land."[2] The tithe was God's tax, not a gift to God. The state was limited to a tax resembling the tithe, a tax on increase, not on the land itself.[3] God as sovereign confiscated the land when the Israelites became apostate, even as He dispossesses and destroys all peoples for their failure to acknowledge His dominion and sovereignty. The marks of a tyrant and a supplanter of God's kingship over a people was specified as oppressive taxation, and the confiscation of land by eminent domain (I Sam. 8).

For the state to claim the right of eminent domain is therefore a claim to *divine right*. Eminent domain is not, as some jurists would hold, a pragmatic and necessary law, but a lively survival of the ancient claim to divinity by the state. The fact that people are not aware of the significance of eminent domain does not reduce its significance to the slightest degree. The state, in claiming eminent domain, is simply asserting "sovereign power over all the property within the state," to cite Webster again, and compensation for such seized properties is "incident to" but not an essential part of "the right of eminent domain." And today, in the average American

[1] H. B. Clark: *Biblical Law*, no. 128, p. 88, Second edition. Portland, Oregon: Binfords and Mort, 1944.
[2] Howard B. Rand: *Digest of the Divine Law*, p. 111. Merrimac, Massachusetts: Destiny, 1943. For a summary of biblical land laws, see Roger Sherman Gaber: *Old Testament Law for Bible Students*, pp. 94-106. New York: Macmillan, 1922.
[3] Rand, p. 93f.

city there are about 50 agencies which have the power to confiscate land.[4]

The right of eminent domain, then, is a divine right and power. Moreover, there are no degrees of divinity: divinity is a total concept. A deity is either divine, or he is not; he is either a god, or he is not. Thus, when the state lays claim to divinity, it lays claim to a total power. The right of eminent domain ostensibly limits the state to the confiscation of properties necessary to the common good, or to the public welfare. But the state is the judge of the common good and public welfare, and so the power of eminent domain expands steadily towards the total possession by the state of all properties within the state. The state, being viewed as the higher or supreme power, and the possessor of eminent domain, is seen as the natural guardian and agency of the public welfare. In terms of this presupposition, *private* ownership is seen as hostile to the common good, whereas *state* ownership advances the public welfare. With this philosophy, total confiscation is simply a question of time. The right of eminent domain, therefore, by associating a "necessary common use" or good with the state, makes the state into a benevolent god whose control and ownership are necessary to the welfare of man.

It is impossible to understand the Bible apart from its assertion of God's sole eminent domain over every realm. The cleansing of the Temple by Jesus, both at the beginning and end of His ministry, was an assertion of His eminent domain over the church. His condemnation of Jerusalem (Matt. 24:1ff.), His declaration that the Kingdom of God was taken from Israel and given to another (Matt. 21:43), His assertion of divine Kingship before the Sanhedrin (Matt. 26:64), and His declaration of His Kingship before Pilate (John 18:33-37), were all assertions of eminent domain over the state, whether Judea or Rome. His triumphal entry into Jerusalem was begun with an act of eminent domain and confiscation. Disciples were sent to a neighboring village to get a colt. There was no promise of payment or return. They were merely to assert: "The Lord hath need of him" (Luke 19:28-48). He blasted the fig tree

[4] Glenn J. Manley, "Eminent domain and your property," in *House Beautiful*, April, 1966, vol. 108, no. 4, pp. 58, 60, 62.

(or Israel) later in the week, asserting His eminent domain over both nature and the state. The "vineyard" or Kingdom of God was His to bestow, and man's life was His to bless, or to destroy (Luke 22:9-16).

Sovereignty and eminent domain are inescapable concepts. Denied to God, they will accrue to men. Today Caesar is taking the sovereignty men will not give to God. Sovereignty is supremacy in rule and power, and eminent domain is an aspect of sovereignty. Sovereignty cannot be avoided: it will either be transcendental, or it will be immanent. It will either be reserved to God, or it will accrue to men. With the anarchists, sovereignty is reserved to the individual man; with the statists, it is reserved to the state. In either case, it is tyranny.

Because the state has claimed sovereignty, and therefore divinity, it has supplanted Christianity as the new yet ancient religion of man. Problems of state are now essentially religious problems, and the program of the state is social salvation, and individual salvation as well by means of mental health plans. Forell has described the change in man's life:

> If one would define the crucial problem of the 16th century as the problem of religion and the crucial problem of the 18th century as the problem of the truth, and it could be said that the crucial problem of the 20th century is the problem of the state. The decisive question on which everything depended for the 16th century man was the decision between the contending religious forces. Later the decisive question became the belief in the supremacy of reason and the truth which reason can supply over all other values and standards. It has been left to the 20th century to place the state and man's political decision in the center of his existence. The conflicts of our age are not religious, if religion is to be interpreted as relating man directly to God, and they are not in the realm of truth or science. All these matters are now subordinated to the state. Right, orthodox, wise, and true is the man who holds the accepted view of the state, even though everything else about him may be questionable. He may have the wrong religion—or no religion at all, he may be ignorant or untruthful; if he shares our view of the state, he is acceptable. Whether we realize it or not the political problem has become the central problem of our life. No longer is our

question, "What is your God?" or "What is your Truth?" but it is now "What is your State?" [5]

John Dewey openly made the state man's religion. "State consciousness" he saw as an achievement of the Greeks which the United States had come "to profit by." "The state life . . . is of more importance than the flourishing of any segment or class." Moreover,

> In such dim, blind, but effective way the American people is conscious that its schools serve best the cause of religion in serving the cause of social unification; and that under certain conditions schools are more religious in substance and in promise without any of the conventional badges and machinery of religious instruction than they could be in cultivating these forms at the expense of a state-consciousness.[6]

For Dewey, state-consciousness was the new form of God-consciousness.

Because the state has become the new form of man's catholic religion, the purpose of the state, whether the United Nations, the Soviet Union, or the United States, has come to be man's salvation.

Especially with World War I and thereafter, the state, in its warfare as well as its legislation, came to be messianic. Historians delight in showing their contempt of Christianity by calling various past conflicts "holy wars," usually with scant excuse. But certainly modern warfare has become holy warfare, and each new war a holy war to save mankind from some demonic forces, usually an opposing form of statism.

The framers of the U. S. Constitution echoed the colonial American horror of human sovereignty and avoided entirely all reference to the concept as illegitimate. For them sovereignty was an attribute of God, not the state.[7] The return of the concept of state sovereignty is thus a rejection of the American heritage as well as of the triune God.

[5] George W. Forell, "The State as Order of Creation," in Warren A. Quanbeck, editor: *God and Caesar, A Christian Approach to Social Ethics*, p. 31. Minneapolis: Augsburg, 1959.

[6] John Dewey: *Intelligence in the Modern World*, p. 707ff. Modern Library, 1939.

[7] See R. J. Rushdoony: *This Independent Republic*, pp. 33-40. Nutley, New Jersey: The Craig Press, 1964.

Because sovereignty is an inescapable concept, it is also an undiminishable concept. Total sovereignty always remains. Its locale is simply shifted as man's "ultimate concern" shifts from God to the state. The undiminished sovereignty remains. That undiminished sovereignty today stands in open manifestation in the form of the state. Man will either acknowledge the sovereignty and eminent domain of the triune God, or he will be compelled to bow down to the pseudo-sovereign state, with its claim to undiminished and total power. But, whatever man or the state does, God's sovereignty remains, and men will meet Him, either as their King or as their Judge.[8]

[8] For the economic arguments in favor of abolishing eminent domain, see the Santa Ana, California, *Register*, Saturday, August 27, 1966, p. C3, "Eminent Domain Should Be Abolished."

6

THE BIBLICAL DOCTRINE OF GOVERNMENT

One of the most revealing and deadly linguistic errors of our time is the equation of the word "government" with "state." When the average person, and indeed almost every man, hears references to government, he immediately thinks of the state. This usage is a relatively modern one. There was a time when, in common usage, especially among the Puritans, the term for the state was "civil government." Government in itself was a much broader concept.

Government meant, first of all, the self-government of the Christian man. The basic government is self-government, and only the Christian man is truly free and hence able properly to exercise self-government. A free social order rests on the premise that self-government is the basic government in the human order, and that any weakening of or decline in self-government means a decline in responsibility and the rise of tyranny and slavery.

Second, next to self-government is another basic form of government, the family. The family is man's first state, church, and school. It is the institution which provides the basic structure of his existence and most governs his activities. Man is reared in a family and then etablishes a family, passing from the governed to the governing in a framework which extensively and profoundly shapes his concept of himself and of life in general.

Third, the church is a government and an important one, not only in its exercise of discipline but in its religious and moral influence on the minds of men. Even men outside the church are extensively governed in each era, even if only in a negative sense, by the stand of the church. The failure of the church to provide biblical government has deadly repercussions on a culture.

Fourth, the school is a government, and a very important one. The desire of statists to control education rests on the knowledge of the school's significant part in the government of man. For formal education to be surrendered to the state is thus a basic surrender of man's self-government.

Fifth, a man's vocation, his business, work, profession, or calling, is an important government. A man is governed by the conditions of his vocation or work. In terms of it, he will educate himself, uproot his family and travel to another community, spend most of his waking hours in its service, and continually work therein to attain greater mastery and advancement. Vocations are both areas of government over man and at the same time a central area of self-government.

Sixth, private associations are important forms of government. These can include a man's neighborhood, his friends, voluntary organizations, strangers he must meet daily, and other like associations. A man dresses, speaks, thinks, and acts in an awareness of these associations, with a desire to be congenial, to further a given faith or cause, or to enhance his social status. These associations have a major governing influence on man, but they can also be means and areas whereby he exercises his government over others, influencing or directing them.

Seventh, another area of government is civil government, or the state. The state is thus one government among many, and to make the state equivalent to government per se is destructive of liberty and of life. The governmental area of the state must be strictly limited lest all government be destroyed by the tyranny of one realm. The issue in the persecution of the early church was the resistance of the Christians to the totalitarian claims of the state. The Christians were asked to sacrifice to the genius of the emperor, i.e., to offer incense to him. This, in its earlier forms, was not a recognition of the deity of the emperor, because only the dead emperor was deified upon approval of the senate. It was a recognition that the state, in the person of the emperor, was the mediating and governing institution between the gods and men, and that all life and government was under the jurisdiction of the state. Religious liberty was available to the church upon recognition of that premise. The

Roman Empire, in other words, like the modern state, assumed that it had the right to deny or to grant religious liberty because religion, like every other sphere of human activity, was a department under the state. The church denied this. Christians defended themselves as the most law-abiding citizens and subjects of the Empire, ever faithful in prayer for those in authority, but they denied the right of the state to govern the church. The church, directly under God, cannot submit itself to any government other than that of Jesus Christ. This was the issue.

Abuses of order within the church are no more under the government of the state than abuses within the state are under the government of the church, and the same is true of every other realm of government—family, church, school, business, and the like. Reformed theologians restricted the right of rebellion against an unjust order within the state to a legitimate order within that state, i.e., to other civil magistrates, who in the name of the law moved to correct the abuses of civil order.

The various spheres are inter-locking and inter-dependent and yet independent. Thus, Deuteronomy 21:18-21 deals with the death penalty for a juvenile delinquent. The parents do not have the power of the sword, i.e., of capital punishment. Upon reporting the incorrigible nature of their son to the city elders, the parents carried their governmental authority to its limits. The elders, upon confirmation of the charges, then assumed their jurisdiction, capital punishment for what was now, upon report, a civil offense. Clearly, the various spheres do not exist in a vacuum; they are interlocking, but the integrity of each is nonetheless real.

The resistance of the church to taxation is based on this independence. The church is an independent sphere and kingdom, and, although residing within a state, is not a part of that state: it has extra-territorial status. It is comparable to a foreign embassy: the law of the church alone is applicable on that soil. The Roman Catholic Church, better than Protestantism, has understood the implications of maintaining this extra-territorial status. The existence of the church as a church is at stake.

Similarly, biblical law did not recognize the legitimacy of a land

tax, because *a land tax destroys the independence of every sphere of government and makes each and every sphere subordinate to the state.* The land, in biblical law, was free from taxation. Rand's summary is accurate:

> It was impossible to dispossess men of their inheritance under the law of the Lord as no taxes were levied against land. Regardless of a man's personal commitments he could not disinherit his family by being dispossessed of his land forever. Millions of people today have no inheritance in the land and are pauperized in a country where hundreds of thousands of acres of land lie idle and unused. Because taxes are levied against the land instead of being levied against the increase from that land, men cannot afford to possess land. Through a system of debt that impoverishes the many and enriches the few the tendency has been to dispossess the many in our refusal to keep the law which states that "ye shall not therefore oppress one another" and we penalize, through taxation, those who should inherit the land! [1]

The tithe was the original pattern of all taxation. It was a tax on "increase," on production, on income. A man paid a double tithe annually, to the Lord's work, for charity, and to rejoice before the Lord with his family. The religious tithes were of three kinds. First, an annual tithe of the increase was claimed by God (Lev. 27:30-33) and was to be given to the Levites (Num. 18:21-24). The second tithe (Deut. 14:22-27) was again of the yearly increase of the land, and was to be used at the place of worship to eat and rejoice before the Lord. The third tithe (Deut. 14:28f.), every third year only, "was to be laid up at home. This tithe was to be shared by the local Levite, the stranger, the fatherless, and the widow." [2] Thus, religious duty, holiday, and charity were taken care of by the tithe.

The words tithe and tax were once equivalent: they referred also to the same thing, a tax on increase. When God, in declaring to Samuel the implications of apostasy, outlined the course of tyranny and totalitarianism, He stated that it would lead directly to a land tax (I Sam. 8:14, 15) and a personal property tax (I Sam.

[1] Howard B. Rand: *Digest of the Divine Law*, p. 111.
[2] Henry Lansdell: *The Tithe in Scripture*, pp. 22-36. London: SPCK, 1908.

8:15, 17). It would also involve forced labor as a tax (I Sam. 8:13, 16). The subsequent history of Israel and Judah confirmed this abundantly. The land was divided for purposes of taxation (I Ki. 4:7); forced labor as a tax came into being (I Ki. 5:13), and confiscation of property, also predicted (I Sam. 8:14), came to pass (I Ki. 21). The land tax became an arm of royal power (II Ki. 23:35), and so on.

The basic premise of the tithe is the oft-repeated declaration that "the earth is the Lord's, and the fullness thereof" (Ex. 9:29; Deut. 10:14; Ps. 24:1; I Cor. 10:26, etc.). *A tax on the land therefore is a tax against God*: this is not lawful. God's earth cannot be taxed, but man's labor, his increase, production, or income, can be taxed by both God and man, hence the tithe.

By restricting taxation to production, the Bible restricted severely the powers of the state and preserved the liberty of the family, the merchant, the church, and every other order of life. According to I Samuel 8, the means to totalitarianism, to an absolute state, will always be the extension of taxation to land, personal property, and inheritance. Today, by means of this anti-Christian concept of taxation, the state has gained jurisdiction over every area of life. The state treats religious liberty itself as something it can grant or deny; the tax exemption of the church is treated as a state-bestowed privilege, and some question its advisability or deny it. Meanwhile, anti-Christian churchmen demand the destruction of the church by pleading for the taxation of the church.

In this rise to totalitarian power, the state has smoothed its way at every turn by claiming to act in behalf of man, as the representative of the people. In the name of man, the state has usurped the place of God; it has then turned on all men to demand a tax of them as lord of the earth, as the very creator. God, while claiming ownership, demanded no land and property tax, only a tithe of the increase: the integrity of His creature, man, was thus preserved as God's image-bearer. Judgment could be the outcome, or blessing the reward, but man's course was man's choice. The state denies man the liberty which the Creator grants man. Under God, man is responsible and therefore liable to judgment. Under the caretaker state, man is not responsible nor is he free, for the state alone is free, and the state supplants responsibility with cradle-to-grave security.

The state, in the name of the people, and as their ostensible representative, robs the people of their God-given heritage. Its first step in this process is to convince the people that the state is their representative and agent. Then, in the name of the majority, or, better, the general will as interpreted by the state, the state takes over all government, it controls or owns the earth, and it plays at being god.

The biblical doctrine of civil government, as summarized in Romans 13:1-7, denies that the state has any right to represent the people: it must represent God. All power is ordained of God, and the state is one such power. Man's law must be rooted in God's law; lawlessness in this sense is resistance to God. First of all, civil government is of divine institution. It is ordained of God and is a part of God's kingdom and government (Rom. 13:1, 2). Second, civil government is ordained to promote good by providing conditions for its welfare by punishing criminals and preventing crime. Its essential function is thus justice, godly order (Rom. 13:3, 4). Third, civil government has the approval of Christian conscience. It is an authority, like that of parents and church officers, which is ordained of God, the only rightful source of authority. According to Hodge's comment on Romans 13:1,

> All authority is of God. No man has any rightful power over other men, which is not derived from God. All human power is delegated and ministerial. This is true of parents, of magistrates, and of church officers. This, however, is not all the passage means. It not only asserts that all government . . . is . . . derived from God, but that every magistrate is of God; that is, his authority is *jure divino*.[3]

Paul was aware that various officials were variously appointed in his day; some held their office by heredity, by appointment from the senate, army, or people, by election, and by assumption or usurpation. The means to office were various, but the same principle ap-

[3] Charles Hodge: *Commentary on the Epistle to the Romans*, p. 639. Revised edition. New York: Armstrong, 1893.

plied: their authority was of God in the discharge of their office, to be a terror to evildoers. Every de facto government has this duty, and the Christian has an obligation to be obedient to it as long as it fulfils in some sense this function. Hodge, on Romans 13:2, noted:

> It was to Paul a matter of little importance whether the Roman emperor was appointed by the senate, the army, or the people; whether the assumption of the imperial authority by Caesar was just or unjust, or whether his successors had a legitimate claim to the throne or not. It was his object to lay down the simple principle, that magistrates are to be obeyed. The extent of this obedience is to be determined from the nature of the case. They are to be obeyed as magistrates, in the exercise of their lawful authority. When Paul commands wives to obey their husbands, they are required to obey them as husbands, not as masters, nor as kings; children are to obey their parents as parents, not as sovereigns; and so in every other case. This passage, therefore, affords a very slight foundation for the doctrine of passive obedience.[4]

To obey the state, therefore, when it enters into the domain of the church, whether to deny or to grant it the right of life, or of liberty of worship, or merely to regulate its existence, is to disobey God and to render to Caesar what belongs to God. This the early church refused to do. To obey the state when it enters into the domain of the family, school, business, and other like areas, is again to disobey God and to make a god of the state.

The state which transgresses in this manner incurs the ultimate judgment of God. In Psalm 82, civil magistrates are called "gods" or sons of God, i.e., types of the Messiah, the Son of God, in view of their authority. They have a delegated jurisdiction over men which places great power in their hands, the power of the sword. Jesus declared they were called "gods" or sons of God because to them "the word of God came" (John 10:34ff.), i.e., their office was established by His word, and, insofar as they judged justly, they were administering God's justice. But, upon disobedience, they would die like men, like all creatures of disobedience.

4 *Ibid.*, p. 641.

I Samuel 8:7ff. makes clear, first, that statism is a rejection of God, and the growth of statist power coincides with the decline of the true faith. Second, when men seek their security from the state rather than from God, they lose security and gain slavery. Third, men who will not be God's servants become the state's servants or slaves. Fourth, the day will come when they cry out in agony because of their bondage, but "the Lord will not hear you in that day" (I Sam. 8:18), because it is the just reward for their apostasy.

Because God is sovereign, statism is first of all an attack on God's overlordship. It is an offense against God and an attack on His sovereignty. Second, God has declared that He will avenge himself. Third, man must realize that statism is primarily directed against God and that its essential thrust is anti-Christian. Man's primary remedial measure must therefore be religious, although it cannot be exclusively so.

The Christian has certain duties towards civil government. First, he must esteem and respect civil magistrates as God's ministers (I Pet. 2:13, 14; Titus 3:1). The despisers of authority are denounced (II Pet. 2:10; Jude 8). Second, this respect requires obedience in all lawful things (Rom. 13:1, 2; Titus 3:1; I Pet. 3:13, 14; I Tim. 2:1, 2). Third, he must render service, military or tax, where service is due (Rom. 13:7). Fourth, he must pray even for hostile officers (I Tim. 2:1-3), that they be blessed in their faithfulness and cursed in their lawlessness. Fifth, where a situation requires it, he must obey God rather than man (Acts 5:29).

In the anti-Christian perspective, the function of the state, first of all, is to represent men rather than God. The state denies the sovereignty of God and, in the name of the people, it asserts its own sovereignty. Second, the modern state declares itself to be a human institution whose function is to promote human welfare. With this pretension that human welfare in the broadest sense is the state's concern, the state usurps the right of man to govern himself under God. The state becomes the totality of government, human and divine. Third, justice is now defined as meeting man's needs and wants. From the days of the Roman Empire to the present, the road to statism has been the assertion that "the health of the people is the highest law." In the name of the general welfare, the state institutes general tyranny and slavery. Justice is denied to the citizen and subject in the name of social justice, meeting the needs of men en masse.

But social justice is not justice at all, because it is anti-personal. The requirements of justice are the requirements of the second table of the law, that man's life, home, property, and reputation be respected in word and deed. Social justice denies the integrity of man's life, home, property, and reputation in the name of classes of men, of men as a body, and men as a body means the state! Thus, social justice means the denial of justice because social justice is anti-personal. It is not the property of the individual, nor his life, home, and reputation which count, but the demands of a class as embodied in the state. And, since the state takes over the function of that class, whether the nobility or workers, the class itself loses all individual rights to the state. Social justice is always a paramount and central doctrine of statism, and the pretension to general welfare concerns is an instrument to power.

Whenever a state denies God's law as the fundamental law, it becomes an instrument of lawlessness, because the basic function of the state's law ceases progressively to be justice and becomes power. Law is heaped upon law, regulation upon regulation, executive order upon executive order, all to one end, to increase the power of the state.

But if God is not represented by the state, then man cannot be represented; he will only be used by his rulers. When the state represents God, it must represent men, in that its law now reflects God's concern for justice. Justice is man's best representative. Whether a man can vote or not is not nearly as important as the question of justice: does the law leave him secure in his governmental spheres, as an individual, a family, church, school, or business? Are these free areas of government? And does the civil law function to protect him from evildoers and to grant him justice against civil wrongs? If he lacks these, he will only vote on irrelevant or minor issues.

If men will not have God to rule over them they will have tyrants, because their own sins will become tyrants over them. Godly men are free men and produce free societies. Ungodly men are slaves to sin and create slave societies. This issue is ultimately personal: our states cannot represent God if we do not represent Him first of all. Men are created in God's image, to be God's representatives before and over creation. Christ, by His atonement, recreates His own from their fallen estate and re-establishes them in the image of God. As bearers of God's image, men must represent God, both in their civil government and in every other area of government.

In Christ, they have a threefold governmental office. As *kings*, men must exercise dominion in every realm, always subject to God and His word. As *prophets*, men must speak for God and interpret every area of life in terms of the word of God. As *priests*, men must dedicate all things to God and His glory and represent all of creation in this dedication.

The essence of justice in biblical law is *restitution*. The thief must restore what he stole, plus the exact amount he hoped to profit thereby, i.e., for a hundred dollar theft a two hundred dollar restoration. With livestock, which has the capacity for reproduction and increase, fourfold and fivefold restitution is required. Not imprisonment but either capital punishment or restitution is the premise of biblical law. Today, restitution has largely disappeared from civil law, except for crimes against the state.

Restitution involves the principle of restoration, the restoration of godly order. Behind it stands the broader principle of universal restoration, the undoing of the fall, "the restitution of all things" (Acts 3:21), and then the glorious new creation.

This is the purpose of the law of God, restoration, and the means is faith, or regeneration by the sovereign grace of God. The law is death to the sinner, but in itself "the law is holy, and the commandment holy, and just, and good" (Rom. 7:12), and the regenerate mind serves the law of God (Rom. 7:25), whereby God's order is extended. Man in Christ dies to the law as an indictment and lives in terms of it as his new nature, one written on the tables of his heart (Jer. 31:33; Rom. 7:22, etc.). God's law is the expression of His being, and it is therefore inescapable for man in God's universe. Law, true law, is born of life. The law of God, as revealed in Scripture, is a revelation of the life and nature of God. "He that hath the Son hath life; and he that hath not the Son hath not life" (I John 5:12). When we have the Son, we have life. When we have life, we have the law. Our lives, our various forms and spheres of government, are then revelational of God and His law, of His nature. This is man's fulfilment and his glorious liberty.

The triumph of statism is the death of every sphere of government other than the state and their absorption by the state. But this also means the absorption of man and the destruction of his privacy because man is now socialized. Man's every private feeling must be known so that the state can govern with the same kind of total knowledge God possesses. As a result, "Big Brother" and his servants deny the validity of any private domain in the name of "human need" and its sciences. According to a news dispatch:

> The old science fiction horror of one's behavior being scrutinized constantly by the eye of a "Big Brother" has become a reality.
> At least for 15 families at the Pennsylvania State University it has.
> They take turns living in a model home with flexible interior walls which has been built into a Home Economics building here.
> From the time they arise in the morning until the children are tucked in at night, research assistants watch and record their activities.
> Object of the data gathering is to learn the house preference of different types of families.
> It also will give graduate students working on the project "deeper insight into human needs," according to college dean Grace M. Henderson.
> So far, no adverse psychological effects stemming from the constant observance of the "Big Brothers and Sisters" have been reported by participating families.[5]

We can safely assume this report to be accurate when it states that "no adverse psychological effects . . . have been reported." Inevitably,

---

[5] " 'Big Brother' Eyes Modern Family," Oakland, California, *Tribune*, Sunday, April 25, 1965, p. 20-CM.

only those would submit to such an experiment who are already fully damaged. A blind man cannot become any blinder.

The same is true of those who volunteered for the long years of experiments by an associate professor of obstetrics and gynecology, a man, and his associate, a woman psychologist. These studies involved the observation and color filming of couples during sexual intercourse and involved methods of evaluating "female contraceptive diaphragms, creams, and jellies, and have shown how sexual activity can alter their effectiveness" by "utilizing specialized photographic techniques." [6]

To deny the sovereignty of God over man is to subject man to the sovereignty of men. God knows and governs the hearts of men without violence to their persons or their liberty. When God's sovereignty is denied, men seek total power over one another and total knowledge of other men. The rise of statism means the decline of privacy and the rise of the "peeping Tom" mentality among all men. Having lost respect for himself, apostate man cannot respect other men.

God as God is not simply the ultimate governor of all life: He is its creator, the maker of life by His sovereign word. As men and states seek to be gods, they seek also to create; but they cannot create, they can only deform. As a result, they turn to a substitute form of power over life, *dissection*. The modern state is therefore a *dissecting* state, even as apostate science is a dissecting science which aims at power through dissection. The experiments described above are instances of this kind of lust for power.

The dissecting state, the modern state, because it cannot create life, therefore aims at power by dissecting life, by a suicidal and destructive course whereby both citizens and the state are destroyed in the name of "government." For in no realm is government merely force. As Isabel Paterson pointed out, "the *constituent* element of government is not force." [7]

[6] "Medicine Secrets of Sex," in *Newsweek*, April 26, 1965, p. 58, vol. LXV, no. 17.
[7] Isabel Paterson: *The God of the Machine*, p. 97. Caldwell, Idaho: Caxton Printers, 1943, 1964.

One theory of history asserts that government arises from war, and therefore is force *per se*. This is doubly false since it is a reversal of the true relation. It has been adopted by philosophers committed to the doctrine of the Absolute State, because it is the sole argument they can muster which seems to afford them a factual base; but it rests upon the error of *post hoc, ergo propter hoc.*

Government by force is a contradiction in terms and an impossibility in physics. *Force is what is governed.* Government originates in the moral faculty.[8]

Government in every area is God's order, law, and authority asserted over His creation. In the world of men, God's government, whether in church, state, school, business, or family, is the extension of God's moral order over a fallen world, an assertion, to use an old Calvinist battle-cry, of "The Crown Rights of King Jesus." To reduce government, whether in the family, the state, or elsewhere, to force is to destroy government. Modern government, having forsaken God's law, is essentially government by force, and its force is a killing, dissecting force, a *government by autopsy*. The school therefore dissects the student and builds up an extensive file on the child by means of years of dissection and dissecting tests, under the illusion that dissection and autopsy are productive of education and life. The result instead is death. Apart from the restoration of godly government in every sphere of life, man's only possible future is suicide.

Long ago, God the Son, as Wisdom, declared, "he that sinneth against me wrongeth his own soul: all they that hate me love death" (Prov. 8:36). The lovers of death are today very much with us.

---

[8] *Ibid.*, p. 74.

7

THE MODERN STATE AS PROPHET AND LOGOS

St. John's Gospel begins by declaring that Jesus is the Word of God, by whom all things were made and by whom all things are either remade or judged as darkness (John 1:1-18; 3:18-21). The identification of Jesus as the Word or *Logos* is a significant one; the term is Greek, but the meaning is Hebraic. Lenski has summarized its implications:

> As far as legitimate evidence goes, it is John who originated this title for Christ and who made it current and well understood in the church of his day. The observation is also correct that what this title expressed in one weighty word was known in the church from the very start. John's Logos is he that is called "Faithful and True" in Rev. 19:11; see v. 13; "and his name is called The Word of God." He is identical with the "Amen, the faithful and true witness," in Rev. 3:14; and the absolute "Yea," without a single contradictory "nay" in the promises of God in II Cor. 1:19, 20, to whom the church answers with "Amen." This Logos is the revealed "mystery" of God, of which Paul writes Col. 1:27; 2:2; I Tim. 3:16; which he designates explicitly as "Christ." These designations go back to the Savior's own words in Matt. 11:27; 16:17. Here already we may define the Logos-title: the Logos is the final and absolute revelation of God, embodied in God's own Son, Jesus Christ. Christ is the Logos because in him all the purposes, plans, and promises of God are brought to a final focus and an absolute realization.[1]

The Hellenic concept of the *Logos* was markedly different: the Logos was the impersonal form, idea, reason, or structure of being. This concept of the *logos* has repeatedly invaded and pervaded the church, and it is basic to the world's perspective with respect

[1] R. C. H. Lenski: *The Interpretation of St. John's Gospel*, p. 29f. Columbus, Ohio: Lutheran Book Concern, 1942.

to the universe: either a structure exists in being, in the universe, or else a structure must be given to it or evolve from it in terms of a human order. This *logos* or true order of being is the state as guided by philosopher-kings or social engineers, by the elite, in whom the *logos* of being is realized.

This perspective is basic to modern statism. For the orthodox Christian, Jesus Christ is *the truth*, by whom all things were made. He is the meaning of history, and the source of all meaning. As creator and sustainer of all things, Christ is also the source of true interpretation or meaning. The true meaning of all things is to be derived from Christ's creative purpose. It is the desire, however, of apostate man to provide his own meaning and to derive that meaning from himself, to create his own *logos* or structure and declare that *logos* to be the true meaning of life and of all being. In short, the Word is Man; Man is the reason and the power of the universe. For the anarchist, Man means the individual; for the statist, Man means collective man, the state, the expression of the general will or the democratic consensus. The state, as it finds itself in terms of Man, becomes the creative word or *logos*, "the light which lighteth every man." It becomes the true interpreter of life and being, and the voice of the state is the voice of Man the *logos*, the voice of truth and meaning of being and the source of life's structure. This prophetic state, therefore, sees man's life as unfulfilled and unfree until the state speaks for him and gives shape, structure, and meaning to his life. The state is that order in which man finds himself, in which he finds expression and structure. Wallas, in *The Great Society*, stated:

> When Aristotle said: "Man is an animal adapted for living in a city state" (Politics, bk. i, chap. ii), he meant, not that man was living in such a state when Zeus was born, but that the city-state stimulated his nature to its noblest expression. "For what every being is in its perfect condition, that certainly is the nature of that being" (*ibid.*, bk. i, chap. ii). Even for Zeno's less confident philosophy "Follow Nature" meant not "Go back to the past" but "Examine the conditions of a good life in the present." [2]

[2] Graham Wallas: *The Great Society, A Psychological Analysis*, p. 71. London: Macmillan, 1914.

To create this state is man's task, because he will therein realize his true nature or structure, the reason of his being. It is "the master-task of civilised mankind." [3]

The concept of evolution has been most conducive to the furthering of *logos* statism. Hegel's philosophy of the state rested on a doctrine of social evolution. Biological evolutionary theory added force to the myth. Men began to speak of "the world's indwelling power that makes for righteousness."

> The universe itself all through is a moral agent, not of the kind perhaps always that would win the prize at a Sunday school, or get its practitioner admitted into good society as a model of deportment, but one that has been true to its great principle of doing what would conduce best to the ever higher well-being of itself and its creature; one that has come up from the wild orgies of its saurian youth into the decencies of a nineteenth-century manhood, and from its myriad bloody-nosed rounds of fisticuffs with savages and barbarians to the battle-fields of civilized industry and to the victories of enlightened peace. If its contests were at first only those of brute strength and brute cunning, and its survivals were the survivals only of those that were physically fittest, it was simply to lay the foundations of its final moral structure the more solid and secure, simply because the root of moral right, as we now know, is in a right physical soil. [4]

Morality thus came to be equated with evolutionary survival, not with transcendental law and the righteousness of God:

> The words of Pliny . . . —principle is not above laws, but laws are above principle—and of Aristotle, that the state exists before the individual, and not the individual before the state, expressed the almost universal sentiment. What the world in its early days wanted beyond everything else, wanted with an intensity we can hardly realize now, was stability, a condition of things fixed against change, violence, disorder; and this it had in the state, this is the origin and meaning of its name. Its form at first was naturally imperialism—that of the one strong man who could suppress disorder. . . . But amid all these changes of form the state itself remained, the center of men's hopes, the

---

[3] *Ibid.*
[4] John C. Kimball, "Moral Questions in Politics," in *Man and the State, Studies in Applied Sociology*, p. 516. Popular Lectures and Discussions Before the Brooklyn Ethical Association, a symposium. New York: Appleton, 1892.

object of their devotion, as honored under law as leader, demos as despot. The habit acquired through long ages of reverencing it as the source of all public order and the means of all public good had become a part of our very nature. And so it was almost inevitable when men in the progress of modern civilization came to have great moral questions to deal with that they should look to politics and political action as the chief, if not the only, means by which they could be satisfactorily settled.[5]

Kimball broke with Spencer's idea "of limiting the functions of the state to the punishment of crime and stigmatizing all laws for the direct promotion of a people's welfare as among 'the sins of legislators.' " In Kimball's evolutionary theory, the state was the high point of man's development, and it was Man. "The state is ourselves, what we are, and with only such authority as we choose to let it have." [6] The state thus is Man, and, to use a phrase echoed from Thomas Paine by Hubert H. Humphrey in his book, *The Cause Is Mankind* (1964).

Humphrey presupposes the unity of mankind; he speaks of "the family called man": "We place our faith in the brotherhood of man under the fatherhood of God." Pope John XXIII is enlisted as a leader in this universalism whereby "we are all children of God." [7] The liberalism of Humphrey is that of "Franklin D. Roosevelt, who completed the transformation of American liberalism from its original anti-statism to a doctrine embracing the use of the power of the state to achieve both freedom and a reasonable measure of equality." [8] The goal is "the humanitarian state," and "human rights" for all.[9] This involves, "in the America for tomorrow," an open immigration policy to produce a multi-racial America: "It will be a land of many races and religions, of peoples cosmopolitan and understanding of each other—yet each cherishing their unique traditions." This "day will come," and the world will be cleansed of disease, ignorance, and poverty as we "internationalize our concepts of social welfare and

[5] *Ibid.*, p. 520f.
[6] *Ibid.*, p. 53ff.
[7] Hubert H. Humphrey: *The Cause Is Mankind, A Liberal Program for Modern America*, pp. 11, 28, 127. New York: Macfadden-Bartell, 1965 (1964).
[8] *Ibid.*, p. 19.
[9] *Ibid.*, p. 21ff.

social justice." [10] This is the purpose of foreign aid, and of dis-armament.[11]

Humphrey says, of "my concept of the welfare society," that it was the faith of the founding fathers and of "all religious leaders":

> I believe it to be a twentieth-century version of the society conceived of by our founding fathers, propounded by the most thoughtful of philosophers, sanctioned by the compassionate spirit of all religious leaders.[12]

Those who would deny that this universalism is true Christianity would be classed as the mentally sick by Humphrey, who holds "that racial and religious prejudice is a disease, a mark of emotional disorder." [13] To hold to the superiority of one's faith, or to believe that Christianity alone can offer man the truth with respect to God and salvation is for Humphrey to be classed with racism. His own prejudice against and hatred of the "radical right" he refuses to see as wrong or as an "emotional disorder." To be against the civil rights movement, the United Nations, social security, fluoridation, and disarmament is for him evidence of "emotional disorder." After all, "the cause is mankind," and this is the true faith alone, and the state is the *logos* of this holy cause, the structure of the new hu-manity of Humphrey's religion of humanity. Mankind will be saved, and man will become truly free, truly himself, in and through this humanitarian state. The state thus speaks for Man: it speaks the prophetic word and it creates the prophetic order. The state is the prophet and the *logos* of man.

The developing *logos* is prophetically declared to be a total revo-lution leading to a universal world order.

> The French Revolution was perhaps the first revolution in world history that was intended to be world-wide. It was equipped with a religion, a philosophy, without which, accord-ing to Mazzini, there is no revolution.[14]

[10] *Ibid.*, p. 62.
[11] *Ibid.*, pp. 83, 89, 93ff., 107ff.
[12] *Ibid.*, p. 71.
[13] *Ibid.*, p. 77.
[14] Nicholas Doman: *The Coming Age of World Control, The Transition to an Organized World Society*, p. 72. New York: Harper, 1942.

Revolution thus requires a prior new religion which renders other religions invalid. The new religion, as expressed by Humphrey, declares the adherents of the old religion to be not merely in error but mentally sick as well. The trend of evolution, according to Doman, is from the tribal unit to the city state, to feudal political formations, to the national state, and now to a world state.[15]

The world state must control world economy and finance, for "without full determination to control all phases of the political and economic life we cannot hope to navigate the tides of insecurity." The state will be a democracy in that it will be *for* the people, but this does not mean that the people can themselves determine the policies.

> The decision of the issue is too momentous and the stakes are too great for a world-wide plebiscite to pass judgment upon them. "If we consider the plebiscitary element in democracy, we are justified in saying, after the experience of the last epoch, that of all democratic institutions it has made the largest contribution to the destruction of the system" (Karl Manneheim, *Man and Society in an Age of Reconstruction*, New York, 1940, p. 356).[16]

In other words, democracy is not in suffrage, in voting, or in majority rule: it is in a consensus whereby the general will is realized by the elite, the social engineers.[17] These social engineers will represent freedom with their controls: men are free because this democratic dictatorship declares they are free! Men become "pawns" in a free social order!

> World-wide planning is the road that leads to the incorporation and integration of the objectives of political freedom and economic security. The highest synthesis of political and economic democracy and of political and economic security could be attained with stable control exercised by a democratically inclined supranational political authority. Democratic freedom, as we have seen, is in a precarious situation in an unplanned capitalist society without a supranational political authority imbued with the tenets of freedom. *With a greater control of our eco-*

[15] *Ibid.*, p. 133.
[16] *Ibid.*, p. 266.
[17] See R. J. Rushdoony: *The Messianic Character of American Education*, pp. 235-266. Nutley, New Jersey: The Craig Press, 1963.

nomic structure and social environment we shall be able to enjoy a more democratic atmosphere. But if we are repelled by the magnitude of the conception that we co-ordinate the political, social, and economic spheres on a world-wide scale we shall again become pawns in the free play of those forces.[18]

This is "democratic universalism." [19] This is the new "universal idea" which "is a beacon within the reach of every man who strives for peace and dignity in a better world." [20] This idea or *logos* manifests itself in the social engineers, in a "democratically inclined supernational political authority" which in and of itself defines the democratic will, welfare, and consensus. This elite controls the state and is to all practical intent *the state.* This state as prophet and *logos,* first of all, speaks for man as man's prophet, and, second, as prophet plans and predicts the future. In its *logos* role, this state becomes the structure of man's being. Man is not truly man outside the *logos* state; he is only a shapeless mass seeking to find form and structure. This *logos* state becomes, instead of Christ, itself "the true Light, which lighteth every man that cometh into the world" (John 1:9). It provides cradle-to-grave security and becomes the ostensible creator and sustainer of man and society.

The law of the *logos* state becomes increasingly administrative law, because the administration or bureaucracy best represents the *logos.* Administrative law and executive orders are fiat law, best representing the pure prophetic voice of the state. To the old-fashioned jurist, like the Rt. Hon. Lord Hewart of Bury, Lord Chief Justice of England in his day, administrative law is despotism:

> Arbitrary power is certain in the long run to become despotism. and there is danger, if the so-called method of administrative "law," which is essentially lawlessness, is greatly extended, of the loss of those hardly won liberties which it has taken centuries to establish.[21]

But to the state, such law is the essence of true freedom. True

18 Doman: *Coming Age of World Control,* p. 266.
19 *Ibid.,* p. 278.
20 *Ibid.,* p. 292f.
21 The Rt. Hon. Lord Hewart of Bury: *The New Despotism,* p. 52. London: Ernest Benn, 1929.

freedom exists because the state has obliterated its enemies, and the state is now free, hence the people, who have no right of independent existence from their logos, are free also. According to Stalin, on December 11, 1937,

> Never in the history of the world have there been such really free and really democratic elections. History knows no other example like it. The point is not that our elections are universal, equal, secret and direct, although that fact in itself is of great importance. The point is that our universal elections will be carried out as the freest elections and the most democratic of any country in the world.
> Universal elections exist and are held in some capitalist countries, too, so-called democratic countries. But in what atmosphere are elections held there? In an atmosphere of class conflicts, in an atmosphere of class enmity, in an atmosphere of pressure brought to bear on the electors by the capitalists, landlords, bankers and other capitalist sharks. Such elections, even if they are universal, equal, secret and direct, cannot be called altogether free and altogether democratic elections.
> Here in our country, on the contrary, elections are held in an entirely different atmosphere. Here there are no capitalists and no landlords and, consequently, no pressure is exerted by propertied classes on non-propertied classes.[22]

Soviet elections are merely approvals of a Communist Party selected list of candidates, without any issues or choices involved. Such an election is "free" because it is free from the foibles of men and expressive of the will of the Party, the *logos* of the proletariat. Liberty means in this perspective the triumph and prevalence of the will of the elite group or party.

Similarly, Justice William O. Douglas, in a section entitled "the Rule of Law," discusses, not the abstract concepts of right and wrong, and the rule of justice as the rule of law, but rather the domination of a world court and its total jurisdiction. The rule of law for Douglas is the rule of a world court.

> We on this continent adopted a federation composed of sovereign nations, and we provided the Supreme Court as the tri-

[22] M. R. Werner, editor: *Stalin's Kampf, Joseph Stalin's Credo, Written by Himself*, p. 258. New York: Howell, Soskin, 1940.

bunal for settlement of controversies between them. We can inaugurate the beginnings of a like rule of law in the international field by a few simple expedients. President Eisenhower's proposal to submit all disputes under treaties to the International Court with power on its part to render binding decisions is one place to commence. That device can be evolved to include many types of controversies, including territorial problems that now raise the specter of nuclear war. International institutions can be created to control and administer certain common problems. Nuclear energy is one. We must start now to provide specific procedural devices to adjudicate international controversies and to control and administer such crucial problems as the use of nuclear energy, which all nations have in common. We must in other words carry a "rule of law" beyond the conversation stage and begin to reduce it to specific, concrete forms, if war is to be prevented.[23]

The meaning is clear. For Douglas, the rule of law is wholly incarnate in an institution which is the *logos* and prophet of society. Law is totally institutionalized: it is made fully immanent and transcendental law is wholly ignored.

This institutionalization of the *logos* is so extensive that world leaders have gained the status of demi-gods or gods. The birthplaces of presidents, leaders, and prime ministers become national or international "shrines." Even worldly newspaper men are afflicted with this attitude. Thus, James Abbe, in describing his 1932 interview with Joseph Stalin, wrote:

> As Stalin reached me, he put his hand forward and gave mine a firm clasp. The best I could do was stammer, "Stalin." He seemed surprised, but did not correct me. He smiled, and that revived me. It suddenly struck me the man was human.[24]

Abbe was surprised that a man was a human, not a god, surprised that "the man was human"! Taken in its minimal sense, Abbe's statement is a striking one.

The Greek thinkers held, as in Plato, that behind the constant flux and change of a world of Becoming, a developing world, were

[23] William O. Douglas: *America Challenged*, p. 45. New York: Avon, 1960.
[24] James Abbe, "James Abbe's Wonderful Years, 25 Minutes With Stalin," in the Oakland, California, *Tribune*, Thursday, February 22, 1962, p. 23.

certain permanent, universal, and unchanging ideas, forms, or structures. For the Stoics, the *Logos Spermatikos*, the seminal reason
which was the world-reason, contained within itself the multitude
of *logoi spermatikoi*, the intelligible and purposive forms or ideas
operating within the world. This *Logos* is impersonal. "As regulating all things, the Logos is identified with Fate (heimarmene); as
directing all things toward the good, with Providence (provoia);
and as the ordered course of events, with Nature (physis)." [25] In
this conception, there was a *logos* in the world in each of the many
forms operative in the world, and a general *logos* of the world which
had a pseudo-transcendence. In the modern form of this doctrine,
the *logos* is totally immanent and present in the state and its scientific managers. They are the *logos* incarnate. The world-reason
is embodied in the state, whether called a communist or socialist
state, "the humanitarian state" (H. H. Humphrey), the welfare
state, or "the Great Society." In every case, all forms and structures
are first absorbed into the state, and then absorbed by the state.

Examples of this absorption by the state are much in evidence.
In the Soviet Union, the "Decrees and Constitution of Soviet Rus-
sia" under Lenin abolished "all property rights in the land, treasures
of the earth, waters, forests and fundamental natural resources."[26]
Freedom of movement and emigration was absorbed by the state,[27]
as was freedom of religion. "No church or religious society has the
right to own property. They have no right of juridical person." [28]
By limiting "juridical person" to the state and its agencies, the
Soviet law abolished the right of existence to all other institutions.
The abolition of free trade, the nationalization of banks made economics further subordinate to the state.[29] Marriage and children
were absorbed by the state, and, by abolition of inheritance, the

[25] Glenn R. Morrow, "Logos," in D. D. Runes: *Dictionary of Philosophy*,
p. 184.
[26] The Clayton R. Lusk Committee, Senate of New York State: *Revolutionary Radicalism, Its History, Purpose and Tactics*, Part I, vol. I, p. 262.
Albany: J. B. Lyons, 1920.
[27] *Ibid.*, p. 270f.
[28] *Ibid.*, p. 277.
[29] *Ibid.*, pp. 277f., 299-305. On the abolition of free trade, see Lenin's statement of March 7, 1920, Pt. I, vol. II, p. 1676.

family was abolished as an independent institution.[30] The Red Terror proclaimed the "physical annihilation" of all whom the state deemed to be its enemies. According to two statements of 1918,

> Enough of mildness. *The interests of the revolution necessitate physical destruction of the bourgeois class. It is time for us to start. . . .*
>
> Nay, we have already left the path of all errors and we have found the right tract of struggle with our hated enemies and this tract is—*Red Terror*.[31]

Not only did the Soviet regime destroy or absorb all institutions within the state, in order to make itself the total voice and *logos* of the proletariat, the people, it also worked to destroy all institutions in other states by denying the validity of "bourgeoise legality." In a Manifesto of July 15, 1920, of the International Council of Trade Unions, it was declared that

> It is their duty to create everywhere a parallel illegal organization machine which at the decisive moment will be helpful to the party in fulfilling its duty to the revolution.
>
> In all countries where the Communists, because of a state of siege and because of exceptional laws directed against them, are unable to carry on their whole work legally, it is absolutely necessary to combine legal with illegal activities.[32]

In the Western countries, where the tactic has been more Fabian, the abolition or the absorption of schools, property, family and inheritance, religion, and other once independent spheres has been more gradual, but nonetheless real. By taxes, zoning laws, legislation, and controls, the state has increasingly arrogated unto itself all government, including man's self-government, so that man's life has been progressively identified with the state as his prophet and *logos*. Man has but one voice, and that voice is the state, because every sphere of life has been made or is in process of being made into an aspect of the state.

The fulfilment of this *logos* is in the world state, "an integrated

30 *Ibid.*, Pt. I, vol. I, pp. 285-294.
31 *Ibid.*, p. 306.
32 *Ibid.*, Pt. I, vol. II, p. 1649.

world order." "Every quest for one God, one ultimate Reality, one brotherhood of man, one true faith, and one true commonwealth is a search, against the grain of man's egoism, for world order." [33] The source of world order was once God: "We believed that God created the universe as a cosmos, and not as a chaos: an orderly, meaningful purposeful system of being, regulated in at least its observable modes by a divinely ordained body of natural law." [34] This faith is gone, and we must now listen to "the prophets of world order." [35] The new *logos* of being is the world state, and the exponents of world government are its prophets, and "the ultimate function of prophecy is not to tell the future, but to make it." [36] A new syncretistic religion will be necessary for this world order.[37] This order will be practical: "Western man has moved in the last two centuries from a long era in which he rarely doubted his ability to know the Truth, to the present era, in which he knows he *cannot* know it." [38] There must be a middle course, a "responsible use of freedom to pool our finite truths in a world mind, a racial will, a policy for Man." This is "simply a 'will to agree.' " [39] "Man by nature is a prophesying animal," [40] with a will to *make* the future, to predestinate it. It is possible for this world civilization and state to become "a kind of planetary anthill, a static, changeless, soulless factory." [41] This tyranny can be avoided only by having perpetually new frontiers such as explorations of the mind, extrasensory powers and of outer space. This will keep man "free." [42] In this perspective, man in time is totally absorbed by the state in the present, and his only freedom is to explore the future. Man in space is totally absorbed on earth, and his only "freedom" is to permit the exploration of inner space, his mind, or to "escape," under state control and subsidy, into outer space.

[33] W. Warren Wagar: *The City of Man, Prophecies of a World Civilization in Twentieth-Century Thought*, p. 13. Boston: Houghton Mifflin, 1963.
[34] *Ibid.*, p. 55.
[35] *Ibid.*, p. 58.
[36] *Ibid.*, p. 66.
[37] *Ibid.*, pp. 154-172.
[38] *Ibid.*, p. 242.
[39] *Ibid.*, p. 246.
[40] *Ibid.*, p. 261.
[41] *Ibid.*, p. 269.
[42] *Ibid.*, pp. 270-272.

The practical consequence of all this will be the abolition of man by the state in the name of Man. The prospect is a fearful one, and the attempt will be made, but it shall fail. Man's true prophet is Jesus Christ and none other. And Jesus Christ, as the *Logos* of God, very God of very God, is the incarnate one, very man of very man, two natures but without confusion. Man therefore finds his only true representation in Jesus Christ as his federal head and new Adam, and his fulfilment is in Christ alone. For the state to appear as man's prophet and *logos* is to deify man, to appear as a false prophet, and to parody Christ in the process of warring against Him. Man as the state dreams of making the future as well as predicting or foretelling it, but Christ himself both ordains all things that come to pass, foretold them in His enscriptured word, and himself brings them to pass. In this, Christ's self-appointed and self-determined destiny, the destruction of Babylon the Great, the state as prophet and *logos*, is a central task.

8

THE POLITICS OF SLAVERY

Paul, in Romans 6:15-23, laid down certain biblical premises with respect to servitude or slavery. A *first* premise of all biblical thought is that man is a creature created by the triune God. Men are not gods; this opinion constitutes the satanic temptation and man's original sin (Gen. 3:5). Broadly stated, men are dependent on powers greater than themselves, since they are a creation of ultimate power rather than its creator. Men are thus either servants or slaves of sin, of the powers of darkness and apostasy, or they are servants of God, in "obedience unto righteousness" (Rom. 6:16).

Second, according to Paul, to be the servant or slave of the one is to be free of the other. If we are slaves of sin, we are independent of and free from God's holiness and His righteousness. If we are dependent upon God, and if we serve him as His own slaves (who by grace are adopted in Christ to sonship), then we are to the same degree independent of sin and the powers of darkness (Rom. 6: 17-23).

Third, the one whom we serve takes control over us and is our security. If we are slaves of sin, then sin is our controller and our security. We are then insecure apart from sin. But, if we are servants of God, then God is our controller and our security. The doctrine of eternal security is one aspect of this fact. Man's security in Christian faith rests, not in himself, the state, or in nature, but in the triune God whose total government of all things is the assurance, not of freedom from problems, but of a triumphant conclusion to life's battles (Rom. 8:28).

Fourth, Paul saw humanity divided between these two classes of servants or slaves with a great gulf between the two. The concept of the universal brotherhood of man is alien to biblical thought. All men are one in sin apart from Christ, and all are by natural birth sons of Adam and fallen in nature, but this oneness in Adam is not brotherhood. The sinner is at war with God, and therefore he is at war with his neighbor and at war with himself. The relationship with God is the determinative one, and man's entire life is governed by the nature of this relationship. Men who are in Christ are in the new humanity of the last Adam, the Adam from above, and between the *two humanities* there is no communion. The alternatives are war or conversion, and sometimes both are required, in that some can only be opposed, because of their hostility, and others are open to evangelization. Coexistence between the two humanities means only the death of the new humanity. The old humanity, the slave of sin, has a security derived from this world and from evil. They are thus independent towards God and dependent towards statism, their substitute god and predestinator. On the other hand, the true servants or slaves of God are dependent on God but independent towards statism.

Fifth, it is now apparent that the two positions lead to different politics, the one to the politics of statism, the other to the politics of responsibility under God and independence from statism. Each of these positions produces a particular character. For the statist, the dependence of the orthodox Christian on the triune God is a sign of weak character and an unwillingness to "face the facts of life," and the trust of the orthodox Christian in the Bible as the infallible word of God is seen as a lack of intelligence and an unwillingness to reason. The whole position of the orthodox Christian is dismissed as "unscientific" and therefore intellectually inadmissible. But this ostensibly independent, rational, and scientific man, who refuses to yield this allegiance to God, yields a similar allegiance to the state. For him, the state is the source of personal and social security, and he looks to the state for those controls and guidances which the orthodox Christian holds should come from God. The statist holds trust in God to be irrational, but his trust in the state, with its unbroken record of abuse of sovereign power, is itself by no means a rational faith. The statist claims that his faith in the state is scientific, and a successful scientific experiment requires total control of all factors, but every approach to total state control in human history has at the same time been an approach to total tyranny. A scientific study should point at least to the untenability of the concept of a scientific state, the premise of statism is neither rational nor scientific: it is religious. When men will not have God to be Lord over them, they will create their own gods and fall down before them in abject devotion, and the most common of these idols is statism.

The orthodox Christian, because he believes in the total, pre-destinating government of God, cannot believe in a state which goes beyond the limited boundaries established by the word of God. Predestination, i.e., total planning, prediction, and control, belongs to God, not to man or the state. The state cannot go beyond its prescribed boundaries without infringing on God's prerogatives and thereby defying God, nor can man the scientist trespass his boundaries. The human order must be kept free therefore from at-tempts by man to predestinate man. The implications of the doctrine of divine predestination are thus clearly hostile to socialism and to statism in any form.

Each of the two politics has, therefore, its own declaration of in-dependence. The statist must, by the logic of his position, declare his independence from God and his dependence on the state. The orthodox Christian, if he truly holds to the faith he professes, must declare his independence from statism and statist planning and con-trol and his dependence upon the sovereign and only true God.

The two politics produce different characters. To expect the non-Christian peoples of the world to act in terms of Christian principles is illusory. Their concern is naturally to become free states and not free peoples, to free the state from any restraints and to increase controls over people. The true hope of the politics of slavery, of statism, is simply statism, and the most advanced and refined form of statism is "scientific socialism," or Marxist communism, although Fabian socialism makes a notable challenge to that claim. To at-tempt to save a non-Christian country from socialism of some form is to attempt the impossible: its goal is socialism. It is illusory, moreover, to believe that the United States, after World War II, dedicated itself to fighting socialism by foreign aid. As against the Red China and U.S.S.R. varieties of socialism, the United States exported its own variety by means of foreign aid and military action. Whether this was intentional or not is an interesting question but beside the point: the premise of foreign aid has been statist and socialist to the core. By forcing "democracy" on various countries, the United States furthered their socialization as well as its own.

Christian politics denies that slaves to sin can become free men politically or religiously without regeneration through Jesus Christ. The road to freedom in every domain is Jesus Christ. Today, most of the United States and the Western powers have left service to to Christ for service to sin. They are free from God but in bondage to sin. Our politics reflects our religious condition.

Sixth, the politics of statism makes the state its source of law rather than God. The law of God is not the *source* of life, according to Scripture, but the *condition* of life. The law of God is "ordained to life" but it is "death" to those in sin (Rom. 7:10). *Freedom from God is thus inevitably the freedom to die.* The Second Person of the Trinity, speaking as Wisdom, said of old, "all they that hate me love death" (Prov. 8:36). It is well to note also the full text of Proverbs 29:18, of which normally only the first half is cited: "Where there is no vision, the people perish: but he that keepeth the law, happy is he." True vision is thus associated with the keeping of God's law.

Seventh, apart from Christianity, we will have slavery. If men will not serve God, they will become the slaves of men. The Bible thus regards slavery as a deformation of man and of society, but also as an inescapable reality in a sinful world. The Mosaic law set forth the standard of liberty under God (Lev. 25:10) while regulating slavery as a social evil, seeking by law to limit it as far as possible. The slavery dealt with by Mosaic law was privately owned slaves, and their condition was strictly regulated. The slave became an inferior member of the Hebrew family, with certain rights, including limited inheritance. Slavery has been extensively abolished as a private factor, but it exists today as a state monopoly, and slavery in this sense is more prevalent than ever before in history. State-owned slaves in past history have been either conquered peoples pressed into servitude to the state, or the people of the land, commanded into forced labor by their own state. The really repressive and vicious slaveries of history have been state slavery, lacking as it is in the personal relationship, responsibility, and affection which often alleviated and marked the private ownership of slaves. It has been a statist encouraged illusion of the twentieth century that slavery is on the wane. It has never been more prevalent. The progress of statist slavery has been accompanied by statist self-praise for the liberation of slaves, but in virtually every nation today, statist slavery is advancing or has accomplished its goal. Every increase in security provisions by the state is an increase in slavery. One side of slavery involves involuntary servitude, subjection, or bondage; the other side involves the care, protection, and maintenance of the slaves by the slave-holder. This often involves some solicitude. Prisoners in state prisons are held in a form of slavery; they have no civil rights, they can be worked at the will of the state, and they have nothing except that which the state chooses to grant them, but it can be argued that the care of prisoners is both humane and conducive to their welfare. What they lack is liberty. The slave state can be very repressive to the recalcitrant, as the U.S.S.R. has generally been, or it can be humane, as the Inca empire usually was, but in either instance it is a deformation of man and society.

Slavery increases as orthodox Christianity recedes. The root of the problem is spiritual, religious. Statist slavery is inescapable when men evade the religious issue and seek an easy answer, a political answer. On June 24, 1965, when the economist, Dr. Hans Sennholz, spoke in Los Angeles, during the question period an elderly woman became abusive, demanding that he give them a sure answer as to how to get through the coming economic crisis without any trouble, and insulting because he denied that such an answer was possible. The demand is for some *gimmick* to escape judgment. It involves a rejection of responsibility and a divorce from consequences which is a prerequisite of the slave mentality. To deny judgment as a necessary part of life is to deny responsibility and liberty. The orthodox Christian begins as a Christian by accepting the fact of judgment against himself: the justice of God requires it, and the grace of God provides the atonement for judgment in the person of Jesus Christ. Since God himself refused to set aside the requirements of justice, insisting on them to the point of the death of the only begotten Son of God, it is impossible for a Christian to deny the reality and the necessity of judgment without denying God. Judgment is no less real than grace, and to deny judgment, as antinomianism does, is to deny by implication grace as well. Grace does not stave off judgment: it accompanies judgment where faith and repentance are present. "If my people which are called by my name, shall humble themselves, and pray, and seek my face, and turn from their wicked ways; then will I hear from heaven, and will forgive their sin, and will heal their land" (II Chron. 7:14). A land requiring healing means a land under judgment.

In dealing with the fact of slavery, it is not enough to treat the symptoms alone; the cause must be dealt with, and the basic cause of statist slavery in our day, as always, is religious. The myth of man's autonomy from God is the source of man's slavery to man in the form of the state. The state, as the free order, has absorbed man's freedom. God, as the free and absolutely sovereign Person, is the only ground of man's true freedom, because God's control and pre-destination are not in violation of man's being, but, because God is the Creator, are in fulfilment of man's being. Under God, we are free to be ourselves; it is no violence to our being that we are what we are: this is God's predestination. The state, as an intruder on the scene, and the would-be-re-creator of man, can only predestinate by a con-tinuing situation of coercion. The ideal of the state is the humanistic scientific ideal which requires total control in order to conduct the valid social experiment.

> As long as this mathematical science-ideal had the primacy in modern philosophy, even human society was constructed after its pattern. The given societal order, which still showed many remnants of the medieval feudal regime, did not satisfy the Humanist view of human autonomy. Thus, this societal order, too was subjected to a methodical destruction by theoretical thought. It was dissolved into its supposed elemental com-ponents, the free and equal individuals who were assumed to

have existed in a pre-societal state of nature. From these elements philosophical thought could freely create a theoretical image of human society corresponding to the Humanist mathematical science-ideal, which aims at complete control over the temporal world.

The first concern was to construct a body politic, provided with absolute power over all other societal relationships, in order to dissolve all connection with medieval society. To this end, the state was defined as an artificial body characterized by its absolute sovereignty, excluding any internal sphere sovereignty of non-political institutions such as the family and the church.[1]

The politics of state planning and control is the politics of slavery. The humanistic science-ideal amounts simply to slavery, and the Christian is under obligation to oppose it.

[1] Herman Dooyeweerd: *In the Twilight of Western Thought*, p. 69f. Philadelphia: Presbyterian and Reformed Publishing Company, 1960.

INDEX